Macroeconomic Policy for Emerging Markets

Macroeconomic policies matter for sustainable long-term growth. With global fluctuations, deviation from a stable growth path can be minimized by countercyclical macro policies, if properly implemented. This book examines Thailand's 55 years of experience in macroeconomic management and provides valuable lessons for other emerging economies at various stages of development on what could have been done to avoid economic instability. It also examines how short-term complications can develop into perennial problems obstructing the process of economic development.

The book provides an alternative approach to the study of economic growth through the inclusion of both economic history and institutional context, appealing to academics and economists who focus on economic growth, economic development, international macroeconomics, public policy study, business cycles, and the open-market economy.

Bhanupong Nidhiprabha is Professor in Economics at Thammasat University, Bangkok, Thailand. He was also Dean of the Faculty of Economics between 2011 and 2014.

Routledge Studies in Development Economics

Economic Transformation for Poverty Reduction in Africa
A Multidimensional Approach
Edited by Almas Heshmati

Employment Policy in Emerging Economies
The Indian Case
Edited by Elizabeth Hill and Amitendu Palit

Inequality in Economics and Sociology
New Perspectives
Edited by Gilberto Antonelli and Boike Rehbein

Capabilities, Innovation and Economic Growth
Policymaking for Freedom and Efficiency
Michele Capriati

The Economics of Natural Resources in Latin America
Taxation and Regulation of the Extractive Industries
Edited by Osmel E. Manzano M, Fernando H. Navajas and Andrew Powell

Global Commodity Markets and Development Economics
Edited by Stephan Pfaffenzeller

The Service Sector and Economic Development in Africa
Edited by Evelyn F. Wamboye and Peter J. Nyaronga

Macroeconomic Policy for Emerging Markets
Lessons from Thailand
Bhanupong Nidhiprabha

For more information about this series, please visit www.routledge.com/series/SE0266

Macroeconomic Policy for Emerging Markets
Lessons from Thailand

Bhanupong Nidhiprabha

Routledge
Taylor & Francis Group
LONDON AND NEW YORK

First published 2019
by Routledge
2 Park Square, Milton Park, Abingdon, Oxon OX14 4RN

and by Routledge
605 Third Avenue, New York, NY 10017

First issued in paperback 2020

Routledge is an imprint of the Taylor & Francis Group, an informa business

British Library Cataloguing-in-Publication Data
A catalogue record for this book is available from the British Library

Library of Congress Cataloging-in-Publication Data
A catalog record for this book has been requested

ISBN 13: 978-0-367-50418-2 (pbk)
ISBN 13: 978-1-138-64419-9 (hbk)

Typeset in Galliard
by Apex CoVantage, LLC

Contents

Figures

Tables

Preface

Economic policy is meant to be useful and effective. But when macroeconomic policy is based on false presumptions and hidden agenda, the policy can be ineffective and may produce disastrous results. More than ever before, macroeconomic policy must be adjusted to changing environment and random shocks from internal and external sources. My main motivation in writing this book is to point consequences of good and bad macroeconomic policies. My second motivation is to demonstrate that macroeconomic theories can be applied to understand economic problems in emerging economies. Statistical analysis and graphical illustrations are employed in each chapter so that conclusion from each chapter is based on factual evidence, rather than conjecture or assertion based on political ideology and anecdotal evidence.

Employing times series of macroeconomic data for more than 55 years, I have divided the period of study into three episodes: the early phase of economic development between 1961 and 1990, the resilient period 1991-2005, when Thailand underwent macroeconomic adjustment in response to external shocks, and the period of political turmoil from 2006 to 2017, when changes in political regimes affected long-term growth.

Although fiscal policy, monetary and exchange rate policies are presented in separated chapters, their interrelationship is highlighted throughout the book. Chapters on the financial sector and the capital market are provided to remind readers the interconnectedness between the real and monetary sectors. The book also provides an analysis of dynamic adjustments among macro variables, when they are perturbed away from long run equilibrium paths. In consequence, I have examined how the Thai economy has been affected by military coups. Since growth and price stability are not the only goals of macroeconomic policy, the book sheds some light on the issue of poverty and income inequality and investigate how macroeconomic policy can be properly implemented to correct the problems. Due to rising influence of the Chinese economy on the world economic landscape, the book discusses how emerging economy like Thailand deals with rising influences of the Chinese economy and its impact on the synchronization of the world business cycle.

There are some new hypotheses emerging from my investigation of macroeconomic development of Thailand. I also suggest new measurements of macroeconomic growth and stability, international competitiveness, and financial riskiness caused by potential asset price bubbles. I hope that other emerging economies would learn from Thailand's macroeconomic policy management. We should not underestimate the important policy lessons from the past. If policy mistakes are repeated, people who are in charge of macroeconomic policy have yet to learn from the past mistakes. Until they realize and admit policy blunders, they would continue making the same mistakes over and over again.

This book is the fruit of long teaching experience and the culmination of my investigation of Thailand's macroeconomic policy in last three decades. Many people have helped me in this book in so many ways. I would like to express my gratitude to Peter G. Warr (Australian National University), who provided invaluable comments. I also owe sincere thanks to all my colleagues who have supported and encouraged me in my endeavors.

1 The Thai economy in the early years
1961–1990

1. Introduction

The bad experience of hyperinflation after World War II shaped macroeconomic policy in Thailand in the early 1960s. The fear of hyperinflation raised inflation awareness, which led to conservative fiscal and monetary policy. Price stability was given top priority more than other macro policy goals. It had strong implications on the conduct of fiscal and exchange rate policy in subsequent decades. As an introductory chapter, we discuss causes and remedies of hyperinflation by referring to Thailand's evolution of the banking and trade sectors. Then we move on to discuss the Thailand's macroeconomy during the first three decades of economic development from 1961 to 1990. We will understand how the development of the banking sector helped reduce the pressure on the price level. Nevertheless, expansion of international trade brought along inflationary pressure via rising prices of traded commodities. We will also examine the role of fiscal policy and exchange rate regimes, which are related to a mechanism which tends to correct internal and external imbalances. We can characterize this early period of Thailand's development as a period of strong growth with price stability. However, impressive GDP growth can be misleading unless we take into account of macroeconomic imbalances. Actual GDP growth must be adjusted downward by a certain degree of external and internal imbalances.

2. Hyperinflation and the return to price stability: 1948–1960

For money to perform its role as a medium of exchange and a store of value, the price level must be stable to create public confidence in the value of money they are holding. During World War II, huge spending of the Japanese military force in Thailand was financed by printing money. The rapidly growing money supply led to hyperinflation which peaked in 1945 at 92 percent, while money supply expanded at 76 percent (Figure 1.1). This was the only time when Thailand experienced hyperinflation.

After the war, excessive growth in money supply and the resulting hyperinflation was curbed by issuance of long-term government bonds. As a result, a

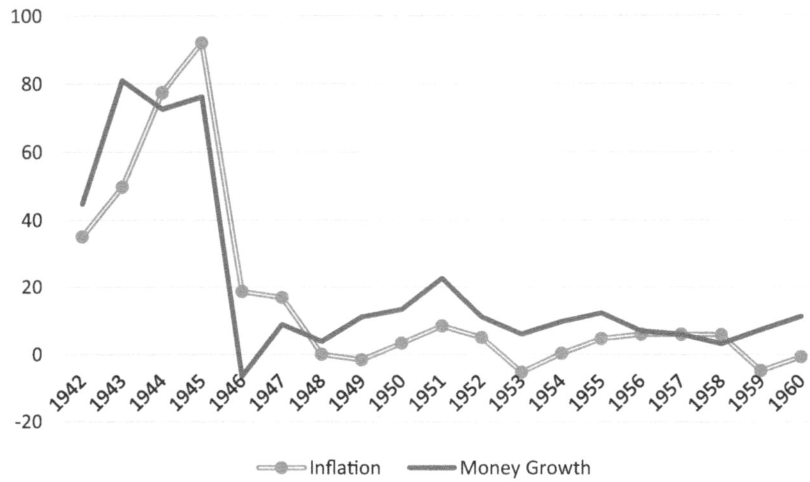

Figure 1.1 Hyperinflation and growth rate of money supply

Source: Bank of Thailand

negative growth of money supply was observed in 1946 together with a plunge in inflation rate (Figure 1.1). This was the result of issuing long-term government bonds to mop up excess money supply. Controlling the money supply is necessary to curb hyperinflation. However, inflation would have not come down unless there was also declining inflationary expectations. The hyperinflation in Thailand was high but not as high as those hyperinflations in Germany during 1920–1923, Zimbabwe in 2011, or Venezuela in 2018. Coomer and Gstraunthaler (2011) attributed reckless spending and exploding budget deficits to hyperinflation in Zimbabwe. Also, the forced seizure of commercial farms almost brought agricultural production to a halt. Zimbabwe's state of hyperinflation culminated into dollarization.

After price stability had been maintained in Thailand in 1948, confidence in the baht was regained. The national currency resumed its role of the medium of exchange and the store of value; commercial banks were able to attract deposits and perform the role of financial intermediaries.

Branches of foreign banks operating in Thailand during this period mainly conducted business related to international trade. Domestic commercial banks did not actively engage in mobilizing savings because the ability of savers was constrained by low income in the aftermath of the war. Commercial banks engaged mainly in financing foreign trade transactions. In 1945, there were only 11 branches of commercial banks. When international trade expanded, it required more banking services and more branches of commercial banks. By 1954, the number of bank branches for the whole country increased to 72. Nevertheless, these branches were not able to attract savings because banking habits among the

Thais had not firmly rooted. Saving was carried out by gold hoarding, because gold was considered a liquid asset and status symbol. As a result, savings and time deposits amounted to only 1 percent of GDP in the period of 1948–1960.

Commercial banks had no incentive to mobilize savings since loan demand was low. Limited investment opportunity did not generate high enough demand for loans to urge banks to mobilize savings. Bank credit amounted to 2 percent of GDP. Moreover, banks were not interested in holding low-yield government bonds. The lack of banks' lending and investment in assets was reflected in a high level of idle cash balances held by banks. According to Yang (1957), the average cash to bank deposits between 1947 and 1954 was around 34.5 percent. Nevertheless, bank excess reserves declined as the economy recovered from recession. Economic recovery in the early 1960s generated higher demand for bank loans and banks were able to reduce their idle cash balances.

Because of subdued inflation, the internal value of the baht was maintained steadily after the war, but the external value of the baht was unstable prior to 1955. The shortage of foreign exchanges led the government to adopt a multiple exchange rate system, in which exporters and importers were subjected to different exchange rates. The exchange rates for essential export commodities such as rice, rubber, and tin were undervalued to discourage exportation, while the exchange rates for imported goods were set closer to the free market rate. The motivation for the multiple exchange rate system was to prevent shortages of essential commodities. The success of the system was the ability to control inflationary expectations. There were some costs associated in terms of inefficiencies arising from disported commodity prices. Black markets and smuggling activities, and disincentives for producers of essential commodities, were natural outcomes of the multiple exchange rates. Once the inflation rate declined, as inflationary expectations died off slowly, there was no need to maintain this distorted exchange rate system.

As a result of the unification of multiple exchange rates into a single exchange rate since 1955, the baht exchange rate remained stable throughout the period 1955–1960. Speculations in foreign exchange markets were eliminated. The stable monetary environment in the late 1950s provided a necessary condition for a stable demand for money corresponding to expanding economic activities.

Investment opportunity and liquidity were improved for commercial banks during the period 1955–1960. New branches of commercial banks were established at the annual rate of 18.5 percent. Between 1955 and 1960, the ratio of time and savings deposits to GDP gradually increased to 3 percent on the average. At the end of 1960, the number of bank branches increased to 324 branches for the whole country. The increasing number of bank branches provided opportunities for financial savings that would otherwise had been put into physical assets or non-productive assets. Since both the ability to save and the opportunity to save were enhanced through rising income and bank branches, the only remaining factor for successful financial deepening was the willingness to save, which depends on positive real interest rates.

The interest rate on government bonds was raised from 6 percent to 8 percent in 1956. Trescott (1971) pointed out that this change led to a great increase in holding of government bonds by banks. Consequently, the government's reliance on credit extended by the Bank of Thailand was reduced. When commercial banks bought bonds to finance budget deficit, the process did not involve increasing the level of high power money. The implication is that government budget deficit can be financed by non-inflationary means.

3. Stable growth path: 1961–1990

The year 1961 was the year in which the first economic development plan was implemented. The focus was on building basic infrastructure. The share of investment to GDP rose from 15 percent to 25 percent in 1968, while the average annual GDP growth rate was 8.1 percent. Despite the high GDP growth, the average annual inflation rate was 2.2 percent. Low inflation and strong growth of per capita income led to substantial increases in deposits in commercial banks. The low inflation rate during this period means that the real rate of return from bank deposits was positive, providing incentive for financial saving. To promote saving, interest earned from saving and time deposits were tax exempted, raising the real net return on bank deposits further. Bank deposits became very attractive long-term financial savings.[1]

From 1961 to 1990, real output increased more or less at its trend growth path of 7 percent.[2] There were some episodes that actual GDP was above the trend, as new growth engines emerged. On the other hand, actual GDP fell below the trend because of the two oil price shocks during the period 1973–1974 and the period 1979–1980 (Figure 1.2). The slowdown in exports in the early 1980s as the result of the real exchange rate appreciation caused the output to drop below

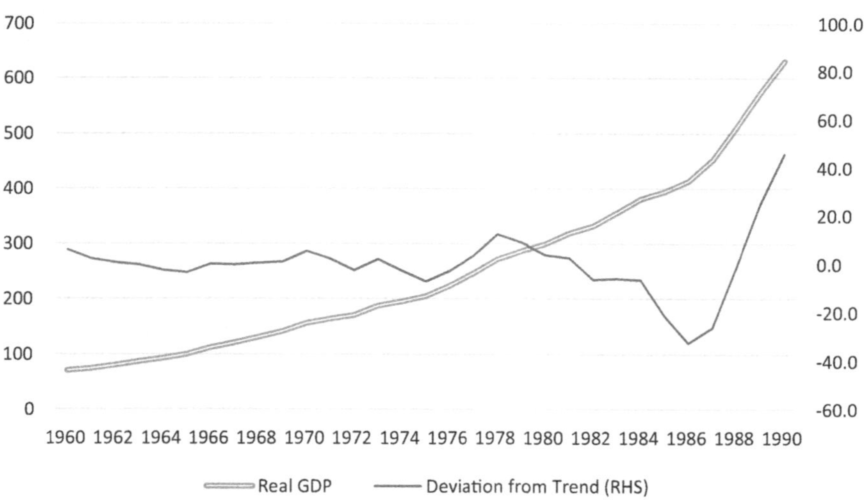

Figure 1.2 Stable growth path: 1960–1990

Source: Bank of Thailand

its potential level. The 1984 devaluation restored international competitiveness and the economy was spurred by rising export demand once again. The Thai economy regained the pre-shock growth path rapidly after 1986.

Policy responses to external shocks such as oil price shocks have significantly influenced the rate of economic growth in developing countries (Balassa, 1985). Thailand engaged in an outward-oriented policy stance at the early 1970s through heavy reliance on export promotion in response to external shocks. The trade policy had favorably affected growth performance. There was a positive deviation of output above its trend from 1988 to 1990.

Figure 1.3 illustrates that growth was driven by investment, exports, and imports. Although imports rose sharply during the oil shocks, both investment and imports were highly correlated. A large part of imports was capital goods. Imported capital goods contributed to productivity improvement in the manufacturing sector, which in turn gave rise to competitiveness and enhanced export capacity.

Comparing the periods 1961–1971 and 1972–1980, the average growth rate between the two periods was almost identical at around 7.2 percent. In the second period, the shock was more severe due to the sharp decline in the terms of trade. The reason why GDP growth was maintained at a high level is the rapid growth of exports. Exports grew every year from 7.6 percent in the first period (1961–1971) to 13.2 percent in the second period (1972–1980). Figure 1.3 shows that other engines of growth, private and public investment, grew less rapidly in the second period.

In the early 1960s, the first economic development plan was launched. As early as the 1960s, important economic institutions were established: the Board of Investment, the National Economic and Social Development Board (NESDB),

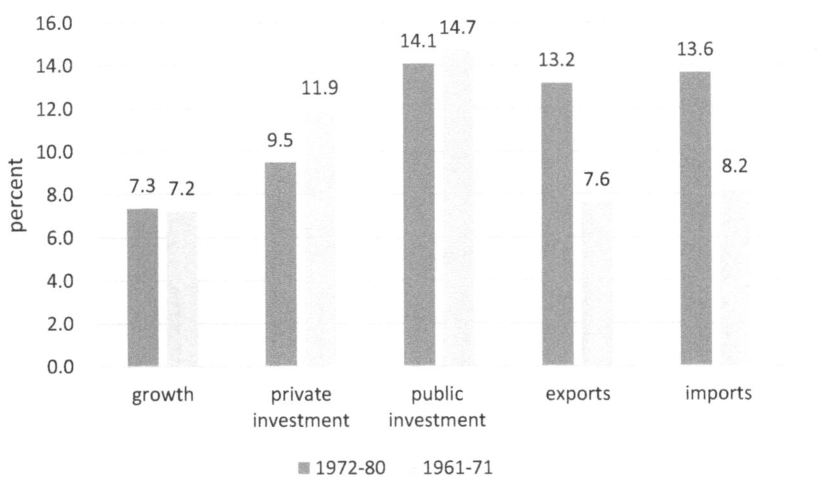

Figure 1.3 Growth of aggregate demand components

Source: Bank of Thailand

the Bureau of the Budget, and the Fiscal Policy Office. Development strategy adopted import substitution policy. This was the period of establishment of quality institutions, which matters for the long-term growth of the economy. The economy was able to grow rapidly without succumbing to high inflation, while maintaining external equilibrium. In the first development plan (1961–1966) the emphasis was given to infrastructure investment and the promotion of private investment. On the average in the period 1961–1971, public investment and private investment grew by 14.7 percent and 14.1 percent, respectively. Growth was driven by exports and investment during this first period.

In the second development plan (1967–1971), import substitution was replaced by export promotion policy; its impact was not obvious until after 1970, when the share of exports in GDP began to rise rapidly, reaching 35 percent by 1990 (Figure 1.4). The rising shares in GDP of exports and investment implies that, for a given level of export and investment growth, the impacts on output growth of increases in investment and exports had become larger.

Balassa (1978) provided the evidence supporting the hypothesis that exports, in particular manufactured exports, are related to economic growth. Exports permit the exporting countries to exploit economies of scale, and allocate and utilize resources as dictated by comparative advantage. Furthermore, pressures from international competition can force local firms to continue improving production efficiency.

The fourth development plan (1977–1981) gave importance to security spending. The political turmoil initiated the development goal of reducing social gaps and restoring natural resources. By the fifth plan (1982–1986), it was realized that Thailand needed public and private cooperation in order to stimulate business investment, while rural development and investment could not be ignored.

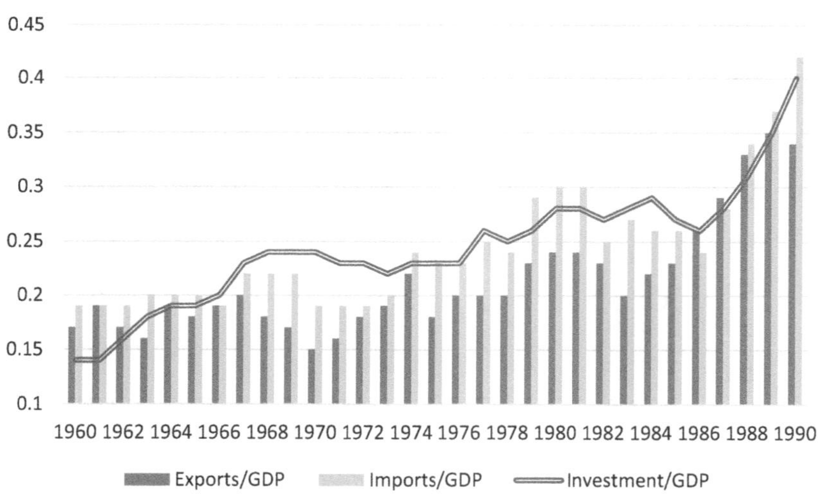

Figure 1.4 Growth drivers: trade and investment

Source: Bank of Thailand

As growth decelerated and fell below the potential path, the sixth plan (1987–1991) shifted back to maintaining economic growth and upgrading quality of life. What is surprising during the first three decades of economic development is that economic growth was achieved without sacrificing price stability.

There is no indication of a trade-off between high growth and the loss of price stability. High inflation was triggered by oil price shocks, which led to slowdown of economic activity. Growth slowdown can be attributed to cost-push inflation, but oil price shocks were followed by high commodity prices. Favorable export prices mitigated stagflation through compensating export demand.[3] Nevertheless, high growth did not lead to high inflation because of the increase in the demand for money, preventing the excess supply of money, which had led to high inflation as it occurred during and after the second world war period. The period of price stability with high growth would not be repeated in the 1990s.

Double-digit inflation episodes can be attributed to the two oil price shocks in 1973–1974 and 1979–1980. The inflation rate came down within a year after the cost-pushed inflation put upward pressure on consumer price levels. External shocks did not cause a runaway inflation as monetary growth rates were moderate. In Figure 1.5, if we exclude 4 years of double-digit inflation, faster growth rates were achieved without accelerating inflation. The terms of trade were also favorable in 1973 when the first oil shock struck. During this period, there was no single year that the economy went into recession. In other words, the economy maintained positive growth – albeit experiencing a slowdown during external shocks.

Figure 1.6 presents the elasticities of consumer price index with respect to import and export prices. Utilizing annual data from 1961 to 2000, the estimated price

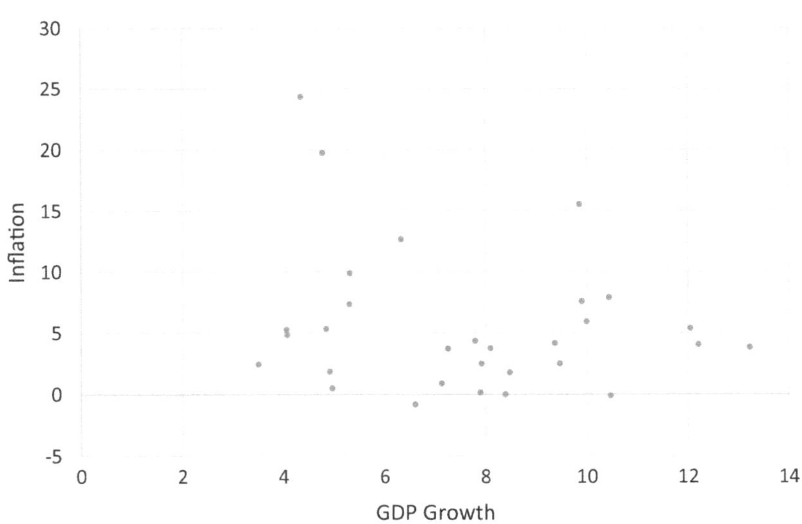

Figure 1.5 Growth and price stability: zero trade-off (1961–1990)

Source: Bank of Thailand

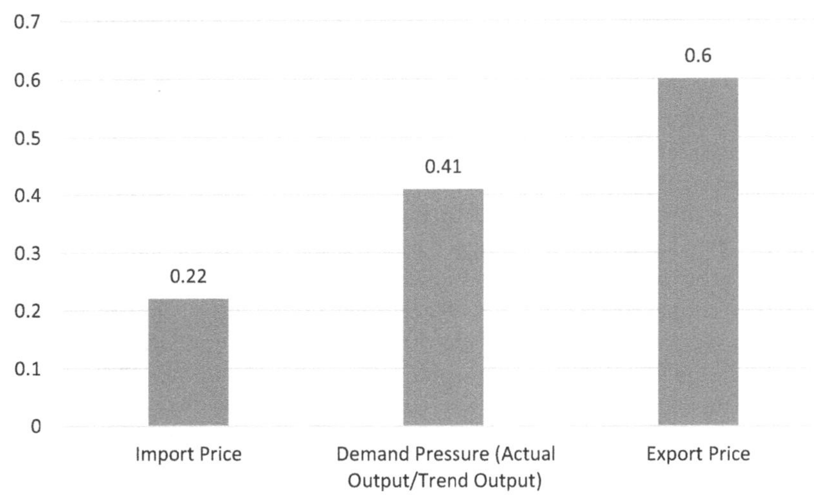

Figure 1.6 Consumer price elasticities

Source: Author's calculation

elasticities are compared between domestic demand and external demand pressures. The strongest price pressure came from the export sector, higher than imported inflation by a factor of three. Consumer price index comprises food categories, in which rice has the highest weight. For rice-exporting countries, rising world prices of rice imply rising consumer prices. When the economy was running above the trend path by 10 percent, it caused a domestic price increase of 4 percent. Since rice was still a major export commodity and household expenditure on food was high, export price inflation was the main culprit for domestic inflation. By keeping a sufficient amount of rice for domestic consumption, the inflation rate remained subdued. The sensitivity of consumer prices with respect to traded good prices suggests that exchange rate policy was a major instrument for controlling inflation.

There were other factors, aside from export and import prices, that contributed to inflation. The traded good prices of exports and imports explained consumer price index by only 44 percent. The rest stemmed from domestic demand pressure and other income and price policies, which involved policy that affected inflationary expectations such as price subsidies and price ceilings of key commodities.

4. Development of commercial banks in Thailand

Conditions for successful financial development include the ability to save, opportunity to save, and willingness to save. The ability to save is determined by income level. At the early stage of development after World War II, when per capital income was low, financial savings were limited. The opportunity to save was available to the public only when banks had expanded branches and established banking habits all over the country. If interest rates offered attractive rates of interest, the public would be willing to part their money in savings deposits. If deposits began to rise faster than output growth, the process of financial deepening would earnestly begin to take place. It is argued here that output growth took place because of the stability in the financial sector that provides sufficient financial resources for efficient private investment.[4]

The quantity of M1 was on average 18 percent of GDP during the period 1950–1954, when bank credit, time, and savings deposits were a small proportion of GDP. Financial institutions had not played the role of financial intermediaries. Private investment was mainly self-financed. If the real interest rate was negative, there would be no incentive to save. Output determines savings, while the real interest rate dictates how much people would allocate their earnings to financial savings. The substitution effect of higher opportunity cost of present consumption dominates the income effect when the interest rate rises. Thus, there is a strong correlation between the real net interest rate and the share of financial saving in total savings.

In 1969, the amount of time and savings deposits exceeded the combined amount of currency and demand deposits (M1). The cross-over point (shown in Figure 1.7) between the ratio of the narrow money and the quasi money indicates a rapid degree of financial deepening. Bank loans also increased faster than the GDP and their path was correlated with bank deposits. Commercial banks performed the full role of financial intermediaries, channeling money from savers to investors. Efficiency of the financial sector contributed to rapid economic

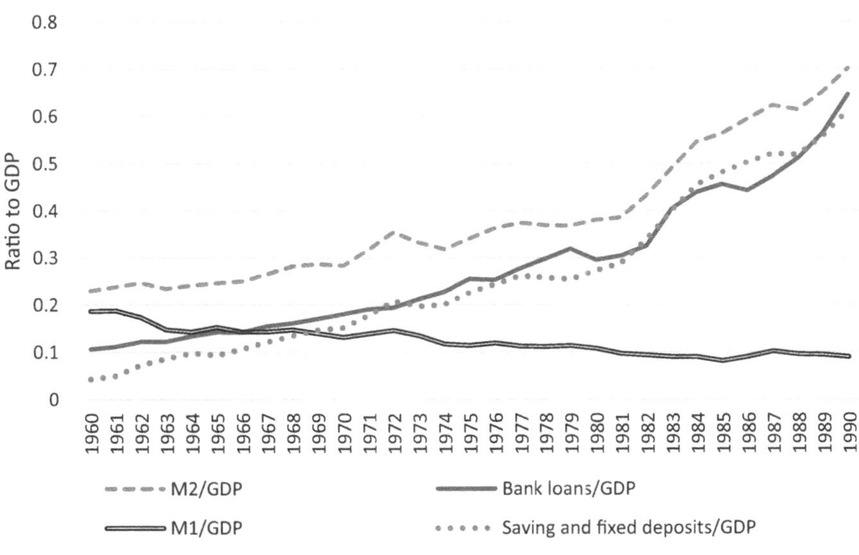

Figure 1.7 Financial deepening: 1960–1990

Source: Bank of Thailand

growth. Thailand has reached a development stage where financial progress made the traditional role of money as a medium of exchange become less important than wealth accumulation through financial savings. This structural transformation has an important implication on the velocity of money. As the country was transformed from a rural agricultural society to the urban manufacturing sector, the demand for money increased considerably, reflecting a higher degree of monetization throughout the country. By then, banking habits had been firmly established, resulting in a rapid increase in the demand for broad money (M2). As the velocity declined, the upward pressure on the price level was reduced, because there was no excess supply of money. Infrastructure investment or money-financed public investment projects did not lead to inflationary pressure. Price stability was secured despite strong economic growth.

From 1954–1969, income elasticity of demand for M1 was 0.7; demand for narrow money increased slower than income level. But during the period 1970–1990, the elasticity rose to 1.7, suggesting that the demand for money for transaction purposes increased a bit faster than income level. Figure 1.7 shows that the ratio of M1 to GDP gradually declined. Considering the same corresponding periods, the estimated income elasticity of demand for broad money (M2) increased from 1.17 to 1.53. This suggests that the demand for broad money increased much faster than income level. Consequently, the velocity of money declined. The income elastic demand for money bodes well for the rising ratio of M2 over GDP in Figure 1.7.

As pointed out by Driscoll and Lahiri (1983), income velocity of money in agricultural developing economies decline as these economies gradually transform into industrializing economies. The estimated coefficients shown in Figure 1.8 provide support for this hypothesis. Thailand was able to grow rapidly without experiencing price instability, thanks to the strength and soundness of its commercial banks which gave incentives to financial savings.

The impact of financial saving on output growth worked through the role of commercial banks as financial intermediaries, allocating limited financial resources to investors. Rapid capital accumulation was permitted by availability of bank credit. The broad money supply had a long-run relationship with bank loans, because banks' main sources of loanable funds were saving and fixed deposits. As banks expanded their lending to the private sector, they mobilized deposits from households. The increase in the loan-deposit ratio indicates the shortage in liquidity in the money markets (Figure 1.9). Since 1973, the volume of commercial banks' foreign liability increased considerably as banks began borrowing from abroad. The amount of foreign borrowings moved in line with the loan-deposit ratio. Financing domestic investment was no longer constrained by domestic savings. Commercial banks borrowed more money from abroad to circumvent low savings in order to supply bank credits to domestic investors. The growth of the economy was no longer constrained by internal resources. Capital mobility through bank borrowing had enhanced output growth. It was not just foreign trade openness but also financial openness that permitted high economic growth during the first 30 years of economic development.

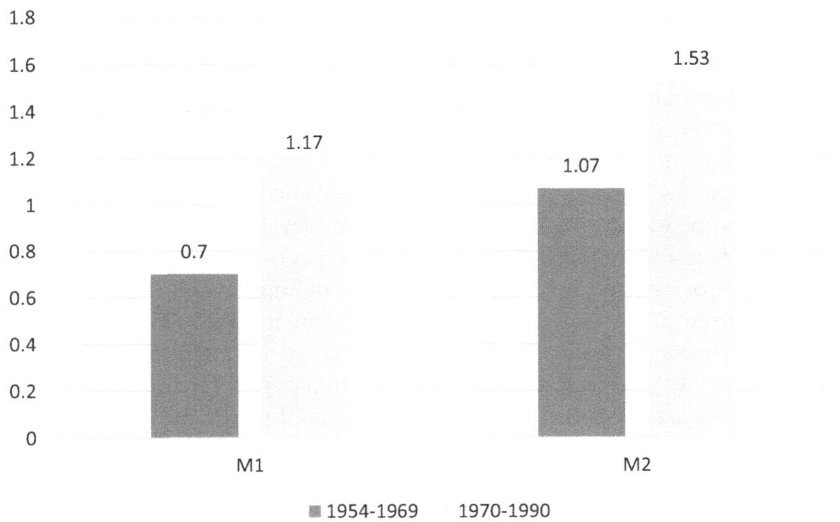

Figure 1.8 Income elasticity of demand for money
Source: Author's calculation

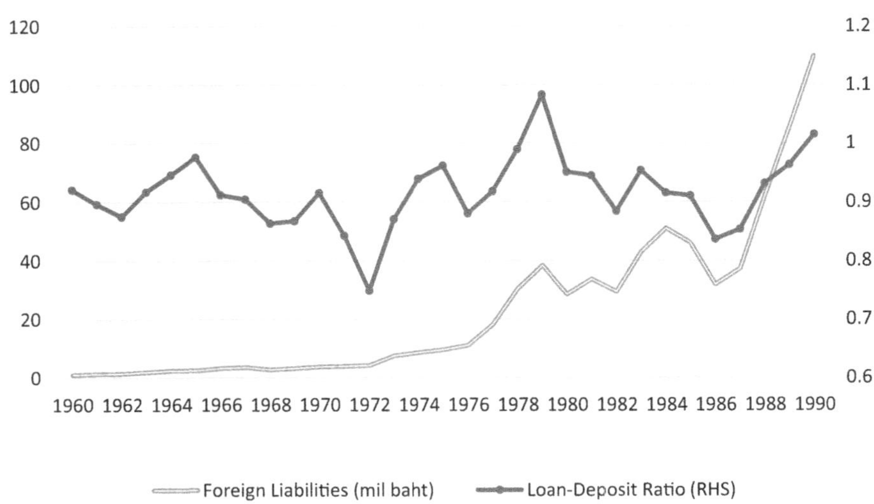

Figure 1.9 Banks' lending capacity and foreign borrowing
Source: Bank of Thailand

5. Development of the trade sector

As Keynes' psychological law of consumption indicates, the average propensity of consumption declines when income rises. Thailand's consumption expenditure share in the GDP declined steadily from 1960 to 1990. The implication on fiscal policy is quite clear; the size of the fiscal multiplier in the early 1960s was higher than the 1990s. Fiscal policy stimulus became less powerful than during the first decade of development. Furthermore, the impact of an increase domestic demand stimulus on output expansion was weakened further due to increased marginal propensity to imports.[5] Rising income levels also gave rise to higher rates of savings and imports, creating more leakages of fiscal expansionary policy.

The share of foreign trade (the sum of values of imports and exports) to GDP increased from 37 percent in 1960 to 76 percent in 1990 (Figure 1.10). An increasing degree of trade openness was related to output growth. Exporters were able to exploit economies of scale and they were forced to improve their efficiency in order to compete in the world markets. Imports can also help propel economic growth since imported capital goods have higher marginal productivity than domestic capital goods. Imported capital goods raised output capacity thereby enhancing long-term growth. It should be pointed out that the degree of openness is a result of trade reform, where tariff and export taxes rate were reduced. Thailand's trade reform was a continuous process which intensified in subsequent decades, when the country established free trade agreements with neighboring countries. The fluctuations in the trade openness index do not imply fluctuations in the degree of opening. It simply reflexed volatility in the trade values caused by terms of trade shocks or world recession.

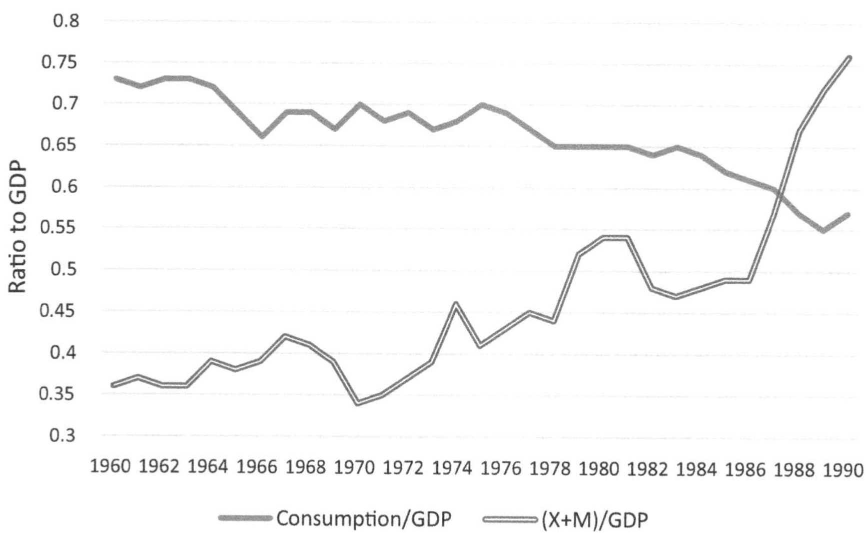

Figure 1.10 Trade openness and domestic consumption

Source: Bank of Thailand

In the first decade of the economic development plan, the trade deficit was insignificant. International trade expanded as the fixed exchange rate provided a conducive environment with zero foreign exchange risk. As the trade deficit enlarged after 1978, the need for exchange rate adjustment became apparent. The second oil shock broke out in 1979–1980 and resulted in substantial current account deficit which required adjustment to correct the imbalances.

By 1990, the amount of trade deficit deteriorated further as the baht appreciated, despite the fact that the public budget was surplus.[6] Thus, the widening trade deficit was caused mainly by the investment-savings gap and the lack of exchange rate adjustment. A high growth rate did not generate savings high enough to close the investment gap, which was financed through foreign borrowings. Because of capital inflows, the balance of payments was in surplus. Despite the trade deficit, international reserves rose rapidly as the result of capital inflows and the Bank of Thailand's desire to maintain a fixed exchange rate. Dealing with excessive capital inflows has been a perennial problem for the Bank of Thailand.

Exchange rate adjustments became more frequent as the trade balance was widening. In May 1981, the baht was devalued against the US dollar by 1.1 percent, which was followed by another devaluation of 8.7 percent in July 1981. Another major devaluation was undertaken in November 1984 by 14.9 percent, followed by another 1.9 percent in December 1985. These devaluations were policy responses to current account deficit and the loss of competitiveness caused by the baht's appreciation against other currencies. The number of months of import-covered international reserves declined steadily before the mid-1981 and November 1984 devaluations. Since the baht was pegged with the US dollar, the appreciation of the US dollar against other currencies implied that the baht was strengthened, resulting in the loss of competitiveness in non-US markets. These devaluations were undertaken as all other measures failed to correct the current account deficit. The ceiling on the issuance of letter of credit in 1983 and the 18 percent ceiling on bank lending were imposed to avoid adverse political consequences of large devaluations. By using indirect measures, the Bank of Thailand did not correct the root of the problem, which was the unrealistic exchange rate.

Devaluations were later proved quite successful as the level of international reserves increased sharply, from the level of USD 2 billion in 1985 to more than USD 13 billion in 1990 (Figure 1.11). Both large devaluations did not lead to inflationary pressure. Nevertheless, a basket of foreign currencies to determine the baht-dollar exchange rate continued providing the stability of the baht-dollar rate. The weight of the US dollar in the basket was more than two-thirds and had been rising over time; as a result the baht-dollar exchange rate remained stable well into the 1990s (Warr and Nidhiprabha, 1996). This practice led to unsustainable current account deficits in the late 1990s. In hindsight, it seems that Thailand had not leaned any lessons from maintaining an unrealistic exchange rate for so long that it outweighed its benefit of having a stable environment to promote international trade.

However, the international trade environment was hardly stable because of the oil price hikes. At the beginning of the 1960s, the terms of trade were favorable

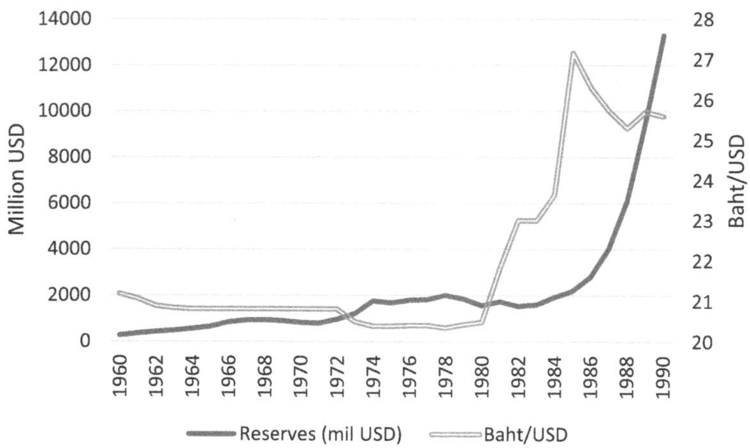

Figure 1.11 Baht-USD exchange rate and international reserves

Source: Bank of Thailand

to Thailand (Figure 1.12). The terms of trade deteriorated marginally in the 1960s. As oil prices rose, export commodities such as rubber also fetched higher prices. The first oil shock in 1973–1974 was compensated by higher commodities prices. Thailand was not affected very much by the oil shocks. In fact, the country experienced an increasing trend of primary commodity exports between 1974 and 1990.

According to empirical evidence provided by Bleaney and Greenaway (2001), terms of trade volatility can adversely impact countries which export primary products. Investment and growth can be depressed when the terms of trade turns against primary exporting countries. Furthermore, growth and investment can increase after the terms of trade improve and real exchange rate overvaluation is eliminated. Prebisch (1959) argued that industrialization is an inescapable part of the process of changes accompanying a gradual improvement in per capita income in poor countries. Because of a relatively low income elasticity of demand for primary commodities, Thailand moved to industrialization and changed the export pattern from agricultural products to manufactured goods so that the country did not have to suffer from long-term decline in the terms of trade by exporting primary products.[7] Figure 1.12 suggests that the terms of trade had turned against Thailand since 1973. When the overvaluation of the baht was corrected, the economy resumed its stable growth path.

6. Sustainability of fiscal position

The conservative fiscal policy of the Thai government in the early stages of development can be viewed from Figure 1.13. The government adhered to balanced budget principles during the General Thanom Kittikachorn administration

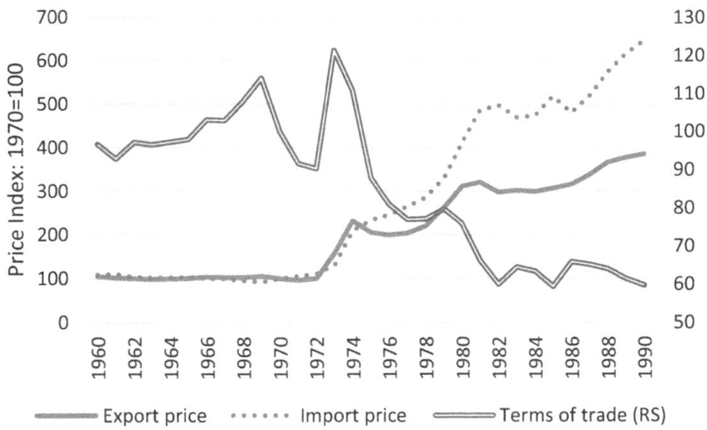

Figure 1.12 Deteriorating terms of trade
Source Bank of Thailand

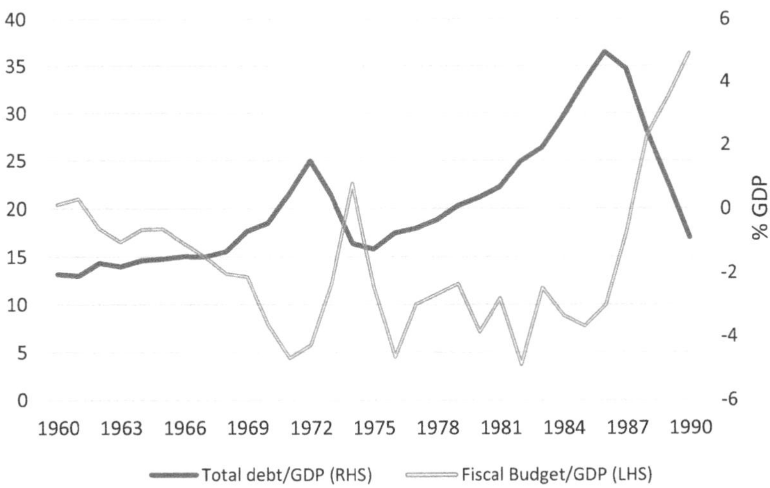

Figure 1.13 Fiscal sustainability 1960–1990
Source: Bank of Thailand

(1964–1974). The size of the budget deficit was larger in the early 1970s but the budget turned into a surplus in 1974 because of the trade tax revenues. During the premiership of MR Kukrit Pramoj in 1975 the budget deficit started growing due to his populist policy that injected money into rural villages. The budget deficit expanded during General Prem Tinsulanonda's regime, which began in 1981. By 1989, the strong growth of the Thai economy generated tax revenues and the country experienced substantial surplus budget, enabling the government to undertake a trade liberalization program through tariff reduction.

Public debt is a mirror image of fiscal position. Figure 1.13 shows that as the public debt increased gradually in the early 1960s, the increasing trend reversed as the budget deficit was curtailed. That reversal was observed again after 1975 when the budget deficit was enlarged and the share of public debt started climbing from 15 percent in 1975 to above 35 percent of GDP in 1986. The ability to cut down the budget deficit led to a sharp decline in the debt to GDP ratio, hence the turnaround in the fiscal position.

The first 30 years of Thailand's economic development shows some valuable lessons. If a country wants to maintain growth and stability, fiscal policy must be flexible enough to ensure fiscal sustainability. In the late 1980s, it was thought that 35 percent debt to GDP was extremely high and the government must use fiscal austerity programs to maintain fiscal stability. A large budget deficit then was considered unhealthy and dangerous to the economy.

For macroeconomic policymakers, growth is only one of the three major ultimate targets. Growth must be consistent with price stability and external equilibrium. The latter can be measured by the position of the current account. A too-high surplus or a large deficit in the current account leads to future problems. A high current account surplus can bring about expansion of money supply if the country is under a fixed exchange rate system. The inflation rate will rise if the central bank cannot control domestic money supply in line with output growth. On the other hand, a too-high current account deficit puts strong pressure on the currency and may lead to inflation after currency depreciation.

It is argued here that a better measurement of macroeconomic objectives must encompass the three macroeconomic objectives: growth, price stability, and current account balances. GDP growth rate can be adjusted by subtracting elements of internal and external equilibrium. If policymakers value price stability more than current account equilibrium, they can assign a higher weight for inflation than the level of the current account deficit. For example, the weighted average scheme gives 0.7 to the inflation or disinflation rate, and 0.3 to the current account deficit or surplus. By adjusting the actual GDP growth rate by the weighted average of the absolute values of the annual percentage price changes and current account, we can obtain imbalance-adjusted growth rates. If both internal and external equilibrium are achieved, the actual GDP growth equals the imbalance-adjusted growth (IAG) rate. There would be no imbalances for policymakers to worry about.

But internal and external balances can hardly exist. Growth will always lead to price pressure, while growth also generates demand for imported goods resulting in current account deficit. Therefore, the actual GDP growth is always higher than the imbalance-adjusted growth rate. But it can never go below the IAG rate, because of the construction of the index which assigns an absolute value of inflation and current account positions. Figure 1.14 illustrates the actual GDP growth and the IAG rates. The former registers positive values over two decades: 1970–1989. Imbalances occurred during the two oil shocks, 1974 and

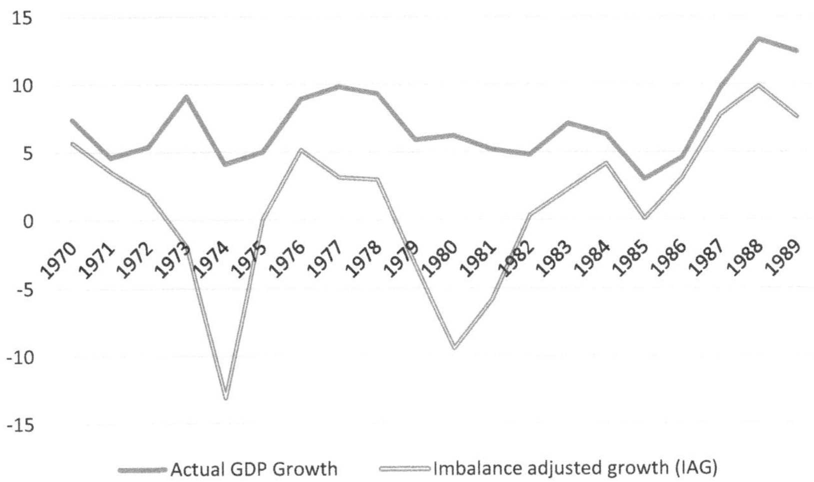

Figure 1.14 Imbalance-adjusted growth (IAG)

Source: Bank of Thailand and author's calculation

1980, causing the IAG to register –13.1 percent and –9.5 percent, respectively. High inflation and a large current account deficit weighed down the IAG rate. There was another turning point which took place in 1985, after a large devaluation gave rise to inflation. Nevertheless, devaluation-induced inflation returned to normality in the following year. The imbalance-adjusted growth was on the uptrend again, suggesting sustainable growth as Thailand entered the 1990s.

7. Concluding remarks

The stable long-term growth of the Thai economy was characterized by an average annual growth rate of 7 percent between 1961 and 1990. The process of financial deepening led to price stability and strong economic growth. There are long-run relationships among real output, money supply, and bank credit. Trade openness has led to rapid growth and transformed the output structure of the Thai economy. During this period, the Thai economy experienced two oil price shocks, when inflation rose to double digits. Nevertheless, the economy adjusted back to price stability within a year. The problem with the current account deficit was dealt with by two major devaluations in 1981 and 1984. After that, the baht-dollar exchange rate under the currency pegging system gradually returned to a fixed exchange rate system, where the weight of the USD in the basket of currencies had increased over the years.

An important lesson can be learned from Thailand's experience during the early development stage. Price stability is the key condition for successful long-term growth. Without price stability, financial development and exchange rate movements can thwart sustainable growth. Without rising demand for money and exchange rate stability, growth can be disrupted. The multiple exchange rate system adopted briefly after World War II calmed down inflationary expectations. Price distortions and price controls are temporary measures, which cannot be employed to an extent that their inefficiency effects outweigh the cost of stabilization. Financial discipline is also a precondition for price stability. The Thai government did not resort to money-financed budget so as to avoid fueling inflationary expectations.

Notes

1 The withholding tax on interest income from fixed deposits was introduced in 1977.
2 Easterly (2001) reported that in 1980–98, median per capita income growth in developing countries was 0.0 percent, as compared to 2.5 percent in 1960–1979.
3 When crude oil prices increase, export prices of natural rubber rise in line with the price of synthetic rubber, a byproduct in oil refinery process.
4 The Granger causality test indicates that, during the period 1950–1990, money supply Granger causes output.
5 Ingram (1971) pointed out that Thailand had high-income elasticity of demand for imports. When exports fell, imports fell immediately by the same degree. This adjustment mechanism preserved the country's trade balance position before 1950.
6 The hypothesis of twin deficits will be discussed in Chapter 6.
7 The share of rice and rubber in total exports declined dramatically from 35 percent and 20 percent, respectively, in 1960, to around 5 percent in 1990.

References

Balassa, Bela. 1978. "Exports and Economic Growth: Further Evidence." *Journal of Development Economics*, 5: 181–189.

Balassa, Bela. 1985. "Exports, Policy Choices, and Economic Growth in Developing Countries After the 1973 Oil Shock." *Journal of Development Economics*, 18: 23–35.

Bleaney, Michael, and David Greenaway. 2001. "The Impact of Terms of Trade and Real Exchange Rate Volatility on Investment and Growth in Sub-Saharan Africa." *Journal of Development Economics*, 65 (2): 491–500.

Coomer, Jayson, and Thomas Gstraunthaler. 2011. "The Hyperinflation in Zimbabwe." *Quarterly Journal of Austrian Economics*, 14: 311.

Driscoll, Michael J., and Ashok K. Lahiri. 1983. "Income-Velocity of Money in Agricultural Developing Economies." *The Review of Economics and Statistics*: 393–401.

Easterly, William. 2001. "The Lost Decades: Developing Countries' Stagnation in Spite of Policy Reform 1980–1998." *Journal of Economic Growth*, 6: 135–157.

Ingram, James C. 1971. *Economic Change in Thailand*, 1850–1970. Stanford: Stanford University Press.

Prebisch, Raul. 1959. "Commercial Policy in the Underdeveloped Countries." *The American Economic Review*, 49: 251–273.

Trescott, Paul B. 1971. *Thailand's Monetary Experience: The Economics of Stability*, New York: Prager Publisher.

Warr, Peter, and Bhanupong Nidhiprabha. 1996. "Thailand's Macroeconomic Miracle." *Stable Adjustment and Sustained Growth.* Washington, DC: The World Bank and Oxford University Press.

Yang, Shu-Chin. 1957. *A Multiple Exchange Rate System: An Appraisal of Thailand's Experience, 1946–1955.* Madison: University of Wisconsin Press.

2 The resilience of the Thai economy

1991–2005

1. Introduction

The Asian currency crisis that followed Thailand's decision to float the baht in July 1997 has become a watershed in the history of Thailand's economic development. We have learned a great deal about what went wrong and what could have been done to prevent the crisis. Pundits warn that history might repeat itself and that we might experience another crisis in the near future, because Thailand has not completely restructured the economy to prepare for the next crisis. Economists are skeptical about the benefits of the pork-barrel spending of the government and fearful of enlarging public debt.

It is argued in this chapter that there exist certain mechanisms in the structure of the Thai economy that would lessen the impact of the next economic crisis, if any, whether the shock was internal or external. It is impossible to rule out various shocks in the future, such as oil price hikes, realignments of major currency values, or some other kind of crisis contagion. Future shocks in the real or financial sector would not have a long-lasting impact. They would simply reduce Thailand's economic growth temporarily below a stable growth path. The Thai economy was resilient enough to regain its pre-shock growth path in a few years after the Asian financial crisis. However, since 2006, when the country succumbed to internal shocks such as military coups and political unrest, the ability to rebound has faded.

This chapter provides an analysis of the underlying changes in the structure of the Thai economy that helped the economy recover immediately after a year of economic crisis.[1] An outward orientation strategy attracted foreign direct investment (FDI) and stimulated growth in industrial production, which led to the transformation of the country's output and export structures.

We explore the relationship between growth, price stability, and the sustainability of current accounts. Fiscal balances and their implication on the public debt are discussed. We outline developments in the financial sector that made Thailand become less vulnerable to future financial shocks. Dynamic aspects of the export sector that made the Thai economy recover rapidly after the currency crisis are presented, while highlighting the importance of the export-led strategy that enabled Thailand to take the opportunity to grow following an upturn in the world business cycle.

2. Growth versus price stability

As discussed in the previous chapter, the Thai economy during the period 1961–1990 expanded rapidly without sacrificing price stability. The development of the banking sector generated demand for money as the economy took off at the early stage of development. In the period 1991–2005, the trade-off between growth and price stability become more pronounced. The main traditional macroeconomic policy goals are growth, price stability, and a sustainable current account deficit. Since there are always trade-offs among these goals, policymakers may have to strike a balance between growth and acceptable levels of internal and external stability. As the Thai economy has become an integral part of the global economy, these goals have become affected by external factors such as world business cycles and oil prices.

Figure 2.1 provides evidence of the trade-off between growth and price stability by excluding the 2 years of the Asian financial crisis in 1997–1998. During this episode, inflation rose while growth rate stalled, due to the impact of massive currency depreciation. There is a positive relationship between growth and inflation.[2] During the double-digit growth in the late 1980s and early 1990s, inflationary pressure began to build up even after the growth rate slowed down. Inflation inertia played an important role in delaying price adjustments. With a moderate growth rate of around 5 percent, the pressure on the price level was not as great as when the economy rose above the trend growth path restrained by existing output capacity. Once inflationary expectations were formed, their impact on wage and price adjustments was felt in subsequent years.

The second oil price shock in 1979–1980 resulted in double-digit inflation, reaching 19 percent in 1980. Another extraordinary year was 1998; inflation

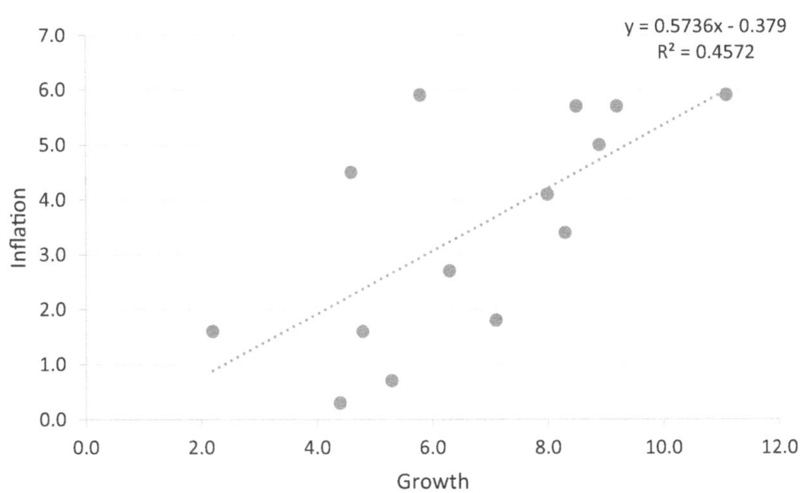

Figure 2.1 Trade-off between growth and price stability, 1990–2005 (excluding 1997–1998)

Source: Bank of Thailand

increased to 8 percent, despite a massive devaluation of the baht. Nevertheless, these two episodes bode well for a low inflation prone economy like Thailand. The inflation rate increased substantially during these two events, but it also came down remarkably well within subsequent years. There was no wage indexation that would allow spiral inflationary expectations. Because of low inflation, there was no need to create interest rate and bond indexation. Printing money to finance a budget deficit was not an option for the Bank of Thailand. When the government ran a budget deficit, most of the deficit was financed through issuing bonds; therefore, there was no expansion of the monetary base.

Considering the trade-off between growth and external imbalances, high-income growth generated higher demand for imported consumer products as well as capital goods. Thus, a high-income growth episode was associated with current account deficit. Even if growth was driven by exports, imported intermediate products are required for production of export goods. During the boom years in the early 1990s, high growth led to a widening current account deficit. However, during a slowdown and moderate growth period, current accounts became surplus (Figure 2.2). High growth induced more imports of capital goods and intermediate inputs for manufacturing production. Because growth is driven by exports and investment, surges in imports and a widening current account deficit became natural consequences of a high-growth episode. When growth collapsed in 1998, Thailand experienced a current account surplus for the first time in the recent history of its economic development. The surplus became smaller and eventually petered out as the Thai economy regained its pre-shock growth path.

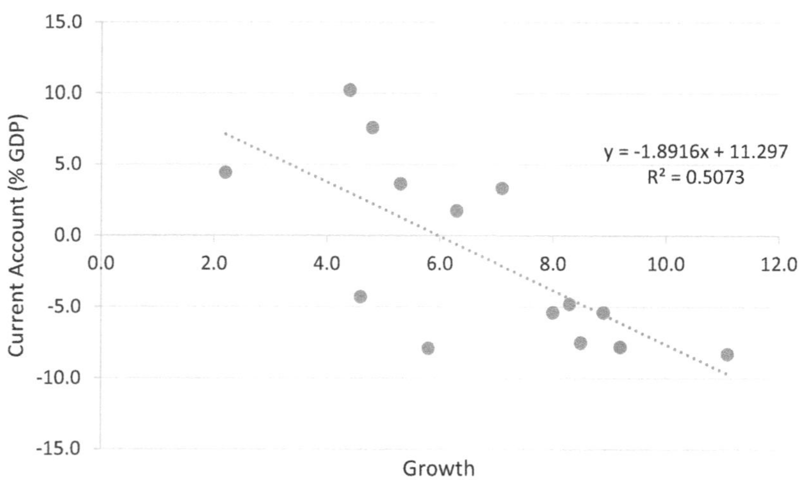

Figure 2.2 Growth and external imbalance: 1990–2005 (excluding 1997–1998)

Source: Bank of Thailand

The negative relationship between the current account surplus, as percentage of GDP, and growth rate depicted in Figure 2.2 can be thought of as a causal relation. The amount of current account surplus also depends on inflation. High inflation induces more imports and depresses exports. Thus, current account deficit was consistent with high GDP growth and high inflation.[3] The policy implication is quite clear: If growth can be achieved with price stability, there would be no complication with the external imbalances.

In the previous chapter, Figure 1.20 illustrates the IAG (imbalance-adjusted growth) rate of the period 1961–1990. The conclusion is that growth rate during the early years of development was sustainable. Using the same method of calculating the IAG for the period 1991–2005, it is found that the IAG was negative only in 1998 (Figure 2.3). This is not surprising because the actual output growth contracted by 10 percent, while inflation was high and current account was deficit.

The IAG rebounded quickly into positive territory in 1999, indicating a very high degree of resilience. From 1999 to 2005, the IAG rate remained positive. As pointed out earlier, the key macroeconomic variables, growth, inflation, and current account, interacted among each other through feedback effects and lagged responses. The IAG captures the three dimensions of the macroeconomic goals.

To the policy question on how to maintain price stability, the answer is the ability to manage food prices. Figure 2.4 suggests a positive relationship between the consumer price index (CPI) and the food price index. It is not surprising that food price index is highly correlated with the CPI, simply because of the high weight of food prices in the household consumption basket.

For low income households, food amounts to a very high percentage of household expenditures. High food prices can hurt the poor in urban areas. On the other hand, they can be a boon to farmers in rural areas. In the early years of

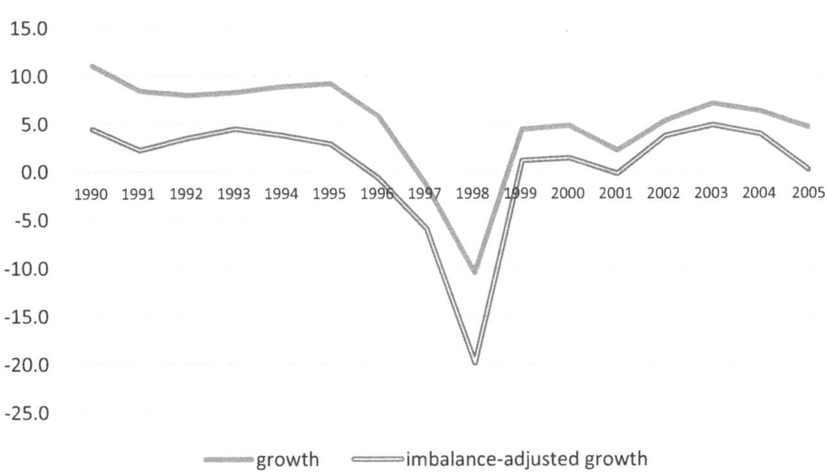

Figure 2.3 Actual and imbalance-adjusted growth (IAG) rate: 1990–2005

Source: Author's calculation

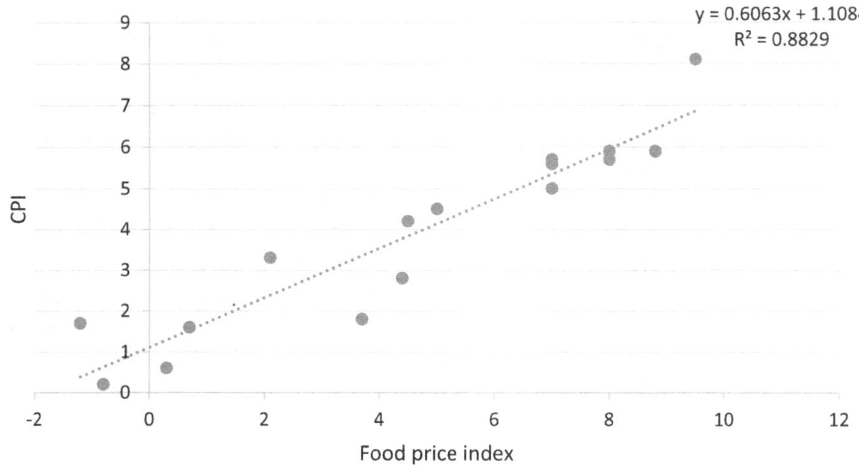

Figure 2.4 CPI and food price inflation 1990–2005

Source: Bank of Thailand

development, inflation was affected by export prices of commodity such as rice. During the period of 1990–2005, the structure of exports changed in such a way that manufactured goods dominated food exports. The ability to control food prices lies in price and income policies, which directly affect inflationary expectations. Since food prices are affected by energy prices, fuel price controls are a means to control inflationary expectations.

Figure 1.7 in the previous chapter indicates that in the early period of development domestic inflation was affected by exported and imported inflation and the pressure from external demand was stronger than the domestic demand pressure. When actual output grew faster than potential growth rate, the excess demand pressure gave rise to domestic inflation.

But during the crisis years between 1997 and 1998, there was a collapse in domestic demand. Investment and private consumption expenditures declined by 36.4 percent and 6.5 percent, respectively (Figure 2.5). Thus, it was the cost-push inflation caused by currency depreciation that was responsible for high inflation during the crisis years. When the exchange rate was stabilized in subsequent period 1999–2005, the inflation rate returned to its normal level. The growth rate of domestic demand for private and public consumption did not rise above 5.5 percent, while investment growth rebounded to 9.7 percent. This suggests a degree of resilience of the private aggregate demand, in particular the increase in investment to 9.7 percent on the average, which was at the same as the pre-shock growth rate between 1991 and 1996. By 2005, growth accelerated and so did inflation and current account deficit. The IAG was near zero level, suggesting imminent macroeconomic problems, which required the government to initiate a stabilization policy.

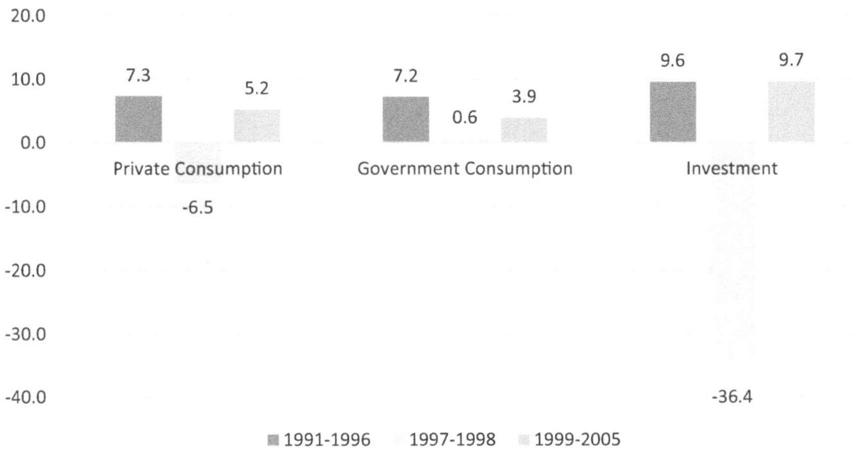

Figure 2.5 Growth of domestic demand

Source: Bank of Thailand

3. Strengthening fiscal position

After PM Thaksin Shinawatra came into office in 2000, populist policy programs were employed by injecting money into rural areas and the grassroots economy. These programs provided social safety nets and targeted poverty reduction. The Thai government attempted to reduce reliance on external demand by boosting domestic demand through promoting local enterprises and developing indigenously owned production capacity. Housing projects for the poor, village funds, and one-village-one-product projects were examples of this dual track development strategy. The shift to domestic demand-led growth can be compatible with export-led growth, in particular when there is a weak demand for exports from the rest of the world. The Thai government's focus was on five sectors where Thailand would develop market niches: a world center of graphic design; the Detroit of Asia; tropical fashion; kitchen of the world; and tourism capital of Asia. Within these five competitive areas that the government wanted to develop, the economy could not depend solely on domestic demand because of the inability to exploit economies of scale. Critics argued that this kind of spending to promote competitive strength and social safety nets was ineffective, inefficient, and would lead to chronic fiscal imbalances.[4] After 4 years in power, the Thaksin government's budget deficit turned around into a marginal surplus in 2003, thanks to rapidly rising tax revenue buoyed by economic recovery.

As shown in Figure 2.6, both spending and revenue declined after the 1998 recession, but they trended upward after rapid recovery in the early 2000s. However, revenue rose faster than spending, resulting in a narrowing budget deficit. This came about as a result of the fact that utilization of the allocated budget was

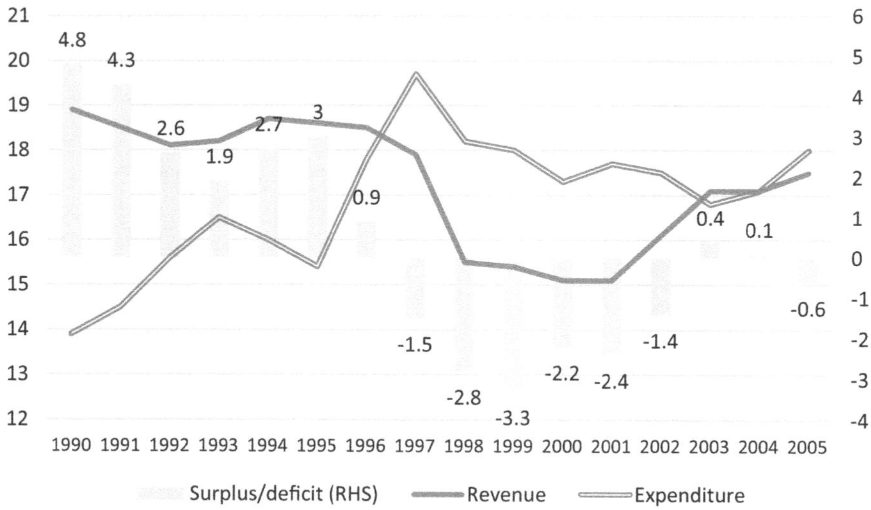

Figure 2.6 Fiscal balance 1990–2005

Source: Bank of Thailand

not high. A new rule was introduced to ban the budget to carry over into the next fiscal year.[5] As such, planned expenditures were always greater than actual budget spending. On the revenue side, the buoyancy of the revenue always guarantees that tax revenues rise faster than the GDP level.

Despite the fact that the value added tax rate has been maintained at 7 percent, instead of returning to the pre-crisis tax rate of 10 percent, value added tax revenues increased rapidly as a result of strong growth in consumption.[6] Between 1999 and 2005, annual private consumption increased on average 5.2 percent – a big jump from a reduction by 6.5 percent between 1997 and 1998 (Figure 2.5). Trade reform has been undertaken since the early 1970s by slowly dismantling tariff walls that protect domestic industries. The surge in imports enhanced revenue collections, although tariff rates have been reduced regularly in line with trade liberalization and the establishment of free trade areas with ASEAN countries.

Achieving high GDP growth of around 6 percent for three consecutive years, from 2002 to 2004, guarantees that the budget deficit is sustainable. It should be noted that inflationary pressure from money-financed budget deficits is not plausible in the context of the institutional setting in Thailand, due to existing laws limiting the size of the deficit and the ceiling on public debt. In 2004, the public debt ceiling was reduced from 55 percent to 50 percent of GDP, while the debt-service ceiling was set at 12 percent of the annual fiscal budget. This fiscal discipline was institutionalized to prevent ballooning of the budget deficit.

Figure 2.7 shows that, as a result of the rapid growth achieved after the 1998 output contraction, fears of explosive public debt were exaggerated. External

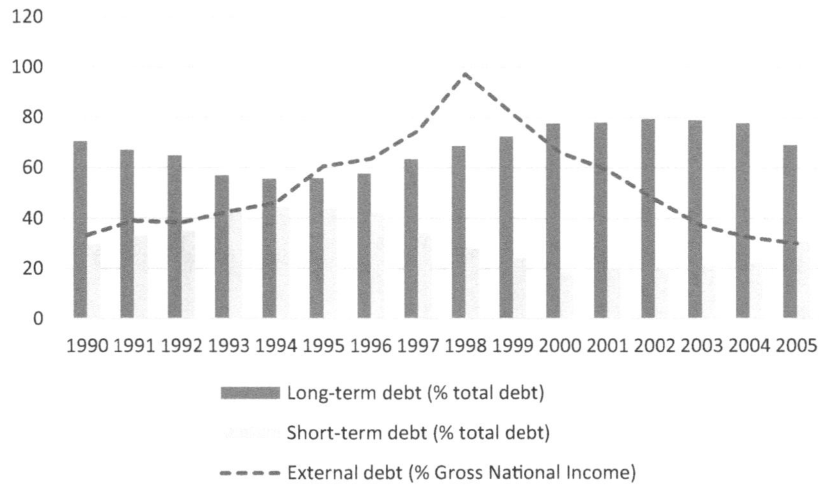

Figure 2.7 External debts: short and long terms

debt, as a percentage of GNI, peaked in 1998 and started to decline rapidly. Reliance on foreign debt was reduced, thanks to the development of the government bonds markets, during the time when domestic interest rates were low. In addition, the composition of foreign capital flows changed in favor of long-term flows or a cold type of foreign capital. Heavy reliance on short-term foreign borrowings, which are more volatile than foreign direct investment, has been cited as a cause of the currency crisis. By 2001, long-term debt amounted to almost 80 percent of total external debt. The short-term debt, which was heightened to 46 percent, began to decline gradually. By 2000, the short-term debt amounted to only 20 percent of total debt. As such, the vulnerability of a sudden capital flight was greatly diminished.

4. Impact of financial liberalization

Portfolio investments from abroad can stir up activities in the stock market, but they are simply short-term capital flows. Capital flight can occur with rapid changes in investment sentiment caused by random arrivals of good news and bad news. Figure 2.8 illustrates this point. The movement of stock prices is a leading economic indicator because stock prices are determined by expectations of dividends. The expected payments are affected by expectations of corporate performance in the future but, in the short run, stock prices are subject to volatilities caused by random shocks of good news and bad news.

The declining trend of interest rates has had important impacts on the Thai economy. The decline encouraged the boom in the bond markets as investors looked for alternative assets to hold as sources of fixed income. The bond market

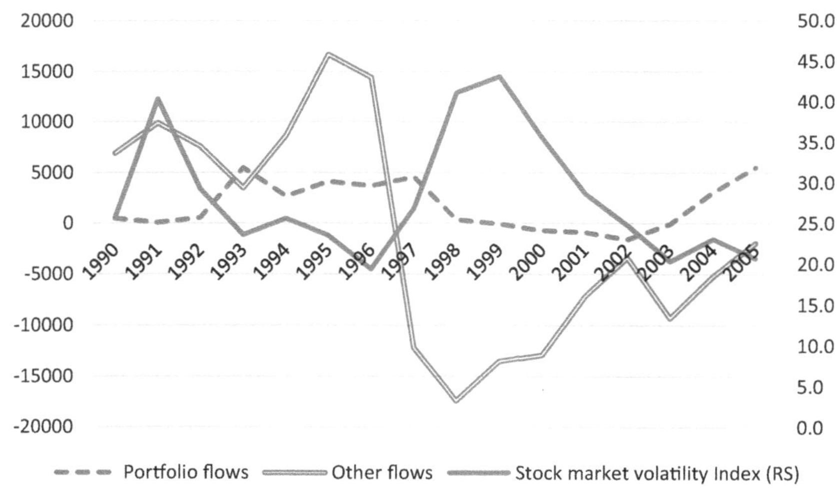

Figure 2.8 Capital flows and market volatility

Source: Bank of Thailand

has emerged as an alternative source of financial resources for firms. Although Thailand is still basically a bank-based economy, availability of resources from the capital market can provide funds when bank loans are not available during a credit crunch. Households also enjoyed high fixed incomes from holding bonds as the real interest rates from bank deposits became negative. Holding bank deposits becomes exceedingly unattractive when fixed deposit rates are below 1 percent, notwithstanding a 15 percent withholding tax rate on interest income. Consequently, the bond market has performed remarkably well during the period of low interest rates. The fact that the government budget deficit is financed by issuing bonds has helped the bond market through establishing the benchmark for bond yields with various maturities. The reference yield curve was not available during the years when the government ran a budget surplus in the 1990s.

High interest rates are the results of high inflation and an overheated economy. The prime lending rate was on the rise in 1995 but it was too late and too little to curb excessive investment. When it was realized that the tight monetary policy applied in the aftermath of the crisis was too severe, causing a contraction in bank credit, the Bank of Thailand relaxed its restrictive monetary policy as the world interest rates began to fall. The prime lending rate of commercial banks had been declining since 1999 until 2003. Because low inflation translates into low interest rates, economic growth can be sustained if the interest rates can be maintained at low levels for a considerable period.

The period of low inflation and low interest rates in Thailand coincides with the general trend in the world. Low interest rates in Thailand enable large corporations to refinance their external debt with cheap loans from domestic banks.

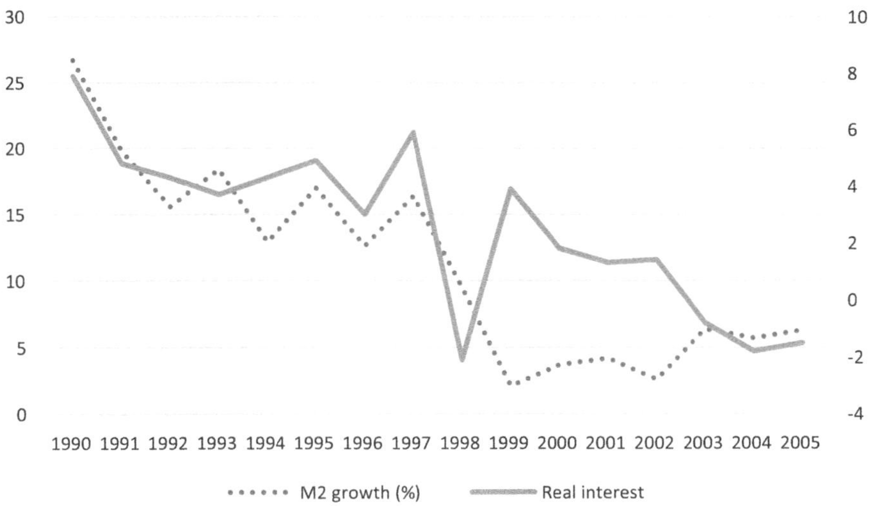

Figure 2.9 Financial savings and real interest rates

Source: Bank of Thailand

Consequently, the vulnerability to currency shocks in the future has been reduced considerably. This is true for both the private and the public sector. Declining inflation and interest rates have paved the way to future sustainable recovery.

The real deposit rates trended downward, because of excess liquidity in the banking sector. Investors were not willing to borrow, while banks were still embedded with large non-performing loans. The resulting excess liquidity led banks to cut their lending and deposit interests. As a result, M2 growth rate decline sharply in line with the real interest rate (Figure 2.9). Note that the interest spread between the two rates remains rather constant. Profit in the banking sector depends crucially on the interest spread and, in turn, profitability in the banking sector indicates the solvency of the entire banking system. Banks have begun seeking non-interest income from services to compensate for the shortfall in their interest income due to sluggish lending activity.

The continued decline in interest rates has also stimulated households' consumption as financing durable goods have become cheaper. Credit availability induces households to consume more by using future resources, while liquidity-constrained borrowers enjoy additional financial resources which were not previously available to them. This means that the recovery of the Thai economy becomes possible once consumers have regained their confidence and started spending on durable items such as automobiles and housing.

The amount of commercial loans extended to consumption increased gradually as the economic recovery became permanent. On the other hand, credit extended to the real estate sector has been shrinking since the property bubble burst after 1998. The decline in manufacturing loans became stabilized and showed signs of recovery in 2004. Credit allocated into this sector will increase gradually as long as many industries have not increased their capacity utilization above 75 percent. With expansion in export demand, the utilization rate was raised to 70 percent in September 2004. It is not surprising that agriculture receives smaller amounts of credit compared to other sectors because of its smaller size in GDP and its lower capital-labor ratio.

Speculative bubbles are largely created by over-confidence and reckless investment during a period of continued rises in property and share prices. However, sustainable increases in asset prices are made possible by credit expansion. Thus, an early warning signal of asset price bubbles is property credit. With available funds, property developers engage in land transactions and start building new housing projects and condominiums. The number of new housing units and condominiums in Bangkok and surrounding areas increased rapidly prior to the bubble burst in 1998. Between 1995 and 1998, housing price increased faster than the export price, indicating the sign of the Dutch disease (Figure 2.10). However, after the AFC, export prices rose faster than housing price. The values of land transactions as well as the credit extended to the property sectors by commercial banks declined sharply until 2002, when the first signs of recovery appeared in the property market. After 5 years of a long slump, the property sector began its recovery and slowly regained strength over the following decade.

The boom in the property sector gave rise to a demand for intermediate inputs. The linkages to other sectors are high both backwards and forwards. The sector itself depends crucially on bank lending, and low interest rates have given rise to greater demand for housing. Nevertheless, the Bank of Thailand is trying not to repeat the mistake made during the previous boom when bank credit expanded at an alarming rate.

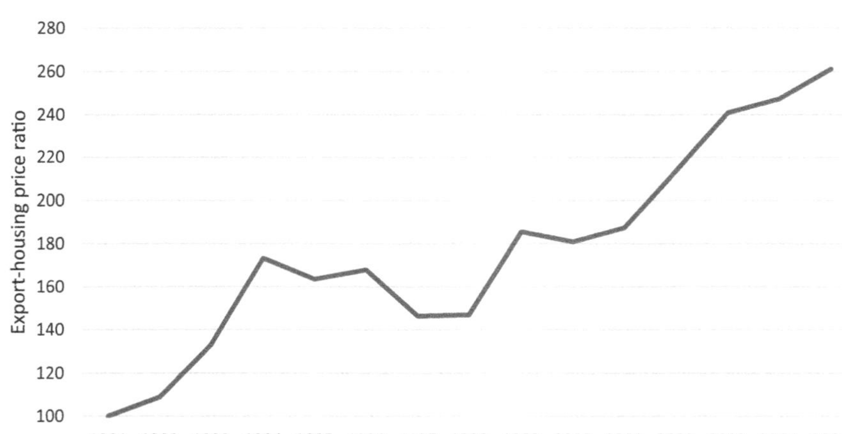

Figure 2.10 Detecting the Dutch disease export-housing price ratio

Source: Bank of Thailand

5. Dynamism of the export-oriented industry

In 1997, Thailand witnessed its lowest level of unemployment rate (1.5 percent), although the official figures seem to be biased downwards and may not take proper account of open and seasonal unemployment in the economy. Notwithstanding the natural rate of unemployment, the series of official unemployment rates can be used to trace the movement of unemployment over time. Incidentally, the rate of industrial capacity utilization moves in an opposite directly with unemployment rate (Figure 2.11). The output contraction in the non-agricultural sector of 11.4 percent in 1998 corresponds with high unemployment in the same year. However, the resilience of the Thai economy has become apparent and the unemployment rate has been declining steadily and gradually since 1999. Flexibility in wage rates is a major contributing factor which prevented Thailand from suffering massive unemployment after the economic crisis. There has been no downward rigidity in both real and nominal wage rates in Thailand; both real and nominal wage rates were cut during the high unemployment. Although there are minimum wages, they are largely nonbinding in the sense that some workers are paid above the minimum levels. In addition, lags in adjustment of the minimum wage levels result in a delay in wage adjustment during tight labor market conditions and rising inflationary expectations.

Compared with the level of per capita income in 1997, the crisis led to a fall in per capita income, but by 2000, the Thai economy was able to regain its previous peak income level. By 2003, income increased by 20 percent from the peak in 1997. Because of the dynamism of the agricultural sector, agricultural income increased at a higher rate than the non-agricultural sector from 2000 to 2003. The agricultural sector has been able to respond effectively to rises in commodity

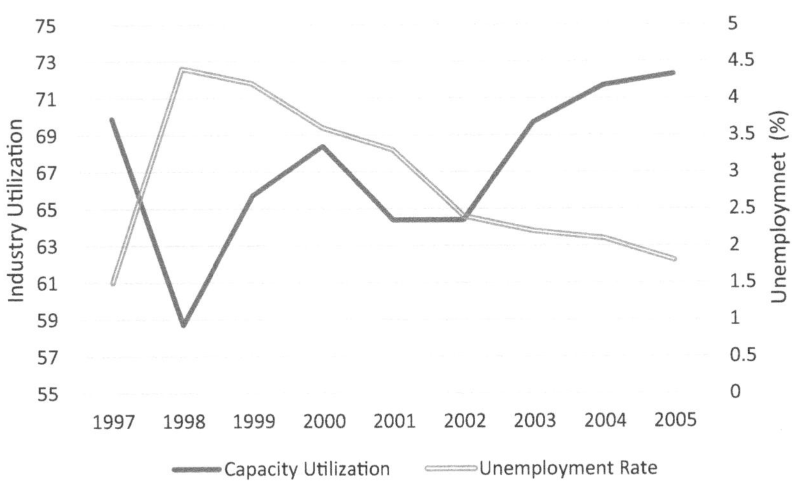

Figure 2.11 Economic recovery after the Asian financial crisis

Source: Bank of Thailand

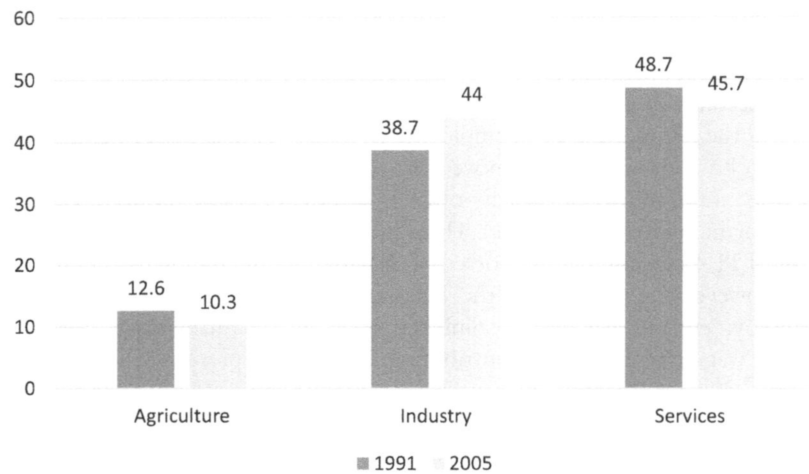

Figure 2.12 Changing output structure
Source: Bank of Thailand

prices in recent years because of the improvement in the sector's productivity. Nevertheless, agricultural sector share in GDP declined from 12.6 percent in 1991 to 10.3 percent in 2005, while industry output share increased from 38.7 to 44.0 percent (Figure 2.12).

Except for the iron and steel industry, all sectors have achieved solid recovery. Using 1995 as the benchmark, the total manufacturing output declined by 3.5 percent in 1998. Vehicles and components suffered a dramatic output fall of 65 percent in 1998, while petroleum, textiles, and jewelry registered strong growth due to the exchange rate depreciation. By 2000, all sectors, except the steel industries, which still suffered from the collapse in the property sector, had recovered and expanded their output (Figure 2.13).

Propelled by the increased exports, manufactured outputs in jewelry, electronics, and electrical appliances, such as air conditioners, have been rising continuously at a very high growth rate. Textile products did not experience output expansion significantly due to the problem with export quotas and high production cost.

It becomes clear that sectors that depend more on exports can rebound successfully and faster than domestic oriented industries. The automobile industry suffered during the slump because the industry relied heavily on domestic markets. Now that the industry has become more export-oriented, it is in a better position to take advantage of the expansion phase of the world business cycle. Output of passenger cars, commercial vehicles, and motorcycles moved in the same direction since they are sensitive to the growth of domestic demand. The industry experienced a gradual reduction in output in 1997 and a sharp fall in 1998, because of its reliance on domestic sales, but after the industry became

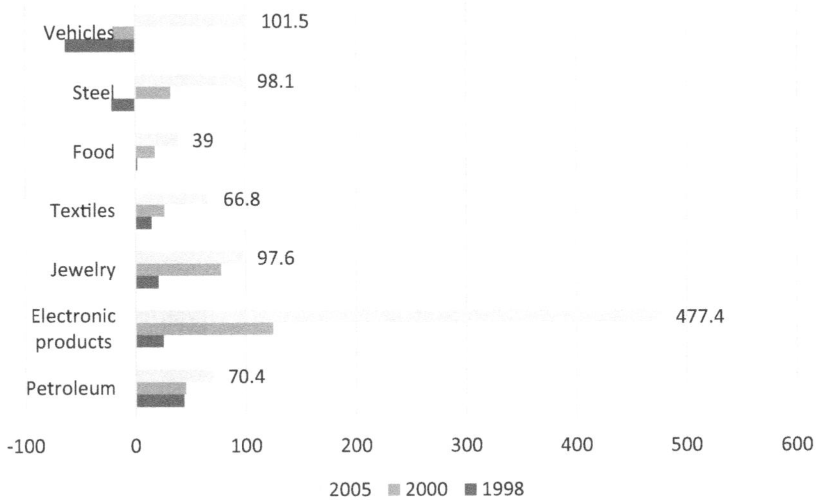

Figure 2.13 V-shaped recovery of industrial output (percent change of manufacturing product from 1995 level)

Source: Bank of Thailand

Note: Manufacturing production index (2000 = 100). Low: Export less than 30 percent of total production, Moderate: Export between 30 percent and 60 percent of total production, High: Export more than 60 percent of total production.

more export-oriented, production growth rates were even higher than their past decade's average growth.

The growth of the manufacturing sector has been driven by exports. Regional integration can enhance market excess of Thai exports to countries in Asia. Export growth also depends crucially on output capacity. The inflows of foreign direct investment over the past three decades have enabled the Thai industry to build up export capability. Industrialization in Thailand followed the development path earlier taken by other newly industrialized economies, along the lines of the flying geese model described by Akamatsu (1962). However, the inflows of FDI have started to decline, in particular the flows of FDI into the industrial sector. FDI has been diverted to China, while other countries in Asia are also experiencing drying up of FDI.

Exports contribute to growth because firms can exploit economies of scale by expansion of production runs to fill demand from external markets. In addition, firms are subject to a competitive environment, so they must constantly improve their efficiency in order to compete abroad. The demand constraints in industrial countries can be ameliorated by a progressive shift of industries and in successfully developing countries into more capital-intensive exports; they would in turn import skill-intensive manufactures from other developing countries at a lower level of development.

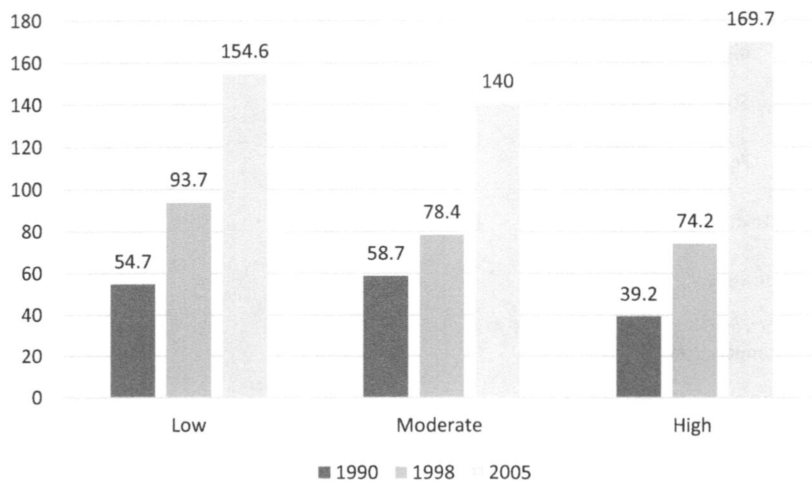

Figure 2.14 Manufacturing production index (2000 = 100)

Source: Bank of Thailand

When analyzing the performances of firms classified by their degree of export-orientation, we find that firms which exported moderately less in the recession of 1998 and were able to recover faster than firms with a lower level of export dependency. Firms classified as moderately export-oriented in 2005 were able to produce 40 percent higher output than the post-crisis level of 2000, while those classified as having a high export-orientation were able to raise output by 70 percent above the level of 2000 (Figure 2.14). Nevertheless, the low export-orientation group was able to raise its output by 54.6 percent during the same period. This level was even higher than the level achieved by the moderate orientation group because the automobile sector was classified in the low export-oriented group by taking their situation in 1995, when domestic markets were still the main focus of that sector.

Exports depend on imported capital goods and intermediate inputs. It is not surprising that imports move together with exports over time as they exhibit a non-stationary time series. To see the long-term relationship, we have to subtract the time trend elements from the level of exports and imports by focusing on their rates of change. The rates of change of both imports and exports are highly correlated. In other words, there exists a long-term relationship between the two series. In addition, the demand for imports of Thailand is highly income elastic in the sense that percentage changes in imports are always greater than the percentage changes in GDP. Rates of change in imports are usually larger than exports. During the recession in 1998, imports fell sharply, resulting in a larger current account surplus than Thailand had ever experienced before; this is not surprising since Thailand has never experienced such a severe contraction in output. During the expansion path of the business cycle, imports tend to grow faster than exports. In consequence, current account deficit will always accompany periods of high economic activity. Current account surplus is a sign of weakening economic activity, and thus a current account deficit indicates the strong growth of the Thai economy. Furthermore, tax revenues are generated from excise taxes and customs can make the tax revenue move anti-cyclically, thus providing a stabilizing effect during the boom.

We have discussed the supply factors that make Thailand's exports respond to an increase in demand from the world market. Given the elastic supply response of Thai exports, growth in export demand very much depends on market access and on demand factors. Because key exchange rates did not change significantly, the major determinant of Thailand's robust exports after the Asian financial crisis was basically the increasing income levels of industrial countries. Changes in world GDP positively affected Thailand's exports between 1996 and 2005. The strength of global markets has a strong impact on Thailand's export performance. This observation remains valid well into the period after the global financial crisis.

The agricultural sector supported the economic growth of the Thai economy by generating high income throughout the early 1990s. Agricultural output responded positively to high prices of world commodities. In turn, the growing agricultural sector generated demand for manufactured products and provided a steady pool of labor for the manufacturing and service sectors. By the early 2000s, agricultural output growth was declining due to unfavorable terms of trade and supply side problems. It was the non-agriculture output growth that propelled growth of the overall economy until it faded after 2006 (Figure 2.15).

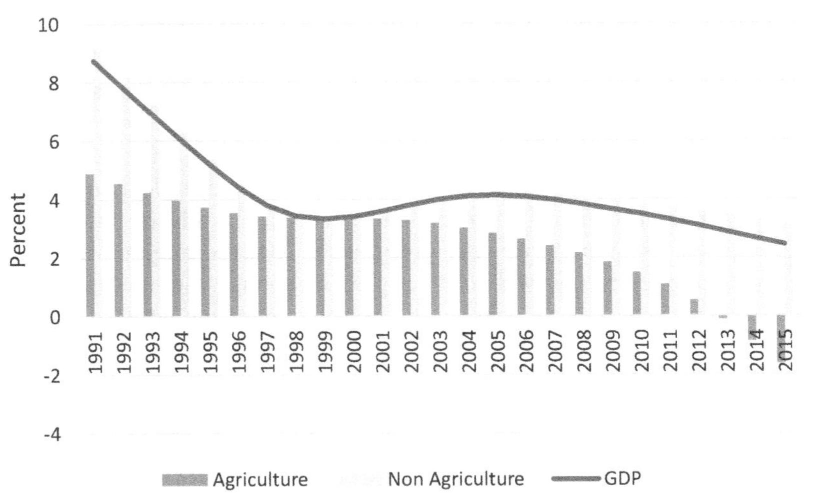

Figure 2.15 Trend growth paths

Since then the Thai economy has begun to slow down significantly. The long-term growth rate fell below 4 percent per year and it kept on declining. We can conclude that up to 2005, the Thai economy showed signs of being resilient. The loss of the ability to maintain high long-term growth can be attributed to the dysfunction of growth engines.

6. Concluding remarks

Since 1998, unemployment had been declining as the economy slowly recovered from the severe slump. Inflation remained subdued compared with global inflation and the resulting fall in domestic interest rates enabled Thai firms to restructure their foreign debts, thereby reducing the degree of vulnerability to a future currency crisis. Furthermore, the development of bond markets should reduce the heavy dependency on bank loans, which was a factor that led to sharp output contraction when Thailand suffered from a banking crisis.

The dynamism of export-oriented industries, which have focused more on foreign markets, has raised the output level far above the pre-crisis period. These industries are able to respond to the growing demand generated by the upturn in the world business cycle.[7] The role of FDI is crucial to Thailand's industrial development. The consistent open policy towards FDI has contributed to continued flows of technology transfer and spillover effect into local industries. It is most vital for Thailand to maintain steady flows of FDI.

The fiscal budget deficit is under control, thanks to the built-in automatic fiscal stabilizer of taxation and the nature of budget utilization. The reorientation of public expenditures provides social safety nets and targets poverty reduction. The financial crisis has given valuable lessons to good corporate and banking governance. The banking sector has become efficient as a result of industry restructuring and getting rid of the problem of non-performing loans. Adherence to international financial standards has improved the quality of bank loans. The Bank of Thailand has been aware of the possibility of asset bubbles and has taken precautionary measures.

Although the Thai economy seems to be resilient, riding on the expansion of world trade, there are still some structural problems. Its dependence on imported oil makes Thailand vulnerable to oil price shocks. The adverse impact of the oil shocks was postponed through public subsidy, but the surge in inflation and the loss in competitiveness will become apparent as wage and prices adjustments begin to take place. For this reason, the exchange rates should have been more realistic with little intervention so as to cushion the economy from external disturbances.[8]

Notes

1 For detailed analysis of Thailand's macroeconomic policy adjustments to external shocks prior to the Asian Financial Crisis (AFC), see Warr and Nidhiprabha (1996).

2 Strictly speaking, there is a lag effect of the demand pressure on the price level. A strong growth rate in the current period will not give rise to a higher price level

right away. Similarly, a lower growth rate in the current year will not reduce the price pressure until the following year. Also, there is a lag adjustment of inflationary expectations, where inflation in the current period is affected by inflation in the previous year. Dynamic inflation process will be discussed in detail in Chapter 8.

3 In a simple ordinary least squares estimation of the determinants of current account, using annual data from 1990 to 2005, it was found that current account position is negatively related to both GDP growth and inflation rate. The estimated coefficient of the two variables are −1.1 and −1.9 respectively. Both coefficients are statistically significant at 0.01 level and the explanatory power of the equation is 0.81.

4 As it turns out, the critics were wrong. Nevertheless, in hindsight, the idea of promoting automobile hub, tourism, and processed food industries proved to be the right policy focus. Providing the social safety net through subsidized medical care for the poor turned out to be a success story.

5 This rule was changed after 2006 to allow the government to set a multiyear budget so as to carry out spending for long-term programs.

6 In 2018, the value added tax still remains at 7 percent due to the fear that raising the rate back to 10 percent might derail the fragile recovery.

7 See Nidhiprabha (2013) for the discussion on the issue of domestic demand versus export-led growth.

8 See Nidhiprabha (2015) for further analysis on macroeconomic policy in Southeast Asia during the global financial crisis.

References

Akamatsu, Kaname. 1962. "A Historical Pattern of Economic Growth in Developing Countries." *The Developing Economies*, 1: 3–25.

Nidhiprabha, Bhanupong. 2013. "Thailand" in Hal Hill and Maria Socorro Gochoco-Bautista (eds.) *Asia Rising: Growth and Resilience in an Uncertain Global Economy*. Cheltenham: Edward Elgar

Nidhiprabha, Bhanupong. 2015. "The Global Financial Crisis and Macroeconomic Policy in Southeast Asia" in Ian Coxhead (ed.) New York: Routledge Handbook of Southeast Asian Economics.

Warr, Peter G., and Bhanupong Nidhiprabha. 1996. *Thailand's Macroeconomic Miracle*. Washington, DC: The World Bank, Oxford University Press.

3 Political instability, the coups, and the underperforming economy 2006–2017

1. Introduction

We have so far traced Thailand's long-term economic development since the early 1960s, when the economy progressed smoothly with strong growth and low inflation. In the first three decades of development, economic institutions were established in such a way that the economy could be managed properly via the conduct of monetary and fiscal policy. Chapter 1 explains how the fixed exchange rate regime was interrupted by two major devaluations, which effectively restored external balances. In Chapter 2 we discussed how Thailand dealt with the currency and financial crises. The abandoning of the fixed exchange rate in 1997 turned Thailand into a full-fledged export-led growth economy. In this chapter, we examine various shocks which affected the economy from 2006 to 2017, during which political turmoil, global financial crisis, and China's slowdown have fundamentally changed Thailand's economic landscape. As economic growth depends on capital deepening and technological progress, if these shocks affect long-term capital formation, the country's potential growth could be adversely affected. It will be clear from the analysis in this chapter that politics matters for economic performance. The standard of living of the Thai people is conditional upon the quality of institutions. The military coups and the impaired quality of governments have deteriorated the competitiveness of the nation through misallocation of resources and undermining the growth potential of the country.

2. The economy before and after the coups

There were three coups in the 1970s and two in the 1980s. There was only one coup in the 1990s, when the PM Chatichai was overthrown by General Suthorn in February 1991. In the early 1990s, the Thai economy expanded rapidly with double-digit growth. This was the period when Thailand had returned to democracy and trade reform was installed to spur economic activity by improving economic efficiency. It was thought that coups were a thing of the past and the country had politically matured. Then came the September 2006 coup, when General Sonthi Boonyaratglin staged a coup against PM Thaksin Shinawatra, who was accused of corruption. The military government was in power until the new constitution was proclaimed. After the general election, Ms. Yingluck Shinawatra was elected as the prime minster in 2011. During the time of political turmoil, she also was removed by the constitutional court on charges of dereliction of duty for failing to stop corruption from the rice pledging scheme. There was 35-billion-baht damage from the scheme that she was ordered by the government committee to pay. General Prayuth Chan Ocha staged a coup on May 22, 2014, and formed a new government and embarked on social and economic reforms.

If we use the year 2005 as a benchmark for comparison of the relative success of economic development from 2005 to 2016, Thailand has slowly raised per capita GDP when compared with other East Asia and Pacific region countries (excluding high-income countries). Based on the constant 2011 international dollar in purchasing power parity (PPP), Vietnam and Indonesia were able to raise the 2016 per capita income by 75 percent and 57 percent respectively, from the level in 2005. The progress of Thailand pales in comparison with other countries in Asia (Figure 3.1). Successful economic development depends on the country's ability to sustain growth without being interrupted by shocks.

In a series of economic and political shocks, Thailand was not able to maintain steady growth and suffered from a series of setbacks caused by internal and external shocks. The level of per capita income rose by 49 percent from the level in 2005. External shocks such as the subprime crisis and China's slowdown badly affected Thailand's exports. But these events created temporary shock to the economy, which was resilient enough to rebound. In 2011, the Thai economy experienced a natural disaster, the great floods, and suffered from a temporary decline in exports. These kinds of shocks are temporary in nature; therefore, the impact dies off slowly. However, a shock by military coups can cause permanent damage to the structure of the economy. Political upheavals such as airport shutdowns and Bangkok's shutdown, which led to political violence and a subsequent military coup in 2014, disrupted the steady growth process. This can prolong the

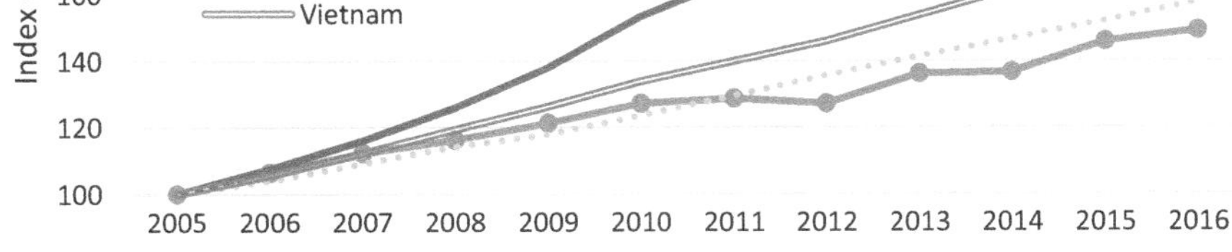

Figure 3.1 GDP per capita PPP (constant 2011 international $)

Source: World Bank

period the country gets stuck in the middle-income trap. Thailand can never get out of the middle-income trap unless it can break out of the military coup trap.

The growth rate of Thailand's per capita income was lower than its ASEAN partners, despite a lower population growth rate, because GDP grew slowly in the aftermath of the November 2006 coup. It can be said that Thailand has entered a new normal growth period. Figure 3.2 clearly demonstrates that Thailand's GDP growth in 2007 was below the world growth rate of 5.1 percent. The developing East Asia region GDP expanded 5.3 percent, while Thailand's economy grew 4.8 percent. Other ASEAN countries experienced rising exports, thanks to the 11.3 percent growth of the Chinese economy. Thailand also benefitted from the strong growth of China's imports but could not generate high economic growth. The problem stemmed from the dismal growth of domestic demand. It is an internal problem, not external one.

If Thailand can maintain growth rate as high as the average growth of the world of 5.1 percent, the gap between the actual growth rate of 4.8 percent can be used as a proxy of the cost of the military coup. Nevertheless, there is merely a short-run cost. Since the impact on the economy lasts longer than a year, there would still be impacts in the medium term for a few years after the coup event. In the longer term, if investment and capital formation slow down, the impact of the coup will be felt on the long-run growth path. In particular, if the coup affects foreign direct investment, this will have adverse impact on export capacity and considerable cost to long-run growth, because exports are a principal growth driver of the economy.

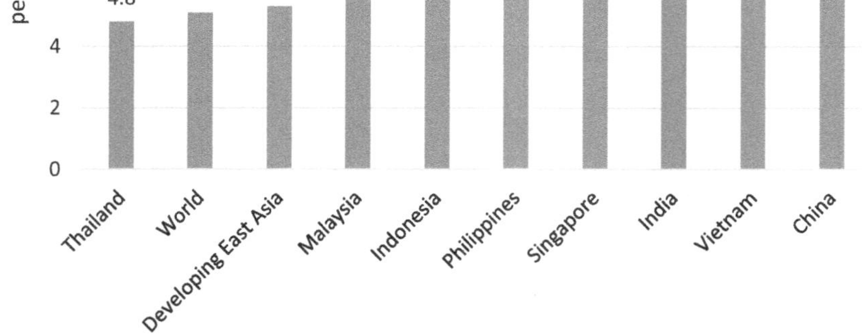

Figure 3.2 Comparison of GDP growth in 2007 and after the coup in November 2006

Source: ADB Key Indicators

When General Prayuth staged a coup in May 2014, the Thai economy had already been weakened by political turmoil. In 2014, the Thai economy expanded at the slowest speed in the region, at 0.8 percent – the same rate when the economy was hit by the great deluge in 2011 (Figure 3.3). In 2015, despite the return to peace under the tight control of the military government, economic growth rebounded to 2.8 percent, marginally exceeding Singapore's growth of 2 percent. Exports of Singapore, Malaysia, and Thailand grew at 0.6 percent, 2.5 percent, and 0.2 percent, respectively. Vietnam was the only country in ASEAN that grew faster in 2015 than 2014, thanks to hefty exports growth of 12.6 percent.

Despite a dramatic decline in exports growth, many ASEAN economies managed to register high growth rate. Expansion in domestic demand in these economies explains why output still expanded despite disappointing export growth. Consumption expenditures grew marginally in Thailand and so did its export growth. In 2014 and 2015, Thailand's exports expanded just 0.2 percent. While other countries also suffered from export shortfalls,[1] their GDP growth did not collapse as much as Thailand, because of the remaining strength of domestic demand. When consumption barely increases at 1.3 percent in 2015 (Figure 3.4), a meager export growth of 0.2 percent contributed to the poor performance of the Thai economy.

Household consumption was around 50 percent of Thailand's GDP, so when consumption grew slowly in 2007, growth sagged to 4.8 percent. That happened when consumer confidence plunged after the 2006 and 2014 coups. Other rapidly growing ASEAN economies—Cambodia, Philippines, Vietnam and Indonesia—have a higher average propensity to consume, implying that their fiscal policy would be more effective in response to external shocks.[2] When the share of trade

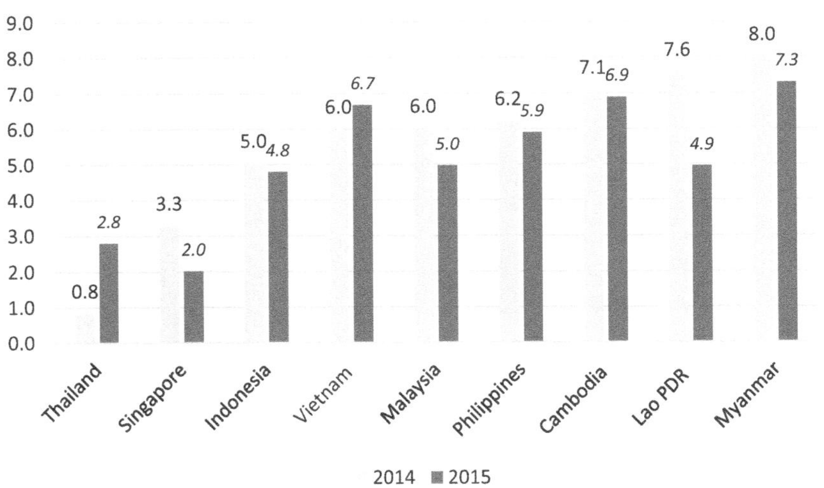

Figure 3.3 Comparison of ASEAN GDP growth after the coup in May 2014

Source: ADB key indicators

sector in GDP is high in countries such as Singapore, Thailand, and Malaysia, these countries must employ fiscal policy to compensate declining exports. More importantly, domestic demand must be sufficiently stimulated through public spending and tax policy measures. However, these stimulus measures are useless if consumers do not have confidence in the future state of the economy.

There is a long-run relationship between consumption and investment. When consumption expenditures are growing slowly, investors postpone investment. Only when investors anticipate a permanent increase in consumption spending do they begin purchasing capital goods and expand existing plant sizes. The collapse of consumption expenditures and output growth in the 2 years after the coups led to a slowdown in investment. Investment expenditure increased only 1.3 percent in 2007 and dropped by 12.5 percent in 2015 (Figure 3.5). The 2015 collapse in investment can be attributed to the slowdown in output growth, which retarded consumer spending.

The year 2007 witnessed rapid expansion of investment in the CLMV (Cambodia, Lao PDR, Myanmar, and Vietnam) countries. By 2014, the growth rate of investment in these countries slowed down significantly. Singapore had a high level of investment growth of almost 17 percent in 2007, but the positive growth rate swung into –2 percent in 2014 (Figure 3.5).

The dismal performance of the Thai economy was a combination of external shocks as well as internal problems that precluded healthy investment and strong household spending which could have lifted the economy out of sluggish growth during the time of China's slowdown.

Figure 3.6 illustrates that Thailand was 2.5 percent and 3.7 percent below the average growth of ASEAN-5 in 2007 and 2008. The Thai economy could have

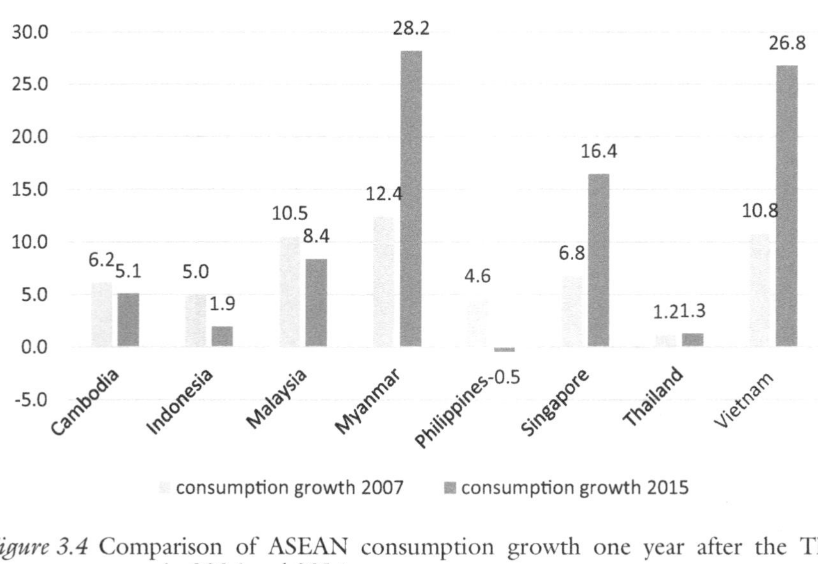

Figure 3.4 Comparison of ASEAN consumption growth one year after the Thai coups in 2006 and 2014

Source: ADB Key Indicators

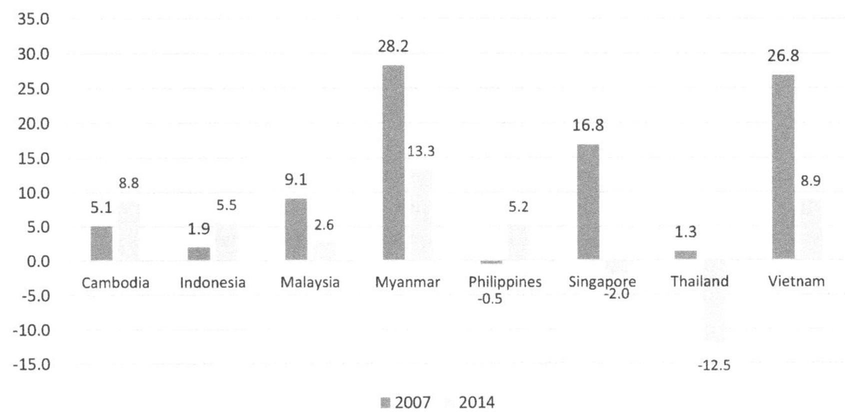

Figure 3.5 Domestic capital formation (percent change)

Source: ADB Key Indicators

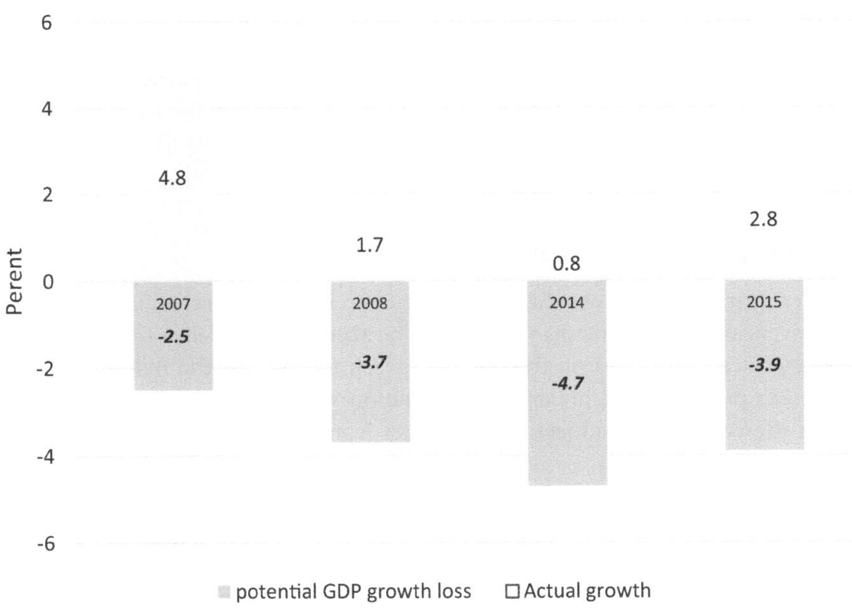

Figure 3.6 Potential growth losses: 2 years after the coups

Source: ADB key indicators and author's calculation

managed to register high growth but ended up growing 4.8 percent and 1.7 percent, respectively. If Thailand is to attract FDI, it must be able to grow at least at the same rate of other ASEAN-5 countries, which are competing with each other to raise the standard of living. If not higher, at the average growth, Thailand's competitive position can be secured, and it would not be left behind in the lower ladder of development of comparable living standards.

When the most recent coup took place in 2014, the potential growth loss was higher than the 2006 coup (Figure 3.6). Admittedly the estimates might be overestimated because the export slowdown originated from external factors. Nevertheless, export performance is related to FDI inflows, which are related to investors' perception of risks. Moreover, unlike a democratically elected government, military-backed governments do not command effective policy implementation in terms of directions and speed to respond to external shocks.[3]

Table 3.1 provides estimates of the cost of the coups in terms of the loss in GDP, based on the counterfactual assumption that Thailand was able to maintain growth rate as high as the average growth rate of the ASEAN-5 countries in the 2 years after the coups, which took place in 2006 and 2014. Since the 2006 coup took place in November, we examined the impacts on GDP in 2007 and 2008, while the 2014 coup broke out in May, so we can still observe the short-run impact on GDP growth in 2014 and 2015.

The opportunity cost of the coups was staggering, much higher than the external shocks caused by the 2004 tsunami or the oil price shocks (Nidhiprabha, 2006). The cost of the coups depends crucially on the duration of time required for the economy to return to the pre-coup growth path. The cost grew higher as the economy deviated from the ASEAN-5 growth of that particular year. The long-run cost will be staggering if investment does not improve significantly. There is also a significant lag effect before the improvement in business sentiment and consumer confidence translates into real investment spending.

3. Business sentiment and the real sector

One cannot underestimate the cost of the coup because it has an impact on the effectiveness of economic management. The absence of criticism of government policy under restrictions on freedom of speech means that the military government can push forward policy implementation without opposition, particularly when the economy is subject to challenges from a changing environment and shocks.

Table 3.1 Estimated loss of real GDP in the aftermath of the coups: the short-run impact

	Billion Baht	*Billion USD (constant 2010)*
2007	179.7	7.45
2008	280.4	11.6
2014	429.9	17.8
2015	359.9	14.9

Source: Author's calculation based on the assumption of GDP growth at the average rate of growth of ASEAN-5 countries

With limited freedom of expression and the absence of public scrutinization of the directions of fiscal policy undertaken by the military government, that policy may go so wrong that it leads to inefficient programs and wasteful spending. This is dangerous because the military government can lead the country into heavy debt and inefficient infrastructure development, as the ability to control corruption is limited. Worldwide governance indicators show that Thailand's index of voice and accountability took a sharp decline after the 2006 coup, rising temporarily when democracy was restored (Figure 3.7). The index took a nose dive when the 2014 coup broke out. With all these political upheavals, the incidence of violence and terrorism intensifies and threatens political stability. Without freedom and accountability, there is no doubt that the control of corruption was weakened together with degenerating the quality of the rule of law.

For the business sector, risks and uncertainties affect investor decisions. The business environment was badly affected by the coups. The business sentiment index echoes consumer confidence, which in turn affects consumer spending. Business investment expands in response to high consumers spending. As discussed in the previous chapter, investment and consumer expenditures are related. High investment generates jobs and income, which stimulate consumer spending. On the other hand, when people lose confidence, they tend to postpone spending. Consequently, investment spending is delayed until there is a sign of surge in consumer spending.

The Bank of Thailand provides an index of business sentiment based on surveyed data from business enterprises. The index itself corresponds to consumer confidence. It is argued here that changes in the level of sentiment matter for investment decisions. The Hodrick-Prescott filter is applied to the business sentiment index (BSI) to obtain its trend and cyclical components. The first difference

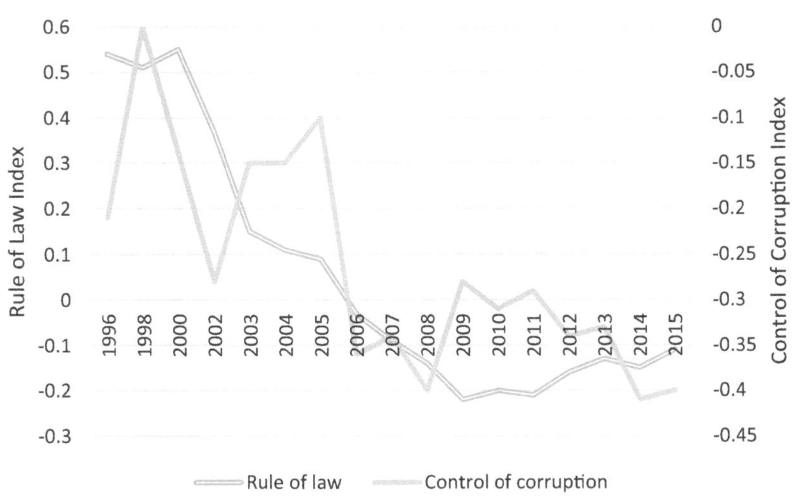

Figure 3.7 Deteriorating rule of law and losing corruption control

Source: Worldwide Governance Indicators

on the Hodrick-Prescott trend component can be thought of as a change in the trend of business confidence. There will be no responses from investors unless they are certain about changes in the business conditions; investors and consumers will make sure that changes are permanent before they react to new information. Figure 3.8 clearly suggests that changes in of the trend of investment index lag after changes in business confidence by about 18 months. There exists a lead-lag relationship between the perception of confidence and the long-term investment. Similarly, the Hodrick-Prescott filter is applied to the personal consumption expenditure index, constructed by the Bank of Thailand. The Hodrick-Prescott trend is employed to capture permanent consumption rather than transitory consumption. Figure 3.8 clearly demonstrates the powerful role of expectations. The BSI, which to some extent captures consumer confidence, is leading changes in trends of consumption expenditures.

The underlying hypothesis is that consumer spending is influenced by the changing business environment through waves of optimism and pessimism cycles. This hypothesis is akin to Keynes' concept of animal spirits, which was further extended by Akerlof and Shiller (2010). Consumers do not spend and businesses do not want to invest when animal spirits are low. Keynes' idea was that swings in confidence are not always logical and the business cycle is to some extent driven by animal spirits. The economic booms are the period when people have substantial trust and associated feelings that contribute to an environment of confidence. On the contrary, when people have lost their confidence in the future state of the economy, private spending plummets. The military coups in Thailand, which caused loss of investor and consumer confidence, have a long-lasting impact on the capital deepening process.

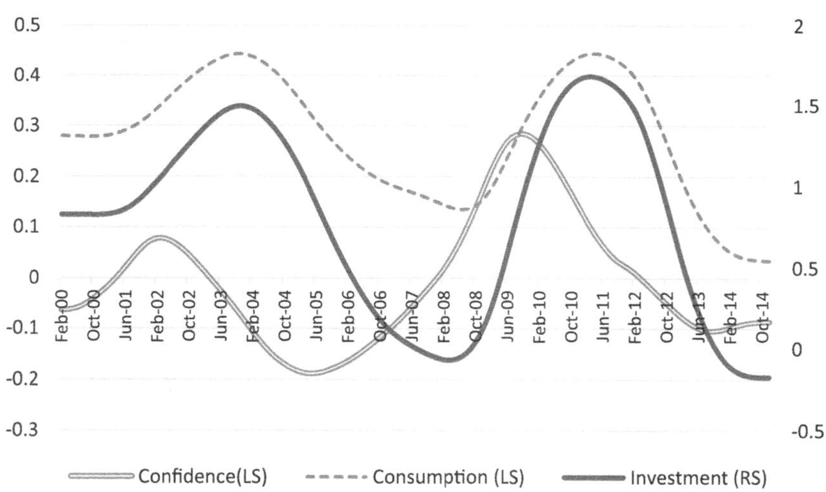

Figure 3.8 Cycles of optimism and pessimism: impact on long-term investment and consumption (change in long-term trend values)

Source: Bank of Thailand

4. Military business cycle

Many developing countries have experienced military coups in the past three decades. However, the frequency of the military coups has declined as countries have embraced democracy. Little did the coup leaders know that their actions would have a long-term impact on economic growth. Leon (2014) observes that *coups d'etat* are common in developing countries, resulting in changes in leaders and institutions. Successful coups increase military spending more than failed attempts. Furthermore, coups are more likely when military spending as a share of GDP is relatively low. A study based on Nigeria's experiences with military coups shows that increased defense burden is harmful to the Nigerian economy, and there exists a negative long-run relationship between defense burden and growth of real output (Ajefu, 2015). The impact of defense burden remains negative in the short-run and long-run, because of a negative crowding-out effect on private investment. In Turkey, there were three military coups between 1950 and 1984. Each coup pulled the Turkish economy 10 years back (Berberoğlu, 2016). Kim et al. (2013) analyze military spending in different regimes from 1960 to 2000. Their empirical results indicate that military regimes allocate more defense budget than other regimes and that military rulers brought into power through military coups or who have experienced military coup attempts against them increase their military resource allocation.

The opportunistic political budget model predicts higher fiscal spending by incumbent democratic governments before an election to gain votes. In the case of Thailand, rapid rises in defense spending come after military coups (Figure 3.9), akin to a military business cycle spending (Nidhiprabha, 2015).

If spending on military hardware is wasteful, there are enormous opportunity costs to the country. In addition to misallocation of resources, it can retard long-term growth. Furthermore, large military procurement can be subject to corruption and dangerous if the equipment is ineffective. There are many cases of military procurement that turned out to be ineffective. Examples abound: the balloon ship, Chinese tanks, Ukraine personal carriers, and bomb detector GT200, to name a few. Some of them are underutilized and costly. The same mission can be accomplished by using lower-cost hardware. It turns out that military spending on hardware can become a burden as these war machine require high maintenance and operating costs.

In a democratic government, in which the rule of marginal cost and benefit is more or less observed, the budget allocated to economic services should have a larger share than military spending. The ratio of defense-to-economic service spending declined sharply from the high level in the late 1980s. From 1998 to 2013, the defense-economic budget ratio stabilized at 0.4. This was when Thailand enjoyed the long period of democracy – so long that people thought Thailand would never go backward to a military regime.

But giving the defense budget a lower share can be dangerous to democracy, since the military would not be happy about the low priority given to modernization of the military force. From time to time, there were requests for

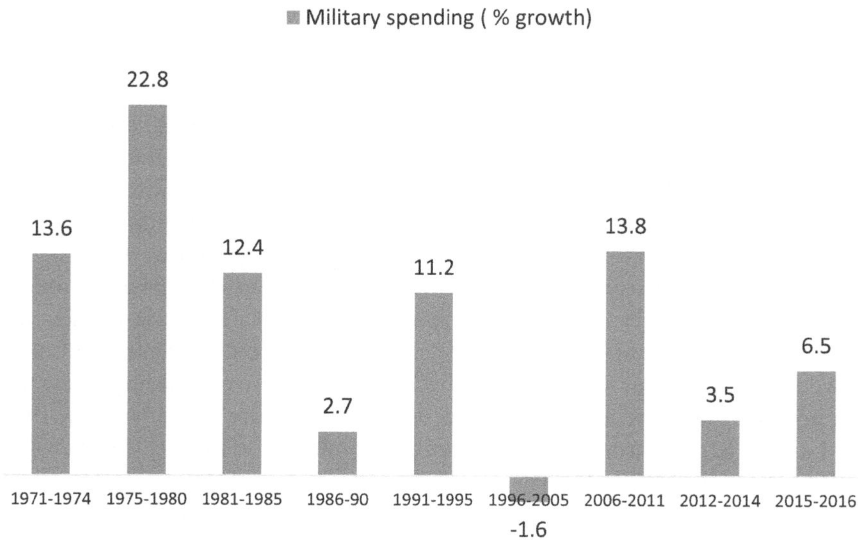

Figure 3.9 Military business cycle

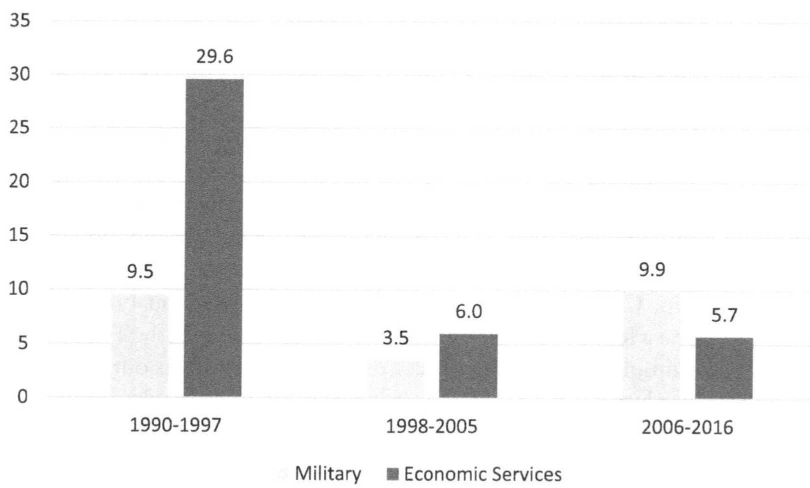

Figure 3.10 Fiscal expenditures (average annual percentage increase)

Source: ADB Key Indicators

buying submarines, but the proposals were turned down. One of many reasons why coups keep repeating can be attributed to insufficient military spending (Figure 3.11). In March 2017, the country's National Legislative Assembly (NLA) approved 211 billion baht for the defense budget and cut the education budget by 4.7 percent.

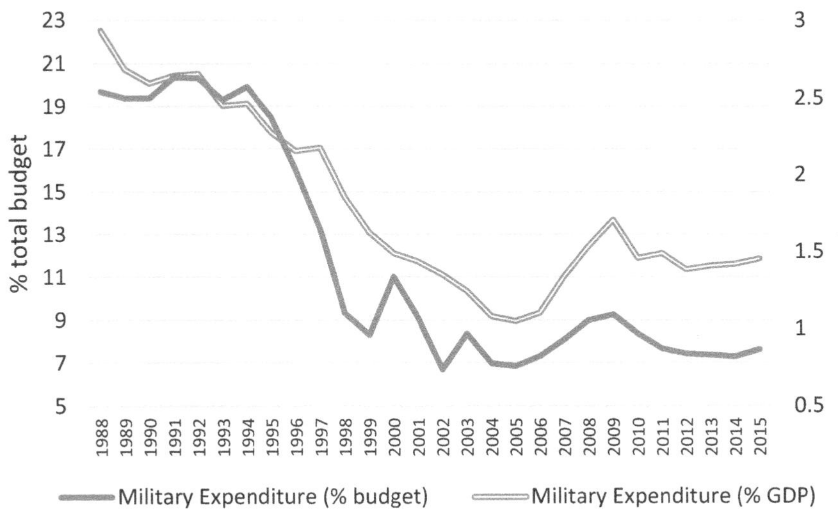

Figure 3.11 Shares of military expenditure

Source: World Bank

5. Underperforming economy

Although there are some country-specific characteristics which contribute to growth performance, there is growing evidence that developing countries with democratic institutions experience superior growth performance (Butkiewicz and Yanikkaya, 2006). Maintenance of the rule of law can promote growth. FDI inflows to Thailand increased steadily when democratic government was in power. But the rising FDI trend plateaued in the third quarter of 2014, following the declining investor sentiment in the aftermath of the military coup in May 2014. By 2015, the impact of China's slowdown was more pronounced and deepened the FDI slump further.

The quality of democratic institutions can be captured by the index of governance indicators. Figure 3.12 depicts the ability of citizen to voice their opinions and the degree of the government accountability. This index registered a positive value under the democratic regime between 1996 and 2004. The index plunged deeply in 2006 and it has remained in negative territory since then. The evidence provided by Rodrik (2003) suggests that countries which experienced the sharpest drops in growth after 1975 were those with divided societies. Thai society has been divided by political views and socioeconomic disparities, which led to political instability and rising violence; this is captured by the declining index of political stability and the rising violence and terrorism. The lack of voice and accountability reinforces political instability, damaging investor confidence and consumer confidence. Rodrik (2005) provided evidence that democracy and the rule of law are both growth promoting, but the rule of law has a much stronger

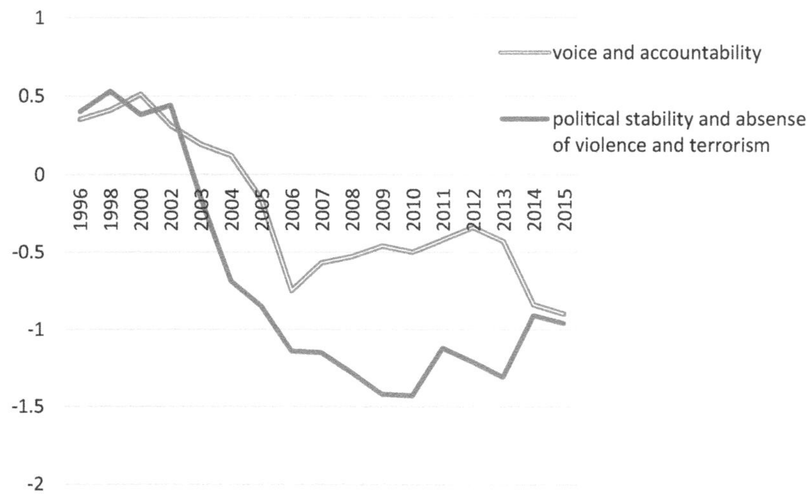

Figure 3.12 Democracy and political stability score range: –2.5 to +2.5

Source: Worldwide Governance Indicators

impact on income. Thailand's declining institutional ability to manage social conflicts is clearly demonstrated by this worldwide governance indicator. Without that institutional capacity, Thailand has entered a dismal growth era.

We can establish that the long-run impact of political instability induced by military coups led to poor growth performance of the economy. Examining the diversion of FDI flows from Thailand to other countries in the region, we observe from Figure 3.13 that ASEAN countries were competing with each other to attract FDI. Consider the level of FDI from 1992 to 2015, which we divide into two periods: before and after the 2006 coup. Between 1992 and 2006, Thailand was able to attract FDI around 9.3 percent of total FDI which went to China. Among the ASEAN countries, Thailand was the second largest recipient of FDI. During the same period, Malaysia and Singapore attracted 11 percent and 8 percent of China's FDI level, respectively. With internal political problems, Thailand and Malaysia faced dwindling level of FDI to around 4 percent of China's in the period 2007–2015. The Philippines faced a similar problem with a relatively declining FDI share. On the contrary, countries with stable governments during the second period enjoyed increasing share of FDI. Singapore, Indonesia, and Vietnam were able to attract FDI at the expense of politically unstable countries.

Over a long duration, we can average out abnormal years of extreme values. Utilizing twelve data points from six countries' average values of the two periods 1992–2006 and 2007–2015, we can relate the FDI inflows with the average index of political stability and absence of terrorism and violence. There exists a positive relationship between FDI level and the peaceful political environment among ASEAN countries (Figure 3.14). The policy implication is obvious.

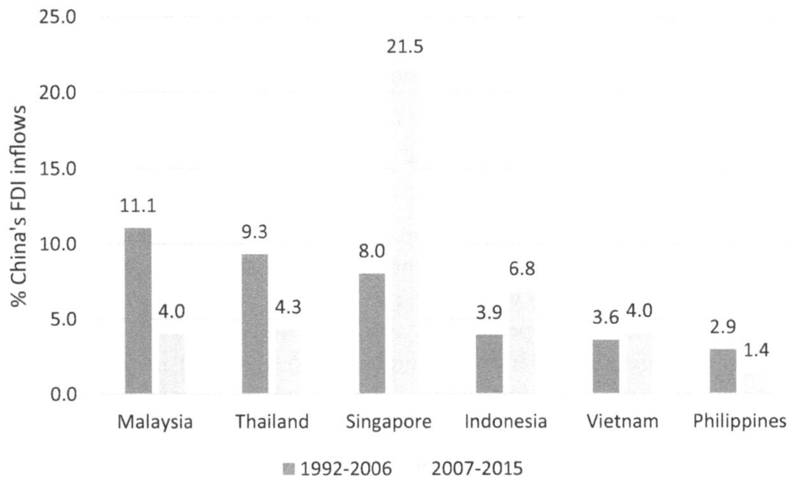

Figure 3.13 FDI inflows to ASEAN countries

Source: ADB Key Indicators

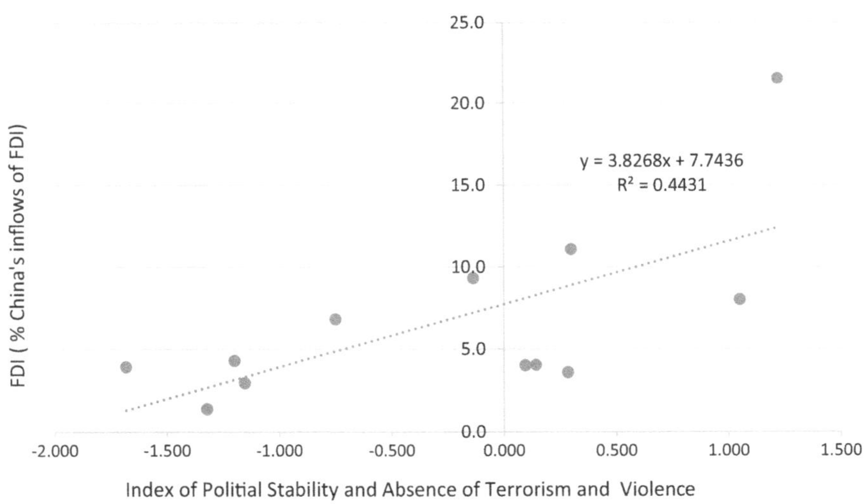

Figure 3.14 ASEAN FDI inflows and political risk

Source: ADB Key Indicators and Global Governance Indicators

Countries with stable and effective governments can attract a higher level of FDI than countries beset by government instability, terrorism, and violence.

The slowdown in FDI means that Thailand will not be able to rely on export-driven growth as much as it did in the past. With political instability compared to other ASEAN countries, Thailand will not be able to compete as a dominant FDI receiver. This is the long-run economic cost of political instability and military coups. If export capacity diminishes over time by the declining level of FDI, growth may not be sustainable in the long run.

6. Comparative macroeconomic performance: 1970–2016

Figure 3.15 illustrates comparison of macroeconomic performance in three key variables: growth, inflation and current account position. In the first period, 1970–1989, output growth was highest at 7.1 percent, followed by the second period, 1990–2005, at 5.2 percent on average. The period 2006–2016 was the lowest growth episode. Inflation was highest at 6.9 percent in the first period, due to external shocks and devaluation. The second period inflation was moderate at 3.9 percent, and the third period inflation averaged only 2.3 percent. Price level is therefore procyclical; this is different in the case of current account, which is countercyclical in the sense that low growth generates current account surplus, and high growth generates current account deficit.

As discussed in Chapter 1, when measuring growth rate, we need to include internal and external imbalances. The imbalance adjustment growth was constructed by adjusting growth by inflation and current account position. In other words, information shown in Figure 3.15 can be aggregated for comparison on the average basis shown in Figure 3.16. In the period since the 2006 coup, the index fell below the zero level in 2008 and 2009. The index mostly tracks the current account position. The low IAG index reflects strong growth and high current account deficit. High GDP growth induces more imports, reflecting

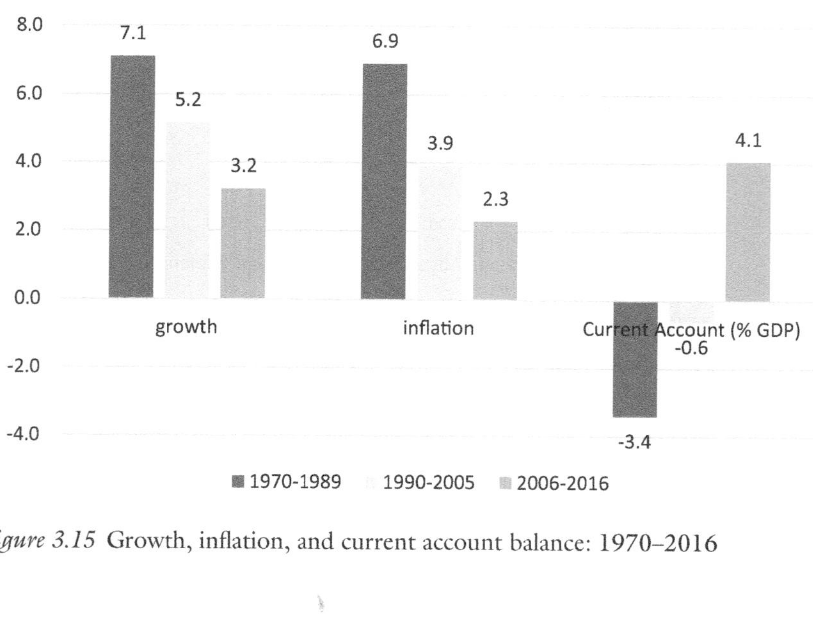

Figure 3.15 Growth, inflation, and current account balance: 1970–2016

strong potential growth, in particular if capital goods are major components of imports. On the other hand, an underperforming economy with slow growth would discourage capital imports and the economy would become trapped in a low growth, low inflation, and high level of current account surplus.

Low growth, low inflation, and high current account surplus are the characteristics of the period 2006–2016. The inflation rate was subdued thanks to the oil gluts and weak petroleum prices. The IAG rate during this period was the highest among the three periods (Figure 3.16). The strong current account position caused the baht to appreciate and eventually slowed down exports. Consequently, long-term growth would be affected. The country was not affected by the currency crisis as there was no pressure on the exchange rate. Nevertheless, we come to the conclusion that the average annual IAG rate in the period 2006–2016 was the lowest among the three periods in comparison. When growth rate is low and imbalances are high, the economy is on a precarious growth path. The period average IAG index has declined consecutively since 1970. In the following chapters, we will discuss what caused these imbalances and low GDP growth rates and what the policy responses were during these three periods in terms of monetary, fiscal, and exchange rate policy.

7. Concluding remarks

Business sentiment and consumer confidence matter for private spending and long-term economic growth. The coups have disrupted the steady growth path of the Thai economy. Poor quality of institutions does not bode well for the investment environment. Thailand is stuck in the military coup trap, which can be

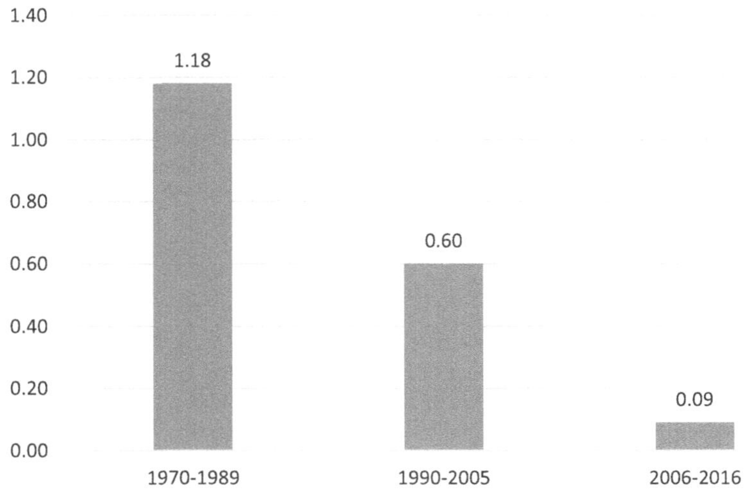

Figure 3.16 Imbalance-adjusted growth (period average)

Source: Author's calculation

repeated all over again as long as people do not see the importance of the rule of law. The instant gratification of the seemingly peaceful situations brought about by the coup has come with the sacrifice of democracy and long-term growth. Worse still, Thailand's addiction to military coups to solve political problems can perpetuate the state of slow output growth, low competitiveness, rampant corruption, and inefficient allocation of public resources.

According to Rodrik (2003), high-quality institutions through sociopolitical arrangement – from the legal system to political institutions – matter for economic growth. Good institutions provide property rights, appropriate regulatory structures, and ensure quality and independence of the judiciary and bureaucratic capacity. The coups have shattered the foundation of long-term growth.

The overthrow of the legitimate government by military coup has resulted in considerable damages in terms of economic losses. The rule of law, good governance and good institutions, and both legal and democratic infrastructure are required to nurture the economic environment suitable for long-term development to raise living standards. In Thailand, pre-2006 military coups did not destroy investor confidence, thereby leaving intact the country's economic strength. The latest coup, however, destroyed democratic underpinning of the stability of the political and economic structures, sapping the economic strength of the economy. The long-term growth of the economy and social welfare is threatened as the government budget is allocated to non-productive spending. Infrastructure public investment and human capital–related spending was curtailed for the sake of defense. The Thai economy has stepped backward, losing opportunity to grow as the world economy recovered from global recession. Alas, the May 2014 coup may not be the last one.[4]

Notes

1 Between 2010 and 2015, the annual average export growth rate in Malaysia and Singapore slowed down to 2.8 percent and 3.4 percent, respectively.
2 In 2015, share in GDP of consumption expenditures in Cambodia was 77.1 percent, the Philippines 73.8 percent, Vietnam 68 percent, and Indonesia 55.9 percent.
3 The capital control measures in response to rapid capital inflows that strengthened the baht against the dollar will be discussed in the exchange rate policy chapter.
4 General Prawit Wongsuwon, the deputy PM in General Prayut Chan Ocha government, stated that the coup might return if people ask for it in the future.

References

Ajefu, Joseph Boniface. 2015. "Impact of Defense Spending on Economic Growth in Africa: The Nigerian Case." *Journal of Developing Areas*: 227.

Akerlof, George A., and Robert J. Shiller. 2010. *Animal Spirits: How Human Psychology Drives the Economy, and Why It Matters for Global Capitalism*. Princeton: Princeton University Press.

Berberoğlu, Bahar. 2016. "The Analysis of the Effects of Military Coups on Gross National Product in Turkey: 1950–1984." *Romanian Journal of Political Science*, 16: 31–62.

Butkiewicz, James L., and Halit Yanikkaya. 2006. "Institutional Quality and Economic Growth: Maintenance of the Rule of Law or Democratic Institutions, or Both?" *Economic Modelling*, 23(4): 648–661.

Kim, Hong-Cheol, Hyung Min Kim, and Jaechul Lee. 2013. "The Post-Coup Military Spending Question Revisited, 1960–2000." *International Interactions*, 39: 367–385.

Leon, Gabriel. 2014. "Loyalty for Sale? Military Spending and Coups D'etat." *Public Choice*, 159 (3–4): 363–383.

Nidhiprabha, Bhanupong. 2006. "The Buffeting of Thailand by the Unholy Trinity of Avian Influenza, Tsunami, and the Oil Price Shock." *Asian Economic Papers*, 5 (2): 117–129.

Nidhiprabha, Bhanupong. 2009. "The Thai Economy after the Coup." in John Funston (ed.) *Divided Over Thaksin: Thailand's Coup and Problematic Transition*. Singapore: Institute of South East Asian Studies, 172–189.

Nidhiprabha, Bhanupong. 2015. "Lessons From Thailand's Fiscal Policy." *Asian Economic Papers*, 14: 110–125.

Rodrik, Dani (ed.). 2003. *In Search of Prosperity: Analytic Narratives on Economic Growth*. Princeton: Princeton University Press.

Rodrik, Dani. 2005. "Growth Strategies." *Handbook of Economic Growth*, 1: 967–1014.

4 The banking sector

Adjustments to financial crises and business cycle

1. Introduction

The Asian financial crisis started on July 2, 1997 when the Bank of Thailand floated the baht, giving up the fight with currency speculators and hedge funds. The abandonment of the fixed exchange rate, after experiencing chronic current account deficit since the early 1990s, led to a contagion effect in other Asian countries. The Asian currency crisis intertwined with the banking crisis as Asian banks had substantial dollar-denominated debts. In effect, it was a crisis that involved both foreign exchange markets and the financial sector. A large number of Thai financial institutions were closed down, consolidated, merged, or sold to foreign banks after 1997. Some underwent painful adjustments and emerged stronger. The crisis opened a window of opportunities for banks to become healthy and more resilient.

Ten years after the Asian financial crisis, the credit crunch in the US in July 2007 spread to other countries when US mortgage-backed securities sold to investors around the world turned sour as US property values declined sharply. Marer (2010) examined the global economic impacts on Eastern Europe and found different impacts on ten Eastern European nations depending on exchange rate regimes, exposure to foreign currency borrowings, and monetary and fiscal policy responses. Kenc and Dibooglu (2010) found evidence that the risk premium of the subprime crisis was comparable to the risk prior to the Great Depression. Simpson (2010) attributed the rampant impact of the global financial crisis to integration of the global financial markets because of the interdependence of the global banking industry. Nevertheless, Thailand also embraced an open capital market in the early 1990s and has since become an integral part of the global financial system. The adverse impact of the global financial crisis on the real economy was substantial, but not significant for the banking sector. The 1997 financial crisis gave a valuable lesson to the Thai financial sector. Financial reform through strengthened rules and regulations has prepared the banking industry for the global financial crisis. After undergoing structural reform and enhancing capital adequacy, the Thai banking sector has become more efficient, leading to impressive performance.

Thailand is a bank-based economy, where savings mobilization and credit distribution are conducted mainly through bank intermediaries. The ratio of bank credit to deposit approximates investment and saving imbalances. In the early 1960s up to the early 1970s, the ratio was stable at around 80 percent (Figure 4.1). Bank credit amounted to 80 percent of financial deposits at banks. After the first oil shock and commodity price hikes in 1973–1974, the ratio increased steadily and peaked at 126 percent in 1979, when the second oil shock occurred and the world economy went into recession. The ratio declined steadily as bank credit expanded faster than bank deposits. The slowdown in the economy implies lower demand for loans for consumption and investment. After the recovery in the late 1980s, the demand for credit soared once again, fueled by cheap credit from international markets. The ratio peaked in 1997 at 182 percent and started declining, thanks to growth collapse as the Thai economy gravitated back toward external equilibrium. Since 2001, the credit to deposit ratio has been stagnant and remained below 100 percent. Bank credit expansion corresponds to real output growth. The slow rise in bank credit relative to bank saving indicates weak investment and low consumption demand.

In this chapter, we examine how the banking sector and the economic crises are closely intertwined from the Asian financial crisis to global financial crisis. The Thai banking sector must adjust in order to survive and thrive during the boom and bust influenced by external and internal shocks.

2. The Asian and global financial crises

When the economy is strong, there is no urgent need to restructure the financial system to improve efficiency. Structural weaknesses of the financial system do

Figure 4.1 Bank credit to bank deposit ratio

Source: Federal Reserve Bank

not reveal themselves until the economy is subject to shocks. In a mild business cycle, efficient financial firms with conservative lending policies can survive temporary losses, but some aggressive banks fail because of excessive risk-taking behaviors. In a deep business downturn, even good banks with cautious lending policies can succumb to losses and bankruptcy. To prevent a system-wide crisis, the central bank must step in to restore public confidence during deep recession. The intervention to bail out troubled financial institutions therefore depends on macroeconomic fundamentals, which are intricately related to the soundness of financial institutions.

Before allowing capital convertibility, prudential rules and regulations should have been established. An open capital account is inconsistent with the fixed exchange rate regime and independent monetary policy. Strengthening the legal framework and corporate governance are required to guard against adverse consequences of liberalization. Unless liquidity-constrained firms can rely on bond markets, strict prudential rules can thwart the recovery of a fragile economy.

Financial liberalization in Thailand began in the early 1990s with the abolishment of interest rate ceilings. Thailand accepted Article VIII of the IMF agreement in May 1990, relaxing capital controls and restrictions on capital account transactions. Consequently, capital inflows rose rapidly. Maturity composition of capital inflows changed dramatically from cold to hot flows prior to the 1997 crisis.

Between 1990 and 1996, the share of foreign borrowing in total capital inflows was 60 percent, while share of portfolio investment flows was 27 percent (Figure 4.2). These numbers indicate the domination of hot monetary flows over cold money, which was represented by the 12.4 percent share of foreign direct investment (FDI).

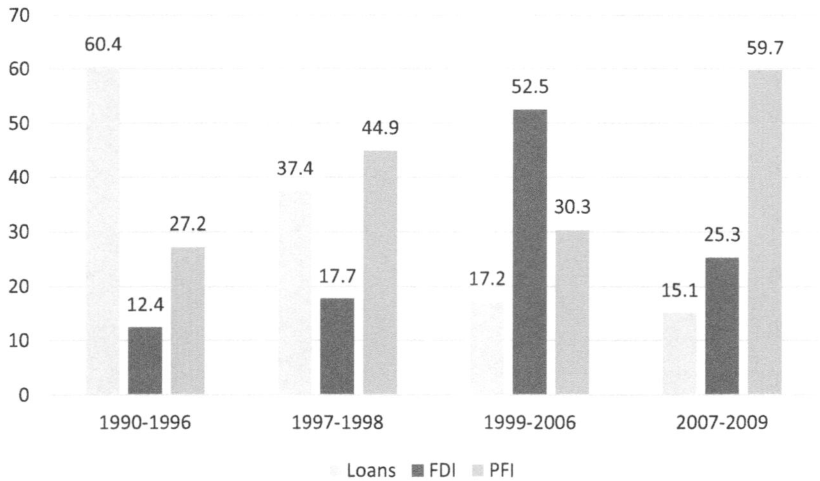

Figure 4.2 Hot vs. cold capital flows: 1990–2009 (percent of total flows)
Source: Bank of Thailand

Liberalization of external accounts may lead to a financial disaster. As in the case of Thailand, capital account liberalization was premature. Capital control was relaxed when Thailand's interest rates were much higher than the world market rates. The relaxation should have occurred after adequate prudential rules and regulations had been established. Open capital accounts led to large and fast inflows, however, building institutional infrastructure, due to its time-consuming nature, could not cope with the huge inflows. The bond market was not sufficiently developed to allow the central bank to sterilize capital inflows. The Bangkok International Banking Facility (BIBF) encouraged borrowing in foreign currencies during the time when large interest differentials between domestic and international interest rates prevailed. Loans extended by BIBF grew from Bt200 billion in 1993 to 1.88 trillion in 1997. At the end of 1999, the BIBF borrowing volume declined to just Bt600 million.

The precarious borrowing structure foretold a financial distress that would come when foreign lenders changed their perception about Thailand's risk. Capital flights followed, causing liquidity problems to Thai financial institutions. Currency and maturity mismatching led to a financial disaster. During the financial turmoil in 1997–1998, the share of foreign borrowing in total capital inflows declined to 37 percent (Figure 4.2). Portfolio flows became the largest part of capital flows. FDI share rose from 17.7 percent during this period to 52.5 percent during the period 1999–2006. Part of the increase was due to brown field investment. Large capital inflows came in the form of acquisitions of assets from troubled banks that simply ran out of capital funds after their huge bad debts were written off.

In 1996, short-term borrowing of finance companies amounted to 95 percent of their total borrowing, while their long-term credit was 40 percent of total lending. This was a technical mismanagement in terms of maturity mismatching between asset and liability. It is not surprising that these finance companies experienced liquidity problems when their short-term borrowing could not be rolled over during the period of financial turmoil. Another technical problem involved currency mismatching, because Thai financial institutions and large corporations borrowed heavily in the US dollar but extended credit in the Thai baht.

The poor performance of the Thai economy deteriorated the balance sheets of the financial institutions, leading to problems of illiquidity and insolvency. The risks of these financial institutions intensified after the 1997 massive devaluation of the baht. Their ability to obtain funds was severely reduced when foreign banks' perception of their risk deteriorated. Technically, commercial banks in Thailand were insolvent because the level of non-performing loans exceeded that level of capital funds. Forty-five percent of assets in financial institutions held were non-performing in 1998. Non-performing loans (NPLs) of private banks and state-owned banks were 40.5 percent and 62.4 percent of their total assets, respectively (Figure 4.3).

To recapitalize, Thai banks were allowed to increase foreign shareholders from the maximum of 25 percent to 49 percent. Bangkok Bank of Commerce (BBC) was the only bank which was closed down. Other bad banks were intervened with

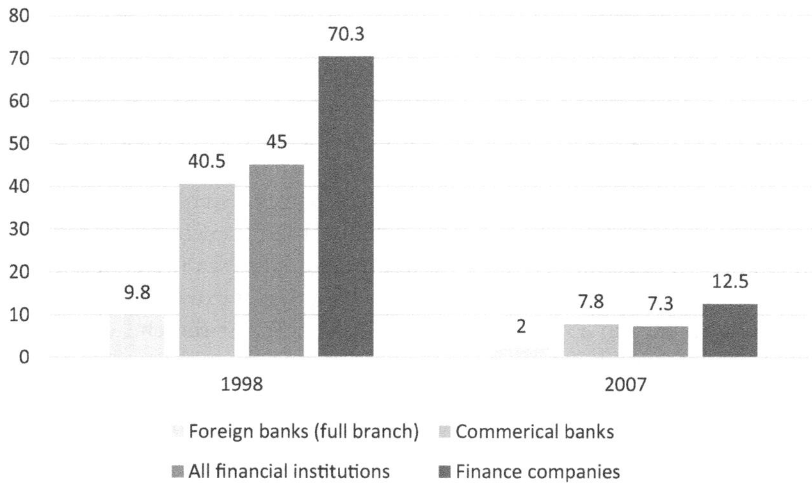

Figure 4.3 NPLs: ten years after the Asian financial crisis

Source: Bank of Thailand

and integrated with the public-owned Krung Thai Bank. Some other troubled banks were merged with stronger banks or sold to foreign institutions.

After 56 finance companies collapsed following the 1997 economic crisis, the Financial Sector Restructuring Authority (FRA) assumed the assets of these defunct financial companies. By August 1998, the closure of the operation of the FRA took place after the auction of the FRA's assets into the Global Thai Property Fund, which was established by Lehman Brothers after paying Bt11.52 billion for the Bt24.62 billion corporate loans extended by troubled financial institutions. Other hedge funds such as GE and Goldman Sachs joined Lehman Brothers by investing in the fund. Ironically, 10 years later, these investment banks suffered from the same fate similar to the Thai finance companies after the burst of the property bubble in 2007.

Because Thai firms and banks borrowed heavily from abroad in the early 1990s, they were exposed to foreign exchange risks. The domestic savings rate was high, but not as high as the investment rate. Investment was financed mainly through borrowing from domestic as well as foreign banks. The average debt-equity ratio of Thai firms was above 8 at the height of the financial crisis, while the economy was exposed to extreme currency depreciation risks. The collapse of the economy in 1998 provided an opportunity for firms and banks to restructure while adhering to good corporate governance and avoiding technical mismanagement.

3. Capital injection and foreign entry

In the aftermath of the financial fiasco, the Thai banking system turned around and raised capital funds. Thanks to capital injection by foreign banks and by the

Financial Institutions Development Fund, managed by the Bank of Thailand, capital adequacy was enhanced. Despite the declining trend of NPLs, the risk-weighted capital adequacy ratio increased substantially, reflecting the strengthened capital funds that can provide safety cushion for depositors.

From 2004 to 2009, capital adequacy ratios (CAR) had been raised in banks of all sizes. Large banks are classified as banks which have more than 7 percent of total assets in the banking system. By this definition, there are four large banks. Small banks had the highest tier 1 capital risk assets ratio as a result of foreign capital injection. The medium-sized banks had the lowest tier 1 capital, although their CARs were raised from 10.9 percent in 2004 to 14.9 percent in 2009. Thus, all banks had capital funds well above the Basel II requirement of 8.5 percent. The most vulnerable banks were medium-sized banks, which had a very high proportion of loans to related parties. It is not surprising that their NPLs increased marginally from 6.7 percent in 2004 to 7 percent during the same corresponding period, while other banks were able to reduce their NPLs from 10 percent to around 4.5 percent. In addition, it was large banks that provided allowances for bad loans more than the amount required by regulations. Thus, large banks tend to be more conservative than small banks, which were the most aggressive in lending; their loans-deposits ratio rose from 93 percent to 137 percent. Medium banks' loan exceeded deposits by 8 percent in 2009, but large banks, on the contrary, cautiously balanced their loans and deposits.

The assets of these small banks are lower than 3 percent of total assets in the banking system. As such, they are competing with disadvantages because they, unlike large banks, cannot exploit economies of scale. Nevertheless, some small banks do have some advantages as they are backed up by huge capital funding from world-class financial institutions. Molyneux et al. (1998) found evidence that foreign bank performance in the US depends mainly on capital strength, in addition to industrial loan growth and asset composition. Berger (2007) provides evidence that foreign-owned banks are more efficient than domestically owned banks in developing countries because of managerial expertise, access to capital, and the use of new technology. In the case of Thailand, foreign banks can compete against state-owned banks because the latter have to comply with the government's objectives, which may not be consistent with profit maximization.

The economic slowdown during the period 2007–2009 was caused by weak consumption and sluggish investment. As a result, financial institutions could not speed up the reduction of their non-performing assets. Since the real estate and manufacturing sectors are sensitive to business cycles, NPLs in these two sectors decline only when the economy regains its strength. All banks have already set aside reserves for loan losses which are larger than the amount required by regulations. The painful experiences of the past have taught commercial banks well in avoiding loan concentration and high-risk exposure. Thanks to the adoption of Basel II, banks are more prepared to deal with global slowdown due to oil price shocks and subprime mortgage problems.

It is believed that local banks should have better information about local clients than foreign banks. As such, they should be less subject to the problem of asymmetric information. That turns out not to be the case, since Thai commercial banks (both private and public) experienced NPLs at 40 percent of total loans in 1998, much higher than the 9.8 percent of foreign banks' total lending (Figure 4.3). By 2007, commercial banks' NPLs declined to 7.8 percent, which was still much higher than the 2 percent of foreign banks. Finance companies' excessive lending led to 70 percent NPLs in 1998, which led to their collapse. Finance companies remained the weakest financial institution in 2007. They were burdened by high NPLs of 12.5 percent, well above the average 7.3 percent of total NPLs for all financial institutions (Figure 4.3).

The ranking of NPLs classified by type of financial institutions in 2007 remained more or less the same as in 1998, although the level of NPLs was much lower than it was 10 years ago. Foreign banks are still the banks which had the lowest non-performing assets, whereas finance companies still had the worst asset quality. Private banks registered in Thailand still could not fully get rid of their NPLs.

There is evidence from transition economies that foreign-owned banks are more efficient than domestic-owned banks because of a transfer of banking know-how and better corporate governance exercised by foreign shareholders (Weil, 2003). The cost efficiency of foreign-owned banks, after taking into account size and structure of activities, does not come from differences in risk preferences between types of banks. Arun and Turner (2004) argue that corporate governance reform is prerequisite for successful divestiture of government ownership and suggested that increased competition resulting from the entrance of foreign banks may improve the corporate governance of banks in developing countries.

There was no significant rise in the banking concentration after the 1998 financial crisis. However, the market share of the top four banks was around 65 percent in 2007, while the largest six banks' combined assets were close to 80 percent of total banking assets. The lack of competition due to increased monopoly power can increase the banking system's profits and increase its solvency. Bank consolidation and conglomeration may not necessarily lead to a safer and more resilient banking system, because consolidated financial firms may take on correlated risks, thereby reducing banks' diversification. There is evidence from the survey of 500 financial firms worldwide in 90 countries that highly concentrated banking systems exhibited higher levels of systemic risk potential than less concentrated banking systems during 1993–2000 and this relationship intensified during 1997–2000 (De Nicolo et al., 2004).

Concentration ratios may not give an accurate measure of the lack of competition since they do not take into account of differences in bank sizes. The Herfindahl index gives a better measure of monopoly power because it gives higher weight to large banks than small banks. The top four banks compete in lending as well as in other services. The ease of entry is also an important consideration of monopoly as excess profit would induce more competition from newcomers. According to Clasessens (2009), the lack of barriers to entry and exit determines effective competition. A banking system with greater contestability in the form of foreign entry and fewer entry and activity restrictions tends to be more competitive.

Small banks cannot compete directly with large banks. They may follow the actions of large banks in setting their interest rates. The solvency of the banking system depends crucially on the health of these large banks. Large banks can take over small troubled banks and subsume small banks' assets and liabilities. Intervention has been a norm in the past through employing public-owned banks to absorb ailing banks. But when bad banks are too expensive to absorb, they must be intervened with temporarily by capital write-off and public capital injection before selling to interested foreign financial institutions. The central bank is subject to the too-big-to-fail syndrome.

The Bank of Thailand has permitted a limited scope of competition for foreign banks through permission of full branch status (only one branch) or subsidiaries of foreign banks. Competition from foreign penetration is weak as the number of branches is limited to four branches for each foreign subsidiary. Because of the ability to exploit economies of scope, large banks were able to obtain non-interest income higher than medium and small banks. Hence, foreign banks are at unit cost disadvantage to local banks. According to the Bank of Thailand, at the end of the first quarter 2010, the outstanding loans of 15 foreign bank branches totaled Bt899 billion. Thai banks' combined loans stood at Bt7.08 trillion, up Bt200 billion over the same corresponding period in the previous year. Bank sizes matter in the exploitation of economies of scale in banking business. Small banks can also achieve their minimum efficiency scale if they focus on the banking segment in which they have comparative advantage. The problem mainly falls on the medium banks since their medium size faces competition from both ends.

Foreign banks have played a dominant role in strengthening Thailand's financial institutions. The Thai banking industry, heavily protected from new competition, has been penetrated by foreign financial institutions through the presence of foreign banks' full branches, establishing foreign partnership, or being taken over. In 1999, the Bank of Thailand encouraged banking consolidation and permitted foreign capital injection, allowing the share of foreign capital to rise above the previous 25 percent limit to 49 percent of total equity. As a result, some ailing Thai banks have stayed solvent by foreign capital injection.

Foreign penetration is prevalent from large- to small-size banks. The average share of foreign ownership in large banks increased from 22 percent in 1997 to 38.5 percent in 2007 (Figure 4.4). Small banks' foreign ownership shares rose from the average 6.4 percent to 55.6 percent during the same corresponding period. The foreign share in medium-sized banks declined to 9.5 percent as the government injected money to bail out these banks. But later on, the share of foreign ownership continued increasing to 37.6 percent in 2007. The need for foreign capital was obvious during recapitalization and when the economy was so weak that it could not generate capital funds. The government has already had considerable financial burden from bailing out bad banks. By opening the banking sector to foreign institutions, the Bank of Thailand has lessened public burden and also maintained public confidence in the banking system. Although some banks failed and disappeared, their deposits were transferred to the government-owned KTB bank, which has assumed liabilities and assets of the failed banks.

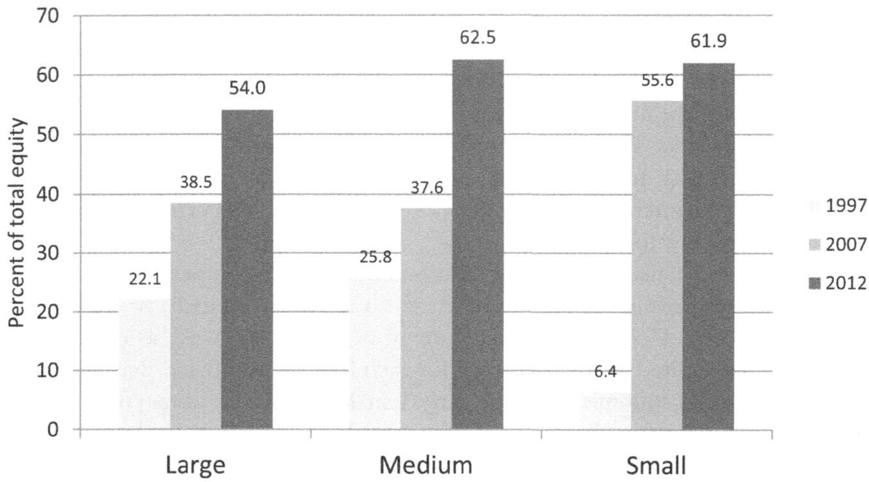

Figure 4.4 Foreign ownership in Thai banks

Source: Bank of Thailand

Among the four largest banks, two banks had foreign shares close to the maximum level of 49 percent permitted by law. The public-owned bank (KTB), after absorbing failed banks, had to accept foreign capital injection. Bank solvency was achieved through reducing the barriers to foreign investment in the financial sector. Although the other top three banks are efficient and profitable private banks, they cannot resist foreign capital participation because of the benefit from having foreign strategic partners. The capital adequacy ratio of all banks must be raised above the 8.5 percent as required by Basel II regulations. By 2007, all banks were able to satisfy the condition. Without foreign capital participation, it would be impossible for banks to maintain high level of capital fund. Unlike large banks, the tier-one capital fund to risk asset ratios of smaller banks were higher than those of large banks due to their limited ability to raise other types of capital funds. The need for foreign capital partnership is greater for small and medium-sized banks.

Medium-sized banks have encountered high non-performing loans and related parties lending. Recapitalization through public money would cost more unless there is a change in management and business strategy. This is precisely the reason why the Bank of Thailand, through the Financial Institution Development Fund (FIDF), would want to sell shares of these medium-sized banks to foreign institutions to reduce their burden after they were bailed out. Unlike medium-sized banks, small banks were easily taken over by foreign institutions that wanted to have their presence in the Thai financial markets. Their quality of assets is better than those of medium-sized banks and they need only relatively small capital injections to boost the capital adequacy ratio to the Basel II standards. Both United Overseas Bank and Standard Chartered Bank have taken absolute control of two small Thai banks and converted them into full-fledged foreign banks bearing their own names. The other four small banks in this group were either consolidated among finance companies or upgraded themselves into commercial banks. At the height of the financial turmoil in 1997, 56 finance companies were closed down. The remaining finance companies were strong enough to undergo structural adjustments during difficult times. They emerged as strong contenders in the financial sector and subsequently were upgraded into banks. Similarly, these newcomers need foreign capital participation in order to compete in the new competitive environment of universal banking system. They tend to concentrate on retail business and real estate lending.

Small-sized banks can be profitable and efficient if they do not compete directly with large banks. They concentrate their operations in their niche areas. The Bank of Thailand allows finance companies to upgrade into banks with a specialization in retail banking. This can create more competition among banks.[1] Competition has been intensified and widened into different kinds of services, including investment in securities, foreign exchange services, fees, and services income. Their numerous branches throughout the country mean smaller banks find it difficult to compete. Most of medium and small banks' non-interest income is in the form of fees and services. In 2007, some medium and small banks suffered losses from investment in collateralized debt obligations (CDO). Nevertheless, such investment was small and did not threaten the stability of any bank's solvency.

In general, foreign banks' branches maintain higher capital funds than Thai banks (Figure 4.5). But there has been a significant difference of about 3 percent since 2014. Because of impaired capital funds in 1998, the amount of capital

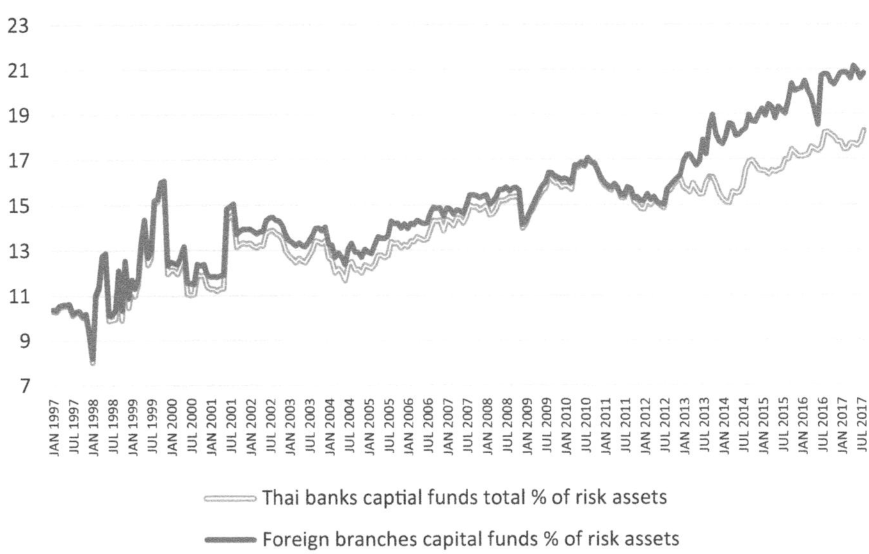

Figure 4.5 Capital adequacy: Thai banks and foreign banks' branches

Source: Bank of Thailand

funds as percent of risk assets dropped closer to 7 percent. Nevertheless, there has been a significant increasing trend since then. The capital adequacy ratio of foreign banks' branches rose to 20 percent by 2017, exceeding Thai banks' 17.8 percent. The rising level of capital funds relative to risk assets can be attributed to the desire to strengthen capital funds or the inability to extend credit during a time of slowdown in economic activity.

A sharp difference in the loan-deposit ratios was apparent when examining the loan-deposit ratio between Thai banks and foreign banks' branches, whose total loans extension is about 10 percent of Thai banks' lending volume. Figure 4.6 depicts a sharp decline in the loan-deposit ratio of foreign bank branches from the peak of almost 220 percent in June 2011 to 104 percent in January 2018. A slowdown in trade credit for exporters and importers partly explains the sluggish growth of lending activities. As for Thai banks, a stagnant loan-deposit ratio bodes well for the slow growing demand for credit from the manufacturing sector.

In January 2016, the Bank of Thailand replaced the 6 percent reserve requirement of bank deposits by the loan coverage ratio (LCR), which adopts a forward-looking approach to liquidity. The ratio measures not just cash reserves, but also stock of liquid assets which can cover the expected cash outflows in the next 3 months. The minimum requirement is 100 percent coverage, but both Thai banks and foreign banks' branches can meet the target without difficulty. Foreign bank branches' LCRs have been higher and more volatile than Thai banks' (Figure 4.7). Higher LCR implies higher excess reserves, and higher opportunity costs in trying to meet unexpected withdrawals of deposits. The implication on deposit creation is quite clear. This measure is meant for maintaining bank liquidity and solvency. It can never be used as the conventional legal reserve ratio to stabilize the economy during upswing and downswing. There is no loss in monetary policy instrument, because the Bank of Thailand has never used the legal reserve ratio for stabilizing purposes in recent history.

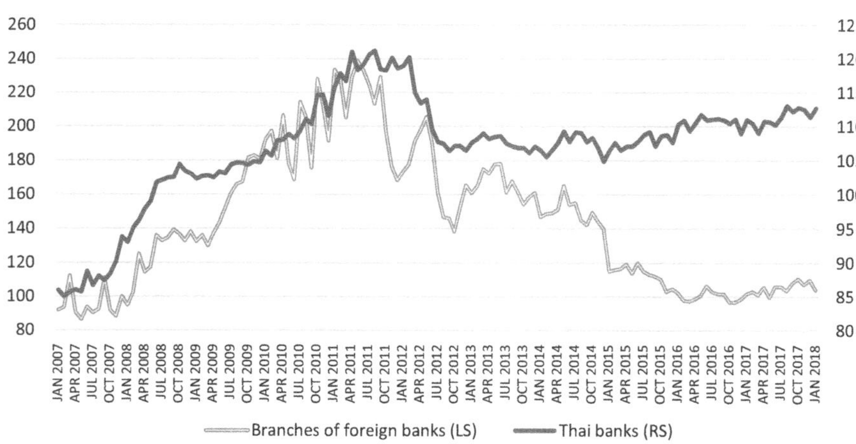

Figure 4.6 Loan-deposit ratio (percent)

Source: Bank of Thailand

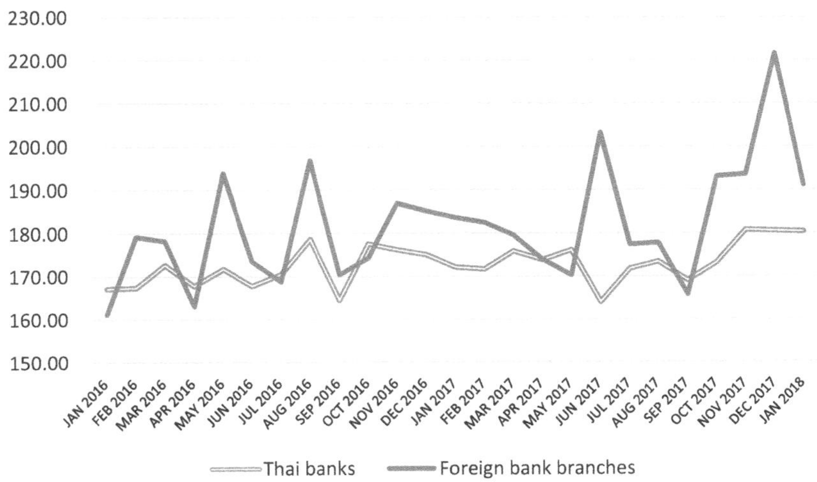

Figure 4.7 Loan-coverage ratio

Source: Bank of Thailand

The global financial crisis in 2007–2009 led the Fed to continue maintaining the low interest rate policy. While the US prime lending rate declined further in November 2008, the Thai commercial banks' minimum lending rate (MLR) was also reduced with a few months' lag. The excess liquidity of the Thai banking system due to the lack of loan demand caused a temporary departure of the domestic interest rate from the world interest rates. The cost of bank funding was reduced since Thai banks also reduced the deposit interest rates when the lending rate was cut. The widening interest spread between the time deposits and minimum lending rates improved the profitability of Thai commercial banks. In particular when the loan-deposit ratio increased after the economic recovery, Thai banks experienced larger interest income. The 5 percent interest spread indicates that Thai banks have monopoly power. Had there been more competition, there would have been a narrower spread. The net interest margin (NIM) of Thai banking in 2010 was close to 3 percent, suggesting the ability to earn larger profits when loan demand expanded in response to a rapid growth rate, which also improved the quality of bank loans.

4. Resilience of the banking sector

The Thai economy experienced a severe recession in 1998 and was able to recover within a few years after the crisis. As pointed out by Bonin and Huang (2002), countries that had strong financial institutions and undertook more rapid restructuring of the banking systems were more successful in coping with the financial crisis. The Thai banking sector has prepared well for the global financial crisis. The global recession led to a declining world trade volume in 2009. The consequent slump of Thailand's exports contracted the GDP by 2.3 percent. Moreover, political violence disrupted the normal policy response of the government, causing a decline in public spending and dampening business confidence. As the economy slowed down, the demand for loans was sluggish and lowered the quality of bank assets. As a result, the amount of risky assets increased, necessitating banks to raise capital funds and increase loan-loss provisions. Figure 4.8 illustrates that by the first quarter of 2017, Thai banks' capital adequacy ratio was raised higher than 14 percent, which is above the Bank for International Settlements (BIS) requirement. The Thai banks have prepared well for the next financial crisis.

In an extreme case, when all non-performing loans turn into bad loans and banks have to write them off from the balance sheet, commercial banks still have sufficient level of capital funds to protect depositors. Figure 4.8 reveals that the equity level of shareholders was much larger than the level of NPLs, which was already on the declining trend since 2007. Although it did not decline below 2 percent, it reached its trough in 2013 and did not rebound above 3 percent in 2017. It is difficult for non-performing loans to fall further as long as GDP growth is still sluggish. It boils down to the strength of the economy, which can lower the NPLs further. The quality of bank assets in the financial sector is a mirror image of the condition in the real sector.

A comparison of the commercial banks' asset quality in 2004 and 2017 reveals that Thai commercial banks have gained strength considerably despite undergoing the global financial crisis and global recession. Banks' tier 1 capital as percentage of risk assets increased from 8.7 percent to 14.8 percent (Figure 4.9). The amount of loans to related parties as percentage of total loans declined from

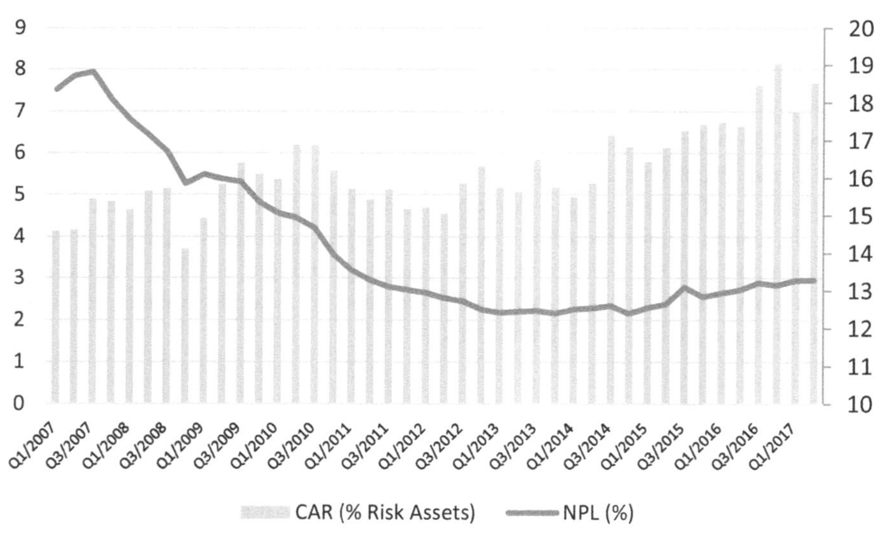

Figure 4.8 Non-performing loans (NPLs) and capital adequacy ratio

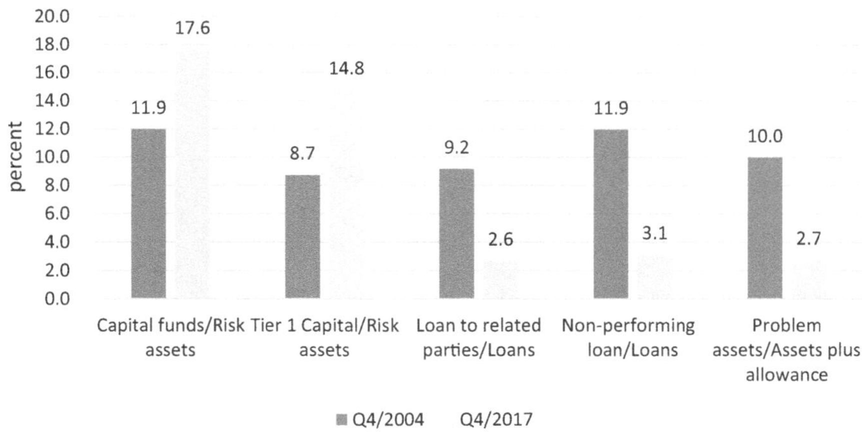

Figure 4.9 Commercial banks' asset quality

Source: Bank of Thailand

9.2 percent to 2.6 percent. During the same corresponding period, NPLs were reduced from 11.9 percent to just 3.1 percent, while problem assets dropped from 10 percent to 2.7 percent of total assets plus allowances for bad debts. This remarkable achievement happened despite the dismal growth performance of the real sector. Banks have to adjust in times of difficulty by improving the efficiency of their operations. Similarly, in time of economic buoyancy, banks should not be complacent and should continue to improve their operations to strike a balance between profitability, efficiency, and solvency.

From 2004 to 2017, the average salaries of bank employees increased from 500,000 baht to 980,000 baht – that is, they almost doubled in 13 years (Figure 4.10). Consumer price index increased 34.2 percent during this period. Since the nominal wage increased faster than the price level, there has been a substantial rise in the real wage. Higher cost of living and improved productivity of workers explain this rise. Other indicators of bank efficiency through the ability to generate net profit and net assets per employee show significant improvement, reflecting higher efficiency per bank branches. Banks pay their workers by the value of their marginal product. There has been a tendency for banks to reduce the number of bank branches. The trend has become clear since 2017 as banks started to cut operating costs from having a large number of branches. Internet banking and new applications on smartphones will have a profound effect on bank employees in the near future.

In the aftermath of the global financial crisis, loan growth declined substantially from the level in early 2000. Commercial banks' net profit per branch and per employee increased. In 2004 real GDP expanded by 6.3 percent and slowed down to 3.3 percent in 2017. Bank loan growth was 5.5 percent and 4.6 percent during the same corresponding period. Net profit and operating profit increased

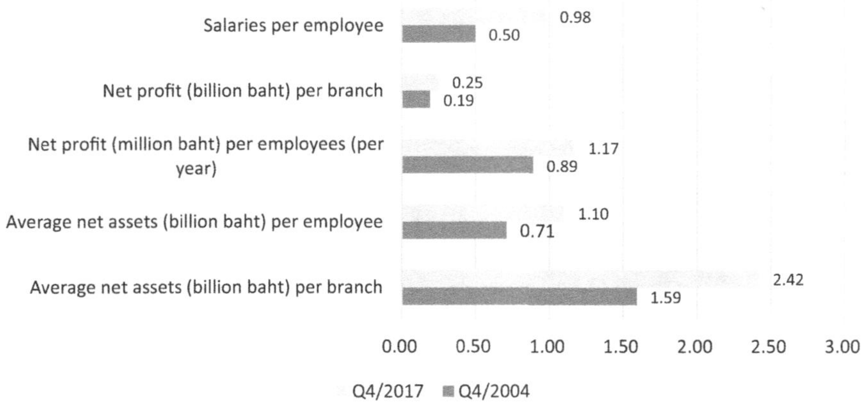

Figure 4.10 Bank efficiency

Source: Bank of Thailand

when measured as a ratio of net assets. This can be attributed to the ability to raise non-interest income, despite the rise in interest expenses. Interest income and dividends also increased (Figure 4.11).

In 2007, operating expenses was 80 percent of net interest income and dividend. It declined to 77.7 percent in 2017. This was a minimal improvement, thanks to higher salaries which jumped from 34 percent to 42 percent of operating expenses during the same corresponding period (Figure 4.12). Banks have found the way to increase non-interest revenues, which rose from 25.3 percent to almost 30 percent. These are revenues obtained from fee and services income, whose share in total non-interest income rose 55.7 percent to 68.5 percent. The relative importance of non-interest income from investment in securities declined due to poor performance of the stock market and gains from foreign exchanges did not increase much due to stable exchange rates.[2]

The interest to expense ratio declined temporarily in 2011 and hit its trough in the following years (Figure 4.13). By 2013, after the economy had regained its momentum, the ratio was increasing. The slowdown of the economy in 2015 caused the interest income to rise slower than banks' expenditures. Nevertheless, the net interest income increased gradually, reaching 110 billion baht by Q2/2017.

Interest income rose steadily despite the slowdown of loan growth, thanks to the trend of widening interest gap since 1992 (Figure 4.14). The larger spread between lending and deposit allowed banks to make a profit despite the low growth volume. It also suggested that the price competition among banks was not high enough to narrow the spread, despite the fact that there are 30 commercial banks, domestic banks, and branches of foreign banks in Thailand. One can argue that a contributing factor to the large spread is the high level of required

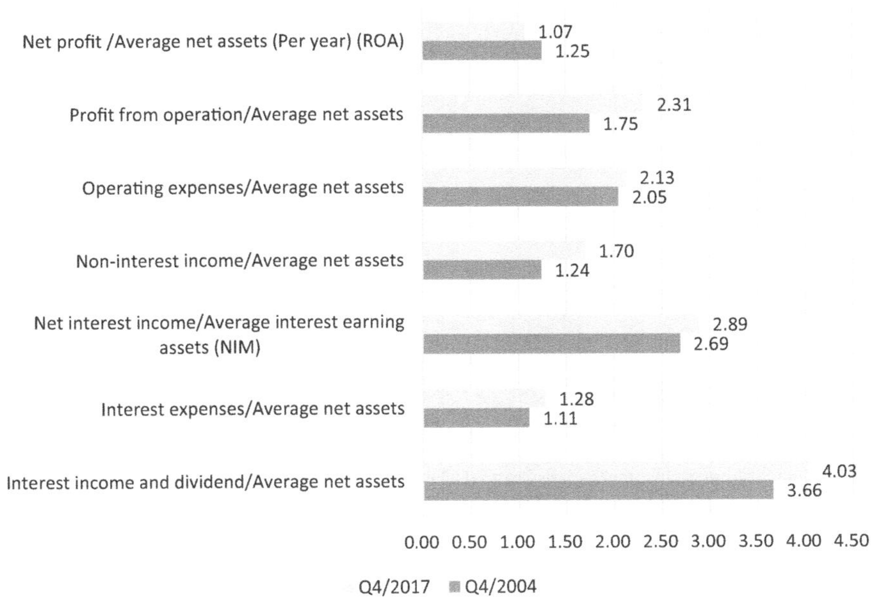

Figure 4.11 Bank profitability

Source: Bank of Thailand

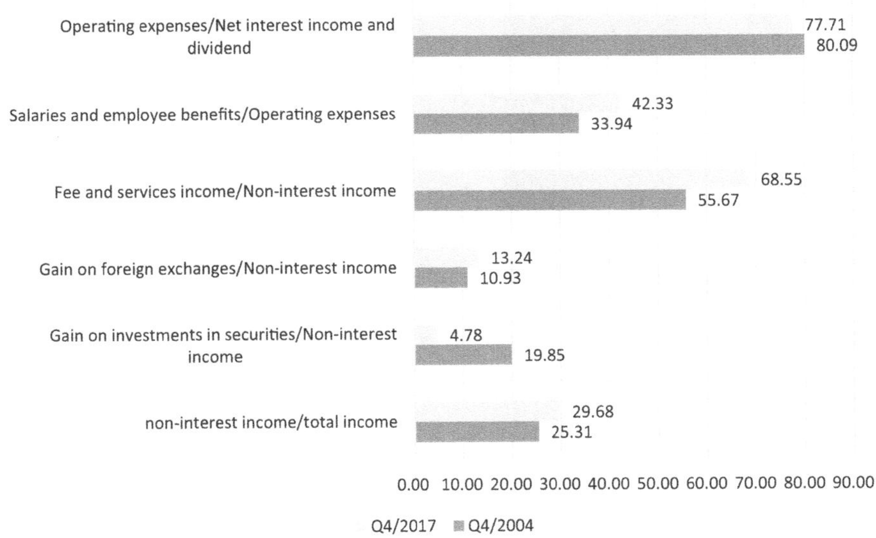

Figure 4.12 Banks' structure of income and expenses

Source: Bank of Thailand

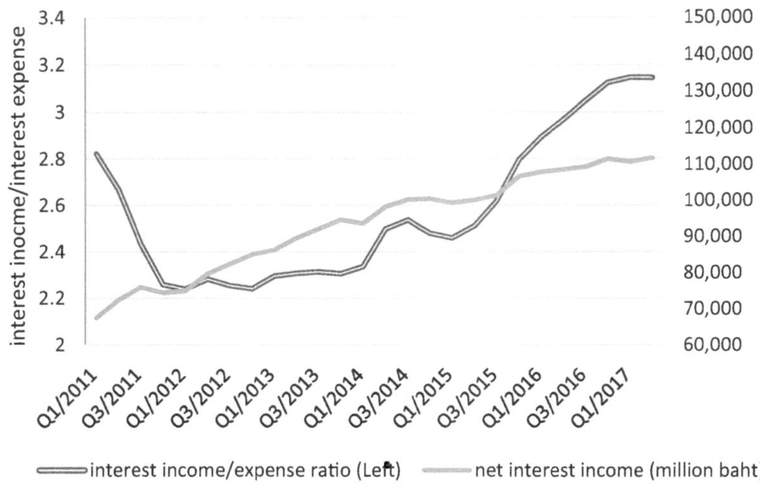

Figure 4.13 Rising interest income

Source: Bank of Thailand

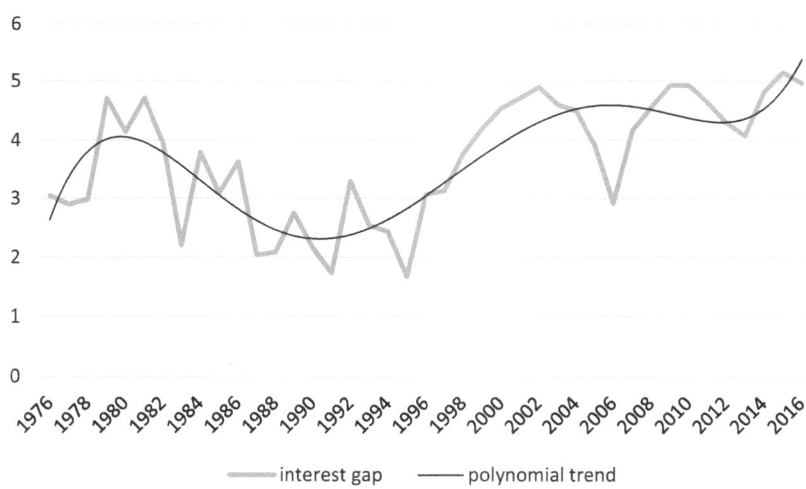

Figure 4.14 Interest gap

Source: Bank of Thailand

reserve and the requirement of banks to contribute 0.01 percent of total deposits to Financial Institution Development Fund (FIDF). We cannot deny that Thai banks enjoy hefty profit from their operations. A proxy for bank efficiency from a social perspective is the size of the interest gap. Viewed in this light, social welfare has declined since the 1990s, as welfare gains were reduced by the loss of consumer surplus of depositors and borrowers.

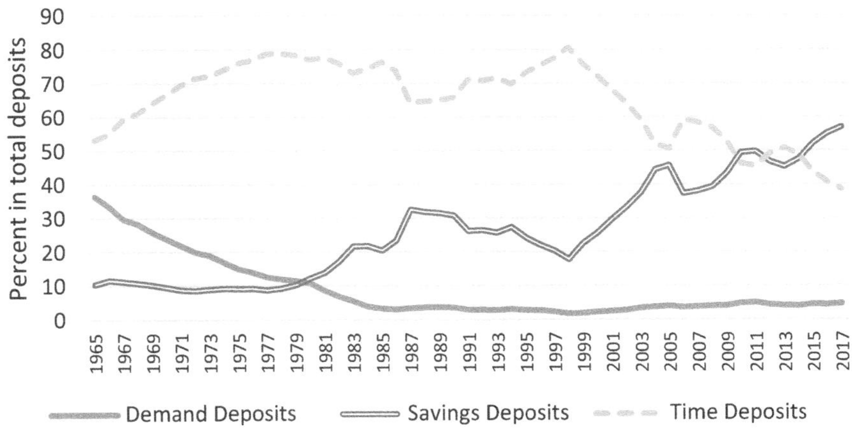

Figure 4.15 Structural change in bank deposits

Source: Bank of Thailand

There was a significant structural change in household portfolios, which affected bank operation and change commercial banks' strategy. Demand deposits have dwindled since 1965 and amounted to less than 5 percent of total commercial deposits since 1985. Similarly, the share of time deposits, which increased substantially to almost 80 percent in 1978, declined to 64 percent in 1988. The final surge in the share of time deposits appeared in 1998 before it resumed a declining trend well into 2017. There has been a portfolio reallocation, shifting away from time deposits to savings deposits. Low interest rates offered by time deposits and more liquidity for savings deposits are the major reason for the shift.

Savings deposits are close substitutes of currency, thanks to the popularity of debit cards and widespread use of ATM machines. Figure 4.16 illustrates that the turnover ratio of savings deposits rose rapidly, while that of time deposits remained stable and less than unity. Commercial banks must prepare ample liquidity for the very high turnover ratio of savings deposits. This is precisely the reason why the regulation on required reserves has been changed into the liquidity coverage ratio. If commercial banks hold excessive amount of liquidity, above the requirement of 100 percent, changing the level of LCR ratio would not be effective in restraining the overheated economy.

As the economy hit its trough near the end of 2016, output started to rise together with the demand for loans. Shown in Figure 4.17, the cyclical movements of bank credit (CYLOAN) and manufacturing output index (CYMPI) are positively correlated. If we remove these cyclical components from their actual values, we obtain trend values of loans and output paths. We can calculate the elasticity of the demand for loans with respect to output, using the trend values of loan and output, by ignoring other factors such as changes in interest rates. The obtained semi-elasticity of the demand for loans with respect to output is in

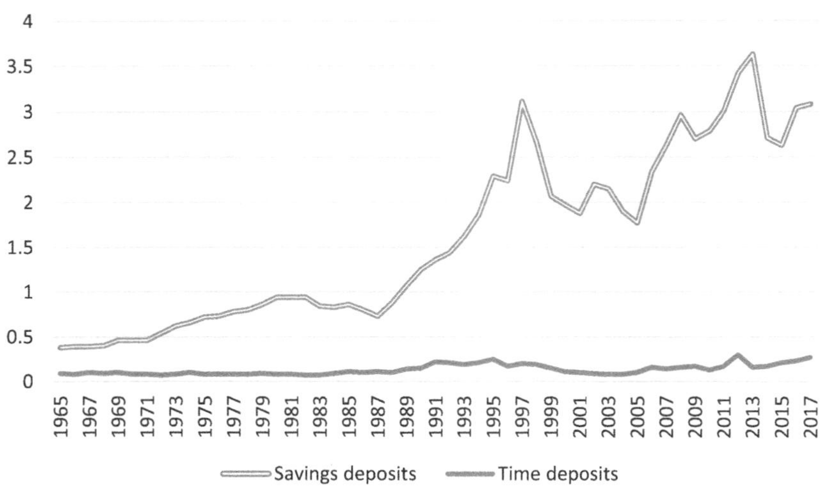

Figure 4.16 Deposit turnover ratio

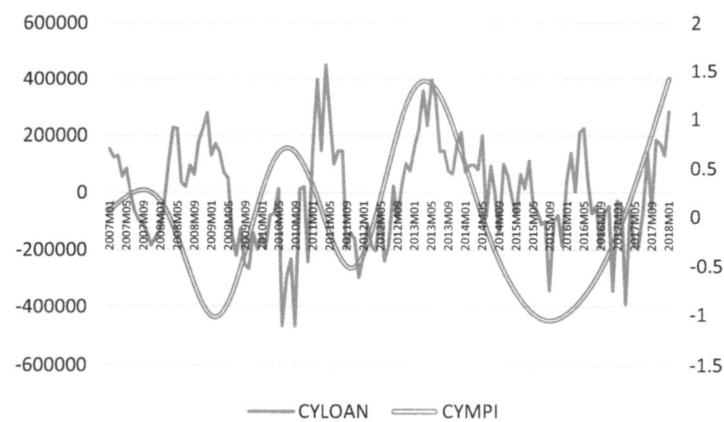

Figure 4.17 Cyclical movements of industrial output and bank loans

Source: Bank of Thailand

the neighborhood of 3.0, indicating that the demand for loans is highly sensitive to industrial output growth.

For banks to remain profitable, they must seek higher profit from a wider interest gap as well as seeking higher non-interest income. During the upturns, credit growth rises faster than the manufacturing output. Bank profit increases substantially if both loan volume growth and the interest gap are high. Bank profits depend on loan growth and the gap between lending and deposit rates. During the downturns, credit growth drops much faster than manufacturing output. This

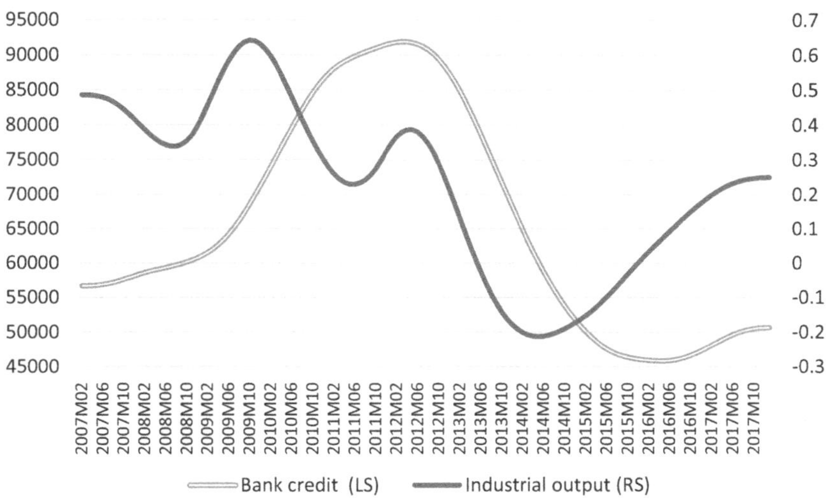

Figure 4.18 Changes in credit and output trends

explains why loan growth is highly sensitive to changes in output growth. When output growth slowed down in early 2010, credit still expanded and then petered out about 24 months later. The lag adjustment of loans to output change is about 2 years. Similarly, when output picks up during the recovery phase of the business cycle, it takes another 2 years before we see a solid recovery of loan growth. There is a systematic relationship between credit cycles and business cycles.

The Granger causality test between bank credit and industrial output, represented by manufacturing output index, confirms that changes in output lead to changes in bank credit. Figure 4.18 depicts such a lead-lag relationship between output cycles and credit cycles. A boom in the economy, fueled by strong growth in manufacturing output, is followed by credit growth. The empirical evidence points to the conclusion that bank profitability depends on loan growth generated by a booming economy. During a downturn, it takes a while before credit growth slows down; hence, bank profit is adversely affected by dismal growth of economic activity.

5. Concluding remarks

The Thai financial sector was vulnerable and weak in the late 1990s. The lack of prudential regulations and sufficient capital funds meant capital control relaxation in the early 1990s was a premature liberalization. The ensuing fast and large capital inflows led to financial turmoil. The Thai financial sector emerged from the 1998 crisis and became stronger and more resilient, thanks to foreign capital injection, good governance, and strengthened financial rules. The rapid economic recovery, despite the political turmoil in 2010, provided opportunities for banks to expand their credit and enjoy the benefits of rising interest rates. In addition, the strong performance of corporate sector enabled banks to reduce NPLs further.

The large interest margin between lending and deposit rates bodes well for the monopoly rent of commercial banks. The transfer of wealth from consumers to banks can be reduced via allowing foreign entry in line with liberalization of the service sector. Financial institutions and their regulators cannot resist the global trend of foreign penetration. By opening up the financial sector to foreign participation, the financial sector has become more efficient, benefiting from competition and technology adaptation. With foreign capital injection, the monetary authorities can maintain system solvency while lessening the burden of financial bailouts.

Since the 1997 financial crisis, the Thai economy has been closely integrated to the world economy through international trade and capital flows. As such, it cannot completely shield itself from external shocks. The global financial crisis during 2007–2009 led to export collapse and output contraction in 2009. The crash of the world's financial institutions and stock markets in 2008 had a negative impact on the Thai stock market. However, the adverse consequence on the Thai banking sector was minimal. Thai banks were able to make profits during difficult times. Most of them did not invest in CDOs nor focus mainly on property lending. The level of NPLs continued to decline, while banks enhanced capital strength and provided sufficient loan-loss provisions. The exploitation of economies of scale and scope improved efficiency in their operations. All of these factors were the result of the financial reform undertaken after the financial crisis in 1997. Thai banks were well prepared for the global financial crisis as they learned a valuable lesson on being conservative and obeying stringent rules and regulations. It remains to be seen how vulnerable and resilient the Thai banking system is during the Eurozone problems and the fears of US double-dip recession. As cautioned by Blanchard et al. (2010), the effectiveness of macroprudential policy must be further evaluated during the next financial crisis.

We have seen the resilience of Thai commercial banks over periods of macroeconomic shocks. Strengthening rules and regulations have made Thai banks stronger. The banking sector underwent global financial crisis, the slowdown of China's economy, and depressed consumer spending during political turmoil and various internal shocks. The main conclusion is that macroeconomic environment matters for bank profitability. Even in times of sluggish economic activity, banks can survive and thrive by riding the business cycles through improving productivity and seeking higher revenue from non-interest income. Technology improvement is a must if banks are going to survive in the world of fast-changing technology. Electronic payments, rising wages, and financial technology are the new order of the day. Failure to adapt to the changing environment spells trouble for some banks which are left behind.

Notes

1 Kubo (2006) estimated Lerner index for Thai banking system after the Asian Financial Crisis. The index shows a possibility of a decline in bank competition, despite reduction in family ownership of banks and the arrival of new foreign banks.

2 See Nidhiprabha (2011) for comparison of large-, medium-, and small-sized banks in terms of efficiency and profitability between 2004 and 2007.

References

Arun, Thanakorn G., and John D. Turner. 2004. "Corporate Governance of Banks in Developing Economies: Concepts and Issues." *Corporate Governance: An International Review*, 12 (3): 371–377.

Berger, Allen N. 2007. "International Comparisons of Banking Efficiency." *Financial Markets, Institutions & Investment*, 16 (3): 119–144.

Blanchard, Oliver, Giovanni Dell'Ariccia, and Paolo Mauro. 2010. "Rethinking Macroeconomic Policy." International Monetary Fund, Research Department Working Paper.

Bonin, John P., and Yiping Huang. 2002. "Foreign Entry into Chinese Banking: Does WTO Membership Threaten Domestic Banks?" *The World Economy*, 25 (8): 1077–1093.

Clasessens, Stijn. 2009. "Competition in the Financial Sector: Overview of Competition Policies." *The World Bank Research Observer*, 24 (1): 83–118.

De Nicolo, Gianni, Philip Bartholomew, Jahanara Zaman, and Mary Zephirin. 2004. "Bank Consolidation, Internationalization, and Conglomeration: Trends and Implications for Financial Risk." *Financial Markets, Institutions & Investment*, 13 (4): 173–217.

Kenc, Turalay, and Sel Dibooglu. 2010. "The 2007–2008 Financial Crisis, Global Imbalances and Capital Flows: Implication for Reform." *Economic Systems*, 34 (1): 3–21.

Kubo, Koji. 2006. "The Degree of Competition in the Thai Banking Industry Before and After the East Asian Crisis." *ASEAN Economic Bulletin*, 23 (3): 325–340.

Marer, P. 2010. "The Global Economic Crises: Impacts on Eastern Europe." *Acta Oeconomica*, 60 (1): 3–33.

Molyneux, Philip, Eli Remolona, and Rama Seth. 1998. "Modeling Foreign Bank Performance and Lending Behavior." *Financial Markets, Institutions & Investment*, 7 (4): 26–41.

Nidhiprabha, Bhanupong. 2011. "The Global Financial Crisis and Resilience of the Thai Banking Sector." *Asian Development Review, Asian Development Bank*, 28 (2): 110–132.

Simpson, John L. 2010. "Were There Warning Signals From Banking Sector for the 2008/2009 Global Financial Crisis?" *Applied Financial Economics*, 20 (1): 45–61.

Weill, Laurent. 2003. "Banking Efficiency in Transition Economies: The Role of Foreign Ownership." *Economics of Transition*, 11 (3): 569–592.

5 The stock market and macroeconomy

1. Introduction

As Thailand's financial development progressed further, new forms of savings became available in response to rising demand from wealthy households. Unlike traditional bank depositors, who seek low risk and stable interest rate income, investors in the stock markets prefer higher returns since they can accept a higher degree of financial risks. Bonds are new portfolio options for savers and investors who are willing to give up liquidity for the sake of stable returns in order to diversify assets. The development of the stock market has an important impact on Thailand's macroeconomy. In this chapter, we examine how the activity in the stock market is related to the real sector. Rising stock prices exert a wealth effect on consumption spending, as households feel richer during the booming stock market and vice versa during market slump. A bull market encourages firms to boost physical capital stock because it is less expensive than acquiring shares of listed firms. Consumption and investment expenditures therefore respond to stock market booms and busts. Other factors such as expectations, business sentiment, and the Dow Jones index, can also cause volatility in the stock market. It is important to understand the sensitivity of the stock market to shocks of macro variables. Furthermore, volatile movements of international stock markets affect the Thai stock market because international investors wish to diversify their portfolio into Asian shares. In the event of financial shocks, there can be a contagion effect via the interconnectedness among asset prices in Asia.

2. The capital market and Thailand's financial development

As the Thai economy gradually moved from a low-income to middle-income country, households' propensity to save increased. Because output growth rate is positively related to a high savings ratio, Thailand's high growth rate prior to the Asian financial crisis (AFC) generated high savings, which provided financial resources for investment. Nevertheless, deceleration of Thailand's economic growth after the AFC caused a considerable decline in investment rate. The excess savings led to declining interest rates, but the resulting decline in the cost of investment did not correct the trend of declining investment. The rate of return from savings was not high enough to attract saving and time deposits (quasi money) in commercial banks. The slowdown in economic activities in Thailand in the 2000s caused quasi money to rise slowly relative to GDP expansion. As the process of financial development continues, households have alternative forms of saving through stocks and bonds. Government bonds and bank deposits are complementary, since both have low risk and a stable rate of returns. Bonds and fixed deposits are assets with long maturity, providing a safe asset for long-term investors who are risk averse. Stocks are more liquid and higher risk than quasi money and bonds. As such, stocks can be considered as substitutes for bank deposits and government bonds.

The relatively high risks from holding equities can be seen from the volatility of market capitalization (Figure 5.1). While the share of bonds to GDP increased gradually over time, except in 2008 during the global financial crisis (GFC), market capitalization as percent of GDP fluctuated from year to year, reflecting movements of share prices. The ratio of bonds to GDP rose steadily from 27 percent in 2000 to 74 percent in 2015. Bonds, in particular government bonds, provide safe financial assets to wealth holders. For majority of the Thais, bank deposits are still the most important assets; deposit yields are lower, but they are considered as safe assets. Savings and time deposits increased from 89 percent in 2000 to 117 percent in 2015. This increasing trend indicated the rising degree of financial deepening in Thailand. The low rate of return from deposits is regarded as high after adjusting for the risk of bank failure. There has been no bank failure in the recent history of Thailand's banking system. For some households, memory of the stock market crash in the 1996 still remains fresh. Figure 5.1 illustrates that from 2000 to 2010, savings and time deposits to GDP remained below 100 percent.

There might be a substitution effect away from bank deposits to other form of savings such as gold, land, and real estate, which are alternative assets to hold for

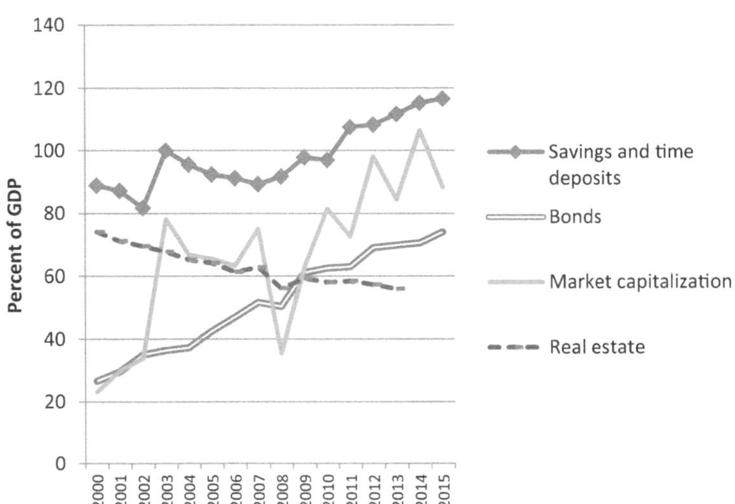

Figure 5.1 Mode of savings

Source: Bank of Thailand and NESDB

inflation hedging and speculations. The capital stock of real estates as percentage of GDP did not increase as fast as other financial assets. Land prices have increased rapidly in the last two decades, because of the excess demand caused by genuine demand for residential development and speculative demand. Liquidity is the main problem with real estate, despite the rapidly rising value of housing. Real estate is an illiquid asset and is not a close substitute for financial assets.

To conclude, there has been substantial development in the capital market since 2000, when the market capitalization was just 30 percent of GDP. By 2014, it rose above 100 percent, despite its ups and downs through various internal and external shocks. The rising importance of the capital markets has slowly shifted the pattern of financing from indirect to direct investment financing. Bank loans are relatively less important to finance large firms, which are able to issue bonds and shares in mobilizing funds for investment.

Bank credit dominates other forms of investment financing mode. Thailand is still a bank-based economy, where domestic firms rely heavily on bank credit to finance investment. From 2004, bank credit slowed down from 95 percent of GDP and reached its trough at 86 percent in 2007. As the Thai economy recovered slowly, bank credit started to grow faster than GDP. By 2015, it reached 117 percent. The ongoing financial deepening process also allows firms to tap financial resources from the local bond market, in addition to domestic and foreign borrowing. Figure 5.2 indicates that Thai firms can issue bonds to finance investment in local currency. The trend is encouraging as it steadily rose from the low level of 5 percent in 2000 to 18 percent in 2015. Within 15 years, the Thai bond market more than tripled its size.

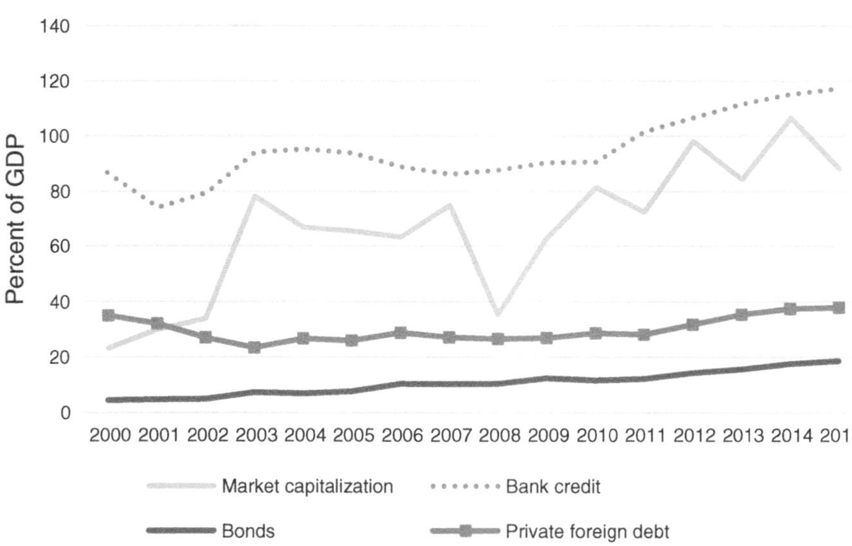

Figure 5.2 Mode of financing

Source: Bank of Thailand

Thai firms borrowed abroad, but resources from foreign savings declined sharply from 35 percent of GDP in 2000 to 23 percent in 2003. The decline was due to lower demand for foreign borrowing, in line with domestic borrowing. In addition, local firms substituted local bank borrowing for foreign loans, thanks to declining interest rates. Foreign borrowing incurs foreign exchange risks, while excess savings in the domestic market allowed firms to borrow domestically at lower costs. From 2006 onward, it seems that foreign borrowing and domestic bank loans were complementary. By 2014, private foreign borrowed increased to the same level as it was 14 years ago. Low interest rates in the US and the strong baht during this period gave rise to more foreign borrowing. In addition to the three sources of funds discussed earlier, firms can offer shares to the public in the stock market. As shown in Figure 5.1, this direct method of financing, which connects savers directly to investors, has become increasingly important. Rising market capitalization is related to future growth potential of the economy.

3. Stock prices and the macroeconomy

Non-neutrality of money is the short-run nature of monetary policy; monetary authority can exert impact on the real economy. In the long run, money supply cannot affect real variables such as output and inflation. Money is neutral in the long run because prices and wages are flexible. When expectations are fulfilled, and there is no trade-off between unemployment and inflation. Friedman (2005) pointed out that a natural experiment of the US monetary policy conducted during the last 80 years leads to a conclusion that the quantity of money determines output fluctuations and the level of the stock market prices. For a small open economy, inflows of foreign capital affect the local stock prices. Liberalizing restrictions on international portfolio flows tends to enhance stock market liquidity, which accelerates economic growth primarily by boosting productivity growth (Levine, 2001). Sawalha et al. (2016), using data from developed and emerging economies from 1980 to 2012, provide evidence that the initial foreign direct investment (FDI) and foreign portfolio investment (FPI) have a positive impact on growth. In the longer term, FDI poses a positive and significant influence on growth, but FPI can exert a negative influence on growth. This hypothesis may hold for the early stage of financial liberalization in Thailand, where capital control liberalization took place in the early 1990s. The unrealistic dream of establishing Bangkok as a financial center in the region led to premature liberalization, which was followed by a stock and economic boom prior to the collapse in the 1997.

Examining daily stock prices from January 2017 to February 2018, it is found that Dow Jones and Nasdaq Indexes Granger cause the SET index, while stock market prices in London, Nikkei, and Hang Seng do not affect movement in the Thai stock market. The Thai stock market is more related to the US stock market than any other markets, because of the expectations that the Thai markets would move up and down together with the Wall Street (Figure 5.3). The Thai economy relies heavily on exports. The bull market in the US signifies the strength of the US economy and its demand for Thailand's manufactured exports. The

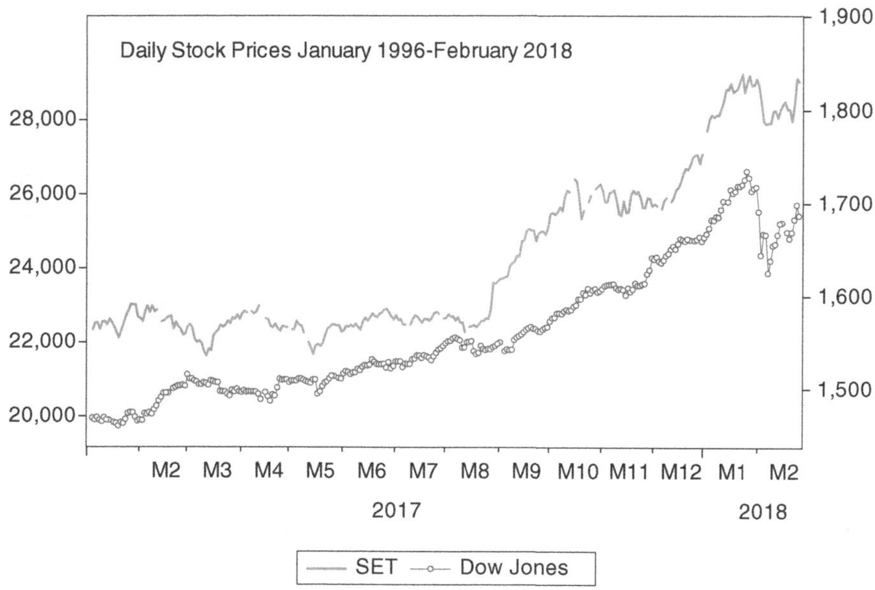

Figure 5.3 Dow Jones and the SET indexes

SET index therefore responds to favorable news from the Wall Street. However, domestic investor sentiment also matters.

In January 2017, foreign investors accounted for 28 percent of total transactions at Thailand's stock market. The combined share of local institutions and proprietary trading was 22 percent, lower than foreign investors. Local individual share was 50 percent, almost twice the size of the share of foreign investors, but it is easily swayed by foreign investors. It is obvious that share prices in the region move in line with Wall Street. Asian share prices move in tandem with the Dow Jones Industrial Average (DJIA). The important role of expectations on DJIA on Thailand's share prices is quite clear, as expectations moved portfolio investment from low-return markets to high-return markets in Asia in the aftermath of the GFC.

Net portfolio investment plunged after the 2006 military coup, rebounded, and peaked at 1.7 percent of GDP in 2011, after the country had returned to democracy with an elected government. FPI pushed up Thailand's share prices when the rate of return in advanced countries declined in line with the Great Recession in 2008. The emerging economies recovered rapidly in 2010, while Europe and the US were still coping with recession. There was a jump in net portfolio investment from 2009 to 2011. Since then the net FPI declined rapidly, turning from positive to negative from 2013 to 2014. Since then the PFI outflows continued, reaching 4.1 percent in 2015.

There is a channel which transmits shocks from the domestic stock market, or from the Dow Jones fluctuations, to affect domestic output. When share prices rise in the Thai stock market, it induces inflows of FPI. As a result, the baht appreciates, which can lead to negative impacts on exports and output. The slowdown in output leads to lower investment, which in turn depress long-term growth of the country. Portfolio inflows cause the baht to appreciate, unless there is a strong intervention by the BoT. Any factors that set off panic and capital flight will lead to currency depreciation. Similarly, outflows of FPI cause the SET index to fall, and the baht becomes weaker. Therefore, capital flights or sudden portfolio flows can cause output contraction or expansion through the baht movement. Stabilization policy of the central bank becomes more complicate with burgeoning capital markets that attract foreign capital. Using monthly data between 2000 and 2017, we can observe the impact of the stock market boom and bust on the baht-dollar exchange rate in Figure 5.4. Performing pairwise Granger causality tests by using the same 216 observations, we find that SET index Granger causes the baht exchange rate, but not the other way around. Movements in the baht exchange rate cannot accurately predict the movements of the SET index. The fluctuations of the latter, of course, reflect the influence from external factors and internal factors – investor sentiment.

With improving investor sentiment, or strengthening fundamental factors of the Thai economy, a boom in the domestic stock market led to more capital inflows and baht appreciation. The baht appreciated when portfolio investment inflows pushed up the stock prices, adding additional supply of the dollar to the foreign exchange market. Just like the case when domestic interest rate increases and attract capital inflows, a boom in the SET or domestic bond markets might require the central bank to stabilize the baht exchange rate.

The return from holding stocks is a leading indicator of manufacturing output growth. This can be explained by the underlying theory that stock prices

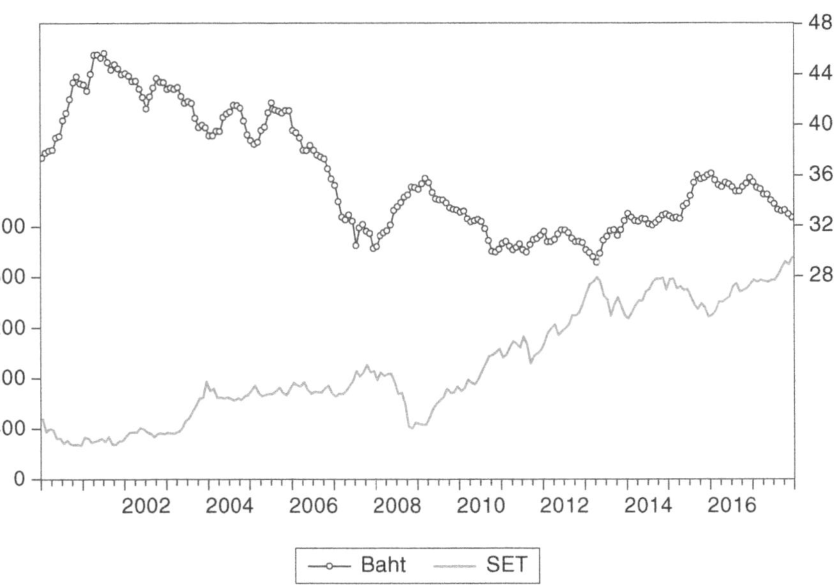

Figure 5.4 Correlates of the SET and the baht-dollar exchange rate: 2000–2017

are discounted present values of the expected return from holding stocks from dividend incomes and expected capital gains. An expansion of output reflects increases in sales and profitability, which give rise to anticipation of high dividend payoffs. Thus, a rise or fall in the stock prices can predict the future path of the economy.

After removing cyclical fluctuations from the trend paths of monthly stock prices and manufacturing output, through the Hodrick-Prescott filter (HP), we can examine the long-run relationship of the two variables by examining changes in the cyclically adjusted stock prices and manufacturing output. The former is represented by the SET index, the latter is captured by manufacturing production index. Applying the Granger causality test on 294 observations between 1993 and 2017, it is found that movement of SET index Grangers causes manufacturing output.

Figure 5.5 depicts such movement from 1993 to 2017. It is clearly demonstrates that the return on stocks can predict the future path of the economic activity, both the upturns and downturns. It is worth noting that there are no feedback effects from output to stock market prices in the Granger causality sense, which is understandable since there are other coherent factors that influence the prediction of stock prices: business sentiment and investor confidence.

By performing the same experiment using broad money supply (M2), rather than manufacturing output, the empirical results indicate that the stock prices also Granger causes broad money supply. The liquidity in the stock market is related to stock market activity (Figure 5.6). As discussed earlier, higher stock prices are the result of capital inflows, which tend to strengthen the baht. It is

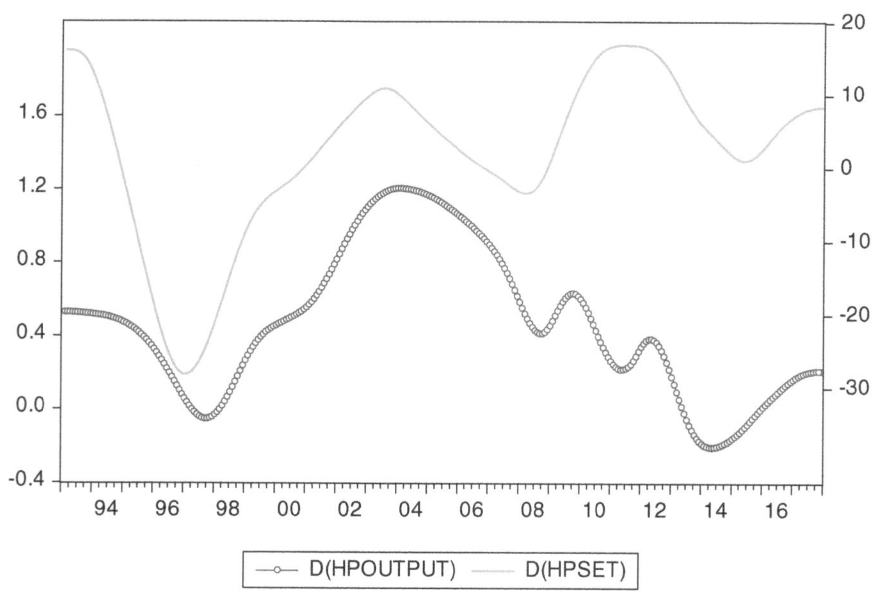

Figure 5.5 Stock prices and manufacturing output (cyclically adjusted)

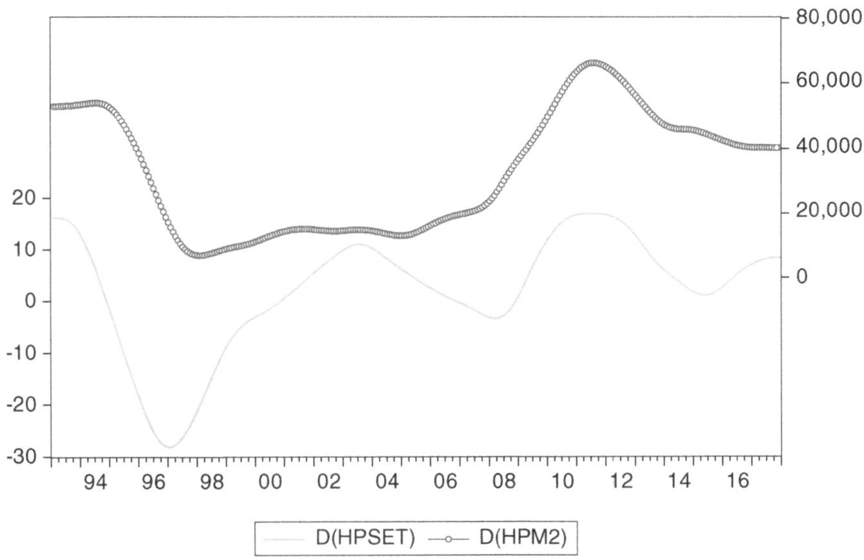

Figure 5.6 Stock prices and money supply

obvious that intervention in the foreign exchange markets to keep the baht stable enlarges that monetary base and hence the stock of money supply.

Viewed in this light, rising stock market liquidity driven by foreign capital results in monetary expansion. Indeed, activity in the stock market has an important implication on the conduct of monetary policy. All of these complications are the result of the desire to maintain the stability of the baht. Similar to the findings of the previous experiment, just like manufacturing output, the movement in broad money (HPM2) does not Granger cause the yield in the stock market.

After removing the cyclical components from the broad money supply and the set index through the HP filter, we obtain the cyclically adjusted quantity of broad money and the cyclically adjusted SET index (HPSET). Using the difference HP trend, D(HP) to capture the structural changes of these two variables, we can observe from Figure 5.6 that there is a co-movement of the two series. There exists a long-run relationship between money supply and the stock price.

Strong correlation between output growth and lagged stock returns can be found in a panel study of emerging market economies and advanced economies (Mauro, 2003). The strength of the correlation between output growth and lagged stock returns is significantly related to high market capitalization to GDP ratio. It should be noted that there is a rising trend of market capitalization in Thailand (Figure 5.2). As such, the relationship between stock market returns and output growth should intensify over time. In a nonlinear panel data mode of 27 countries, Henry et al. (2004) found that stock returns are most useful in predicting growth when the economy is in recession. In the Thai context, using monthly data from 1993 to 2016, the statistical evidence shows that the stock price Granger causes manufacturing production. The Bank of Thailand also employs the SET index as a component of leading economic indicators, which can be used to predict manufacturing output.

Stock prices can be thought of as a present value of future streams of income derived from holding the stocks. Expectations play a crucial role in determining stock prices. The SET index responds to changes in domestic and foreign conditions, which shape expectations about future stock returns.

The Bank of Thailand provides the expectations index of business sentiment (EBSI). If we remove the cyclical components from the time series using the HP filter, we obtain cyclically adjusted variables. To remove non-stationarity, we use the first difference of the HP series of SET and EBSI. Changes in the cyclically adjusted magnitudes of business sentiment and stock prices are shown in Figure 5.7. Employing 220 observations of monthly data from 1999 to 2017, the two series are founded to be co-integrated and to have bi-directional Granger causations. This is different from the previous finding of pairwise Granger causality tests between stock prices versus broad money, exchange rate, and manufacturing output, where causation ran in one direction only from stock prices to broad money, exchange rate, and output. The bi-directional causal relationship between stock market volatility and expectations provides an important understanding of the underlying nexus between the stock market and macro variables.

Volatilities in the stock market can be caused by changes in Expected Business Sentiment Index (EBSI), which in turn affect stock market activity. Figure 5.7 depicts the booms and busts in the stock market from 1999 to 2017. The stock

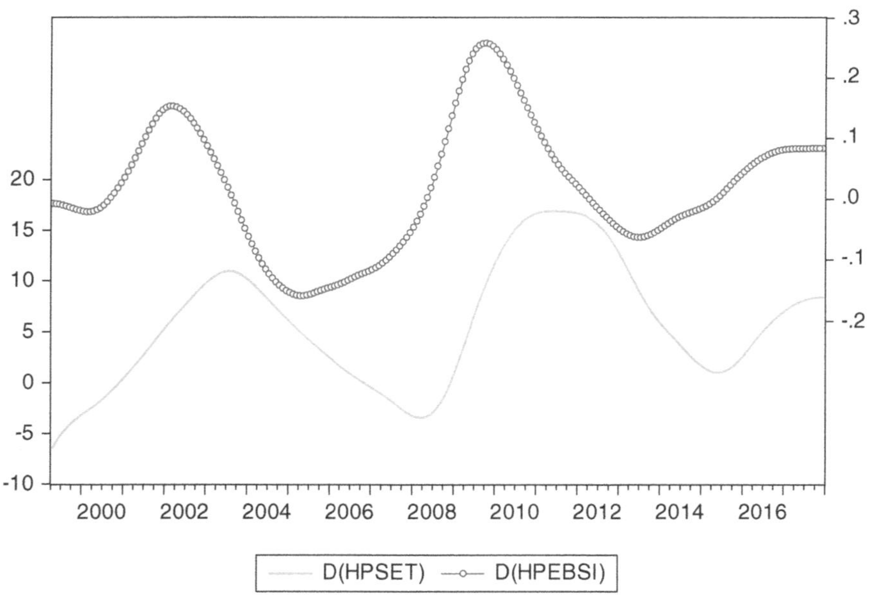

Figure 5.7 Stock prices and business sentiment: 1999–2017

price volatilities are echoed by the swings in expectations of the future part of the economy. A shock occurring in the stock market has psychological repercussions on the future expectations of economic agents. On the other hand, perception of future unfavorable events which might take place, such as political turmoil or trade wars, directly affects market sentiment. Anticipation of favorable economic policy outcomes perceived by economic agents can lead to rising share prices. The success of maintaining the bull market depends partly on the controllability of news. We need to explore the factors affecting business sentiment, which in turn affect the movements of those factors. There are spillover effects from the stock market to the real economy via the expectations channel.

4. Dynamic spillovers

As discussed earlier, Thailand's stock prices reflect expected returns shaped by Wall Street and investor sentiment. The Bank of Thailand does not use the interest rate policy to influence the stock market. The BoT did not attempt to cool down the stock market boom by using the interest rate policy. The goals of output stabilization and price stability are key priorities of monetary authorities. Nevertheless, monetary policy can indirectly affect the stock market by its exerting influence on money supply over output growth. There is a question whether the BoT should sacrifice growth objectives in order to deflate the stock bubbles.

If there is no close relationship between the boom in the real sector and the asset markets, then there would be no trade-off between growth and maintaining stability in the asset markets. It turns out that there is a strong correlation between output and stock prices (Figure 5.5), and there is a long-run relationship between the stock prices and money supply (Figure 5.6). Viewed in this light, controlling the appropriate level of money supply can contain the bubble in the stock market, which in turn would restrain excessive output growth. Thus, there is no conflict between stabilization policy objectives and avoiding bubbles in the asset markets.

There are various reasons why the central bank should prevent the stock market from getting overheated. When stock prices rise, the Bank of Thailand has to cope with the impact of capital inflows on the baht exchange rate. This can lead to baht appreciation and result in the expansion of the monetary base, due to intervention in the foreign exchange market to prevent baht appreciation. The strong baht can hamper export growth and encourage more capital inflows for speculation in the foreign exchange markets. Furthermore, the stock market boom would spur speculation in the property sector and derail the stabilization policy of the central bank.

If there are sufficient reasons for the central bank to intervene in the stock market, then there is a further question whether the Bank of Thailand can actually influence the stock market prices. How high and how often should the Bank of Thailand raise the interest rate or contract the monetary base to achieve the target of slowing down the rise in the stock price? Raghavan and Dungey (2015) examined monetary policy and stock markets in Singapore, Malaysia, Thailand,

Indonesia, and the Philippines and concluded that any attempt to prevent asset inflation caused by speculative bubbles may derail the basic objective of the central bank: output and price stability.

Unless the central bank intervenes in the foreign exchange market to maintain the exchange rate stability, there can be a contractionary impact on output when the Bank of Thailand attempts to deflate the bubbles. Thus, whether the central bank should prick the bubbles depends on whether the economy is near full employment. If so, the attempt to cool down the economy is consistent with deflating the bubbles. On the other hand, if the economy is sluggish but the asset markets are booming, due to speculative bubbles and the spillover effect from irrational exuberance in Wall Street, deflating the asset price bubbles would inadvertently choke off output recovery.

To provide empirical evidence to support the above conjecture, a vector autoregressive (VAR) model is employed to analyze monthly data provided by the BoT. The period of the study covered January 1999 to December 2017. There are seven variables included in the model. The number of automobiles sold (Car) represents durable consumption expenditure, which is determined by expected output or permanent income of households. The amount of new capital investment, or registered capital (Investment), is affected by business sentiment and expectations of output sold. The areas permitted for construction in square meters (Construction) are proxied for construction investment, which is also influenced by the expected yield from the property sector. The strong expansion of the economy and the favorable investment sentiment would drive the growth of this type of investment. Output variable, represented by manufacturing production index (MPI), captures current economic activity. The upturn of MPI signifies the expansion of the economy and the downturn of the MPI indicates economic recession. These economic activities are largely determined by the magnitude of investment and consumption expenditures. Broad money supply is included in the VAR so that we can examine whether the BoT can use monetary policy to curb asset bubbles. The final variable to be included in the model is the expected business sentiment index (EBSI), which is the key driving force of stock and the market as well as decisions to consume and invest. The SET movement is strongly dictated by expectations of the state of the economy, represented by changes in EBSI, followed by money supply and output (Figure 5.8). In turn, the expectations of the economy or business sentiment are determined by the amount of money supply (liquidity), the level of permanent or expected output, and the direction of the SET index. Rising stock prices signal economic booms, while falling stock prices signal economic contraction.

The number of automobiles sold is a proxy for permanent consumption expenditure, which is mostly affected by changes in business sentiment and expectation. Output (MPI) expansion also leads to higher sales of automobiles. Liquidity in the stock market, proxied by SET index movement, also has a positive wealth effect on car sales. Fluctuations in money supply also lead to rising car sales, but their impact is not as strong as expectations of the state of the economy, output expansion (income effect), and stock market movement.

Private investment spending is captured in the model by the amount of newly registered capital. It is mostly affected by, in descending order, expectations (EBSI), stock market liquidity (SET), output level, and money supply (Figure 5.8). Business expectations, output, and stock market prices are positively influenced by construction activity, which is proxied by the area permitted for construction. The positive impact of money supply expansion is short-lived and turns to negative impact after 3 months. A rise in output level leads to increasing money supply, while higher liquidity in the stock market drains the amount of money supply. If monetary policy is accommodative enough, demand for money rises along with the output expansion path. There is a complex relationship between stock market prices and the level of money supply, due to capital inflows and the central bank's intervention in the foreign exchange market.

What explains the business expectations or consumer confidence is the increase in output and stock market activity. Nevertheless, these impacts die off after a quarter. Broad money supply has a long-run positive impact on business sentiment, which is maintained as long as there is sufficient amount of liquidity in the money market. Both business expectations and SET index change gradually as they move by inertia forces of shocks in the past. When these variables change slowly, it creates dynamic spillover of shocks into the real sector of the economy. Changes in stock market liquidity are driven mainly by expectations, while the latter's effects on the former is smaller. This is because there are other factors contributing to business sentiment, much more important than stock market prices. Broad money and output affect stock market prices as expected by theory.

The conclusion from this VAR experiment is that stock market movements matter for the real economy through their impacts on consumption and investment. Another important factor is business expectation, which is partly affected by the stock market. The stock market liquidity and business sentiment are important factors determining real variables in the macroeconomy. Furthermore, money supply is related to stock market activity. This finding points out that the central bank can use preemptive monetary policy to curb asset markets from creating bubbles. This issue will be further examined in Chapter 8, which discusses monetary policy for stabilization.

5. Possibility of financial contagion

The AFC started in 1997, when the Bank of Thailand floated the baht exchange rate. Some countries in the Asian region, including South Korea, were affected by the contagion effect of massive currency depreciation and capital flight. Twenty years later, an increasing degree of interconnected trading countries implies that shocks from one country can be easily transmitted to other countries through export booms and busts. Similarly, when capital accounts are liberalized, financial shocks from a large country can be felt in other countries, whose trade and financial sectors are highly exposed to that large country. China's trade activities have become increasingly important to Thailand, replacing the role of the US, Japan, and European nations.

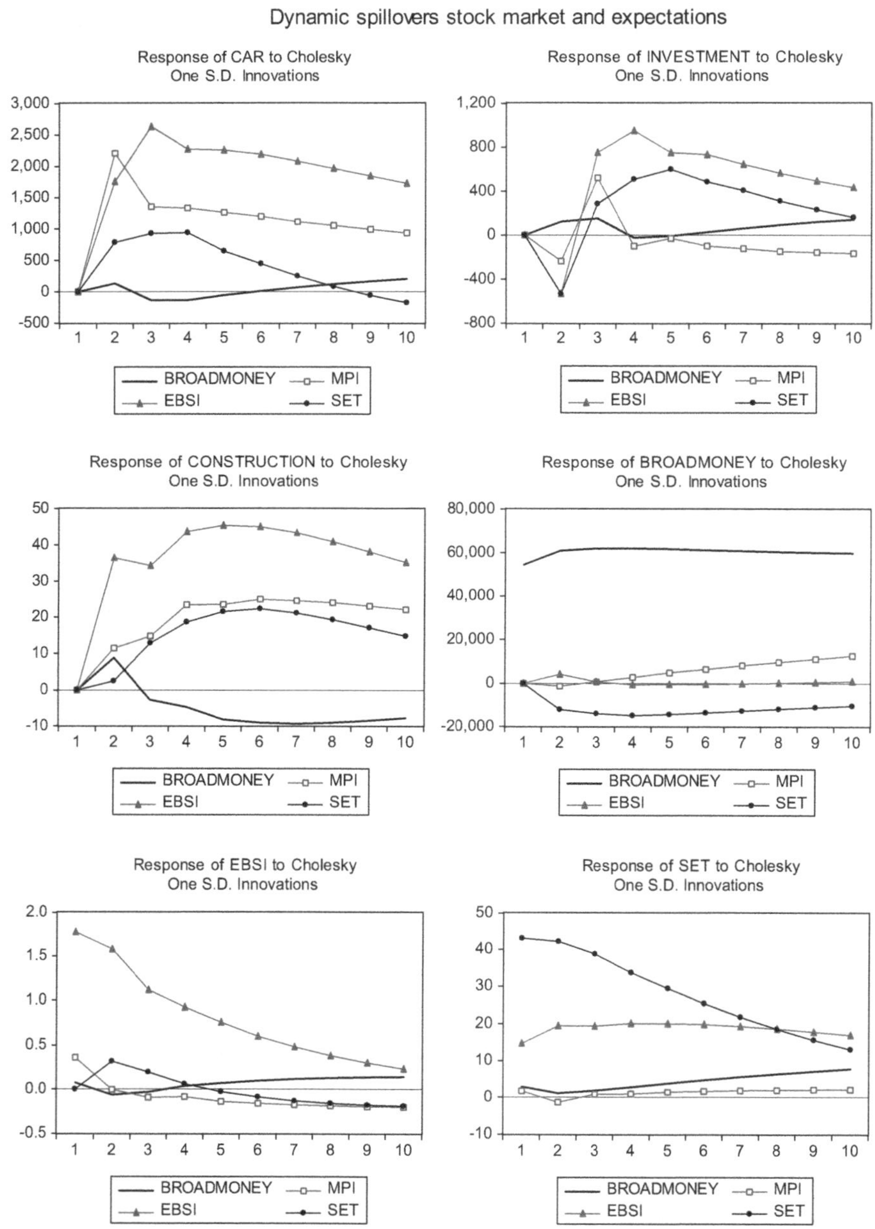

Figure 5.8 Dynamic spillover of shocks in the stock market

The stock markets in ASEAN-5 countries responded in different directions and degrees to business cycle shocks in China and other emerging economies, but they were more aligned with growth fluctuations in developed economies (Teng et al. 2013). According to You et al. (2014), financial liberalization in China can lead to financial contagion and regional financial crisis. As a result, there is a strong correlation between stock returns in China and major stock markets around the world. The risk of a stock market collapse exists if the People's Bank of China cannot reign in the property market booms. If so, the hard landing of the Chinese economy and its subsequent stock crash in China would exert strong impact on regional stock markets.

As shown in Figure 5.9, Thailand's stock market performance is related to China's stock market as well as other ASEAN stock markets. Judged by the correlates between stock market returns in Thailand vis-à-vis Singapore, Malaysia, Hong Kong, and China, the degree of interconnectedness increased over time from 2002 to 2012. The Thai stock market was mostly related to activity in the Hong Kong market, where the correlation rose from 0.66 in the period 2002–2006 to 0.92 in the period 2007–2012. During the same corresponding periods, the correlates with the stock market in China increased from 0.20 to 0.71. The correlation with Japan increased marginally from 0.58 to 0.66, which was still lower than the correlation with the Singapore market between the period 2002 and 2006. This statistical evidence suggests that the Thai stock market has been closely related to Southeast Asian neighboring countries. However, the degree of connectedness increased considerably after the Chinese stock market became more open and China's economic dominance more pronounced.

This new development in regional stock markets heightens financial risks, due to contagion effects of financial shocks. Thailand's stock market is increasingly vulnerable to disturbance of external shocks. International investors perceive the

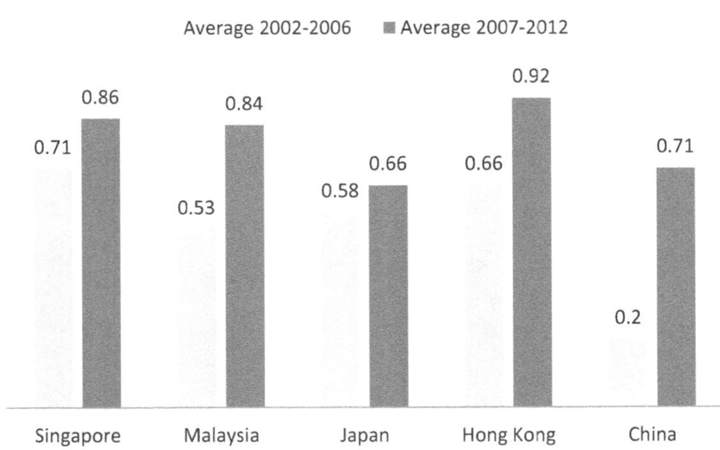

Figure 5.9 Thailand's stock market: correlation coefficients of returns

Source: ADB Asian Bond Integration Center

Thai stock market as an integral part of the Asian markets. In times of financial crisis that originated outside Thailand, in some Asian markets, foreign investors would move funds out of Thailand's stock markets, causing baht depreciation in response to capital flights. On the other hand, when there is a boom in the Chinese stock market, foreign investors may also pour money into Thailand's stock market, causing the baht to appreciate. Thailand's well-developed stock market can be exposed to such shocks and complicate the conduct of monetary policy, which also needs to maintain large international reserves to cushion external disturbances.

For long-term investment, bond yields indicate the cost of long-term borrowing. Bond holders must be compensated for the loss of liquidity, which reflects in the upward sloping yield curves. Each country has its own specific risks, which make bond yields differ from one country to another. Since the risks are not uniformly distributed, there will be less correlation among the bond returns than stock market returns. Stocks are more liquid and they are traded more frequently than bonds.

When considering the integrated relationship of the Thai bond markets to other Asian markets, we have a different picture of development. The return correlation of the bond yields has declined (Figure 5.10). Because of the country-specific risks, the return on the Thai bonds market correlates less with other Asian markets. Unlike investors in stock markets, bond investors are more concerned with long-term growth prospects of the countries issuing bonds. During the periods 2002–2006 and 2007–2012, there has been a significant decline in the correlation of Thailand's return on bonds with those in Japan, Hong Kong, and Singapore. The reason behind the declining trend is quite clear. The Thai bond market reflects a specific country risk which makes the Thai long-term capital market become distinctive from other markets. Unlike the stock market, the Thai

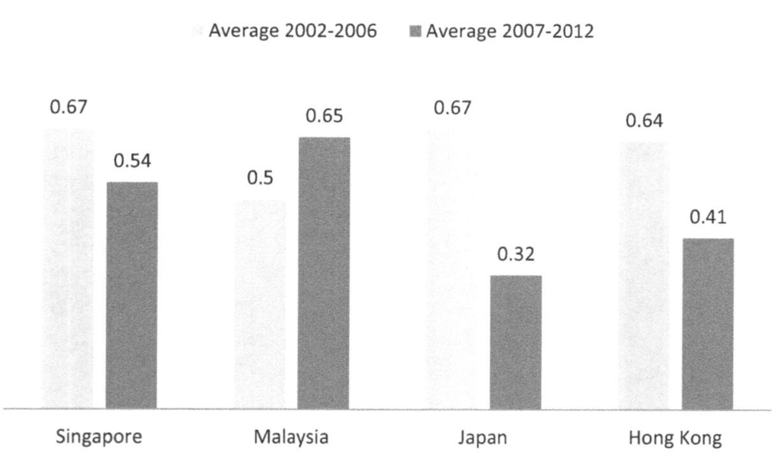

Figure 5.10 Thailand's bond market: correlation coefficients

Source: ADB Asian Bond Integration Center

bond market did not move closely in line with other Asian markets as in the early 2000s, except for Malaysia where the correlation increased from 0.50 to 0.65. Thailand's bond market has been less integrated to other Asian bond markets because of its own deteriorating prospect for long-term growth after 2006.[1]

To counteract the declining long-term growth, the government must consider fiscal stimulus through infrastructure spending, which is being earnestly employed in many Asian countries. Thailand's inadequate infrastructure development has slowed down long-term growth of the economy. Another motivation for the big push for infrastructure development is to counteract the slowdown of world trade expansion. Huge infrastructure projects would require the Thai government to issue bonds to finance construction. The success of such massive infrastructure development depends crucially on financing the projects. Unless political risks decline substantially, such infrastructure bonds must be offered with high returns to attract domestic and foreign investors. The only way to keep down the borrowing cost of financing infrastructure development is to maintain low inflation and reduce risk premium. Price stability is not difficult to achieve, judging from Thailand's historical record of low inflation. To keep risk premium low is more difficult. Progress in capital market development is not independent from political stability. Absence of political turmoil and social conflicts reduces anxiety and perception of political risks, thereby reducing the risk premium in issuing long-term bonds.

There is an asymmetric integration development in Thailand's stock and bond markets vis-à-vis Asian markets. While integration with other regional stock markets has been increasing, integration with other regional bond markets has declined. Specific risks in the bond markets make Thailand's bond markets decouple from other markets. Viewed in this light, the bond market is subject to less financial contagion than the stock market.

6. Concluding remarks

The rising level of market capitalization in Thailand reveals a process of physical capital deepening as the stock market performs the critical role of more efficient allocation of financial resources to investors. Although the Thai capital market has been integrated more to the world financial markets, it has been exposed more to external shocks and would act like a conduit transmitting financial shocks to macroeconomic variables.

In the classical world, the real economy is separated from the financial sector in the sense that money supply does not affect the real sector. The only function of money supply is to determine the price level, but it does not impact output and employment. A dichotomy between the real and monetary sectors exists in the classical world, where prices and wages are flexible. In the Keynesian world, the two sectors are connected via the interest rate. The empirical evidence provided in this chapter indicates that there is also another channel through which real and monetary sectors are inseparable. The stock market is another channel linking the monetary and real sectors.

Expectations about the future direction of the state of the economy, or business confidence and sentiment, affect stock market liquidity. The wealth effect from the stock market affects consumption and investment expenditure, providing the linkage between the real and financial sectors. Monetary expansion enhances liquidity in the stock market and stimulates private investment and consumption. A rise in private expenditures increases the level of output and raises output expectations, thereby creating physical and financial capital deepening. It is plausible that output and price level stabilization goals are not in conflict with the central bank's objectives of keeping the lid on the overheated asset markets. The empirical evidence suggests a possibility that the Bank of Thailand could implement a preemptive monetary policy before the stock market can formulate bubbles, which can send ripple effects to the real sector.

Note

1 Eichengreen and Hausmann (1999) advance the "original sin" hypothesis to explain the relationship between financial fragility and exchange rates, emphasizing the inability to borrow in terms of its own currency in international markets.

References

Eichengreen, Barry, and Ricardo Hausmann. 1999. "Exchange Rates and Financial Fragility." Proceedings – Economic Policy Symposium – Jackson Hole, Federal Reserve Bank of Kansas City, pages 329–368.

Friedman, Milton. 2005. "A Natural Experiment in Monetary Policy Covering Three Episodes of Growth and Decline in the Economy and the Stock Market." *Journal of Economic Perspectives*, 19 (4): 145–150.

Henry, Olan T., Nilss Olekalns, and Jonathan Thong. 2004. "Do Stock Market Returns Predict Changes to Output? Evidence From a Nonlinear Panel Data Model." *Empirical Economics*, 29 (3): 527–540.

Levine, Ross. 2001. "International Financial Liberalization and Economic Growth." *Review of International Economics*, 9 (4): 688–702.

Mauro, Paolo. 2003. "Stock Returns and Output Growth in Emerging and Advanced Economies." *Journal of Development Economics*, 71 (1): 129–153.

Raghavan, Mala, and Mardi Dungey. 2015. "Should ASEAN-5 Monetary Policy-Makers Act Pre-emptively Against Stock Market Bubbles?" *Applied Economics*, 47 (10–12): 1086–1105.

Sawalha, Nabeel N., Mohammad I. Elian, and Adil H. Suliman. 2016. "Foreign Capital Inflows and Economic Growth in Developed and Emerging Economies: A Comparative Analysis." *Journal of Developing Areas*, 50 (1): 237–256.

Teng, Kee Tuan, Siew Hwa Yen, and Soo Y. Chua. 2013. "The Synchronization of ASEAN-5 Stock Markets With the Growth Rate Cycles of Selected Emerging and Developed Economies." *Margin: The Journal of Applied Economic Research*, 7 (1): 1–28.

You, Jiaxing, Chun Liu, and Guqian Du. 2014. "With Economic Integration Comes Financial Contagion? Evidence From China." Emer*ging Markets Finance and Trade*, 50 (3): 62–80.

6 External imbalances and macroeconomic adjustments

1. Introduction

As Thailand's process of global integration of goods and capital market continues, its business and inflation cycles have become synchronized with the rest of the world. When Thailand's global dependency becomes more intensified, the effects of external disturbances on the Thai economy become more pronounced than they were in the early decades. It is more difficult for a small country like Thailand to employ its own monetary and fiscal policy instruments to mitigate the impact of external shocks. The economy has become increasingly sensitive to monetary and fiscal policies undertaken by large economies such as the US, Japan, and China. The benefits from increasing integration require a sacrifice in terms of economic policy independence. The country must come up with an optimum policy mix between fiscal and monetary policies to mitigate external shocks. The optimal mix of monetary and fiscal policy depends on the degree of exchange rate flexibility and capital mobility.

In the early stages of economic development, Thailand experienced current account deficit, while maintaining high economic growth. Foreign savings were used to overcome shortages of domestic savings to deepen capital formation. For some countries, the current account deficit phenomenon is a temporary situation. Because imported capital goods can be used for building export capacity, at the later stage of economic development current account deficit would turn to surplus with rapid economic growth driven by exports. However, this conventional wisdom ignores the fact that surplus current account does not necessarily imply economic strength. Likewise, a rapidly growing economy can experience worsening current account deficit. When investment exceeds domestic savings, during strong economic growth, foreign savings are necessary to sustain capital accumulation and long-term growth. As long as Thailand experiences sufficiently large surplus in capital accounts, there is no problem with unsustainability. In the globalization era, with rapid movements of portfolio flows and foreign direct investment, capital inflows can sustain high output growth despite current account deficit. Current account deficit can go along with the strength of the economy.

This chapter outlines development of Thailand's external imbalance by focusing on its determinants. Current account and capital account disequilibrium may be persistent rather than temporary. In general, if an equilibrating mechanism exists, output, exchange rates, and the price level can restore external equilibrium. It is possible that external imbalances are persistent, because some of the current account determinants do not change or are not flexible enough to restore external equilibrium. There are various channels through which equilibrium can be restored after facing external shocks: output changing and expenditure switching policy adjustments via the price level, interest rates, and the exchange rate. Only in the long run can the economy gravitate back to equilibrium. The speed of the adjustment depends on how quickly those equilibrating variables are allowed to adjust. If some variables are not permitted to perform their equilibrating roles, the burden of the adjustment falls on other uncontrolled variables. If fundamental adjustments are prolonged, costly adjustments in terms of output loss would occur.

2. External and internal disequilibrium

Internal equilibrium implies that there is no excess demand or excess supply in the goods market. Hence, there will be no tendency for output or price levels to change from the existing level. If there is a discrepancy between supply and demand, adjustment takes place through output adjustment, rather than the price level. This is because prices are sticky in the short run. External equilibrium implies that current account and capital account offset each other in the sense that there is no surplus or deficit in the balance of payments. When the balance of payments is in disequilibrium, there would be adjustments in the exchange rate and the output level to correct the imbalances. Therefore, external and internal balances are interconnected though the movements in the exchange rate and output level. In the long run, prices levels are flexible enough to correct the disequilibrium. But in the short run, exchange rate and output would adjust to restore both internal and external equilibrium.

Thailand rarely experienced a deficit balance of payments, thanks to capital inflow. In the years of balance of payments deficits, the current account was actually in surplus (Figure 6.1). It was capital flight that caused the balance of payments deficits. Those years were unusual as there were random events that caused capital outflows. In the years prior to the Asian financial crisis, the chronic deficit current account was camouflaged by surges in capital inflows. When the current account deficit became fundamentally serious and could not be concealed by the seemingly healthy balance of payments, there was a sudden stop of capital inflows and reverting capital outflows. These capital flows are determined by pull and push factors (Eichengreen et al., 2018). In times of prosperity, capital inflows were attracted by pull factors such as Thailand's high GDP growth and high rate of return from investment. In time of crisis, capitals were pushed out by rising foreign interest rates and expected baht devaluation.

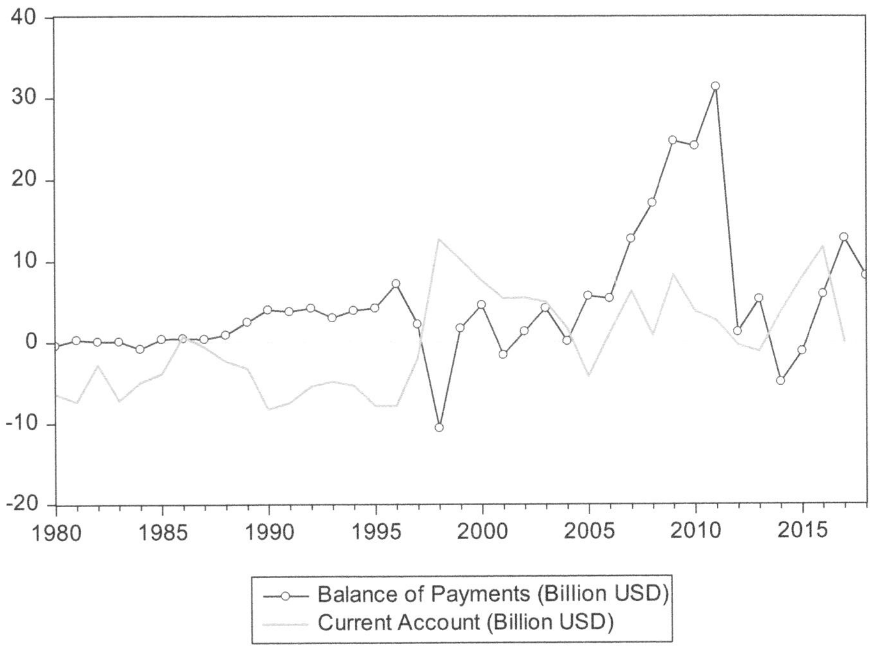

Figure 6.1 External imbalances: 1980–2016

Net capital inflows helped finance the current account deficit, which was caused by investment booms. From 1980 to 1996, current account deficit was on the average 5 percent of GDP, but the baht depreciated only 1.4 percent (Table 6.1). On the other hand, between 1999 and 2006, current account surplus was 4.1 percent of GDP, but the baht appreciated only 1.1 percent. This implies that the foreign exchange markets were heavily intervened with by the Bank of Thailand. The baht exchange rate was not allowed to correct the external disequilibrium.

In an early attempt to explain the currency crisis, the fixed exchange rate system was the main culprit. Fiscal deficits are linked to balance of payments deficit, losses of international reserves, and financial crises. Bird and Mandilaras (2006) found that fiscal deficits have exerted a significant impact on foreign exchange pressures in Latin America but not in Asia. During the boom period of 1980–1996, Thailand's fiscal balance was not in deficit, but it was a small surplus of 0.1 percent of GDP (Table 6.1). Similarly, during the slow growth period of 1999–2006, public deficit amounted to 1.1 percent of GDP, while current account was in surplus on the average of 4.1 percent. It can be concluded that Thailand's fiscal imbalances were not the cause of external disequilibrium.

The impact of internal disequilibrium on external imbalances stemmed mainly from investment and saving imbalances. During the financial crisis between 1997

Table 6.1 External and internal imbalances

	Current account/ GDP	*Fiscal balance/ GDP*	*Exchange rate (%)*	*GDP growth*	*Inflation*	*Net capital flows//GDP*
1980–96	-5.0	0.1	1.4	7.8	5.5	8.0
1997	-2	-1.9	23.8	-1.4	5.6	-4.4
1998	12.7	-2.5	31.9	-10.5	8.1	-14.7
1999–2006	4.1	-1.1	-0.9	4.9	2.2	-1.9
2007–2016	4.4	-2.1	0.59	3.1	2.0	-04

Source: Bank of Thailand

and 1998, due to output collapse and massive exchange rate depreciation, external equilibrium was restored. A huge current account surplus of 12.7 percent of GDP was experienced in 1998. From 2007 to 2016, because of the current account surplus around 4.4 percent, the baht continued appreciating, although less than 1 percent annually. While GDP growth averaged 3.1 percent during this period, inflation rose to 2.2 percent. The nominal exchange rate depreciated by 0.6 percent during the same corresponding period. This implies that the real exchange rate appreciated by about 1.2 percent and there was a slight net capital outflow of 0.4 percent of GDP. At the same time, fiscal balance was in deficit by 2.1 percent, a level which was still manageable. These are intricate relationships among fiscal policy variables and internal and external disequilibrium.

In general, interest rates play an equilibrating role in the credit market. During the boom, the excess of investment over savings should lead to a rapid rise in the interest rate. But the rise in the domestic interest rate would not be able to curb the rising demand for loans, because the inflows of foreign capital weakened the equilibrating role of domestic interest rates. During economic slumps, when investment is lower than savings, interest rates would insufficiently fall to reduce the savings gap, because capital outflows would take place. Domestic interest rate adjustments are relatively slow as they are affected by foreign interest rates as well as domestic market conditions. Table 6.1 shows that growth was associated with high inflation. The period 1980–1996 can be described as a high-growth episode with higher inflation. The annual economic growth averaged 7.8 percent and was consistent with 5.5 percent inflation rate. On the contrary, when output growth declined to 4.9 percent during the period 1999–2006, consumer price levels increased on the average 2.2 percent. The crisis period 1997–1998 was an exception because output declined by 10.5 percent and the inflation rate went up to 8.1 percent because of the cost-push inflation triggered by massive currency depreciation of 23.8 percent and 31.9 percent in 1997 and 1998, respectively. We can conclude that external and internal disequilibrium are interconnected through adjustments in output growth, the price level, and the exchange rates. When growth rate is altered, it affects investment and saving. The gap between investment and saving creates disequilibrium in the current account.

3. Investment-saving gap

If the budget deficit is small, current account deficit is largely determined by the investment-saving gap. Because of national income identities, foreign savings, or the trade deficit, is the difference between investment and domestic savings. Feldstein and Horioka (1980) suggested that we can measure the degree of capital mobility by examining the responsiveness of investment to changes in domestic savings. If capital mobility is high, investment to GDP ratio should not depend much on the domestic savings rate. On the other hand, if capital mobility is low, investment must be subject to availability of domestic savings. For the case of Thailand, capital mobility is far from perfect. Despite the capital liberalization attempt in the pre-crisis period, domestic investment has not been financed by external savings to the extent that domestic savings have been. Domestic savings are important financial resources for investors via financial intermediaries. Bank loans and the cost of borrowing matter for investment.

Table 6.2 shows investment and saving ratios in different episodes. During the boom period (1980–1996), investment was on the average above savings by 19.3 percent. During the slump (1999–2006) investment was below savings by 13.1 percent. Growth and the investment-saving gap are intricately related. The causation can run both ways. Note that the role of financial intermediates is important in channeling household's savings to investors via bank credit expansion. On the average, during the boom period, bank credit grew by 21.1 percent while the minimum lending rate (MLR) for prime customers was 14.1 percent. In 1997, bank credit grew by 30.5 percent and the prime rate was 15.3 percent. Again, we observe a positive relationship between credit and the bank lending rate. Although the demand for credit is negatively related to the cost of borrowing, the rising cost of borrowing was not able to offset the rising demand for credit generated by rapid output growth and high expected rates of return from investment within the country. The year 1998 witnessed investment collapse together with credit contraction by 7.9 percent. The prime lending rate declined from 15.3 percent in 1997 to 11.7 percent in 1998, when for the first time, investment dropped below savings by almost 36 percent. Current account turned around from deficit into surplus. Output adjustment is therefore a very powerful mechanism to correct current account disequilibrium, but it was very costly in terms of output loss.

Table 6.2 Investment-saving gap (period average: percent)

	I/GDP	*S/GDP*	*(I-S)/S*	*Bank credit growth*	*Minimum lending rate*
1980–96	34.3	29.0	19.3	21.1	14.1
1997	33.7	33.1	1.9	30.5	15.3
1998	20.4	31.8	-35.7	-7.9	11.75
1999–2006	25.4	29.3	-13.1	-0.2	7.0
2007–2016	25.0	32.5	-22.3	7.9	6.5

Source: Bank of Thailand and National and Economic Development Board (NESDB)

As Thailand entered a period of recovery in 1999–2006, investment was 13 percent below savings (Table 6.2). This is the episode when bank credit growth was negative by 0.2 percent on the average, while the MLR was 7 percent. Both the interest rate and the rate of credit expansion are procyclical. Since the average propensity to consume falls as income rises, the savings rate must be positively related to income growth rate. At the same time, the investment rate would increase as growth accelerates, due to the accelerating impact of output changes on investment. Figure 6.2 illustrates that the saving rate exceeded the investment ratio after the crisis year and has remained higher since then. As investment contracted further after 2007, the investment-saving gap was pulled down deeper into a negative zone, from –13.1 between the period 1999–2006 to 22.3 percent in the period 2007–2016, when bank credit resumed an expansion path and the MLR declined marginally from 7 percent to 6.5 percent. During this low-investment, high-saving episode, savings exceeded investment by 22.3 percent, corresponding to the high level of current account surplus.

Current account positions and GDP growth are related, because growth has an indirect impact on current account via the investment-saving channel. Whether growth can lead to current account deficit or surplus depends on the net effect of growth on savings and investment. If domestic savings respond more to output growth than investment's response, economic booms can lead to current account surplus. On the other hand, if investment responds more than saving during economic upturns, current account deficit can be widened. The actual

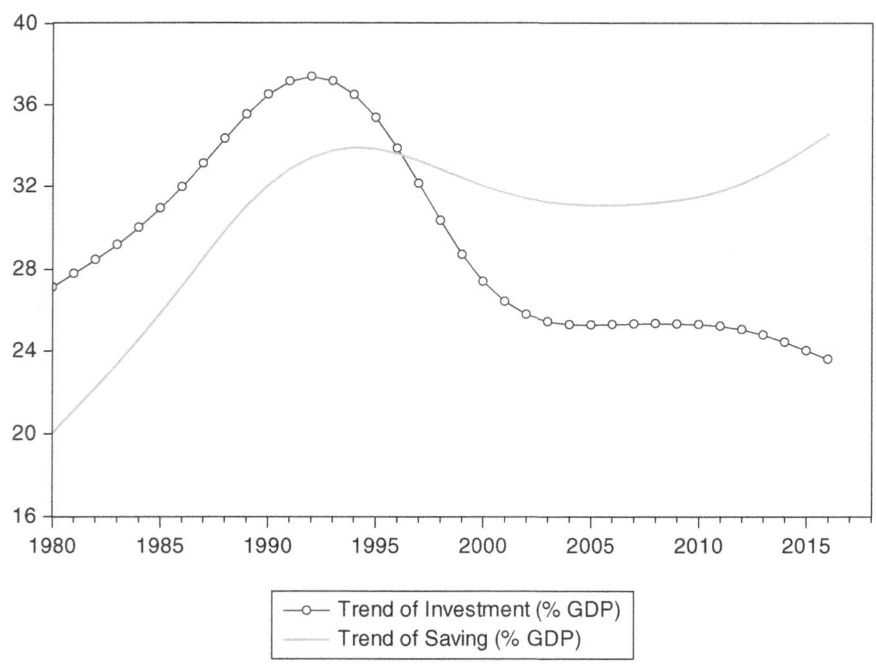

Figure 6.2 Long-term paths of investment and saving

impact of growth on current account is an empirical issue, whether investment or saving responds more to output growth. Can the twin deficits hypothesis explain current account disequilibrium? If so, fiscal policy matters if sustainable current account deficit is one of the macroeconomic goals.[1]

The excess of investment over savings was wiped out in 1997, but the severity of recession was so intense that investment fell below savings by 37 percent. The Thai economy plunged into a downturn cycle with low rate of capital formation in subsequent years. The saving rate gradually declined as GDP growth decelerated. Thailand experienced current account surplus as the investment rate remained consistently below the saving rate. The problem during this slow growth episode was excessive savings over domestic investment. Capital accumulation requires continuity and a slow buildup period. The investment climate must be favorable for investors. The investment rate began to pick up gradually between 2000 and 2005. Banks resumed lending and the investment-saving gap became positive for a brief period in 2005. However, because of internal political upheavals, the investment rate fell afterwards.

4. Resource gaps and growth nexus

Does the investment-saving gap explain Thailand's current account imbalances? How does output growth rate affect the current account position? From 1980–1989, a change in long-term growth path seems to move in line with a change in the long-term current account position. Growth slowed down while current account position was deteriorating.[2] However, the positive relationship seems to disappear in the 1990s. The relationship turned into movements in opposite directions. An acceleration of the long-term growth rate caused declining in current account surplus, while deceleration of the long-term growth led to widening surplus in the current account (Figure 6.3). A permanent increase in output growth induces higher demand for investment and imported capital goods, thereby deteriorating the current account balance. When growth collapses, the demand for investment declines and reduces imported capital goods. Consequently, poor growth performance is associated with an enlarging current account surplus. We conclude that output growth affects the investment gap and vice versa and if growth impact on investment is stronger than growth impact on saving, current account deficit would be widened. On the other hand, if the impact of growth on investment is weaker than on saving, current account surplus will be the outcome of rapid growth.

When the government runs a budget deficit, the increased absorption of domestic output reduces net exports. As such, fiscal imbalance is related to current account situation. However, the causations run in both directions. If trade imbalance is widening, customs tax revenue increases and leads to improvement in fiscal position. Viewed in this light, there is a possibility that fiscal surplus can be either positively or negatively related to current account deficit. We can observe that fiscal deficit correlates with surplus current account and fiscal surplus is associated with deficit current account. If this is the case, the hypothesis of twin

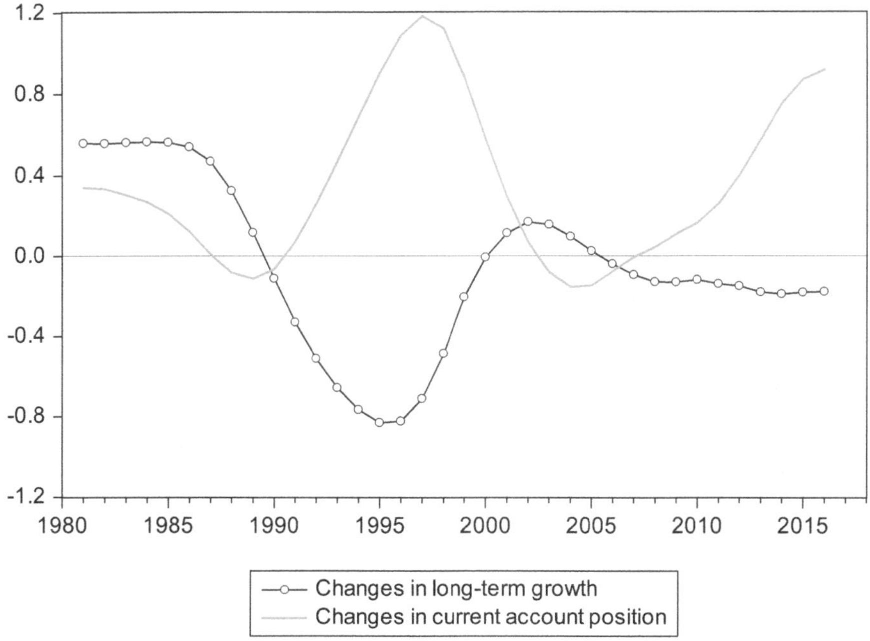

Figure 6.3 Changes in current account and long-term growth rate

deficits in the Thai context would have to exclude budget deficit from explaining current account deficit. Only the excess of investment over saving would be responsible for current account deficit in Thailand.

After applying the Hodrick-Prescott filter to the annual data from 1980 to 2017, we obtain the long-term trends of both series. Figure 6.4 illustrates the long-term paths of fiscal balance and current account position. By discarding the cyclical components of the actual values, we can regard the paths of the filtered series as a long-term path of the two variables. These deviations from the trends stem from temporary shocks due to disturbances such as terms of trade shocks. From Figure 6.4, we conclude that after 1996, there has been a structural transformation of the long-term current account deficit into long-term surplus. Fiscal position turned around from deficit in the 1980s into a brief period of surplus before the Asian financial crisis in 1997. Since then the long-term fiscal position has remained in deficit.

We can examine the twin deficits hypothesis by focusing on the determinants of current account surplus by analyzing the annual data from 1980 to 2016. The change in the real exchange rate is augmented in the twin deficits hypothesis, so as to include the role of the exchange rate in influencing the level of current account. The fully modified ordinary least squares (FMOLS) method of estimation produces correlates of current account vis-à-vis the baht-dollar

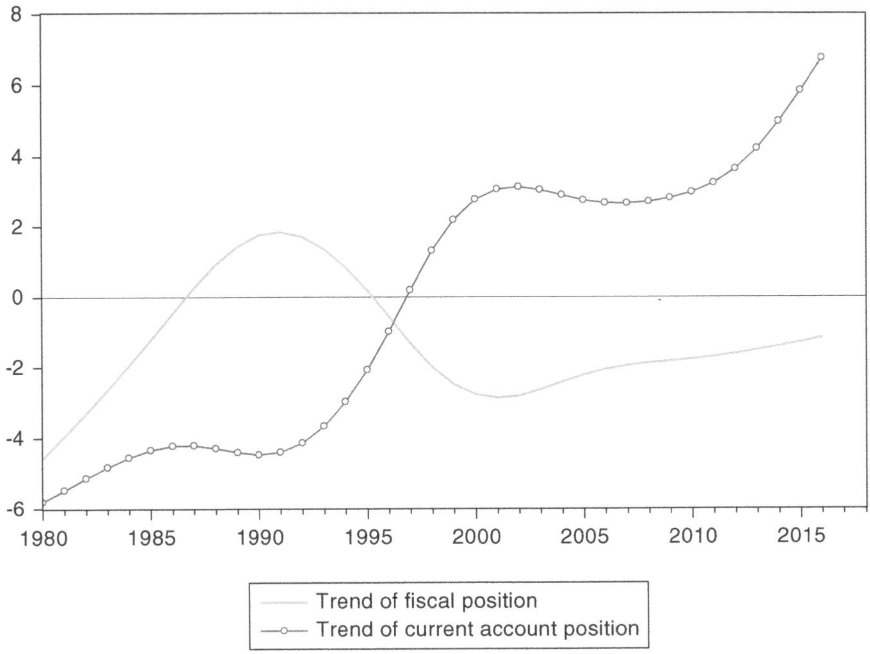

Figure 6.4 Long-term paths of fiscal imbalance and current account

exchange rate, the investment-saving gap, and fiscal surplus, measured as percentage of GDP. The estimated coefficients reported in Figure 6.5 suggest that real exchange rate appreciation and the size of the investment-saving gap are negatively related to current account surplus (Figure 6.4). The negative correlation between fiscal surplus and current account surplus does not correspond to the twin deficits hypothesis. Fiscal deficit does not always bring about current account deficit. These two barometers of the strength of the economy can move in opposite directions. The puzzle can be explained by the third dynamic factor, output growth, which drives current account deficit as well as the fiscal surplus, at the same time.

On one hand, there is a strong positive correlation between output growth and budget surplus. On the other hand, growth is negatively correlated with current account surplus. Growth generates higher demand for imports due to Thailand's high-income elasticity demand for imports. If growth is driven by exports, this type of high growth can also lead to current account deficit if exports are highly correlated with imports.[3] Some types of export commodities, which depend on imported intermediate products, do not add high value to the economy. Thailand's output and export levels are highly dependent on imports.

A rapidly growing economy raises both saving and investment ratio to GDP. But if the impact of growth on the investment rate is higher than the saving rate,

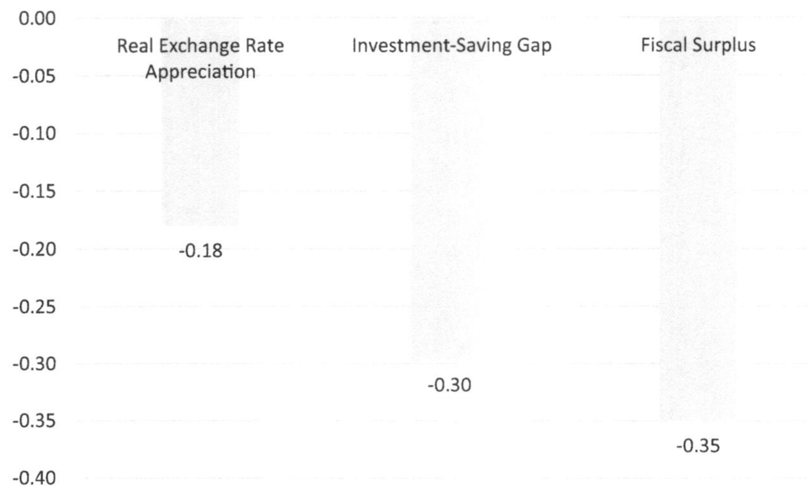

Figure 6.5 Correlates of current account surplus: 1981–2016

Source: FMOLS estimates (1981–2016)

strong growth widens the investment-saving gap. Consequently, strong growth generates high current account deficit, while a sluggish economy causes higher surplus in the current account. Recall that we have created an index of imbalance-adjusted growth rate to measure the sustainability of growth by taking into account internal and external disequilibrium. A dismal long-term growth path adjusted by trend of current account surplus can be a sign of an unsustainable economy.

The positive relationship between growth and investment ratio is supported by the dynamic least squares estimates shown in Figure 6.6. Investment ratio is positively affected by credit expansion and the lending interest rate, measured by the minimum lending rate (MLR). The effect of credit availability allows firms to adjust capital stock to a newly desirable capital stock level faster than when they are credit constrained. An interesting finding from this exercise is that a rising interest rate does not dampen the investment ratio to GDP. Firms are willing to bear the cost of higher borrowing while banks are willing to lend more when the economy is booming. Note that the values of these financial variables are less than unity, suggesting that investment ratio is not very sensitive to changes in credit and interest rate. GDP growth contributes to higher investment ratio, while it also raises the saving ratio – albeit to a lesser extent (Figure 6.7). The estimated elasticity of the investment rate with respect to growth is 0.04, greater than 0.02 of the corresponding estimated elasticity of the saving rate. This implies that the investment-saving gap enlarges during the boom years. It is not surprising that during the phase of economic recovery, current account turns around from surplus to deficit.

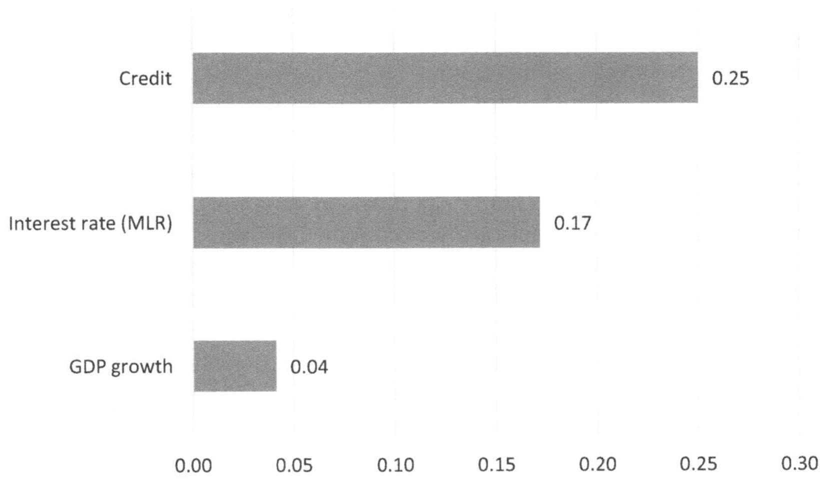

Figure 6.6 Investment rate elasticities

Source: Dynamic least squares estimation (1982–2014)

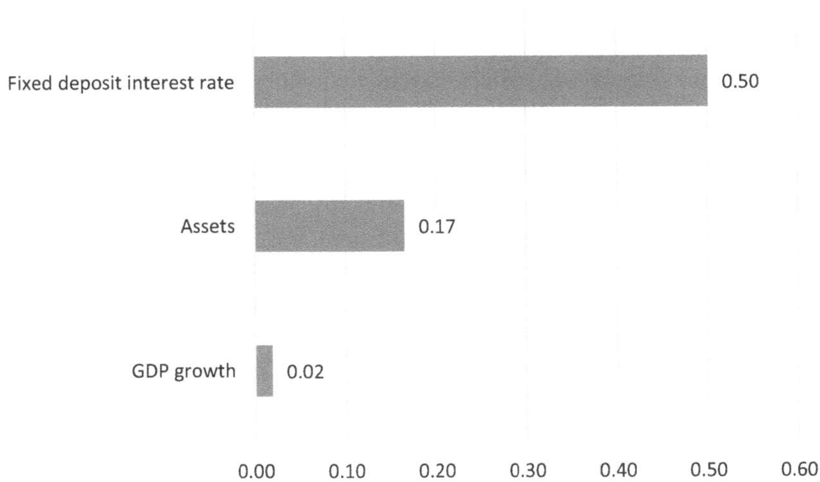

Figure 6.7 Saving rate elasticities

Source: FMOLS estimation (1981–2015)

The saving rate is determined by growth, wealth, and saving incentives represented by the fixed deposit rate. These variables are statistically significant in determining the saving rate. Note also that the response of the saving ratio to deposit rate is higher than the response of the investment ratio to rising lending rate. In effect, during the expansion of the bank lending cycle, the interest rates increase but the increase in the investment rate is less than the response of the saving rate to the increasing deposit interest rate. Hence, at the expansion stage of the economy, when interest rates are rising, the widening investment-saving gap is mitigated by the rising interest rate as saving responds more to saving incentives than the investment rate. On the contrary, when the level of assets rises, its ensuing wealth effect raises the saving rate further, but the impact of increasing credit on the investment rate is more powerful and dominates the impact of increasing wealth on the saving rate. Consequently, current account is widened during financial booms and economic upswings. We have come to an important conclusion that economic growth, activities of financial intermediaries through deposit mobilization and credit allocation, and interest rates are all related. They are fundamental factors contributing to external imbalances.

The hypothesis of twin deficits, which relate current account deficits to deficits in fiscal balance and the resource gap for investment, are too simple to explain the long-term trend of current account position. The hypothesis ignores the complex relationship between important macroeconomic variables such as output growth and other financial variables involving financial savings, credit extension, and interest rates, which affect the investment and saving processes.[4]

5. Exchange rate and external equilibrium

Aside from growth and investment-saving nexus, there is another important macroeconomic variable that affects external equilibrium: the exchange rate. In the short run, when price levels are slow to adjust, output is the equilibrating mechanism. But the exchange rate moves much faster than output to correct disequilibrium in the current account. Cuestas and Regis (2016) found a co-integrating relationship between the real effective exchange rate and the ratio of the current account balance to GDP. The causality runs from the real exchange rate to the current account. Duarte and Schnabl (2015) provide evidence based on data between 1990 and 2013, indicating that nominal exchange rates are not the main determinant of current account positions in 86 emerging economies. For East Asia, sterilization and monetary policy are determinants of current account, while fiscal policy stances are at the core of current account positions. Only in Latin American countries does the exchange rate play an important role in determining current account positions. This evidence seems to be contradictory to the conventional wisdom that exchange rate changes affect the trade balance. We need to take into account the price variable, which can alter the real exchange rate. Eguren (2016) employed data from 1960 to 2007 of 180 countries and concluded that flexible exchange rate arrangements deliver a faster current account adjustment among non-industrial countries. Exports respond to changes in international relative prices, providing a channel through which exchange rates exert their impacts on current account adjustment. A similar finding of the impact of exchange rate adjustment on current account was conducted by Gervais et al. (2016). The real exchange rate adjustment significantly reduced current account imbalances.

The exchange rate crises stemmed from the prolonged overvaluing of the fixed exchange rate, which resulted in unsustainable current account deficit. In the long run, real exchange rate movements facilitate current account adjustment. When export prices rise relative to import prices, the trade balance position can be improved. Nevertheless, it is possible that the trade balance deficit can widen if the demand for imports is inelastic and the demand for exports is rather elastic. An improvement in the terms of trade therefore can lead to deteriorating trade balance.

Since exports are driven by world demand and imports by domestic income, changes to world income relative to domestic output create an income effect on trade balance through imports and exports. If world GDP is growing faster than Thailand's output, an improvement in trade balance occurs. This conjecture is supported by the empirical evidence shown in Figure 6.8.

The result from FMOLS regression, based on annual data from 1980 to 2016, suggests that exchange rate movement can improve trade balance, measured by the ratio of exports to imports (Figure 6.8). Note that the estimated coefficients can be interpreted as trade balance elasticities with respect to terms of trade (PXF/PMF), relative world to domestic output, and the nominal exchange rate. These estimated coefficients are smaller than unity, suggesting that trade and current account adjust slowly to changes in the values of their determinants. Fiscal and monetary policy can affect external imbalances indirectly through their impact on domestic output. The regression results stress the important impacts of expenditure switching and expenditure changing policies. Changes in the exchange rate, the relative price levels, and relative output in Thailand compared to the rest of the world signify the substitution effect from changing price levels and the income effect of economic activity on trade balance. Note that these magnitudes are expressed in terms of the ratios of the two variables.[5]

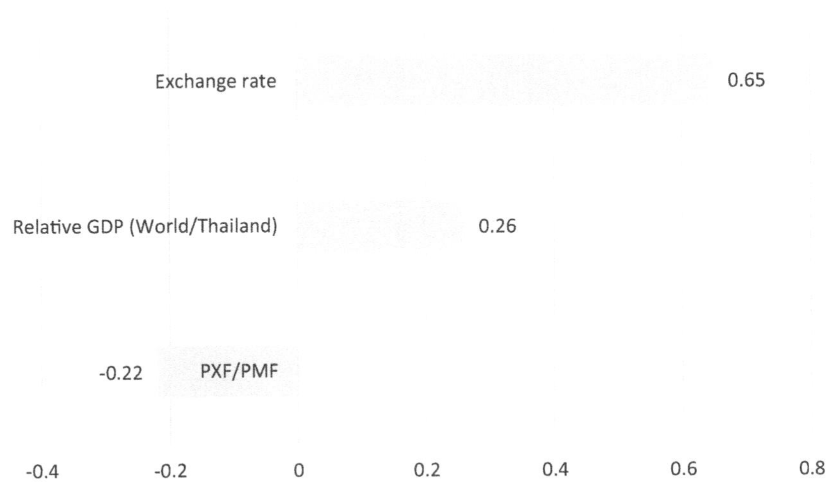

Figure 6.8 Elasticities of trade balance: ratio of exports to imports

Source: FOML estimates: 1980–2016

In sum, the exchange rate, together with domestic output adjustments, can help correct external imbalances, which can be perturbed by trade shocks or fluctuations in the world business cycle. Even if there is no change in the nominal exchange rate, the real exchange rate can be altered to gain international competitiveness if the country's inflation rate is lower than its trading partners' and competitors' in the world markets. Real exchange rates play an important role in adjusting disequilibrium external balances.

Figure 6.9 depicts the dynamics of real exchange rate adjustment and current account position in the long run. The long-run paths can be visualized by applying the Hodrick-Prescott filter to the actual real exchange rate and current account surplus, expressed in percentage of GDP. Changes in the trend of current account surplus lead to appreciation of the real exchange rate in the long run. There could be two-way causations between these magnitudes, for a substantial degree of real depreciation can lead to improvement in current account.

Figure 6.9 shows that there were co-movements, almost simultaneously, between the real exchange rate and current account balance from 1980 to the early 2000s. Current account tended to improve after 2005, while the long-run exchange rate continued to depreciate – albeit at a slower rate. The long-run currency depreciation propelled the expansion of current account surplus. Figure 6.9 provides a clue that there might be a causal relationship between the exchange rate and the external imbalance in the long run and the causations can run both ways. If changes in the exchange rate are in fact an equilibrating mechanism, rapidly rising current account would bring about real exchange rate

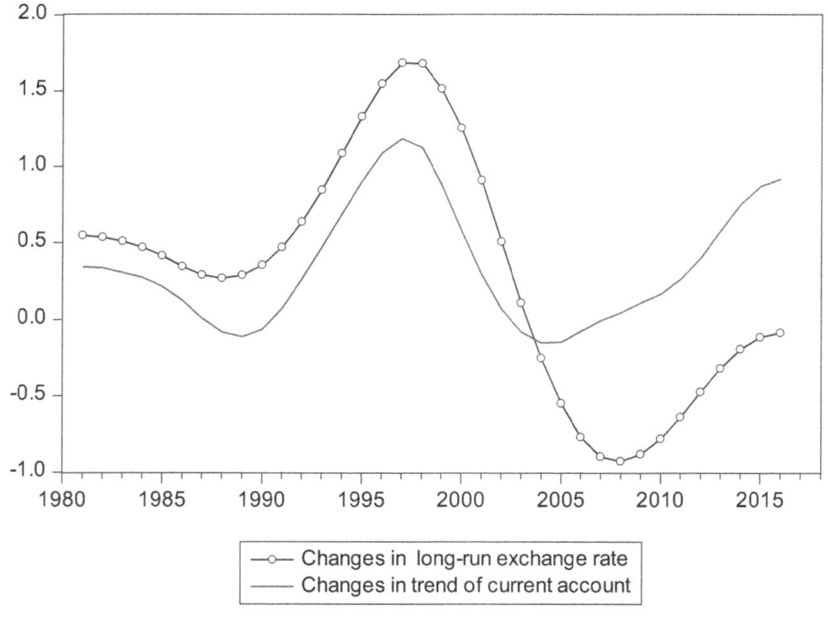

Figure 6.9 Long-run paths of real exchange rate and current account

appreciation. A deteriorating current account position would require depreciation of the real exchange rate.

6. Macrodynamic adjustments to external imbalances

To allow for feedback effects of important determinants of external adjustment variables, a vector autoregression (VAR) model is employed. The annual data utilized are from 1980 to 2017. The model offers an alternative approach to modeling the relationship between external adjustments and macro variables. Because the theory does not provide specification of the dynamic relationship among external and internal adjustments, non-structural VAR models can shed light on the interactions of endogenous variables. The VAR model includes five variables: GDP growth, the real exchange rate, current account deficit, fiscal balance, and the investment-saving gap. The last three variables in the list are expressed in terms of percent to GDP. The Hodrick-Prescott filter is applied to these five variables to obtain the trend variables, which can be thought of as long-term tendencies, since cyclical components of each series have been removed from their actual values. The model employs a change in the levels of these trend values when estimating the VAR model to obtain impulse response functions. We investigate how the structural path or long-term value of the current account is affected by changes in the following shocks: long-term output growth, fiscal budget, the real exchange rate, and the investment-saving gap. The model is perturbed by a shock or an innovation of one standard deviation of the shock variables. We can trace their dynamic impacts on the current account from the impulse response of the current account, reported in Figure 6.10, which shows that acceleration of GDP growth leads to a substantial current account deficit. The unfavorable impact on the current account is stronger than the negative impact from the widening investment-saving gap. Nevertheless, these negative impacts die off slowly and revert to a positive effect on the current account position in the long run. After a sufficient level of capital deepening, induced by strong economic growth, the current account turns into a surplus. As such, the current account deficit may not be unsustainable, if it is caused by strong growth and investment.

Factors that lead to a favorable current account include long-term real currency depreciation and structural budget surplus. Initially, fiscal austerity can lead to improvement in the current account, but in the long run it can lead to a serious problem in the current account deficit.

There is an important policy implication from this impulse response exercise: a sustainable and desirable level of current account as percentage of GDP, either deficit or surplus, can be obtained. Because strong GDP growth simultaneously leads to current account deficit and fiscal surplus, these two opposing forces reduce the likelihood that Thailand will experience an unsustainable current account level. During times of high investment and rapid GDP growth, current account can be improved if the real exchange rate depreciates to restore the external disequilibrium.

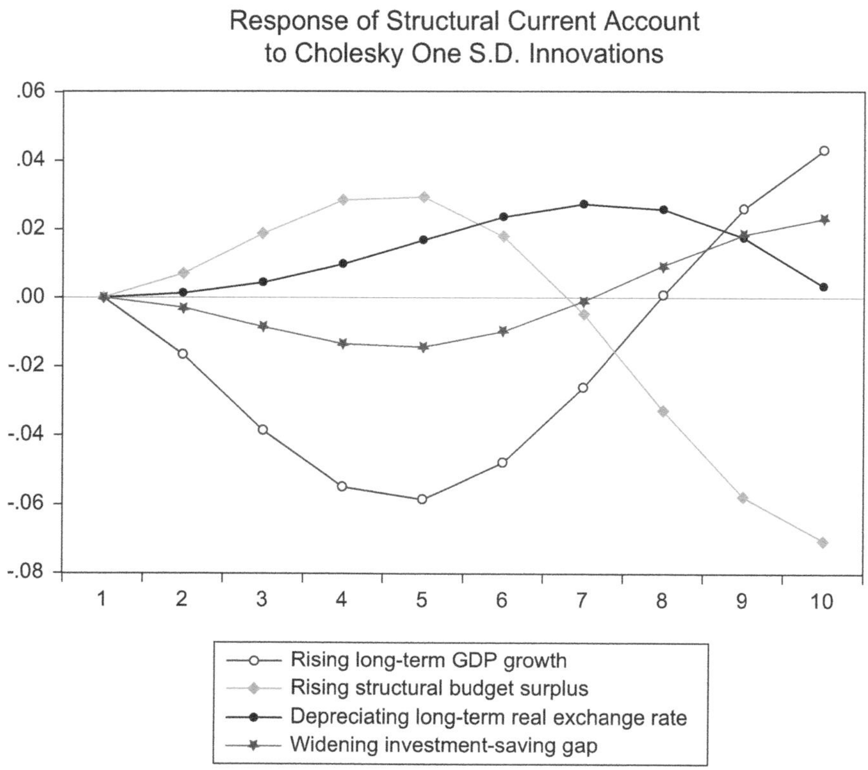

Figure 6.10 Impacts on structural current account

We ask a further question regarding whether there is a mechanism that allows the real exchange rate to appreciate when the surplus in current account is widening. We will use the same VAR model, but this time we will examine how the real exchange rate adjusts to shocks that originate from external and internal disequilibria. The sources of shocks may stem from changing terms of trade, e.g., the rise in oil price, which can lead to sudden current account deficit. In addition, internal disequilibrium can occur by a sharp rise in permanent government spending, e.g., on massive infrastructure buildup, which might lead to chronic budget deficit in the future. Moreover, internal disequilibrium can also occur if there is a sudden change in business sentiment and consumer confidence, which leads to a permanent rise in the excess of saving over investment, when the saving rate declines sharply. The level of the real exchange rate can also be altered by changes in the long-term GDP growth path as a result of shrinking world trade volume. The above-mentioned possibilities are scenarios which would affect the real exchange rate adjustment. The question is whether the exchange rate adjustment would be able to perform the equilibrating tasks if there is no output adjustment. In theory, if output is the only variable allowed to adjust, the economy may be able to achieve either internal equilibrium or external equilibrium. Without the exchange rate adjustment, the economy can gravitate to either side of this equilibrium at the cost of moving away from the other equilibrium.

The impulse response function of the long-run real exchange rate is shown in Figure 6.11. As expected, the real exchange rate appreciates when current account surplus enlarges. We can conclude that the real exchange rate depreciates when the deficit in the current account grows. Indeed, there exists an adjustment mechanism through the exchange rate that corrects the external disequilibrium. When the economy is able to achieve high long-term growth, the real exchange rate appreciates to reflect rising productivity and higher standard of living. Figure 6.10 showed that rising structural budget surplus leads to higher current account surplus. This is consistent with the impulse response of the real exchange rate reported in Figure 6.11, which shows that the real exchange rate appreciates when the structural budget is in surplus. The equilibrating function of the real exchange rate adjustment to correct the external imbalance must be emphasized. Internal imbalance, i.e., the widening of the investment-saving gap, does not cause a substantial exchange rate adjustment. The explanation is that the impact of an enlarging investment-saving gap on current account (Figure 6.10) is not as strong as the impact of changes in long-term GDP growth or the structural budget surplus.

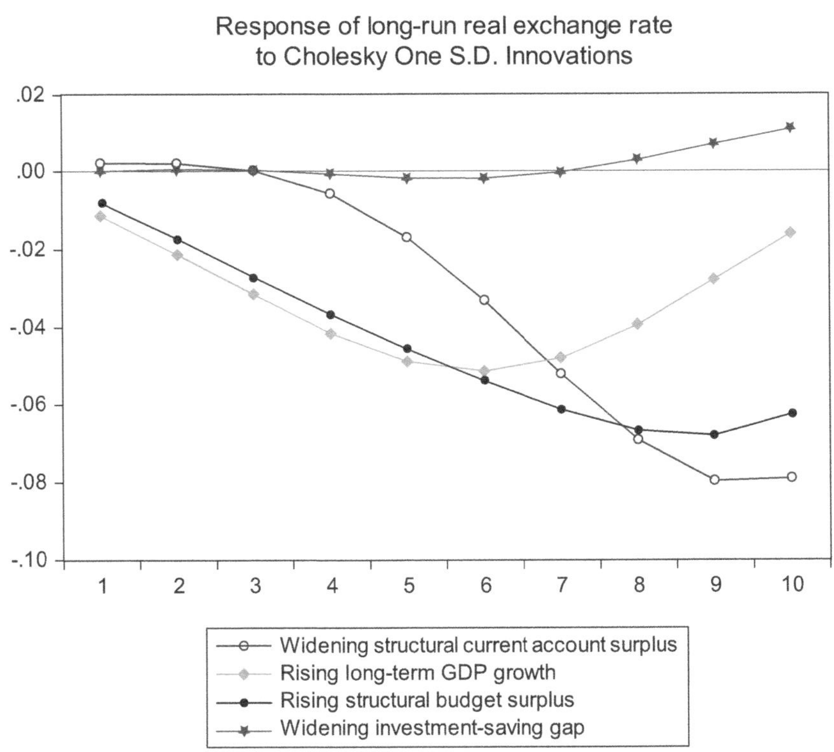

Figure 6.11 Adjustments of the real exchange rate to imbalances

7. Capital flows and their determinants

The current account deficit can be thought of as foreign savings required to fill the resource gap when domestic saving is insufficient to provide financial resources to booming investment demand. Capital inflows are required to fill that gap. Interest parity theorem predicts that there will be no capital movement from one country to another if the rates of return from holding financial assets in both countries are equalized.

Other things being equal, a widening gap between the interest rate in Thailand, represented by the minimum lending rate (MLR), and the foreign interest rate, proxied by the federal funds rate (FFR), should imply increase capital inflows into Thailand. A casual observation from Figure 6.12 suggests that there might be evidence supporting the interest parity theorem. Although there might be a positive correlation between the interest differential (MLR-FFR) and capital flows (Kflows), the relationship is far from perfect. Of course, other things do not always remain constant. Between 1980 and 2017, there were changes in expected currency depreciation and appreciation, risk factors, and capital controls, which would loosen the interest parity relationship. Note that there was a wild gyration of capital flows after 2005. Other factors, in addition to the interest differential, also influence the decisions of investors to move in and out of capital flows: direct investment, portfolio flows, trade credits, and bank flows. Perception of political risks after the two recent coups must be factored into the decision making of international investors.

Changes in the levels of domestic interest rates are partly determined by monetary policy; we will examine in subsequent chapters the effectiveness of monetary

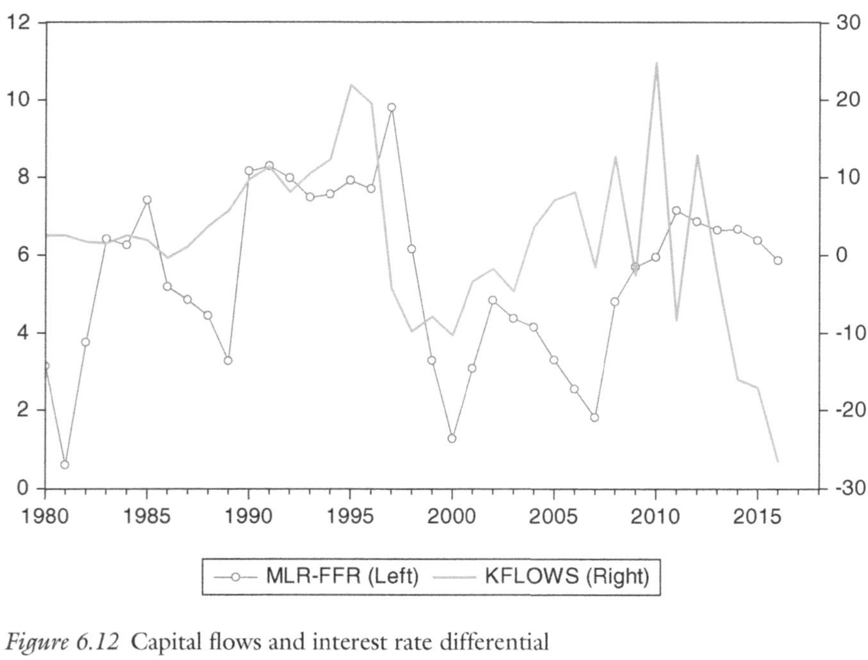

Figure 6.12 Capital flows and interest rate differential

policy in influencing the domestic interest rates, which in turn affect capital flows. The influence of expectations on the exchange rate will be discussed in the next chapter.

Employing annual data from 1982 to 2016 to explain the movement of capital flows (Kflows), we use the FMOLS method to estimate coefficients of the MLR and FFR, 1.85 and −1.87, respectively. Both coefficients are statistically significant at 0.01 level of confidence, implying that interest rate differentials affect capital flows.

$$\underset{}{Kflows} = \underset{(2.6)}{-8.23} + \underset{(3.98)}{1.85MLR} - \underset{(3.61)}{1.87FFR} - \underset{(2.62)}{1.35\,\Delta E^{e}} + \underset{(1.77)}{0.57g} - \underset{(6.38)}{22.7Coup}$$

Adj $R^2 = 0.58$, SER = 7.05

The results indicate that domestic interest rate policy and the Fed's monetary policy are pull and push factors relating to capital flows. Other factors contributing to capital outflows are the expected depreciation of the real exchange rate of the baht, proxied by changes in the real exchange rate (ΔE^e), and a dummy variable (Coup) for the years following the 2006 coup. The empirical evidence supports the conjecture that political turmoil and uncertainty can lead to capital flights. Thus, maintaining the rule of law and upholding the constitution can prevent capital outflows. High growth rate (g) is also positively related to capital inflows, but the growth variable is not highly significant. This reflects the fact that growth is usually funded by domestic savings more than capital flows. The adjusted R^2 is 0.58, suggesting that there are still some specific unexplained variations of capital flows: inflows and outflows of foreign direct investment, portfolio flows, and trade flows. There are some specific determinants of these components of such capital flows, such as wage rates, tariff structures, and market sentiments. These factors are excluded from the above equation.

8. Concluding remarks

An important policy implication derived in this chapter is that current account disequilibrium is the result of an imbalance in the resource gap, arising from excessive investment or excessive savings. Because saving and investment rates respond to growth differently, current account deficit or surplus is a structural problem. The fiscal imbalance is not the cause of current account disequilibrium. In fact, the long-term fiscal position goes in the opposite direction from the current account imbalance. It reflects a working fiscal automatic stabilizer.

When exchange rate adjustments are not allowed to perform their role to equilibrate current account imbalance, adjustments have to take place through output in order to gravitate back to the external equilibrium in the long run. Current account deficit is a problem associated with a booming economy, while current capital surplus is observed during economic slowdown. The problem arises from the excess of savings over investment.

Notes

1 Kim and Roubini (2008) provides evidence from the US showing that the hypothesis is refuted by the US data.
2 This was the period when the country experienced oil price shocks, causing stagflation. Current account surplus declined while output growth contracted. In the early 1980s, exports increased as a result of devaluations, which spurred growth. Hence, there was a positive relationship between output growth and current account improvement.
3 Using annual data from 1980 to 2017, the correlation coefficient between the rates of change in imports and exports is 0.79.
4 This is not to deny that saving rate is affected by population structure. However, the long-term growth rate is affected by population growth. Presumably, the long-term impact of population growth has been captured by the long-term growth rate.
5 In effect, the homogeneity degree is assumed to be behind this formulation. The coefficients of these magnitudes are assumed to be equal but of opposite signs. We will relax this assumption when exploring the exchange rate policy in the next chapter.

References

Bird, Graham, and Alex Mandilaras. 2006. "Regional Heterogeneity in the Relationship Between Fiscal Imbalances and Foreign Exchange Market Pressure." *World Development*, 34 (7): 1171–1181.

Cuestas, Juan Carlos, and Paulo Jose Regis. 2016. "On the Relationship Between Exchange Rates and External Imbalances: Should We Learn From East and South-East Asia?" *Annals of Economics and Finance*, 17: 255–280.

Duarte, Pablo, and Gunther Schnabl. 2015. "Macroeconomic Policy Making, Exchange Rate Adjustment and Current Account Imbalances in Emerging Markets." *Review of Development Economics*, 19: 531–544.

Eguren, Martin Fernando. 2016. "Exchange Rate Regimes and Current Account Adjustment: An Empirical Investigation." *Journal of International Money & Finance*, 65: 69–93.

Eichengreen, Barry, Poonam Gupta, and Oliver Masetti. 2018. "Are Capital Flows Fickle? Increasingly? And Does the Answer Still Depend on Type?" *Asian Economic Papers*, 17 (1): 22–41.

Feldstein, Martin, and Charles Horioka. 1980. "Domestic Saving and International Capital Flows." *Economic Journal*, 90 (2): 314–329.

Gervais, Olivier, Lawrence Schembri, and Lena Suchanek. 2016 "Current Account Dynamics, Real Exchange Rate Adjustment, and the Exchange Rate Regime in Emerging-Market Economies." *Journal of Development Economics*, 119: 86–99.

Kim, Soyoung, and Nouriel Roubini. 2008. "Twin Deficit or Twin Divergence? Fiscal Policy, Current Account, and Real Exchange Rate in the U.S." *Journal of International Economics*, 74 (2): 362–383.

7 Exchange rate policy

Lessons from the past

1. Introduction

Theoretical arguments exist to support intervention in the foreign exchange market. According to Bilson (1985), there is a link between variability of exchange rates and interest rates. Since interest rate fluctuations are a causal factor to the business cycle, as currency risk premiums increase, interest rates must also increase to compensate for the risk. The combination of instabilities of real interest rate and real exchange rate must have an adverse effect on the economy. There are also internal factors such as domestic monetary shocks and political uncertainties which create currency volatility under the choices of a fixed exchange rate regime (Hasan and Wallace, 1996). Furthermore, real exchange rate volatility has a negative impact on private investment (Bhandari and Upadhyaya, 2010). According to Kenen and Rodrik (1986), volatilities of real exchange rates reduce the volume of international trade. Exchange rate fluctuations comprise risks and uncertainties, which can disrupt international trade flow. Exchange rate volatility has a significant negative impact on export flows to the world market (Chit et al., 2010). Even when the nominal exchange rate does not change, the real effective exchange rate can fluctuate as a result of movements of major currencies. Relatively high inflation at home can bring about a loss in international competitiveness. Krugman (1989) argued that gains from international trade are reduced when exchange rate instability blurs price signals which supposedly regulate international markets. If future exchange rates are uncertain, firms are more cautious and delay investments, even when they face increases in demand for exports. This argument for a fixed exchange rate is based on the need to accumulate physical capital at an early stage of development.

Between the 1960s and the early 1980s, Thailand benefited considerably from the fixed exchange rate system. Thailand experienced steady growth while maintaining a stable exchange rate. From January 1982 to October 1984, the baht exchange rate averaged at 23 baht to the dollar, depreciated by 2 percent. From November 1984 to October 1985, the baht exchange averaged 27.3 baht, or devaluation by 18.5 percent compared to the previous period (Table 7.1). From then until June 1997, the baht appreciated to 25.5 baht, or 0.5 percent of the annual average. This remarkable stability became a massive depreciation by

Table 7.1 Period average (year-on-year)

	Baht/USD	*Average percentage change*	*Standard deviation of rate of change (yoy)*
Before 1984 devaluation (1982–Oct 1984)	23.0	2.0	4.3
Nov 1984–Oct 1985	27.3	18.5	2.02
Nov 1985–June 1997	25.5	-0.5	1.84
July 1997–Dec 1998	39.7	40.9	31.8
Jan 1999–March 2018	35.9	-0.28	2.71

Source: Bank of Thailand

40.9 percent between July 1997 and December 1998. From January 1999 to March 2008, the baht exchange rate appreciated by 0.28 percent on the average. There has been a pattern swinging from a remarkable stability to extreme depreciation.

GDP grew steadily at an annual rate of 7 percent. In this period, trade volume rose from 35 percent to 75 percent of the GDP. Rapid economic growth was achieved without sacrificing price stability. It can be argued that the fixed exchange rate system contributed significantly to trade expansion and rapid output growth. In 1963, the baht was initially pegged at 20.8 baht to the US dollar. The baht exchange rate remained at that level until 1973, when the Bretton Woods system broke down and the baht was revalued to 20.0 baht, the rate that had been fixed for another 5 years. Then came the first devaluation in July 1981; the baht was devalued by 8.7 percent to 23 baht to the dollar. In 1984, the second devaluation by 14.7 percent took place. In the 1980s, devaluations were carried out as a last resort when other policies failed to correct the unsustainable current account deficit. Even after external disequilibrium was corrected by establishing a realistic exchange rate, old habits died hard. A system of a basket of currencies, including the US dollar, Japanese yen, West German mark, UK pound sterling, Malaysian ringgit, Hong Kong dollar, and Singapore dollar, was adopted after the baht devaluation in 1984. It was supposed to give the baht more flexibility. It turned out that the dollar weight in the basket gradually increased until July 1997. In reality, the baht had returned to the fixed exchange rate regime despite adopting a currency-basket system. At the end of June 1997, the currency-basket system set the exchange rate at 25.8 baht to the dollar.

After the Plaza Accord, the yen started its long-term appreciation against the US dollar. Consequently, the baht depreciated against the yen because of the baht peg to the dollar (Figure 7.1). Thailand benefited by increasing exports to Japan and rising Japanese FDI inflows. By 1995, the baht was pegged to the dollar, which started to appreciate against the yen. As a result, Thailand's exports suffered from the strengthening of the baht exchange rate against the yen, and the current account deficit was enlarged because the overvalued baht led to rising imports. The Bank of Thailand imposed an 18 percent credit growth ceiling on

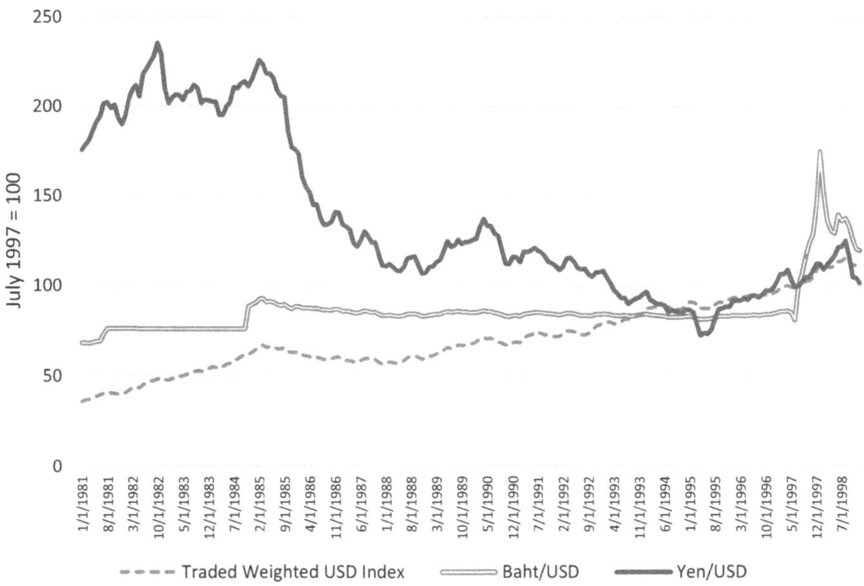

Figure 7.1 Root cause of the baht crisis

Source: Federal Reserve Bank

commercial bank loans. That policy did not work since the root of the problem was the overvaluation of the baht. When the deficit became unsustainable, floating the baht was the only option left.

With increasing integration, the cost of maintaining a fixed exchange rate regime outweighed its benefits. If monetary authorities give priority to maintaining exchange rate stability, intervention in foreign exchange markets may reduce the effectiveness of monetary policy. Establishing baht stability by increasing the weight of the US dollar in the basket caused an appreciation of the baht when the dollar appreciated against other currencies. Overvaluation of the baht resulted in a loss of competitiveness. The exchange rate was maintained by continued intervention in foreign exchange markets. The fear of floating can be seen as a reason for such intervention (Calvo and Reinhart, 2002). Prior to the 1997 financial crisis, Thai financial institutions borrowed heavily in dollars. Allowing the baht to depreciate substantially to correct the current account deficit would have damaged the balance sheets of banks and finance companies. The Bank of Thailand continued intervening in the spot and forward exchange markets despite a substantial loss in international reserves. Adverse consequences of the fixed rate had become more apparent after confidence in the baht was eroded by speculative attacks.

From 1960 to the early 1990s, Thailand grew rapidly because of strong growth in exports and investment. From 1990 to 2008, the share of exports in GDP increased from 40 percent to over 70 percent. After the 1998 collapse of financial institutions, investment ceased to be a growth engine. By 2000, the share of investment in GDP had declined from 40 percent to 20 percent. Before the 2008 global recession, exports remained the main engine of growth. Thailand depends on imported intermediate products to manufacture export goods. When Thailand experiences export shortfalls, imports are curtailed accordingly. Thus, a global slowdown that shrank the demand for Thai-manufactured exports did not lead to current account deficit. Imports always move in line with exports. Therefore, contribution to growth by exports must not be overstated, since a surge in exports simultaneously led to considerable rise in import of raw materials. The content of Thai exports has changed considerably from agricultural commodities to manufactured products since the early 1990s. Imported components of electronic products are required to manufacture hard disks and computers. These industries create lower value added than agricultural commodities and processed food exports, which mainly utilize domestic raw materials. Without realizing this fact, the urge to keep the baht unrealistically weak will remain.

This chapter examines Thailand's exchange rate policy and its macroeconomic impacts in recent decades. It provides a critical review of Thailand's exchange rate policy and draws lessons from past mistakes. Capital controls and interventions in the foreign exchange markets will be discussed.

2. An abrupt exit from the fixed exchange system

In addition to containing foreign exchange risk to promote international transactions, a fixed exchange rate can assure a steady output growth path. Therefore, the central bank regularly intervenes in foreign exchange markets. There are theoretical arguments for choosing a flexible exchange rate system. According to Friedman (1953), speculations are likely to be stabilizing as long as market participants are rational. When markets are efficient, there is no room for destabilizing speculation. Yet, as we have seen from the Asian financial crisis in 1997 and the US subprime loan crisis in 2008, speculative behavior is not always stabilizing. There is no concrete evidence of efficient asset markets. In Thailand, there were periods of departure from uncovered parity, which coincided with a high level of risk premiums. Speculation can be destabilizing, and negative externality provides a reason for intervention.

Pegging an exchange rate can lead to unrealistic values when productivity and price levels change over time. The purchasing power parity (PPP) may not provide a benchmark for targeting the exchange rate. Substantial departures from the PPP, even in a world of flexible exchange rates, can exist in the short run and even over decades (Obstfeld and Rogoff, 1995). With a considerable differential between productivity growth in the tradable and non-tradable goods sectors, a country can experience rising relative prices of non-tradable goods, resulting in the appreciation of the real exchange rate. Therefore, it is impossible to pinpoint the exact equilibrium value of the exchange rate based on deviations from the PPP, nor can the current account deficit indicate the exact degree of exchange rate overvaluation. As discussed in the previous chapter, the investment-saving relationship also determines the current account position. Indeed, intervention in foreign exchange markets to obtain an appropriate value of the exchange rate must be exceedingly difficult, without considering further complications arising from the impact on domestic absorption caused by changes in the exchange. So, one of the arguments against a fixed exchange rate system is that even if it is desirable to fix the exchange rate to provide stability, there is also a question about the level at which a country should choose to peg the exchange rate.

A flexible exchange rate allows the baht to become more flexible in response to fluctuations in world trade volume. Broda (2004) provided evidence that short-run real output responses to real shocks are significantly smoother in floats than in pegs. Coudert and Couharde (2009) found that pegged currencies were significantly more overvalued than flexible currencies.

If the baht appreciated more than other currencies, there must be some other factors in addition to the appreciation of the yen that contributed to its strength. Capital inflows were the source of the strength of the baht. Using the monthly data from January 1994 to June 2017, the correlation coefficients of the real board effective exchange rates between the baht and the US dollar is –0.73, suggesting that the movement of the real effective exchange rate or the overall competitiveness of the baht is influenced by the direction of the US dollar.

When Thailand embraced the IMF's capital account liberalization policy, borrowing in foreign currencies was encouraged. The real effective exchange rate of the baht appreciated more than in trading partners' currencies (Figure 7.2). By June 1997, the real effective exchange rate (REER) of the baht appreciated more

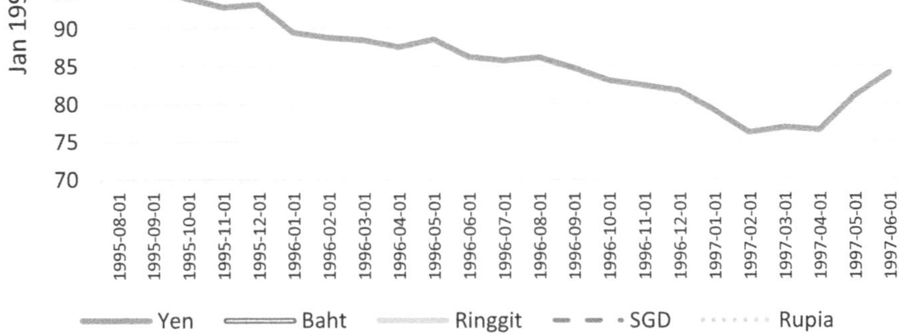

Figure 7.2 Appreciation of the baht REER September 1995–June 1997

Source: Federal Reserve Bank

than the yen, the ringgit, the rupiah, and the Singapore dollar (SGD). The fixed exchange rate of the baht to the dollar did not reveal the erosion of Thailand's competitiveness as much as the REER shown in Figure 7.2.

On July 2, 1997, the Bank of Thailand gave up defending the baht and the exchange rate plunged to 27.4 baht to the dollar. That was just the beginning of the baht's long slide. The value of the baht kept declining and triggered a financial crisis in Asia. Other regional currencies also suffered similar steep declines. When an exchange rate is unrealistically fixed for so long, the cost of intervention soon outweighs its benefits. After floating the baht in July 1997, it depreciated to a record low of 55 baht to the dollar in January 1998 (Figure 7.3).

Capital inflows include FDI, bank borrowings, and portfolio investment. Other capital flows (OTHER) were deposited in non-resident baht accounts, which can be used later for speculative purposes in currency and bond markets (Figure 7.4). These flows were related to speculation that the baht would imminently be devalued. The irregular flow returned to normal after the massive devaluation of 1998. After 2006, there was no wild fluctuation of this type of speculative flow after the baht regained its stability and the speculation died off slowly.

3. Export competitiveness and REER

In 1995, the continued strength of the dollar caused overvaluation of the baht, which needed to be corrected by a free fall of the baht against the dollar in the second half of 1997. Table 7.1 indicates the large swings of the baht after the float in July 1997. By 1999, the baht began to depreciate again, but the degree of depreciation was greater than its appreciation. Apparently, asymmetric

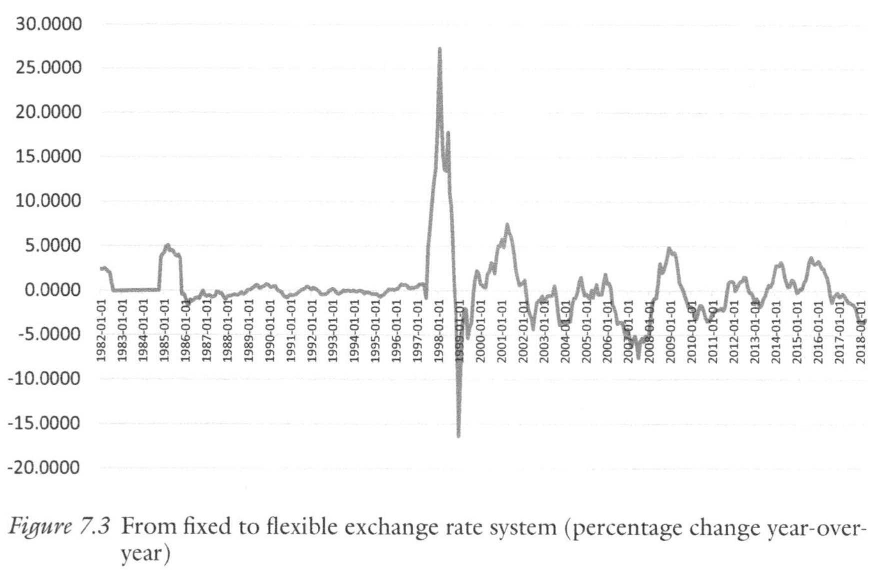

Figure 7.3 From fixed to flexible exchange rate system (percentage change year-over-year)

Source: Federal Reserve Bank

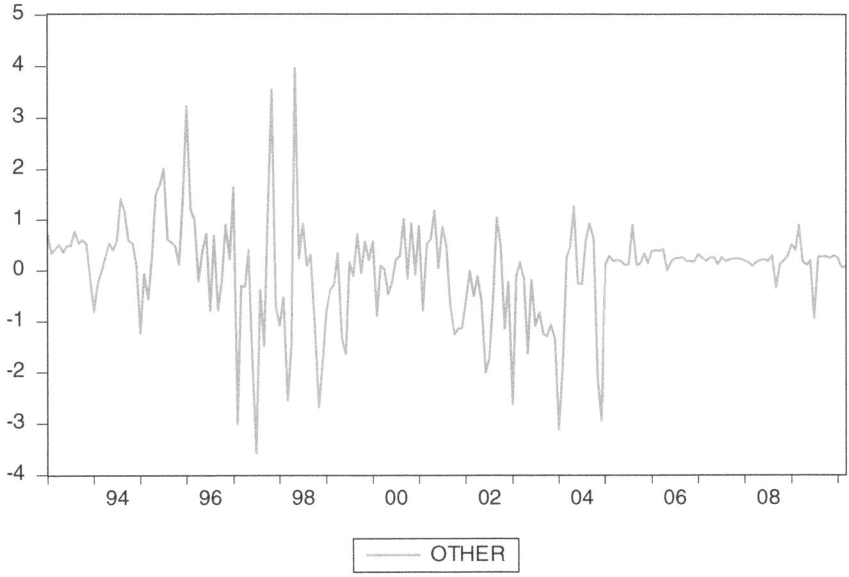

Figure 7.4 Capital flight and the financial crisis

intervention maintained the baht's stability. The Bank of Thailand intervenes less when the baht depreciates and more when the baht appreciates. The fear of appreciation is unwarranted. The Bank of Thailand does not want to hurt exporters, but on the other hand, importers, investors, and consumers can enjoy the benefits of cheaper imported goods.

Apart from the possibility of retaliation by other competitors, devaluation does not ensure a long-lasting effect on international competitiveness, which depends on a productive labor force, savings, and technological progress. A strong currency may be associated with export competitiveness. A country with a high savings rate and rapid productivity growth will experience real exchange rate appreciation, while commanding a considerable degree of international competitiveness. It has always been suggested that Thailand needs a weak baht to help exporters gain competitiveness. Since changes in foreign exchange rates profoundly affect prices of all commodities in the country, we must evaluate the overall impact of foreign exchange rate changes. For example, there is an income distributive issue, which involves income transfer between exporters and importers, tradable and non-tradable sectors, and creditors and debtors in foreign currencies.

Flexibility in the real wage rate could explain why Thailand was able to maintain the fixed exchange rate for so long.[1] According to Obstfeld (1998), before the 1997 crash, Thailand had been a "puzzle" since it is very rare for countries to observe the fixed exchange rate discipline for longer than five years. Flexibility of wages and prices would not require Thailand to rely on flexible exchange rates as a means to correct macroeconomic imbalances. Conservative fiscal policy (fiscal surplus) prior to the 1997 crisis helped mitigate monetary expansion caused by capital inflows. Monetary base growth was prevented from being explosive, threatening price stability under the fixed exchange rate system with an open capital account. With many policy objectives, the fixed exchange rate system, which previously worked well as a domestic anchor, had to be sacrificed.

A depreciation of the real effective exchange rate does not always imply a gain in price competitiveness. Not only the direction of the movement matters, but also the gap between actual and equilibrium real exchange rates. A real depreciation would not improve competitiveness much if the actual real effective rate were significantly overvalued. A real appreciation may not necessarily imply a loss in competitiveness, if it reflects a productivity gain.

Between 2001 and 2005, the real effective exchange rate of the baht depreciated by 10 percent. The weakened baht helped the Thai economy recover from the recession through strong export growth. This depreciation had much to do with the strength of the dollar in the early 2000s. While the real effective exchange rate of the yen depreciated from 2000 to 2007, the weakening of the dollar only began after 2003.[2] Starting in 2005, weaknesses in both currencies gave rise to real effective appreciation of the baht. This episode led to the adoption of capital controls in Thailand in December 2006. By 2007, the yen began to climb and the dollar started appreciating in its aftermath, leading to the depreciation of Thailand's real effective exchange rate and relieving upward pressure on the baht. As the real effective exchange rate appreciated, it encouraged more imports. We have seen the upswings of the importation of goods. However, the real effective exchange rate uptrend did not show a significant effect on movement in the trend of exports. Imports also are affected by rising export trends due to expansion of the demand for parts and components of export products.

The trend of REER, shown in Figure 7.5, indicates that the baht's competitiveness increased right after switching to a more flexible exchange rate system. By 2006, the competitiveness of the baht exchange rate eroded gradually. This episode of the strengthening of the baht did not adversely affect export growth. Hence, there must have been other factors contributing to rapid growth of exports and imports.

When monetary authorities allow the baht to fluctuate more freely, it is difficult to target a specific level of real effective exchange rates, let alone its direction.[3] The real effective exchange rate of the baht always moves in the opposite direction of the yen and dollar, while the impact of dollar movement has become increasingly more dominant. The implication of this long-term relationship is that the interest rate policy employed by that the Bank of Thailand to target the real effective exchange rate may not be useful since the baht's real effective exchange rate is determined by world's key currencies. When the real effective rates of the dollar and the yen depreciate, that of the baht appreciates accordingly. Liew et al. (2009) pointed out that influences of domestic and foreign monetary policies on Thailand's exchange rates cannot be neglected.

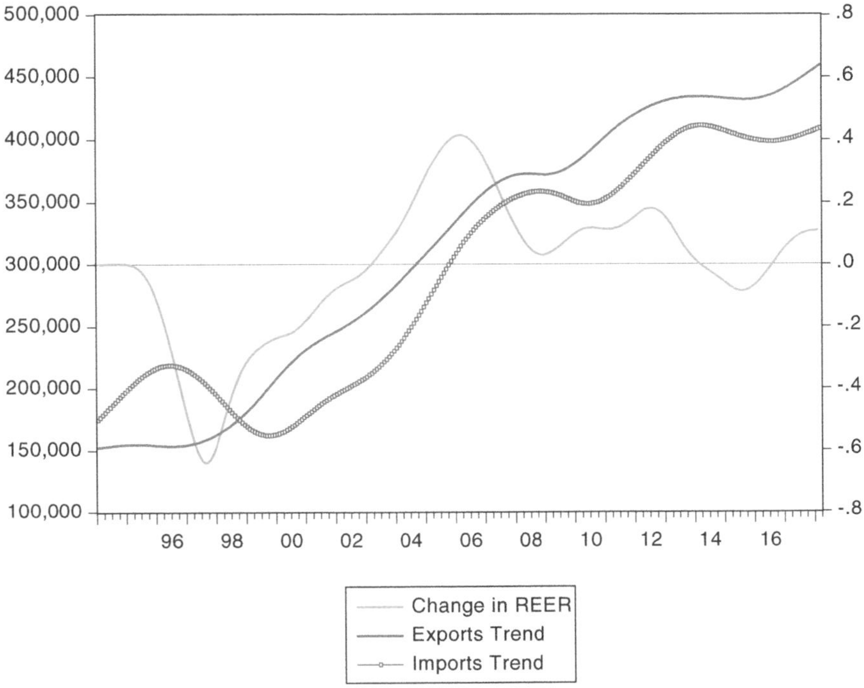

Figure 7.5 Trends of the baht REER and imports

With more open capital accounts, the Bank of Thailand must choose between targeting the exchange rate or the interest rate. If the interest rate is targeted, the Bank of Thailand must stand by to adjust the money supply to bring about the desired level of the interest rates. Capital controls permitted the Bank of Thailand to pursue monetary policy to produce the level of money supply which is consistent with the internal equilibrium condition. At the end of 2006, capital control was employed to delay baht appreciation against the dollar.

4. Intervention in the foreign exchange markets

A fixed exchange rate system together with an open capital market is incompatible with independent monetary policy. Thailand learned this lesson well after the 1997 currency crisis. The fixed exchange rate functioned well with monetary autonomy and a certain degree of capital controls. When capital controls were relaxed in 1993 to liberalize capital accounts, monetary autonomy was sacrificed. Trade reform can improve efficiency and resource allocation. However, as Bhagwati (1998) pointed out, there is a big difference between liberalization of trade and capital flow. Capital account liberalization does not always lead to welfare improvement if financial infrastructure is not ready to cope with capital inflows.

Lack of financial supervision and prudential rules and regulations on financial institutions led to excessive lending and property bubbles. Eichengreen (2000) suggested that Chilean-style capital control should be retained until banks' risk management practices and regulatory oversight have been upgraded. Capital control is found to be sufficiently supported by both economic theory and empirical evidence as a way to address macroeconomic problems associated with short-term capital flow (Montecino and Cordero, 2010).

The exchange rate is determined by trade and capital flow, in addition to external factors and exchange rate expectations. Exchange rate movement can be considered an indicator of country risks. A sharp plunge in baht value would signify governmental mismanagement of the economy. A sharp deterioration of the external value of the baht during the last quarter of 1997 reflected in part the loss in policy credibility of the ruling government during a period of political turmoil.

Since capital controls are costly to enforce and may reduce welfare due to intertemporal consumption, total capital control is impossible. Insofar as excessive short-term capital flow raises the possibility of a financial crisis, hot money flows should be limited by establishing prudential regulations on overseas borrowing by the private sector.

The flexible exchange rate system also sends a signal to the private sector that borrowers of foreign capital must internalize some costs of failing to hedge against unanticipated movement of exchange rates. The need for strict capital controls is reduced as capital flight declines. Flexibility in foreign exchange rates guarantees that there is no serious misalignment of the exchange rate. Therefore, the probability of capital flight would reduce, provided that economic fundamentals and political stability prevail. The evidence provided by Dubas (2009) indicated that an intermediate exchange rate regime between a pure float and hard peg is most effective in preventing exchange rate misalignment. Moreover, the welfare level of a small country under a freely floating regime was generally higher than under other regimes (Akiba et al., 2009).

The effective exchange rate movement is still determined by the dollar-baht rate because of the dominance of the dollar in international trade transactions. Depreciation of the baht against the yen slowed appreciation of the baht's nominal effective exchange rate. Thus, the nominal effective rate did not appreciate as much as the dollar-baht exchange rate. Market intervention cannot maintain competitiveness of the baht (when using the effective rate measurement).

Taylor (2001) observed that the current appreciation of the exchange rate, through inertial effects of exchange-rate transmission and the existence of a policy rule, will result in a decline in interest rate. Even though the exchange rate is not an explicit part of policy rules, because of current appreciation of the exchange rate, it becomes more likely that the central bank will lower the interest rate in the future as inflationary expectations are revised downward. Monetary policy rules that respond indirectly to exchange rate changes might work better than rules which respond directly. Accordingly, if the Bank of Thailand does not resist baht appreciation, there will be less need to initiate interest hikes in order to curb inflation.

Intervention cannot slow down baht appreciation, which is caused by inherent weakness of the dollar. The Bank of Thailand cannot resist the trend of baht appreciation by intervening in foreign exchange markets.[4] Increased intervention, as measured by the ratio of net forward position as a percentage of total reserves, did not halt baht appreciation. As a clear trend of baht appreciation emerged at the beginning of 2006, exporters did not want to hold dollars long after receiving payment. As the dollar's strengthening trend continued, the Bank of Thailand suffered enormous financial losses from buying the dollar forward in order to reduce pressure on the baht. From January 2003, when the net forward position (NFP) was a few percentage points of total reserves, intervention was intensified as the baht appreciated in 2006 and 2007. By January 2008, the amount of net forward position of the Bank of Thailand peaked at 24 percent of total reserves. By 2011, the Bank of Thailand was able to issue bonds without seeking approval from the Ministry of Finance.

International reserves accumulated every month; the Bank of Thailand was obliged to sterilize capital flows by issuing bonds to mop up excess money supply. In doing so, it built up pressure on interest rates. As the federal funds rate was continuously cut to prevent recession in the US, the Bank of Thailand was not able to maintain high interest rates to fight inflation, because widening uncovered interest differentials would further induce capital inflow and currency appreciation.

During December, 2006, in a desperate attempt to prevent baht appreciation, a zero-interest reserve requirement of 30 percent on short-term flows was imposed. In effect, the onshore and offshore markets for the baht were differentiated. Since the baht's strength was caused by portfolio inflow, it was not surprising that the Bank of Thailand attempted to stem the flow of portfolio investment by imposing Chilean-type capital controls. In 1991, the Bank of Chile imposed a 30 percent unremunerated reserve requirement (URR) to curb short-term capital inflow, which tended to cause domestic currency appreciation. Although the URR did not reduce capital inflow or halt currency appreciation, it changed the composition of inflow from short to longer maturity. Forbes (2007) found evidence that the Chilean URR increased financial constraints for small firms and misallocation of resources occurred because the control discriminated against short-term projects and firms that depend heavily on bank credit.

Investors in the stock market were against capital controls because the control measure inhibited capital inflow to the stock market. The URR measure led to a stock market collapse and prompted the Bank of Thailand to exempt portfolio investment from capital controls one day after the measure was announced. The Bank of Thailand further relaxed and exempted debt instruments and forward-covered transactions from the URR.

There is no evidence that the capital controls imposed in 2008–2009 significantly slowed down appreciation, as the Bank of Thailand had hoped. There are also unintended effects of capital controls. Asiedu and Lien (2004) found evidence that capital controls deter foreign direct investment in East Asian countries. In 2007, although foreign investment in Thailand increased, the percentage increase was much lower than in neighboring countries such as Malaysia and Vietnam. Coelho and Gallagher (2010) suggested that, by employing Colombia and Thailand as case studies, there is still a role for capital control to play in the twenty-first century, but such controls should be more sophisticated than in the past. Due to the fact that capital controls are envisaged as anti-globalization by investors, among other policies of a military-installed government, the Chilean-style capital control measures became counterproductive and costly in terms of financial losses to the Bank of Thailand. Moreover, exporters had no incentive to improve efficiency, since they were relying on undervalued currencies. Moral hazard arose as exporters had believed that the government would help them by keeping exchange rates competitive. Figure 7.6 shows deviations of portfolio flows from their trend. In December 2006, portfolio investment fluctuated wildly after the imposition of capital controls.[5]

The Stock Exchange of Thailand recorded the single biggest one-day loss in its history of 820 billion baht – a decline of 14.8 percent – one day after the measures were announced. On March 3, 2008, the Bank of Thailand finally abandoned capital controls, reasoning that the economic situation had returned to normality and they were no longer needed. In late 2009, after the fear of global recession subsided, capital inflow into the stock market resumed and the baht regained strength.

The stock exchange index of Thailand rose to 43.8 percent from December 30, 2010 to February 2, 2011. It is important to understand the macroeconomic policy consequences of this attempt to maintain a weak baht.

In the aftermath of capital controls, wider fluctuation of portfolio investment is to be expected. Notably, foreign investment, which is not supposed to fluctuate

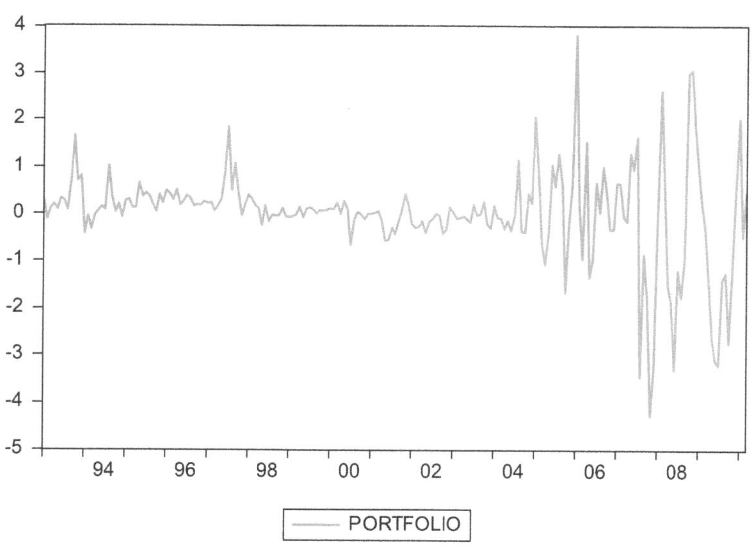

Figure 7.6 Volatility of portfolio flows during period of capital controls (normalized values)

widely, becomes more volatile. This suggests that foreign investors are affected by the Thai government's uncertainty and policy inconsistency after the restriction of capital flow. Capital control was the wrong policy applied for the wrong reason. Previously, Thailand had maintained an open-door policy to foreign investors. Authorities believed that capital controls would not impact long-term investors, since the policy was only applied to short-term flow and for a specific duration. Little did the authorities realize that animal spirits of investors do not distinguish between short-term and long-term control measures. When policy becomes inconsistent with past expectations, risk premium is heightened, resulting in massive capital flight from the stock market.

During the period of continued appreciation of the baht, the Bank of Thailand was under pressure to resist baht appreciation to protect exporters (Figure 7.7). The Bank of Thailand intervenes less in the forward market, thus allowing the baht to appreciate against the dollar. The Bank of Thailand has gradually raised its policy interest rate to discourage inflationary pressure. There is concern that the enlarged interest rate differential between key policy and federal fund rates would induce more capital inflow and further strengthen the baht.

In October 2010, the government revoked the 15 percent withholding exemption on interest and capital gains earned by foreign investors. The motivation of this policy was to prevent baht speculation as there was a capital flow surge in the bond market. Tax instruments were called upon to slow baht appreciation. Again, this policy was likely to fail to reduce capital flow, because the inflow is the result of portfolio investment in response to an anticipation of capital gains in the Thai stock market.

The Bank of Thailand has promoted direct investment abroad to lessen pressure on the strengthening baht. Listed firms are permitted to invest abroad. The ASEAN Economic Community Agreement that went into effect in 2015 eased the restrictions on outward portfolio investments. With uncertainties in the recovery of the US economy and the sovereign debt crisis in Europe, there was more baht volatility. The Bank of Thailand still ponders the use of various kinds of capital control measures to curb capital inflow, hoping that they may have some deterrent effect on speculators.

The baht continued to gain strength against the dollar, which depreciated to correct the US's unsustainable current account deficit. The strength of the baht could have been more spectacular without market intervention by the Bank of Thailand. As the level of international reserves kept rising, the question arose whether the accumulated reserves could be put to uses such as financing budget deficits or repaying debts accumulated from financial institution bailouts. The principal reason for intervention was the unwarranted fear that a strong baht would hurt Thai exports and slow economic growth, and therefore, the central bank must keep the baht at a competitive level. The Bank of Thailand still intervenes regularly to prevent the baht from rapid appreciation. As a result, the amount of international reserves increased from 26.9 billion dollars in 1997 to 138 billion dollars in 2009. During this period, the baht appreciated from 47.2 baht to 33.3 baht to the dollar. By March 2018, foreign exchange reserves increased to 215.6 billion dollars and the baht appreciated to 31.7 baht.

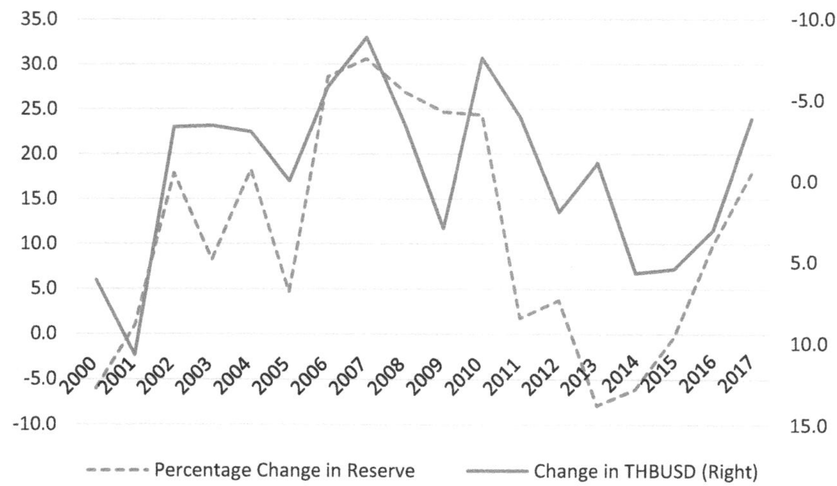

Figure 7.7 Leaning against the wind of strong baht

Source: Bank of Thailand

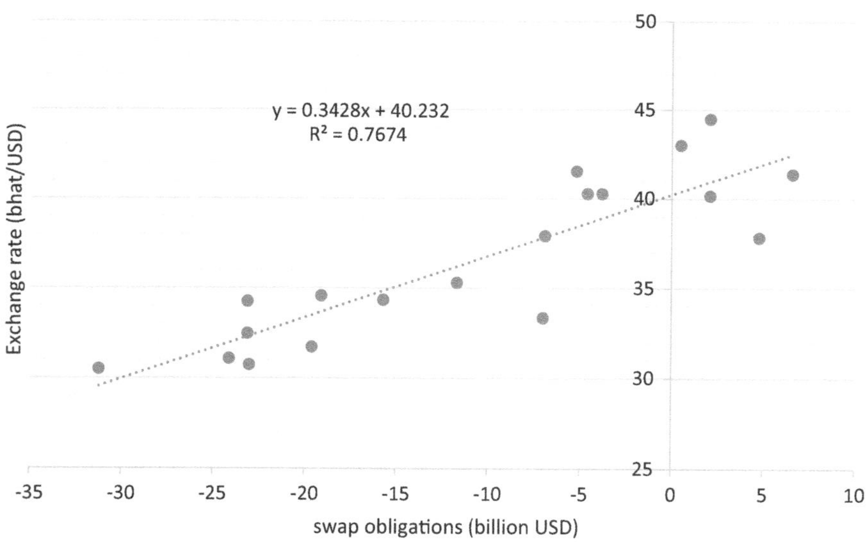

Figure 7.8 Intervention in the forward markets: 1998–2016

Source: Bank of Thailand

Intervention to manage the baht exchange rate to help exports are carried out regularly. Figure 7.8 shows that, between 1998 and 2016, the Bank of Thailand bought the dollar forward (negative swap obligations) when the baht appreciated and sold the dollar forward (positive swap obligations) when the baht depreciated. At the height of the baht appreciation to almost 30 baht to the dollar, the

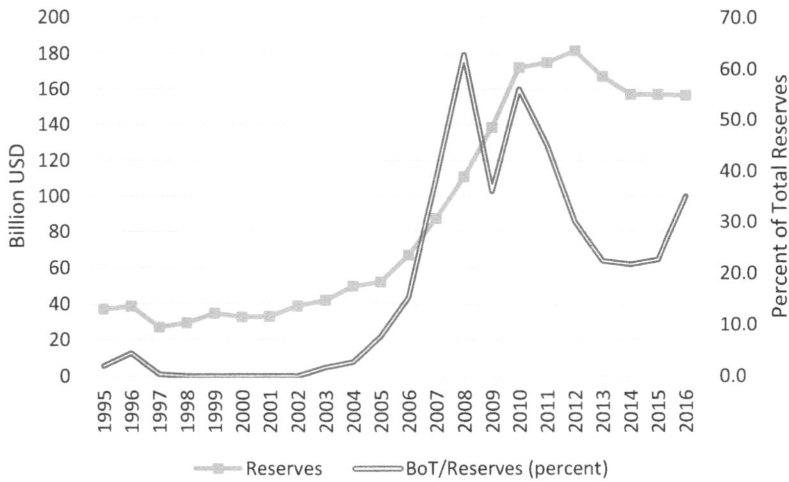

Figure 7.9 BoT bonds: sterilization of capital inflows

Source: Bank of Thailand

Bank of Thailand bought the dollar at the spot and forward markets to prevent the baht from appreciation beyond the 30-baht psychological level. Buying the dollar increases the international reserves, which expands the monetary base. Sterilization of capital flows can be done by selling BoT bonds to absorb the money supply (Figure 7.9).

Exports are largely responsive to output growth. With expansion in capacity output and a greater degree of capital utilization, exports can be increased. Therefore, instead of engineering a weak exchange rate, exports can be increased in the long term through promoting the flow of capital into productive sectors. Any measure that hinders capital inflow and foreign direct investment can reduce export growth in the long run. Political unrest and uncertainty, capital control, protectionism, and policy inconsistency entail the reduction of long-term capital flow and thereby reduce exports in the long run.

If Thai monetary authorities are unwilling to let the exchange rate adjust to equilibrate external imbalances, the burden of the adjustment falls on output. If the real exchange rate is allowed to appreciate in response to surplus in the balance of payments, export growth can slow to prevent the economy from overheating. Likewise, if the real exchange rate depreciates in response to a deficit in the balance of payments, exports can be enhanced to stimulate the economy. The exchange rate is such an important macroeconomic policy variable that we cannot do without its equilibrating role.

5. Trade elasticities: how important is the exchange rate?

Employing monthly data from 1980 to 2016, the trade value elasticities are estimated. The estimated elasticities are obtained from FMOLS estimation

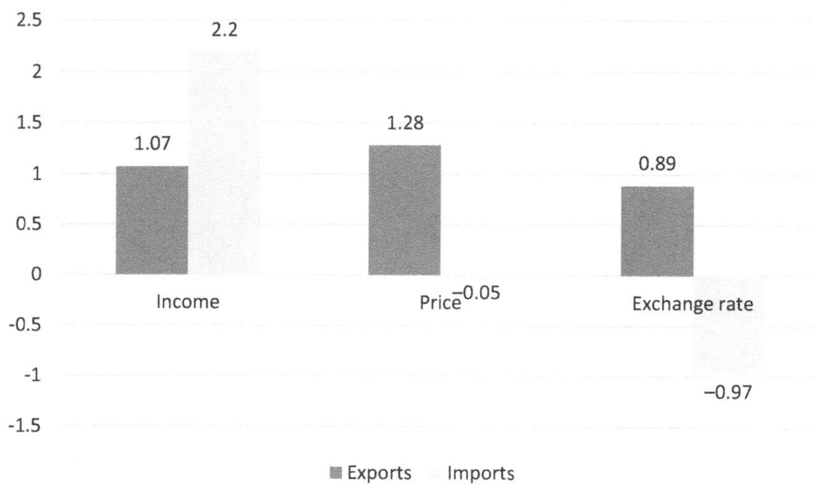

Figure 7.10 Trade elasticities: 1980–2016

Source: Author's calculation

(Figure 7.10). Except for price elasticities, world income elasticity of Thailand's exports and Thailand's income elasticity of imports are statistically significant at 0.05 percent. Although import and export price elasticities are not highly significant, they have the expected signs. Higher indexes of export and import prices increase values exports and decrease import values. As world economic growth accelerates, Thailand's exports value increases by almost the same percentage. Similarly, Thailand's imports expand more rapidly than real output growth – more than double the rate of GDP growth. The Thai economy is highly import dependent; therefore, it experiences current account deficit during strong growth. Exchange rate movements matter for trade flows. The estimated exchange rate elasticity reported in Figure 7.10 confirms the importance of exchange rate policy management. Nevertheless, because income elasticities are larger than exchange rate elasticities, income effects are stronger than substitution effects caused by exchange rate changes. Indeed, exchange rate depreciation increases exports and decreases import values. These estimated income elasticities are higher than unity, while estimated exchange rate elasticities are less than unity. Keeping the baht weak is not a good idea during times of world economic expansion, because exports expand despite a strong baht. During times of world economic recession, Thailand's import and export growth significantly slows down (Figure 7.11), and an attempt to make the baht weaker to stimulate export growth would be futile.

6. Exchange rate policy strategy: the way forward

The baht exchange rate appreciates or depreciates due to external forces. When the trade-weight dollar exchange rate appreciates, the baht depreciates

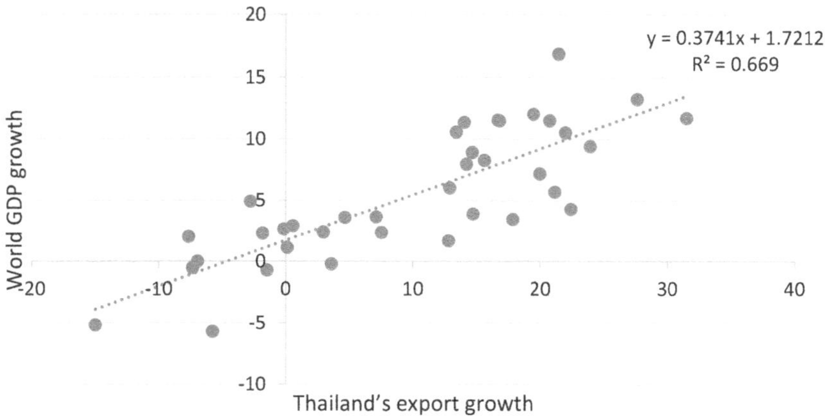

Figure 7.11 Thailand's export and world GDP growth rates

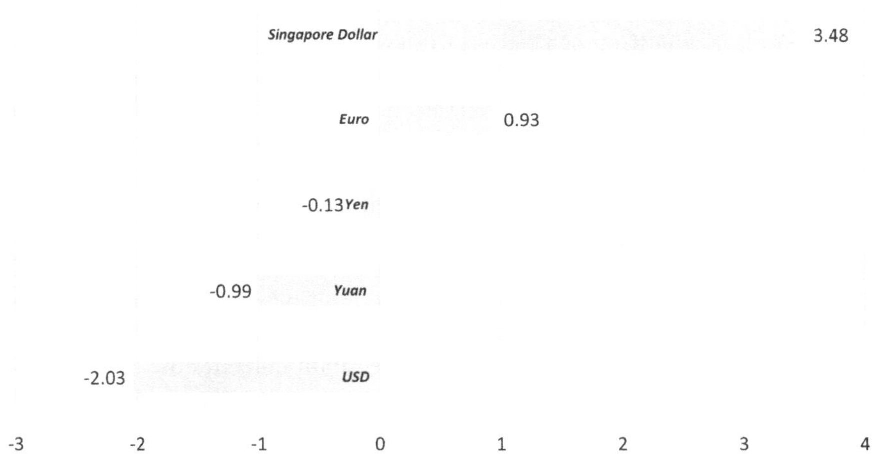

Figure 7.12 Impacts on the baht/USD

Source: Author's FMOLS estimation of elasticity of trend values (monthly data: January 1999–April 2018)

accordingly. The estimated elasticity of the dollar index was close to –2.03, which is much larger than the yuan and the yen (Figure 7.12). Hence, the baht moves in the opposite direction to the currencies of major trading partners. On the other hand, the baht exchange rate moves in line with the Singapore dollar (SDG) and the euro. The elasticity of the baht with respect to the Singapore dollar was about 3.5, implying that the baht moves in line with Singapore dollar and the baht is most sensitive to changes in the SDG exchange rate. The baht also moves proportionately with the euro and USD and also moves proportionately in the opposite direction with the yuan. This finding suggests that the Bank of Thailand has very little room to conduct an independent exchange rate policy.

7. Concluding remarks

This chapter explored whether the central bank can come up with an optimum exchange rate policy that lies between the firmly fixed and the fully flexible exchange rate system – the system that can compromise the benefits to trade transactions under the stable environment provided by a fixed regime and yet flexible enough to maintain the adjustment mechanism of the flexible exchange rate regime.

Between the 1960s and 1980s, because of the zero foreign exchange rate risk, Thailand benefited from the fixed exchange rate system. At this early stage of development, exports were the main growth driver. As the country developed further, investment and consumption became principal growth drivers. Exports contributed less to growth as imports increased in line with exports. There was a tendency to keep the exchange rate at a competitive level to propel export growth. When the country increasingly relied on foreign capital flow to finance the investment-saving gap, the current account deficit became unsustainable. It was difficult for the Bank of Thailand to allow the baht to depreciate, because it would threaten the banking sector, which borrowed heavily in dollars.

Nevertheless, maintaining the overvalued exchange rate of the baht for too long led to a drastic exchange rate adjustment which culminated in currency and banking crises in 1997. In the early 1990s, when Thailand experienced rapid capital inflows, the Bank of Thailand did not permit the baht to appreciate against the dollar. Had the baht been permitted to appreciate, the overheated economy and ensuing economic crisis could have been avoided. From 2006 to 2009, the baht was once again undervalued and the Bank of Thailand did not permit the baht to appreciate by market forces because of the concern that exports and economic growth could be jeopardized. Currency appreciation mitigates the impact of oil price shocks and would have no considerable impact on export growth, which was mainly dictated by world trade volume. An unrealistic exchange rate policy to protect exporters from currency appreciation may result in moral hazard and harm the incentive to enhance competitiveness through productivity improvement obtained from the importation of capital goods.

Interest rate policy cannot be used to target the value of the baht. Foreign exchange market intervention by the Bank of Thailand intensified when the baht appreciated against the dollar from 2006 to 2009. Intervention in foreign exchange markets was ineffective, because the baht-dollar exchange rate is determined by movements of major currencies and capital inflow to the stock market. Attempts to sterilize this flow are costly and ineffective in the long run. When exchange rate changes are not allowed to correct current account disequilibrium, adjustments must take place from the output market. With more flexible exchange rate movement, the burden of adjustment does not fall solely on output fluctuations.

Capital controls are instruments usually employed during currency crises. The 14-month capital control which began in December 2006 was unnecessary and ineffective. It may have had adverse consequences on foreign direct investment if it sent the wrong signal to investors worried about policy commitment to open capital markets. As such, temporary capital control measures can be detrimental to long-term economic growth.

We have come to the conclusion that exchange rate matters for correcting trade imbalances. Too rigid exchange rate stability, in such a way that the exchange rate becomes unrealistic, can cause damages and invite speculative attacks. On the other hand, wide fluctuations of the exchange rate can hamper trade and investment. A combination of adjustable and gradual changes in the exchange rate can be done when the imbalance-adjusted growth enters a critical zone, or when the IAG rate falls into negative territory.

Notes

1 The flexibility of the wage rate continued until the late 2000s. Domestic demand grew by 2.3 percent and 4.1 percent in 2007 and 2008, respectively, while the real wage rate rose by 0.7 percent and 4.8 percent. When domestic demand contracted by 6.6 percent in 2009, the real wage rate declined by 1.6 percent. See Nidhiprabha (2003) for a discussion of wage flexibility and implications of the trade-off between inflation and unemployment.

2 The impact of the dollar decline on the US current account deficit was not apparent until 2008, when the US economy entered into the recession.

3 For evidence on temporary movements of the real dollar rates and interest rate differentials, see Nakagawa (2002).

4 Co-integration analysis indicates that the ratio of net forward position to total reserves moves in line with the rate of change of the baht exchange rate.

5 Similarly, FDI and banks' capital flows exhibited wild gyrations from their trends after the imposition of capital controls.

References

Akiba, H., Y. Iida, and Yoshihiro Kitamura. 2009. "The Optimal Exchange Rate Regime for a Small Country." *International Economics and Economic Policy*, 6: 315–343.

Asiedu, Elizabeth, and Lien Donald. 2004. "Capital Controls and Foreign Direct Investment." *World Development*, 32: 479–491.

Bhagwati, Jagdish. 1998. "The Capital Myth." *Foreign Affairs*, 77: 7–12.

Bhandari, R., and Kamal P. Upadhyaya. 2010. "Panel Data Evidence of the Impact of Exchange Rate Uncertainty on Private Investment in South-East Asia." *Applied Economics*, 42: 57–61.

Bilson, John 1985. "Macroeconomic Stability and Flexible Exchange Rates." *American Economic Review*, 79: 62–69.

Broda, Christian. 2004. "Terms of Trade and Exchange Rate Regimes in Developing Countries." *Journal of International Economics*, 63: 31–58.

Calvo, G. A., and Carmen M. Reinhart. 2002. "Fear of Floating." *Quarterly Journal of Economics*, 117: 379–408.

Chit, M., M. Rizov, and Dirk Willenbockel. 2010. "Exchange Rate Volatility and Exports: New Empirical Evidence From the Emerging East Asian Economies." *World Economy*, 33: 239–263.

Coelho, B., and Kevin Gallagher. 2010. "Capital Controls and 21st Century Financial Crises: Evidence From Colombia and Thailand." Working Paper Series Number 213, Political Economy Research Institute.

Coudert, V., and Cecile Couharde. 2009. "Currency Misalignment and Exchange Rate Regimes in Emerging and Developing Countries." *Review of International Economics*, 17: 121–136.

Dubas, Justin M. 2009. "The Importance of the Exchange Rate Regime in Limiting Misalignment." *World Development*, 37: 1612–1622.

Eichengreen, Barry. 2000. "Taming Capital Inflows." *World Development*, 28: 1105–1116.

Forbes, Kistin J. 2007. "One Cost of the Chilean Capital Controls: Increased Financial Constraints for Smaller Traded Firms." *Journal of International Economics*, 71 (2): 294–323.

Friedman, Milton. 1953. *The Case for Flexible Exchange Rates in Essays in Positive Economics*. Chicago: University of Chicago Press, 157–203.

Hasan, S., and Myles Wallace. 1996. "Real Exchange Rate Volatility and Exchange Rate Regime: Evidence From Long-Term Data." *Economic Letters*, 52: 67–73.

Kenen, P. B., and Dani Rodrik. 1986. "Measuring and Analyzing the Effects of Short-Term Volatility in Real Exchange Rates." *The Review of Economics and Statistics*, 68: 311–315.

Krugman, Paul. 1989. "The Case for Stabilizing Exchange Rates." *Oxford Review of Economic Policy*, 5: 61–72.

Liew, V. K. S., A. Zubaidi Baharumshah, and Chin-Hong Puah. 2009. "Monetary Model of Exchange Rate for Thailand: Long-Run Relationship and Monetary Restrictions." *Global Economic Review: Perspectives on East Asian Economies and Industries*, 38: 385–395.

Montecino, J. A., and Juan Antonio Cordero. 2010. "Capital Controls and Monetary Policy in Developing Countries." Center for Economic and Policy Research Report, April 2010.

Nakagawa, Hironobu. 2002. "Real Exchange Rates and Real Interest Differentials: Implications of Nonlinear Adjustment in Real Exchange Rates." *Journal of Monetary Economics*, 49: 629–649.

Nidhiprabha, Bhanupong. 2003. "Thailand Macroeconomic Policy After July 1997." *Asian Economic Papers*, 2 (1): 158–168.

Obstfeld, Maurice. 1998. "The Global Capital Market: Benefactor or Menace?" *Journal of Economics Perspectives*, 12: 9–30.

Obstfeld, M., and Kenneth Rogoff. 1995. "The Mirage of Fixed Exchange Rates." *Journal of Economic Perspectives*, 9: 73–96.

Taylor, John B. 2001. "The Role of the Exchange Rate in Monetary Policy Rules." *American Economic Review*, 91: 263–267.

8 Monetary policy strategy for long-term growth and stability

1. Introduction

In the process of sustainable economic development, real per capita income must be raised continuously for several decades. Success in economic development can then be observed in rising standards of living and longer life expectancy. Economic growth enhances a government's ability to redistribute income and reduce unemployment. Small differences in growth rates make enormous differences in levels of potential output over a few decades. If the growth rate is maintained at 3 percent over a decade, income rises by 35 percent. If the growth rate is raised to 7 percent, income will double. When 7 percent output growth is continued for three decades, income rises eightfold. The key strategy for long-term development is to keep growth continuous for several decades.

How should monetary policy strategy be applied to maintain growth without disruption during internal and external shocks? Monetary policy is the key macroeconomic tool employed by central banks to maintain economic growth and price stability. To raise real per capita income, inflation must be contained so that interest rates can be kept low. Since inflation is related to interest rates, monetary policy can stimulate capital accumulation by ensuring that investors and savers are rewarded for undertaking risk and saving, respectively. Unstable investment expenditures cause short-term fluctuations in GDP by affecting aggregate demand and its components. Rising investment also generates long-term growth by increasing potential or full-employment national income. Monetary policy can reduce investment fluctuation by controlling the cost and quantity of credit available to investors.

From the early 1960s to 1996, the Thai economy generally experienced low inflation, but high economic growth. Since then, the growth path has been reduced as a result of corrections to macroeconomic imbalances. External and internal shocks have reduced the long-term growth path, although the pre-crisis level of income was regained within a few years after the 1997 financial crisis.

The Bank of Thailand adopted an inflation-targeting strategy after switching from a fixed exchange rate regime to a managed floating exchange rate system. The core inflation target is set between 0 percent and 3.5 percent, although net benefits from targeting core instead of headline inflation are not clear due to problems with measuring core inflation (Quah and Vahey, 1995). Because of global recession and a sharp drop in oil prices in 2008, Thailand experienced price deflation in the first half of 2009. Inflation targeting is subject to a real test of its potency.

As the Thai economy was exposed to globalization, capital inflows influenced monetary aggregates. Evidence points to an increasing degree of financial market integration in East Asia (Jeon et al., 2006). As such, monetary policy must take into account the impact of shocks in world money markets. Since foreign portfolio investment affects domestic money supply and exchange rates, monetary aggregates have not increased at the rate corresponding to a stable output growth, which led to the deleterious effect of fluctuations in monetary aggregates.

We will examine the relationship between money supply and output and explore a trade-off relationship between inflation and unemployment. The reaction function of monetary authorities will be investigated. The effectiveness of monetary policy and its degree of autonomy will be discussed. Finally, we provide monetary policy strategy in dealing with asset price bubbles

2. Monetary aggregates and real output

In the absence of GDP monthly data, manufacturing output index was employed to represent economic activity with high-frequency data. Although manufacturing output cannot represent all economic activities, its importance to GDP has increased over time. While the share of agricultural output has declined, the increasing contribution to GDP from the service sector cannot be denied. It is stipulated that activities in the manufacturing sector are related to the GDP contributed from the agricultural and service sectors.

Monthly data from January 1993 to June 2017 are employed to capture the relationship between manufacturing output and monetary aggregates (Figure 8.1). As the result from a co-integration test indicates, a long-run relationship exists between output and monetary base. To maintain a stable growth path, money supply growth must be kept in line with output growth.

The rate of growth of money supply outpaced growth in output during the boom years before the 1997 financial crisis. There was a steep increase in money supply as output expanded from a manufacturing production index (MPI) of 60 to 90. At this time, monetary shocks led to an excessive unsustainable growth of output.

As the Thai economy recovered from the recession of 1997–1998, the monetary aggregate and output regained their long-run equilibrium relationship. Since 2006, the Thai economy has suffered from internal political upheavals and oil price shocks during which output and money supply again drifted away from the equilibrium path. It was not an excessive boom like the early 1990s, but rather there has been output contraction since August 2008 and slow growth in money supply (Figure 8.2). The economy would not soon return to a long-run equilibrium path between money and output.

Following Hodrick and Prescott (1997), we define cyclical movements as the difference between the actual value of the series and the Hodrick-Prescott filter

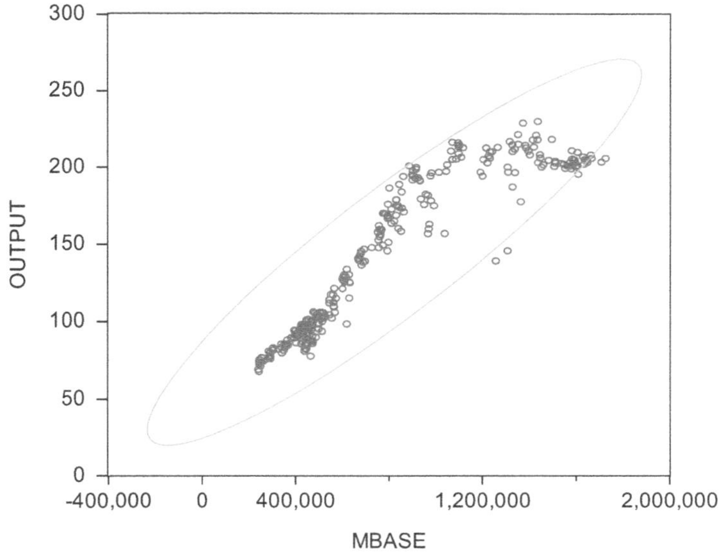

Figure 8.1 Monetary base and output level: the long-run relationship

Source: Bank of Thailand

trend of the series. We observe a remarkable positive relationship between the degree of cyclicality of output and monetary aggregates (broad money supply) in Figure 8.2.

When broad money exceeded its long-run trend, output also expanded at a rate faster than its normal growth path. Similarly, when monetary aggregates contracted below their long-run trend, output growth slowed to beneath its trend. Peaks of monetary growth (lagged 5 months) were associated with peaks in manufacturing output; the deepest contraction in output synchronized with a trough in monetary cycles. The lead-lag relationship of two variables gives us a clue to direction of causation.

There is a long-run relationship in cyclical fluctuations in output and the monetary base, we then perform the Granger causality test, which yields statistical evidence supporting the notion that money supply growth affects economic growth. Changes in output do not contain information useful for predicting future movement of monetary aggregates. However, output growth can be predicted by the growth rate of money supply lagged by 2 months. A rising income level contributes to a higher demand for money. Other forms of financial assets may be used as saving vehicles. Increasing sophistication of the capital market has made bonds and stocks alternative forms of financial assets to be held for investment and saving. Consequently, changes in output have lost their power to predict M2.

Theoretical reasons explain why M2 affects output level. Money balances can be thought of as a factor input in the production function, so an increase in

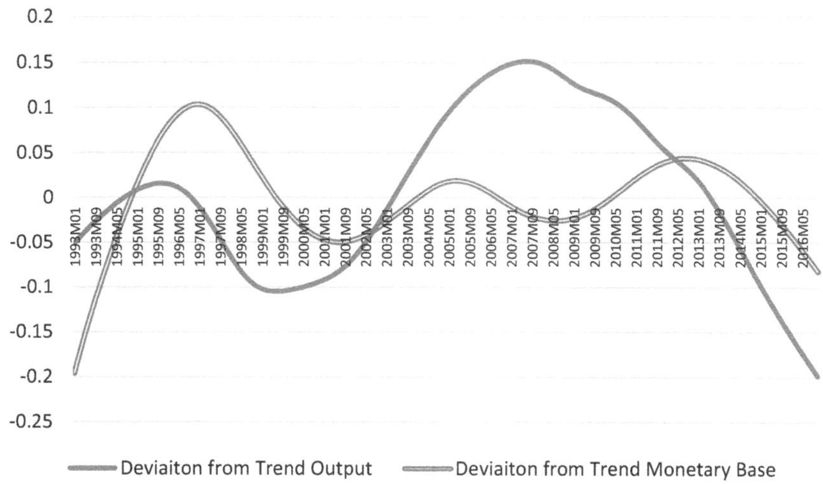

Figure 8.2 Output and monetary base: deviations from trends

Source: Bank of Thailand

money supply provides working capital to smooth the production process. As the economy is increasingly dominated by manufacturing output, money balances and bank credit become inseparable inputs in the production function. Failure to provide liquidity to the real sector could lead to a fall in output. A credit crunch or capital crunch in the banking sector is always associated with a slowdown of the real sector. In this sense, monetary policy impacts output by affecting supply and demand. The impact of credit contraction would be more severe than when money supply is not an important factor for production.

We now turn to the issue of shocks that might originate from the real and monetary sectors. If shocks are defined as actual values and expected values obtained from the long-run trend, output and monetary shocks can be measured by the gap between trends of output and monetary aggregates. Again, we employ the Hodrick-Prescott filter trends to extract the cyclical movement of the two variables. The Granger causality test between two cyclical movements (the difference between the actual and Hodrick-Prescott filter [HP] trend). The causation runs from monetary shocks to output shocks. We have arrived at an important conclusion on the conduct of monetary policy: monetary authorities must avoid creating large swings in monetary aggregates because they could lead to output fluctuations.

Accommodating monetary policy or procyclical monetary expansion can propagate temporary booms as it eventually leads to an overheated economy, requiring both internal and external disequilibrium. Calderon et al. (2004) found the evidence that countries with higher credibility levels are able to conduct countercyclical macroeconomic policies, while procyclical policies are observed when credibility is weak. Inflation, unsustainable current account deficit, and appreciation of real exchange rates would ensue, leading to output collapse and unemployment. Countercyclical monetary policy can be employed to prevent booms or busts through adjustments in monetary aggregates and interest rates.

Since we have established the crucial link and causation running from money supply to real output, we further investigate sources of rapid increases in money supply broadly defined (M2). After 1991, when Thailand accepted IMF Article VIII, liberalizing capital accounts, the rate of growth of the monetary aggregate gained momentum. The establishment of Bangkok International Banking Facilities (BIBFs) to make Bangkok a regional financial center resulted in huge rapid capital inflows. The influx of foreign borrowing was so large that it was impossible to sterilize the expansion of the monetary base. Figure 8.3 shows that net foreign assets (NFA) increased substantially after capital account liberalization and establishment of the BIBFs. Premature liberalization led to huge rapid capital inflows so that the existing antiquated financial infrastructure was unable to monitor and supervise activities in the financial sector.

The Thai economy was able to grow rapidly with low inflation in the late 1980s, partly because the monetary base did not grow too fast. Surplus budget mitigated the rise in the monetary base as claims on government (CG) were negative due to the amount of public debt reduction. Fiscal surplus helped reduce upward pressure on the monetary base. The bailout of financial institutions prior to the 1997 financial crisis was reflected in the rising claims on financial institutions (CF). After the collapse in 1998 of 56 finance companies and a bank, the bailout's impact on the monetary base level gradually eased.

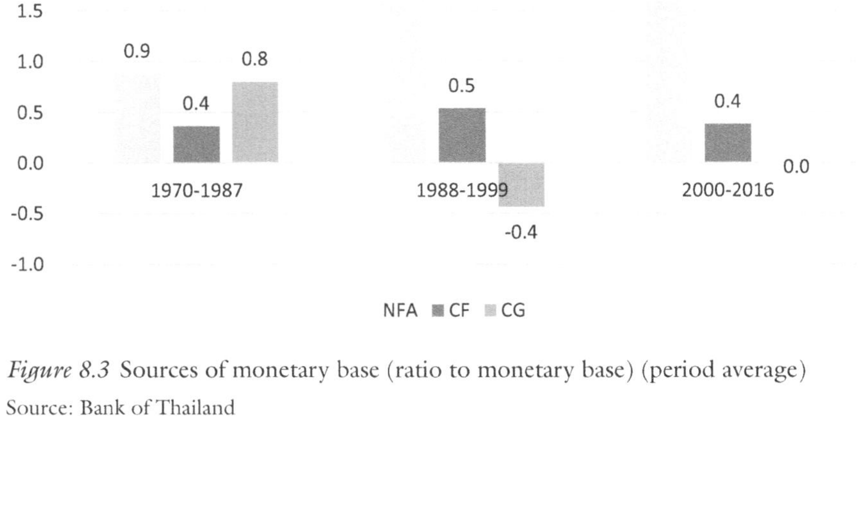

Figure 8.3 Sources of monetary base (ratio to monetary base) (period average)

Source: Bank of Thailand

After the 1998 crisis, the BoT's lending to government and financial institutions declined as the economy returned to its pre-shock growth path. However, as the Bank of Thailand began intervening in foreign exchange markets to prevent baht appreciation, the amount of foreign assets relative to broad money steadily increased. The analysis of monetary policy must consider the implications of the exchange rate regime and capital inflows.

3. The Phillips curve

Under the circumstances of global recession, oil price shocks, and virulent capital flows, how should monetary authorities conduct policy instruments? After baht flotation in July 1997, a new monetary policy strategy was adopted in 2000. The Bank of Thailand announced an inflation target strategy, stipulating the core inflation target between 0 percent and 3.5 percent. Note that the target was not on headline inflation, which includes the prices of fresh food and energy. Since food and energy prices are subject to uncontrollable factors, the Bank of Thailand opted to focus on core inflation.

The relationship between headline inflation and unemployment is shown in Figure 8.4. If there is a trade-off between price stability and full employment, monetary expansion can reduce unemployment at the expense of higher price levels. How high a price must we pay to reduce the unemployment rate? How can the central bank strike a balance between growth and price stability? Which policy instruments are available and effective? The effectiveness of inflation targeting can be evaluated from the linkage between the policy interest rate and commercial banks' lending rates, which would eventually affect investment, price level, and output growth.

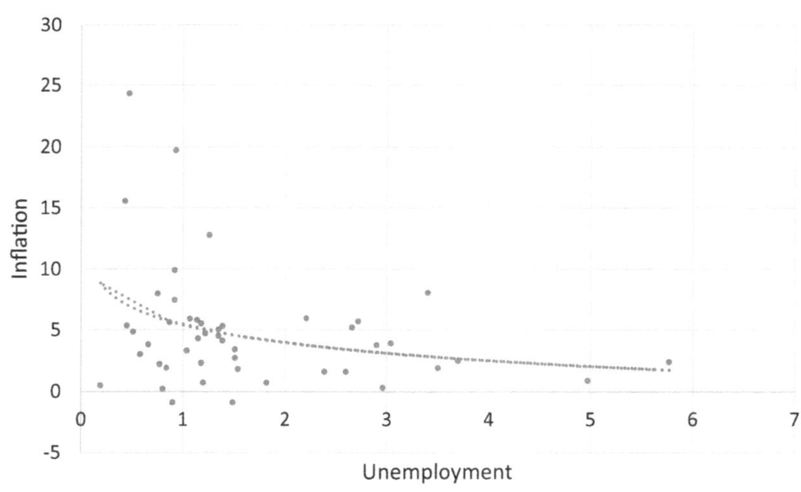

Figure 8.4 The Phillips curve: 1971–2017

Source: Bank of Thailand

The Phillips curve depicted in Figure 8.4 exhibits a negative relationship between inflation and unemployment over the past four decades. Employing annual data between 1971 and 2017, we present a statistical relationship between unemployment rate (U) and inflation rate (π). Unemployment rate is negatively related to inflation. Applying the fully modified ordinary least squares (FMOLS) method to the data, the negative relationship between the two variables is statistically significant. The inflation expectation (π^e) is proxied by the previous period inflation rate. The annual rate of change in the consumer price index is used as the inflation rate.

$$\pi = 10.29 - 1.2U + 0.22\pi^e - 0.18Trend$$
$$(7.99) \quad (4.83) \quad (2.87) \quad (6.29)$$
Adjusted $R^2 = 0.51$

The estimated coefficient of U_t is negative, implying that there is a trade-off between inflation and unemployment. A reduction in unemployment rate results in higher price inflation. The explanatory power of this model is only 51 percent, suggesting that there are some other factors excluded in the model, for example, supply shocks from oil price hikes and devaluations which cause the upward shift in the Phillips curve. During the span of 47 years between 1971 and 2017, there were many changes in Thailand's trade structure and exchange rate systems. The Phillips curve has become flatter as the force of trade reform gives rise to lower prices of imported goods. Hence, the cost of disinflation has been reduced over time.

The cost of maintaining output near full employment level is not high in terms of sacrificing price stability. The model's underlying assumption is adaptive rather than rational expectations. Mankiw and Reiss (2002) criticize the New-Keynesian Phillips curve model with rational expectations that disinflation causes a boom and monetary policy quickly impacts inflation. In the conventional empirical model presented above, expectations are adaptive but disinflation can occur by reducing the inflation expectations (π^e) without embarking on consolidating the fiscal balance or contracting money supply. Inflation expectations can be maintained despite a booming economy if some key commodity prices are temporary regulated. The Thai government has many adjustable ceilings on essential consumer goods such as rice, cooking oils, and gas. Of course, there are some costs in terms of inefficiency, but it may be worthwhile to trade off with maintaining the growth path close to the potential output. The estimated coefficient of the previous period's inflation rate can be treated as the impact of inflationary expectations on the current inflation rate. Alternatively, it can be thought of as the persistent coefficient of inflation (Pivetta and Reis, 2007). If the persistent coefficient is high, the cost of disinflation will be large, as it will take longer to reduce inflation. The estimated coefficient of the lagged inflation rate, or expected inflation rate, is 0.22, suggesting that the cost of reducing the inflation rate is not that high. Nevertheless, the lagged adjustment of expectations help gives some room for monetary authority to maneuver the inflationary target.

4. Interest rate policy reactions

In the basic Taylor's rule, the determinants of the central bank's interest rate are deviations from output and inflation target (Taylor, 1993). The nominal effective exchange rate can be included to make the inflation target more flexible. Ball (2000) proposes the exchange rate be included in the monetary policy reaction function. Chadha et al. (2004) estimated Taylor-type rules that include exchange rates for a number of open economies. The flexible inflation-targeting strategy in response to currency movement can be captured by the reduction in the bank rate in response to baht appreciation. Indeed, the bank rate adjusted to exchange rate changes in addition to output growth and inflation. However, the BoT in the past also resorted to other policy instruments to prevent baht appreciation, such as capital controls and direct intervention in foreign exchange markets.

To examine how the BoT key policy rate reacts to policy goal variables growth, inflation, and the real exchange rate, we apply the dynamic least squares method of estimation to examine the sensitivity of the BoT key policy rate in response to changes in long-term goal variables price level, output, and real effective exchange rate (REER) appreciation. Using monthly data between 1994 and 2017, the actual and fitted values of the model are shown in Figure 8.5. This policy function can be regarded as a quasi-monetary policy reaction function. Rather than measuring how the key policy rate reacts to deviations of actual from the target magnitudes, it measures how the key policy rate adjusts to changes in

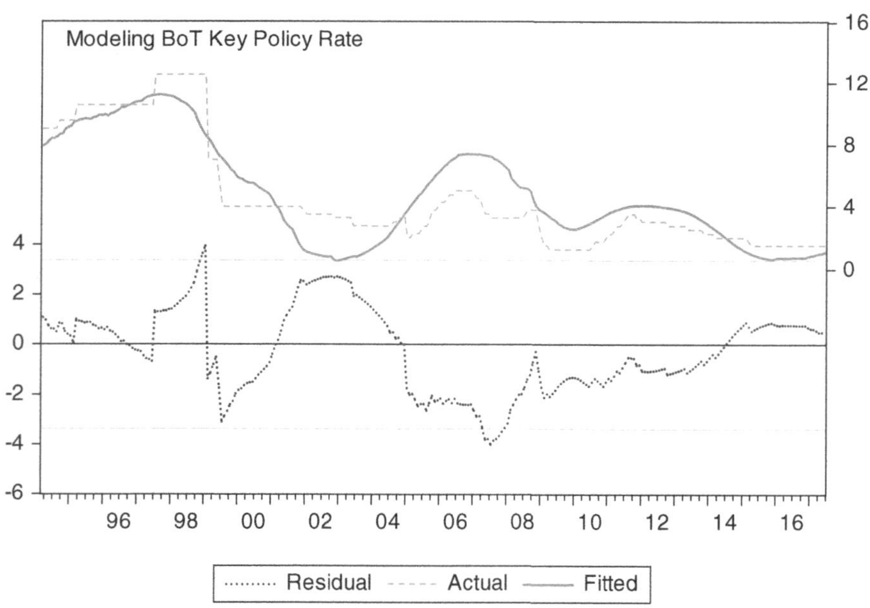

Figure 8.5 A quasi-monetary policy reaction function

Source: Dynamic Least Squares estimates

the trends of price level, output, and the real effective exchange rate. The model tracks well the actual adjustment of the key policy rates in response to changes in the key policy targets.

The normalized coefficient of the reaction functions is shown in Figure 8.6. The BoT responded most to inflation (estimated elasticity of the key policy rate was 1.59) This is in line with the rule that to raise real interest rate, the central bank must raise the nominal interest rate faster than the inflation rate. As far as growth rate is concerned, it seems that the BoT uses countercyclical policy, although the reaction is much smaller than inflation. In other words, the BoT's prime objective is price stability, and the reaction parameter is eight times higher than that of output growth. It could be the fear of dampening effects of a strong contraction policy on private spending. The last variable included in this flexible inflation targeting is the exchange rate. The regression result indicates that the BoT lowers the interest rate when the real effective exchange rate appreciates. There is such thing as the fear of currency appreciation.

During the fixed exchange rate regime, the country's price anchor is the foreign partner's price level. In the long run, the inflation rate in the country should move in line with inflation in the country to which the currency was pegged. As long as the exchange rate remains fixed, the target of inflation remains the trading partner's inflation rate. Before 2000, the bank rate was apparently adjusted to maintain exchange rate stability. Before the crisis, the interest hike was used to keep the baht from depreciating (Figure 8.6). After the 1998 crisis, the monetary policy stance did not respond to exchange rate movement, yet we can observe a constant shifting of monetary policy from easing to tightening. In short, since 2000, the bank rate must have adjusted to other targets.

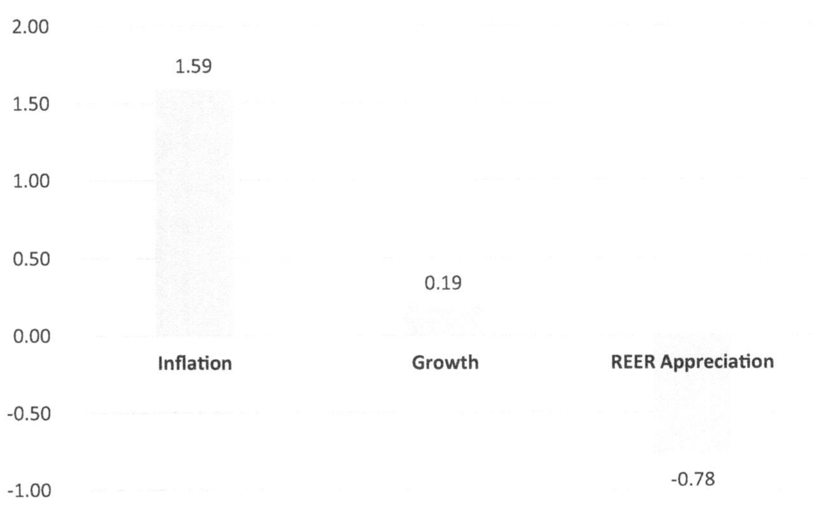

Figure 8.6 Normalized coefficients in the policy rate reaction function

Source: FMOLS estimates

It is a standard practice to describe the stance of monetary policy in terms of short-run nominal interest rate (Clarida et al., 1999). However, Chowdhury and Schabert (2008) found that an assessment of US Federal Reserve policy based on postwar money supply leads to different conclusions about the impact of Fed policy on macroeconomic stability than previous studies indicated.

The bank rate did respond to inflation as anticipated by the inflation-targeting strategy employed after floating the currency. Nevertheless, this adopted inflation target strategy is flexible, since the bank rate also responded to other factors, that is, the federal funds rate and the nominal effective exchange rate.

The Bank of Thailand has demonstrated its policy consistency in intervening in the foreign exchange market using, among other means, the interest rate policy. This is akin to the fear of floating syndrome (Calvo and Reinhart, 2002). The root of the problem is the myth that the exchange rate is the major determinant of trade flows. In fact, the world trade volume, or the output effect, has greater impact on trade flows than the substitution effect caused by exchange rate changes.

5. Monetary policy effectiveness

We may conjecture that the bank rate is affected by the federal funds rate, because of the openness of the capital accounts in Thailand. In an age of financial globalization, a small country may not be able to carry its own monetary policy independently of world market interest rates. The question arises of how long the Bank of Thailand can conduct its own monetary policy while ignoring the Federal Reserve Board's decision to adjust federal funds rates.

The minimum lending rate (MLR) or the prime rate, which commercial banks charge the most credit trustworthy customers, responds to the Fed rate hike with

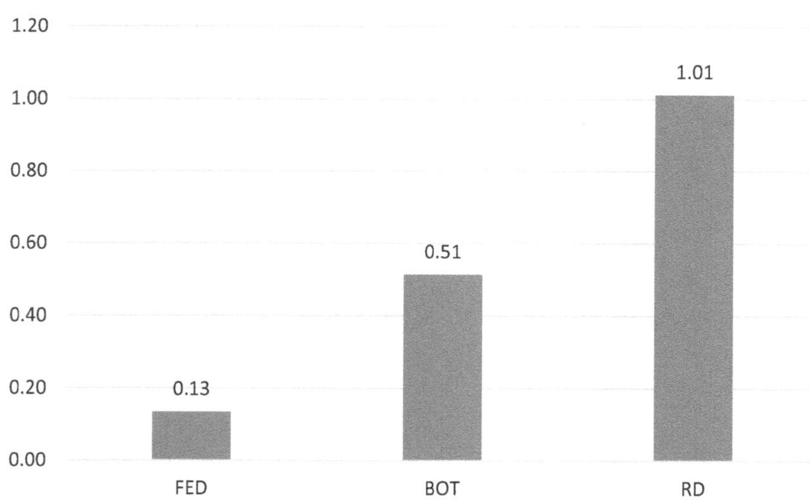

Figure 8.7 Factors affecting minimum lending rate (MLR)

Source: FMOLS estimated coefficients (January 1993–June 2017)

an elasticity of 0.13, which is quite small when compared to the impact of the BoT rate hike (Figure 8.7). There is a certain degree of capital immobility in Thailand. If capital mobility is perfect, the estimated coefficient should be close to unity. For this reason, there is still some room for Thailand's monetary authorities to maneuver its policy stance. The estimated coefficient of the MLR with respect to the BoT's key policy rate is 0.5. This finding suggests that the central bank can somehow influence the direction of the lending rate but not completely control the magnitude of the commercial lending rates. The last factor included in the equation explaining the MLR is the deposit interest rate (RD). The estimated coefficient of the variable is not significantly different from unity. The implication of this empirical finding is that commercial banks' cost of funds matters most as a determinant of the MLR. Because of the unit elasticity, commercial banks can keep the interest gap stable so as to maintain profitability. If deposit rates fall, commercial banks reduce the lending rate accordingly by the same proportion, whilst they raise MLR whenever RD goes up. As discussed in Chapter 4, the lack of competition in the credit markets makes the gap between lending and deposit rates remain stable over time.

Using monthly data between 1978 and 2017, the Granger causality test is used to test the hypothesis that the Bank of Thailand can conduct an independent monetary policy, and is rejected. On the other hand, the BoT policy interest rate can be predicted by the federal funds rate 5 months in advance, but not vice versa (Figure 8.8). Given that the BoT can temporarily conduct monetary policy when world interest rates change in a different direction, a further question arises regarding the BoT's ability to change commercial bank interest rates. Let us examine the relationship between the key policy rate and prime lending rate in the US before further examining the case of Thailand.

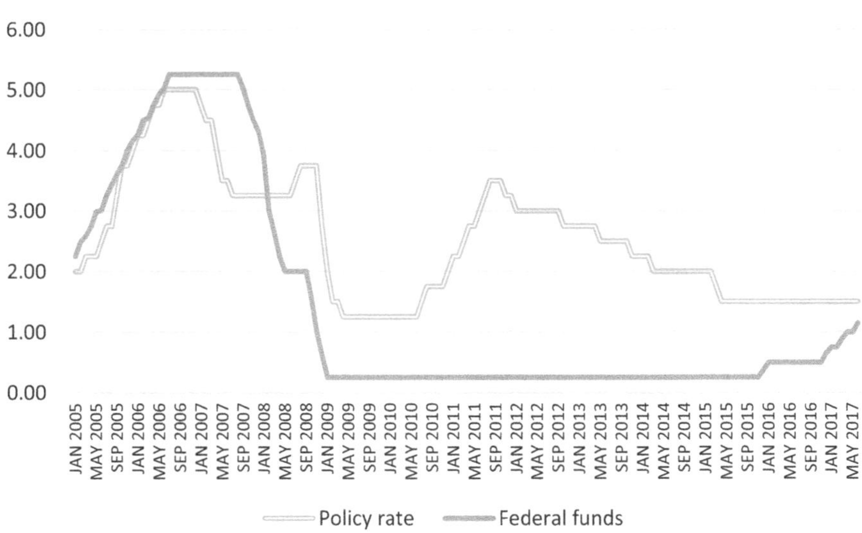

Figure 8.8 Federal funds rate and BoT policy rate

Source: Bank of Thailand

Figure 8.9 shows the US prime rate, which seems to closely follow the federal funds rate. There is a consistent gap between policy rate and bank lending rates. In the US, monetary policy instruments can be used to achieve a desirable lending rate. Underlying institutional factors, including industrial concentration and the sophisticated structure of money and capital markets, determine the predictability of monetary policy outcome.

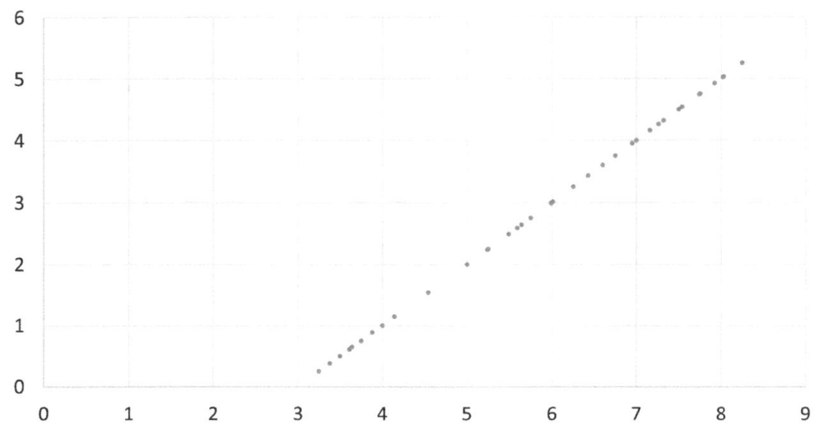

Figure 8.9 Federal funds and prime rates: 2005–2017

Source: Federal Reserve Bank

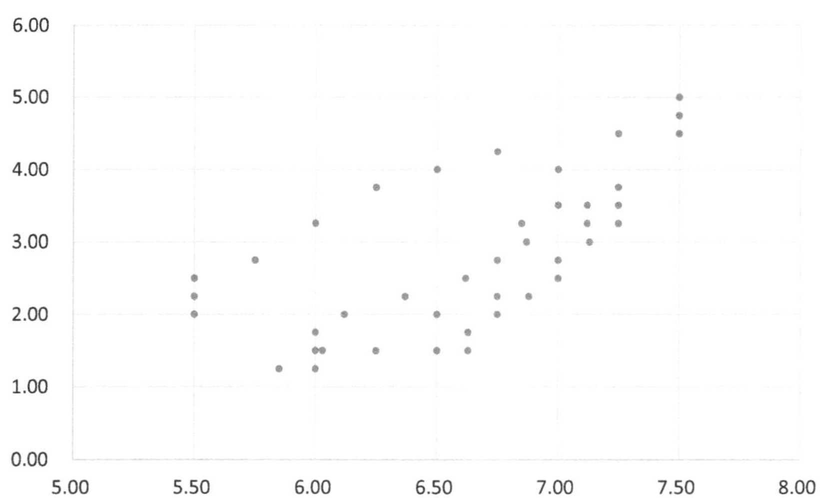

Figure 8.10 BoT policy rate and MLR: 2005–2017

Source: Bank of Thailand

Unlike the federal funds rate, which systematically impacts the prime lending rate of commercial banks in the US, the impact of the rate cut in Thailand is unpredictable and inconsistent, as commercial banks refuse to lower interest rates during recessions (Figure 8.10). High liquidity and rising default risks are used as excuses to maintain commercial bank lending rates. With excess liquidity, cutting the central bank lending rate does not encourage other banks to borrow from the central bank. The slow reaction of the lending rate to the key policy rate cut is also due to a lack of price competition. The Thai banking industry remains highly concentrated. Thus, monetary policy effectiveness is limited during recessions when the central bank seeks to stimulate the economy. Unsurprisingly, Thai banks in 2008 enjoyed high profits despite a slowdown in lending activity.

During recessions, banks are unwilling to lend and investors are unwilling to borrow. Investment is also determined by factors other than the cost of borrowing. Credit availability is an important factor during economic booms since there are many liquidity-constrained investors. Monetary policy effectiveness is enhanced during booms, when the central bank can control credit availability. Business confidence is no problem during booms because investors are likely to be carried away with irrational exuberance. During slumps, by contrast, business confidence erodes quickly. Despite the central bank's low interest rate policy, which influences commercial bank lending rate cuts, investors have no confidence in projects likely to fail if they anticipate a future deterioration of demand. For this reason, business confidence must be taken into account when modeling the impact of monetary policy.

The finding from the response functions indicates that inflation inertia is powerful. It is reflected by the long lag impact of price innovations. The impact of a sudden jump in price level peaks in the third month. Its impact remains strong, albeit at a slower rate, 10 months after the inflation shock. This result is consistent with the estimated coefficient of lagged inflation rate reported earlier. Inflation expectations are difficult to disperse after they begin. Monetary authorities must avoid inflation in the first place. According to van der Ploeg (2009), prudent monetary policy could also mean more aggressive reactions of nominal interest rates to inflation and output gaps.

Business confidence impacts inflationary pressure. The confidence variable is represented by the business sentiment index provided by the Bank of Thailand. When an optimistic outlook is widespread, inflationary pressure will build as consumption and capital spending rise. The bank rate may be used to curb inflation. Nevertheless, the impact on price level will not be apparent until 5 months after implementation. This long lag effect produces some degree of uncertainty about the outcome of monetary policy. The collapse of business confidence has a more powerful impact than any interest rate hike.

An output shock that leads to an excessive supply of manufactured goods can ease inflationary pressure. Expanding manufacturing plants generates more supply, lowering pressure on commodity prices. Positive output and capacity buildup have similar impacts on price levels. Investment in new plants can be captured by the amount of newly registered capital. This is distinct from construction investment, which tends to put upward pressure on price levels.

6. Transmission channels and asset prices

There are various channels through which monetary policy affect the real sector. In the world of flexible exchange rates, monetary policy is more effective than fiscal policy because the exchange rate changes in such a way that it intensifies the initial impact of monetary policy. However, the exchange rate channel is not very important if the central bank tries to minimize its movement. Other channels through which monetary policy can exert its impact on the real economy are the interest rate channel and the credit availability channel.

We investigate the channel in which the BoT can exert its influence on the real sector by estimating the elasticities of consumption and investment with respect to commercial banks' lending interest rate and credit volume. The output level is included in the functions, representing a scale effect. Monthly data on the manufacturing production index are employed to capture the output effect. The BoT provides indexes for both consumption and investment. Employing a double-log form in the estimating equations, we can directly interpret the estimated coefficients, obtained from the FMOLS method of estimation, as the values of FMOLS elasticities. Based on monthly data between 2000 and 2017, the estimated coefficients are shown in Figure 8.11. All variables have expected signs; investment and consumption expenditures increase together with expansion in output and credit, declining when the bank lending rate increases. The estimated output elasticities for consumption and investment are 0.25 and 0.76, respectively. Investment responds to output changes more strongly than consumption. This finding is consistent to the volatile nature of investment spending. Consumption smoothing behavior of households results in more stable consumption behavior than investment, which is more volatile due to fluctuations in business sentiment.

The empirical evidence shown in Figure 8.11 also reveals that both consumption and investment spending respond positively to output expansion and credit

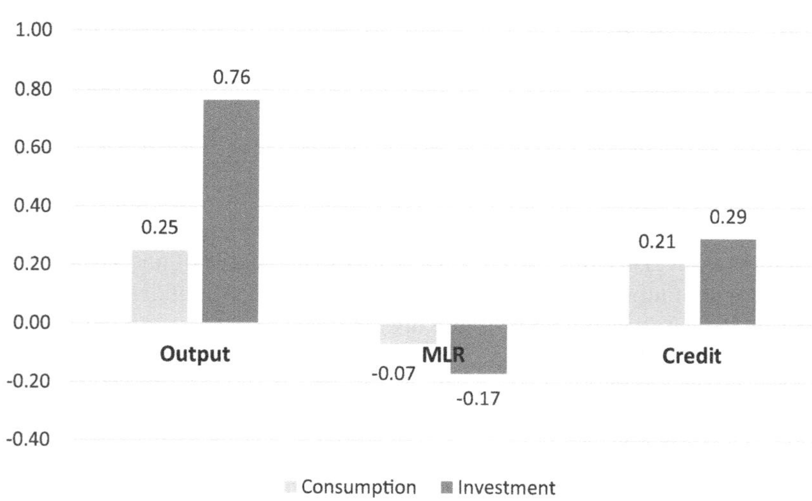

Figure 8.11 Elasticities of consumption and investment (cyclical adjusted)

Source: FMOLS estimates (January 2000–June 2017)

extension. An increase in the MLR dampens investment and consumption. Interest elasticity of consumption and investment expenditures are negative and their absolute values are lower than unity, suggesting that the private aggregate demand function is rather interest inelastic. The response of investment demand is marginally higher than that of consumption demand, which is similar to their responses to credit expansion. An important conclusion from this finding is that the credit availability effect is more important than the interest rate channel in monetary policy. Conducting monetary policy through the interest rate channel is not as effective as the credit channel in both consumption and investment.

During the course of rapid economic expansion, there might be a positive relationship between stock prices and property market activity. Evidence in Taiwan (Chen, 2001) and in Japan (Ito and Iwaisako, 1995) indicates the relationship among asset prices and credit expansion. Through the wealth effect, asset prices can increase the effectiveness of monetary policy used to counteract business fluctuations.

More importantly, another relevant policy question is whether the Bank of Thailand should raise the interest rate to curb activities in asset markets. In a rapidly growing economy, the property sector has high linkages to the real sector through large multiplier effects. The demand for property and securities is related to credit availability. By controlling credit growth, the central bank can ultimately influence speculation in asset markets. In addition, asset markets are linked to foreign exchange markets through foreign capital inflows. Consequently, the exchange rate is affected by inflows of foreign capital attracted by capital gains in the asset markets. The central bank must choose whether to curb capital inflows or to allow the exchange rate to perform an equilibrating role for external disequilibrium adjustments.

The size of the stock price bubble can be captured by the percentage deviation from the HP trend line. Similarly, the size of the property bubble can be

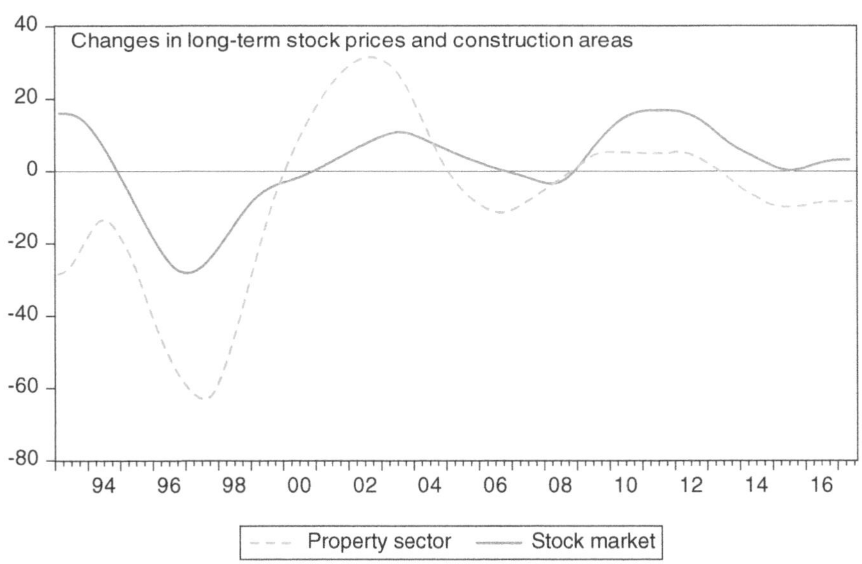

Figure 8.12 Correlates of stock prices and property sector activity

Source: Bank of Thailand

approximated from the deviation from the HP trend of construction activity, approximated by permitted construction in urban areas (Figure 8.12).

Using monthly data from January 1993 to December 2017, the Granger causality test indicates that the SET index (after removing cyclical movements) Granger causes cyclically adjusted construction investment, but not vice versa. We can predict the property bubble from speculative activities in the stock market. In conclusion, measures to curb stock market bubbles are necessary to prevent bubbles in the property sector. This conclusion does not imply that the stock market index should be included in the monetary policy reaction functions. Selective control measures may be used directly to stamp out speculative lending in the stock market.[1]

There is also a question regarding where and when the bubble started. The lead-lag relationship between the two bubbles can shed light on measures to prevent bursting asset bubbles. Speculation happens with a mechanism akin to Ponzi finance, where net assets decline with borrowing to finance acquisition of assets with rising prices. Therefore, extending credit into these sectors propels speculative demand for these assets.

Bank loans expand as the monetary base increases, and other things remain unchanged. Despite the constant monetary base level, bank loans can increase rapidly as banks may become recklessly aggressive, lending when collateral value increases. As a result, the credit multiplier will magnify rapidly during lending sprees as banks become more lenient with credit risk assessment. This actually happened from 1994 to 1998 at the height of the lending boom cycle.

Figure 8.13 shows that the property credit multiplier increased abnormally high prior to the financial crisis in 1997. We can monitor the financial sector's soundness by using the credit multiplier as an early warning indicator for

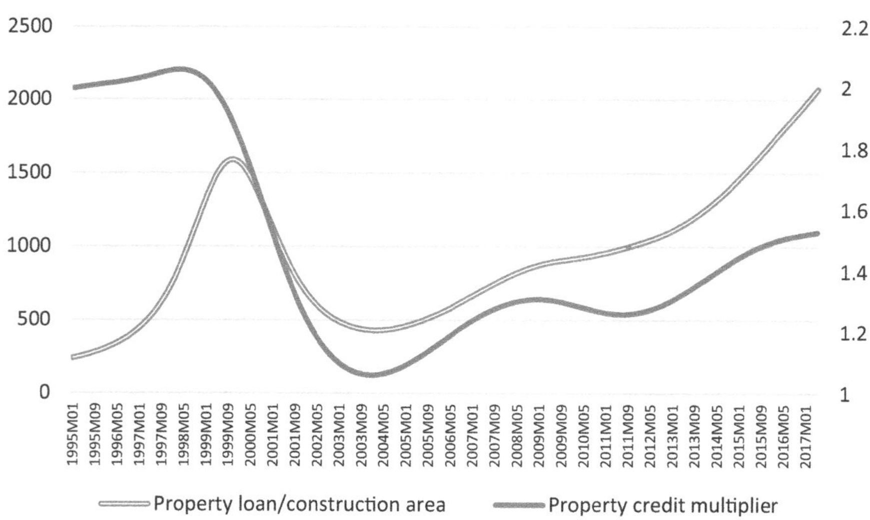

Figure 8.13 Overlending in the property sector

Source: Bank of Thailand

overlending. When the interest rate is high, commercial banks are willing to take more risk to obtain higher returns from assets. If the Bank of Thailand raises the interest rate on its lending facilities, banks are discouraged from lending, thereby causing a decline in the credit multiplier. This conclusion may not hold if commercial banks can get access to cheap foreign sources of funds and the forward exchange market works efficiently.

An increase in the MLR raises the value of the credit multiplier, while the BoT lending rate reduces it. There is a significant degree of lending inertia. A positive shock in the credit multiplier did not entirely phase out after a year. Because of the long lag effects of shocks in lending, it is difficult to curtail rapid growth of credit within a year, to boost credit growth within a short period after the economy experiences a credit crunch.

When the credit multiplier increases, and if the monetary base growth is uncontrollable, the impact on credit growth is excessive. When large amounts of foreign capital flows into the stock market and the Bank of Thailand must prevent currency appreciation, asset price bubbles are likely to appear. Figure 8.14 shows the booms in the property sector. Land prices and condominium prices increased substantially between 2009 and 2018. Similarly, the prices of single houses and townhouses increased, although they moved at a slower pace.

By controlling the level of the monetary base, the BoT can reduce excess supply in the property sector. Estimation of the excess supply of housing can be measured by the ratio of property credit to construction area (Figure 8.13). Property credit extended to property developers enlarges the supply of housing

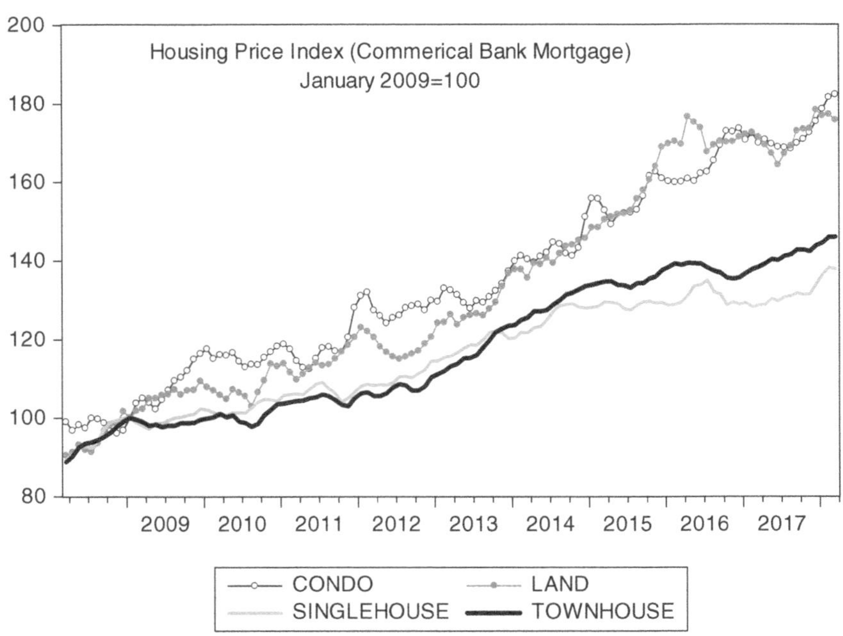

Figure 8.14 Rising property prices

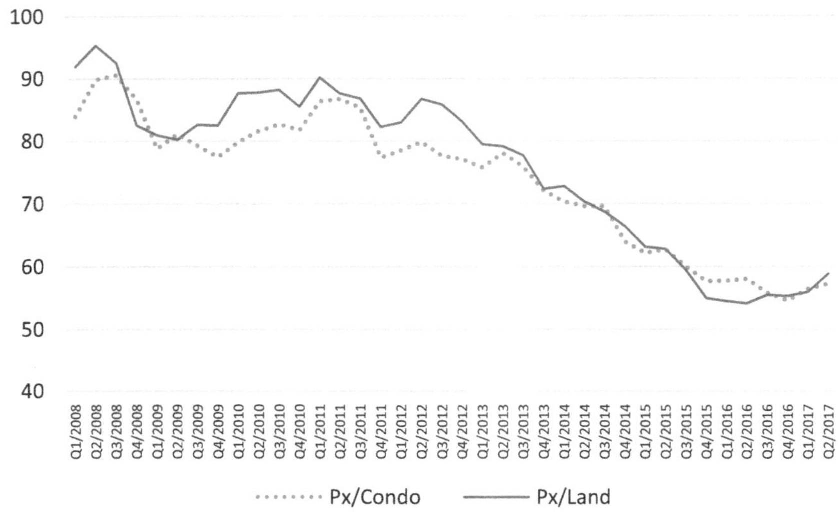

Figure 8.15 Signs of creeping Dutch disease (2008–2017)

Source: Calculation based on BoT data

and commercial spaces. If it rises faster than the construction areas, it indicates an enlarged supply of the property sector, just like the steep increase before the financial crisis. On the other hand, during the downturns of the non-traded sector, the ratio fell sharply until it reached its trough in 2004, before it started rising. The ability to restrain the growth of the monetary base is crucial for successful control of asset bubbles.[2]

An important policy implication is that the BoT can affect the supply of housing and commercial property by controlling the monetary base. The best way to curb asset bubbles is to begin as early as possible when there is a sign of bubble formation, because there is always a lag effect for monetary policy implementation. The sign of such formation can be seen from the index of the Dutch disease. It is proxied by the price ratio of exports to property price indexes. Shown in Figure 8.15, the prices of land and condominiums rose faster than the export price between 2011 and 2017. Note that during the period 1991–2005, there was no sign of Dutch disease (Figure 2.10) and eroding international competitiveness, because the growth during that period was driven by strong export growth. The boom in the property sector occurred at the same time of the export booms; the degree of Dutch disease was less pronounced.

Resources are relocated to the non-traded sector rather than the traded sector, thereby reducing international competitiveness. The slowdown in Thailand's exports can partly be attributed to the supply factor, in addition to the demand factor from the slowdown in the world trade volume. The lack of sufficient investment in the tradeable sector, compounded by the problem of downturns in the FDI inflows, limits productivity growth and erodes the competitiveness of Thailand's exports.

7. Concluding remarks

What are the monetary policy strategies that can ensure stable growth and price stability? The answer to that question is provided in this chapter. There is a long-run relationship between output and monetary aggregates. Monetary policy can stabilize the economy to achieve long-term growth and price stability. Changes in monetary aggregates influence the cyclical movement of real output. If the broad money supply can grow at a stable rate corresponding to output growth, monetary authorities can avoid deep recessions and excessive booms.

Past excessive growth of monetary aggregates was related to capital account liberalization and the fixed exchange rate regime. Despite the low level of claims on government, monetary aggregates increased substantially prior to the 1998 financial crisis. Capital flows and foreign exchange market interventions led to burgeoning net foreign assets. Consequently, the monetary base and broad money supply increased at an excessive rate, causing an unsustainable boom. A general lesson is that pursuing an unrealistic exchange rate target could undermine the fundamental objectives of monetary policy: to sustain growth and maintain price stability. There is a trade-off between inflation and unemployment. The cost of pushing the economy to full employment is not high in terms of sacrificing price stability. Nevertheless, persistent inflation is difficult to subdue after it starts to accelerate.

Given the concentration of the banking industry, monetary easing strategies during recessions may not be able to stimulate the economy back to the long-term growth path unless business confidence can be restored. Tight monetary policy works more effectively during booms when investors are constrained by credit availability. Prior to the 1998 economic crisis, excessive bank lending can be captured by the rising credit multiplier. Consequently, monetary authorities must scrutinize the movement of the credit multiplier, which can be a leading indicator of asset price bubbles. Since stock market bubbles precede property bubbles, it is desirable and possible to burst the stock market bubble with quantity tightening policies to curb excessive output and credit growth. This is not to suggest that stock price indexes be included among monetary policy reaction functions.

Notes

1 Mandler (2009) found evidence of a strong deterioration in the stabilization success of US monetary policy reaction functions that respond to stock market indices.

2 A dynamic least squares estimation of the monthly data between 1995 and 2017 reveals that the elasticity of the property excess supply with respect to the cyclically adjusted monetary base is 0.5, which is statistically significant.

References

Ball, Laurence. 2000. "Policy Rules and External Shocks." NBER Working Paper No. 7559.

Calderon, C., R. Duncan, and Klaus, Schmidt-Hebbel. 2004. "The Role of Credibility in the Cyclical Properties of Macroeconomic Policies in Emerging Economies." *Review of World Economies*, 140 (4): 613–633.

Calvo, G., and Carmen Reinhart. 2002. "Fear of Floating." *Quarterly Journal of Economics*, 17 (2): 379–408.

Chadha, J. S., Lucio, Sarno, and Giorgio Valente. 2004. "Monetary Policy Rules, Asset Prices, and Exchange Rates." *IMF Staff Papers*, 51: 529–552.

Chen, Nan-Kuang. 2001. "Asset price fluctuations in Taiwan: Evidence From Stock and Real Estate Prices: 1973 to 1992." *Journal of Asian Economics*, 12 (March): 215–232.

Chowdhury, I., and Andreas Schabert. 2008. "Federal Reserve Policy Though a Money Supply Lens." *Journal of Monetary Economics*, 55: 825–834.

Clarida, R., J. Gali, and Mark Gertler. 1999. "The Science of Monetary Policy: A New Keynesian Perspective." *Journal of Economic Literature*, 37, 1661–1707.

Hodrick, R., and Edward Prescott. 1997. "Postwar U.S. Business Cycles: An Empirical investigation." *Journal of Money, Credit, and Banking*, 29 (1): 1–16.

Ito, T., and Tokuo Iwaisako. 1995. "Explaining Asset Bubbles in Japan." NBER Working Paper No. 5358.

Jeon, J., Y. Oh, and Doo Yong Yang. 2006. "Financial Market Integration in East Asia: Regional or Global?" *Asian Economic Papers*, 5 (1): 73–89.

Mandler, Martin. 2009. "In Search of Robust Monetary Policy Rules – Should the Fed Look at Monetary Growth or Stock Market Performance?" *Journal of Macroeconomics*, 31: 345–361.

Mankiw, N. G., and Ricardo Reis. 2002. "Sticky Information Versus Sticky Prices: A Proposal to Replace the New Keynesian Phillips Curve." *Quarterly Journal of Economics*: 1295–1328.

Pivetta, F., and Ricardo Reis. 2007. "The Persistence of Inflation in the United States." *Journal of Economic Dynamics and Control*, 31: 1326–1358.

Quah, D., and Shaun P. Vahey. 1995. "Measuring Core Inflation." *The Economic Journal*, 422: 1130–1144.

Taylor, John B. 1993. "Discretion Versus Policy Rules in Practice." *Carnegie-Rochester Conference Series on Public Policy*, 39: 195–214.

van der Ploeg, Federick. 2009. "Prudent Monetary Policy and Prediction of the Output Gap." *Journal of Macroeconomics*, 31: 217–230.

9 Impacts of quantitative monetary easing policy

1. Introduction

The global financial crisis (GFC) of 2007–2008 led to recession in the US in 2009 and a decline in Thailand's exports. Because of Thailand's high market exposure to US and Japanese markets, it was difficult for this export-led growth country to escape from the deflationary impact of the GFC. Although Thai financial institutions were mildly affected, the Thai stock price index was initially dampened by capital outflows and pessimistic sentiment. Unconventional monetary policy conducted in the US and Japan affected Thailand's capital flows, interest rates, exchange rates, and the stock market price. The massive injection of dollar liquidity also brought about booms in Thailand's asset markets, strengthening the Thai baht and complicating the conduct of Thailand's monetary policy. The Bank of Thailand tried to prevent baht appreciation by conducting a low interest rate policy to discourage capital inflows. But this easy monetary stance rekindled inflationary pressure and propagated asset bubbles. In addition, when the US economy showed sigh of sustained recovery, the fear of the Fed's policy reversal created a possibility of capital flights, liquidity risks, and exchange rate volatility in Asia. In July 2015, the baht hit a 6-year low against the dollar. The collapse of China's stock market and the Greece debt crisis created new risks and uncertainty on the baht exchange rates.

The Thai economy experienced record low growth in 2014. Internal conflicts, political uncertainty, and the overthrowing of a democratic government led to deteriorating investment sentiment. Consumer confidence remained poor during the period of political violence and world recession.[1] The government struggled to stimulate the economy through public spending, but it was too little and too late to offset declining private expenditures and exports. The Thai economy is driven by manufactured exports, which account for more than 60 percent of GDP. Declining exports since 2011 reflect the sluggish output growth of manufacturing output, which is shown in Figure 9.1, illustrating the sluggish manufacturing production index (MPI). Between January 2000 and July 2008, MPI and exports increased steadily. The GFC temporarily decreased exports and manufacturing output. The V-shaped recovery was evident in the aftermath of the GFC. Another temporary collapse of exports and output occurred in November 2011, when the floods disrupted production and exports.

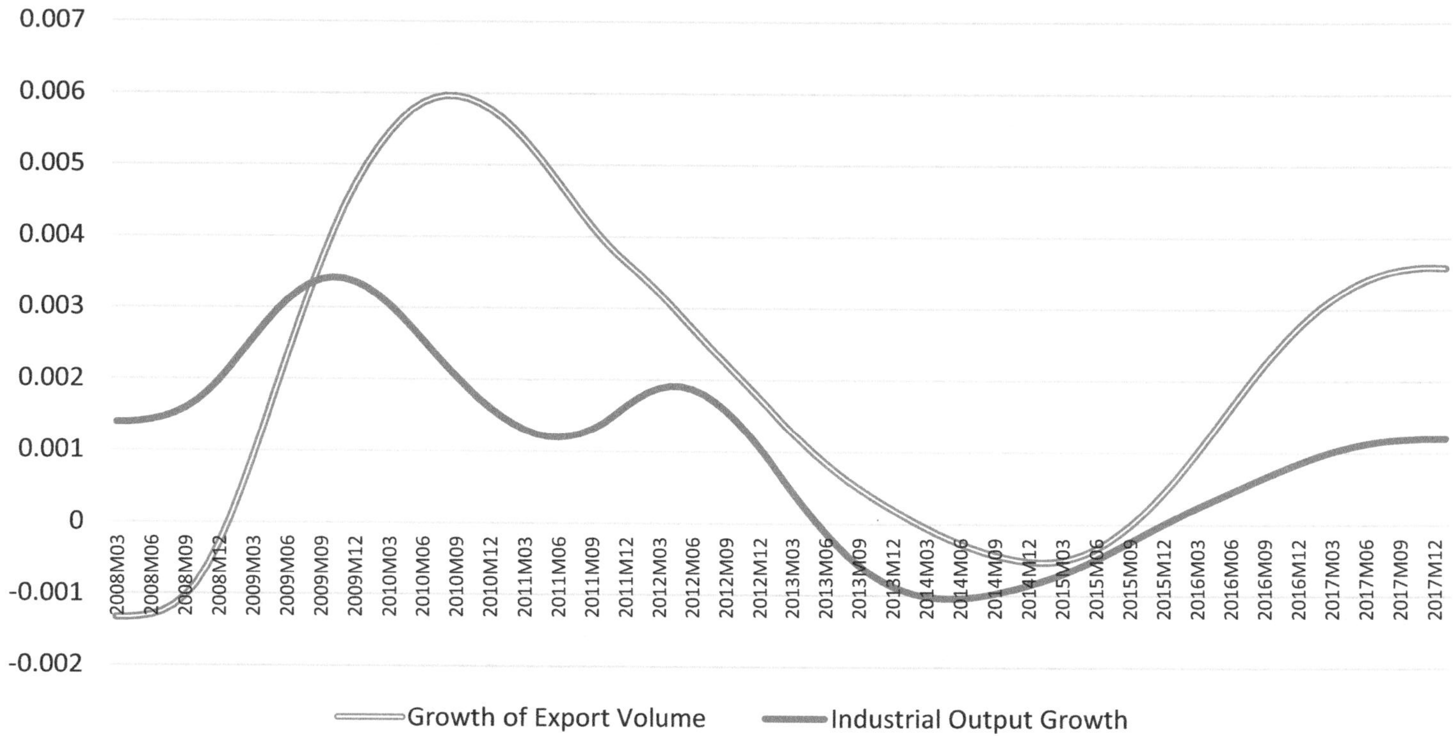

Figure 9.1 Exports and industrial output: long-term growth paths

Source: Bank of Thailand

In the first 4 months of 2015, Thailand exports declined by 4 percent (yoy), as a result of world economic slowdown and weak commodities prices in rice and rubber. According to Tharnpanich and McCombie (2013), changes in the terms of trade had an adverse effect on the growth performance of Thailand. The growth decline following the Asian financial crisis in 1998 was due to the dramatic decline in the world income elasticity of demand for its manufacturing exports.

Despite deprecating of the baht, a negative world output effect on the demand for Thai exports is stronger than the positive substitution effect of baht depreciation. Other currencies of Thailand's competitors also depreciate simultaneously with the Thai baht, thereby weakening the impact of baht depreciation.

The recovery in private spending was apparent after the world economy slowly recovered from the GFC. In 2011, the great deluge substantially reduced automobiles sales, but the rebound was also spectacular as the government employed fiscal measures to support consumer spending. The fiscal stimulus seemed to work and the economy was about to regain its pre-shock growth path. No sooner than the recovery had taken place in 2013 by export recovery and increased private spending, the political confrontation and the subsequent military coup in May 2014 derailed the path to economic recovery.

Automatic fiscal stabilizers on the revenue side have been working reasonably well. With ample space, the governments could have used fiscal policy stimulus through infrastructure development to spur long-term growth. The difficulty of implementing public expenditures lies in frequent changes in the government since the 2006 military coup. New governments could not focus on long-term growth, having to deal with intermediate problems that continuously threatened government stability. After the coup in 2014, the Thai economy experienced the lowest growth among ASEAN countries. The fiscal policy could not effectively compensate for the fall in export demand. The budget spent on economic services was diverted to defense, increasing the public sector's wages, and income transfer payments. Fiscal policy was not able to function to stabilize the economy as there were urgent short-term policy issues the government had to tackle to maintain its power. But monetary policy can still be performed by the Bank of Thailand in time of economic turbulence.

It is well-known that monetary policy has a long and variable lag effect on the real sector. In many cases, monetary policy is carried out too late and too little to cope with shocks in aggregate demand. To increase the effectiveness of monetary policy, the information and decision lags must be minimized. When experiencing a temporary external shock, a gradual approach to monetary policy adjustment is preferable to a sudden shift in monetary policy stance. But when the shocks are persistent, a gradual approach may not be appropriate to deal with permanent shocks, because private expectations have changed to new environments.

The Fed aggressively cut the federal funds rate right after experiencing the subprime crisis. Because of the linkage between short-term and bank lending interest rates, the US prime rate instantaneously declined after the Fed took easy monetary policy stance. There was a constant gap between the federal funds rate and the prime lending rate. Unlike interest rate adjustments in the US, Thailand's minimum lending rate (MLR) did not follow closely with the BoT's monetary stance, signaled by changing the key policy interest rate. Because of the loose connection between the short-term and long-term interest rates, monetary policy in Thailand is not as effective as the Fed's influence on the US financial sector. The federal funds rate was maintained at 0.25 percent from January 2009 to September 2015. Unconventional monetary policy through the Fed's massive injection of liquidity via purchasing of corporate bonds began in 2008. The Bank of Thailand started tightening monetary policy by rising the key policy rate in May 2010 from 1.25 percent to 1.50 percent in September 2010. The rate hike peaked at 3.5 percent in August 2011. As a result, the interest rate differential between domestic and foreign markets widened, encouraging capital inflows. With ample liquidity in the Thai money markets, the MLR did not decline by the same proportion of the BoT's interest rate cut. The MLR declined by 0.75 percent despite the 1.25 percent cut in the key policy rate. The gap between the prime rate and the MLR was widened from 2.75 percent in April 2007 to 3.5 percent by the end of December 2014. Maintaining a long duration of the large interest rate gap complicates the BoT's conduct of monetary and exchange rate policy. The unwarranted fear of baht depreciation and the underestimation of recession probability precluded the BoT from engaging in timely monetary easing to spur growth. By February 2015, the BoT's key policy rate remained at 2 percent, despite easy monetary policy stance employed in more than 10 countries since the beginning of 2015. The central banks in Singapore, Indonesia, India, Australia, and Canada have already cut their policy rates to prevent capital outflows.[2]

Chung et al. (2012), employed the Fed's FRB/US macroeconomic model and found that the large-scale asset purchases (LSAP) reduced long-term interest rate by 50 basis points and raised the real GDP by 3 percent; inflation rate was 1 percent higher than if the Federal Reserve had not carried out the program. Thus the asset purchases prevented deflation in the US. There is a question whether the recovery is still fragile as consumption spending and residential investment remain weak. Furthermore, the question arises about the consequences of the possibility of the Fed's quantitative contraction (QC) after the Fed unloads its assets from the balance sheet, and whether the reversal of the quantitative easing (QE) will lead to global adjustment of capital flows. Capital flights might lead to another round of foreign exchange crisis if the QE measures are abrupt and unanticipated.

Breedon et al. (2012) constructed a counterfactual path of bond yields to estimate the impact of QE. They found evidence that the 2009–2010 QE program significantly lowered government bond yields, through portfolio balance channel, by 50 basis points. According to Joyce et al. (2011), over the period March 2009 and January 2010, the BOE spent 200 billion pounds, representing 14 percent of annual GDP, on government securities. The evidence indicates that QE purchases financed by central bank money have had a significant impact on the British economy. Baumeister and Benati (2010) investigated the macroeconomic impact of lower long-term bond spread during the 2007–2009 recession period. They concluded that a compression of the long-term yield spread has a powerful effect on output growth and inflation. Their counterfactual simulations illustrated that unconventional monetary policy actions in the US and UK averted deflation and output collapses.

The literature seems to suggest that QE has a positive impact on the economy in the medium run. Nevertheless, there is still doubt whether the US and Japanese economies can actually sustain recovery with strong productivity growth that can generate expansionary impact on the world economy. We now turn to discuss the impact of the QE on Thailand's exchange rates and exports.

2. Impacts on exchange rates and exports

Large injection of the dollar to the world liquidity led to appreciation of the yen and other Asian currencies. The yen appreciation against the Thai baht and other Asian currencies increased exports, provided the Japanese market is dominant. Moreover, if QE leads to output expansion in the US and Japan, the income effect from expanding output in these two economies can boost exports in Asia. On the other hand, if their export markets concentrate heavily in the US market, the substitution effect caused by the appreciation of the domestic currency against the US dollar can mitigate the expansionary income effect of the QE.

Because Thailand's international trade is conducted mainly in the dollar, the QE and QC have significant impact on the Thai baht. In general, the price of the dollar is terms of baht trended downward from 2002 to 2014, while the price of the yen in terms of baht fluctuated more than the dollar (Figure 9.2). The reason

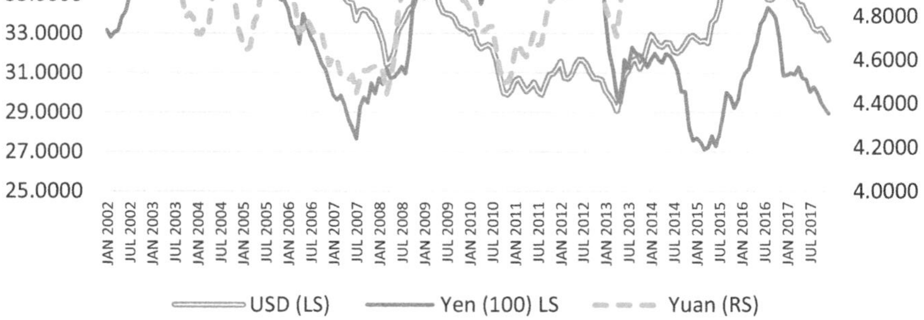

Figure 9.2 Baht vis-à-vis dollar, yen, and the yuan

Source: Bank of Thailand

behind this volatility is that the BoT has intervened heavily to stabilize the baht-dollar exchange rates, allowing the baht-yen exchange rate to adjust accordingly to international arbitrage condition. The BoT attempted to slow down the baht appreciation in order to prevent export shortfalls caused by the rapid baht appreciation against the dollar. The ratio of the bah-USD and the baht-yen exchange rates simply demonstrates the fluctuations in the yen-dollar exchange rate, which is the outcome of the asset expansion of the Fed and the BOJ. The baht depreciated against the yuan largely because the baht appreciated against the dollar less than the yuan.

When the baht appreciated against yen and the dollar simultaneously in 2005–2006 and 2013, the impact on Thailand's export sector was substantial in terms of loss in international competitiveness. As the baht appreciated, the BoT intervened heavily in spot and forward markets. The share of net forward position in total international reserves increased more to 24 percent in 2008 when the baht appreciated against the dollar in June 2005 from to 41.3 baht to 31.5 baht in March 2008, representing a 31 percent appreciation. As the QE liquidity injection slowed down, the baht depreciated marginally before climbing to a new high of 29.3 baht in April 2013, prompting the BoT to intervene heavily once again in the forward market.

Even if the BoT succeeded in postponing the baht appreciation, the BoT would pay a high price in terms of foreign exchange losses as long as the dollar trended upward. In the long run, export firms may get complacent, knowing that the central bank will bail them out when the exchange rate turns again them. This kind of moral hazard will not take place unless the Bank of Thailand refrains from unnecessary market intervention.

By expressing the value of the assets purchased by the Fed and BOJ in the form of an index (2007 = 100), we can see the relative strength of the QE of the two central banks (Figure 9.3). The Fed has been more aggressive than the BOJ in asset purchases. Consequently, the broad effective real exchange rate of the Thai baht appreciated considerably by the sheer force of the QE in 2008, causing the broad real effective exchange rate (REER) of the baht appreciated by 15 percent by April 2014. In case of the US, Warburton (2013) found evidence that the trade-weighted dollar was affected by the interest spread, which tracks QE, although unexpected changes in national financial conditions, the federal funds rate, and the velocity of money account for more variation in the trade-weighted index of the dollar.

The loss of international competitiveness of Thailand can be captured by the sluggish growth of Thailand's exports to the US, Japan, and China. The GFC had already caused a substantial decline in Thailand's exports in 2009; the adverse consequences from the QE exacerbated the export decline. Nevertheless, Thailand's exports did not perform poorly in ASEAN markets (Figure 9.4). Similar to the Thai baht, other ASEAN countries' currencies also appreciated against the dollar after the QE programs. Although Thailand's exports to ASEAN remained flat between 2012 and 2014, Thailand's dependency on ASEAN markets has become increasingly important.[3] From 1995 to 2015, the dependency on the

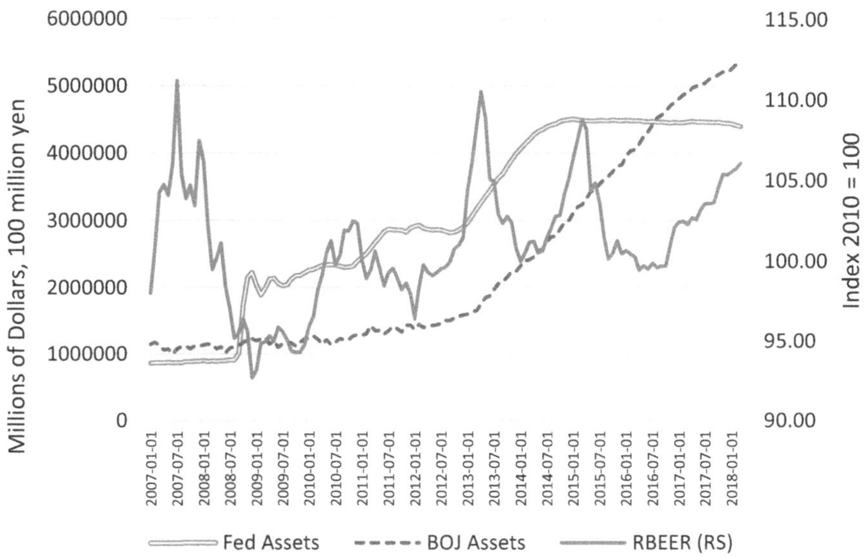

Figure 9.3 QE and the real effective exchange rate of the baht

Source: Federal Reserve Bank

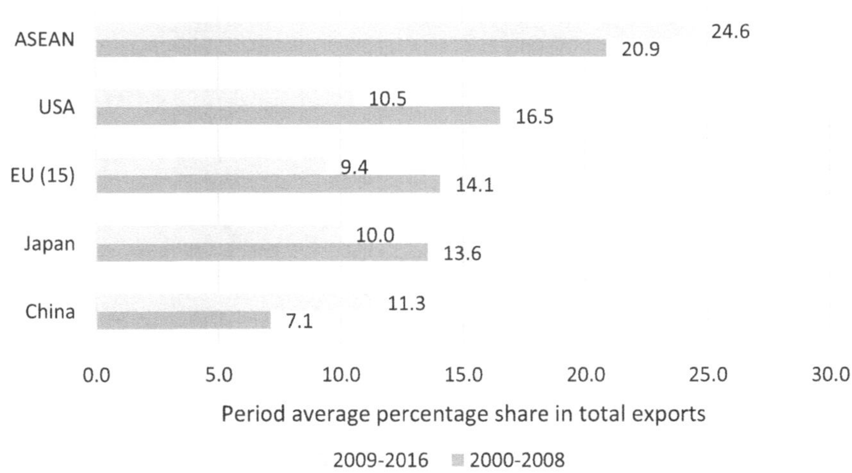

Figure 9.4 Thailand's export destinations: 2000–2016

US, Japan, and the EU has declined to 10 percent, while ASEAN and China have become the major export destinations. The up and down business cycle in China implies China's imports fluctuations and volatility of ASEAN exports.

The poor performance of Thailand's exports can partly be attributed to the expansion of the dollar supply that caused baht appreciation. Export-oriented firms suffered more than domestic market-oriented firms. They ran lower capacity utilization, thereby discouraging them from undertaking capital investment despite the benefits from baht appreciation that cheapened imported capital goods. Viewed in this light, QE programs have a far-reaching impact on investment and long-run productivity growth of the country.

When the renminbi appreciates against the dollar, China's exports growth slows down. In turn, a decelerating growth of output in China means lower demand for Thailand's exports. The medium-run impact of QE works through income effect when the Chinese economy experiences growth slowdown because of yuan appreciation. This leads to the fear of sudden yuan depreciation and another currency war if China needs to stimulate its export-driven economy via yuan devaluations.

The indirect impact of QE via China is in the form of yuan appreciation (Figure 9.5), which caused sluggish exports and economic activity. Nevertheless, yuan appreciation is beneficial to Thailand's tourism industry. However, the slowdown in China's exports as the appreciation of the yuan's real exchange rate sent ripple effects to the rest of the world. China and her major importing trade partners experienced similar growth deceleration.

Because of the appreciation in the real effective exchange rate, China's total export growth slowed down from 20 percent in 2011 to only 6 percent in 2014. Similarly, Thailand's export growth rate declined from 30 percent to 5 percent

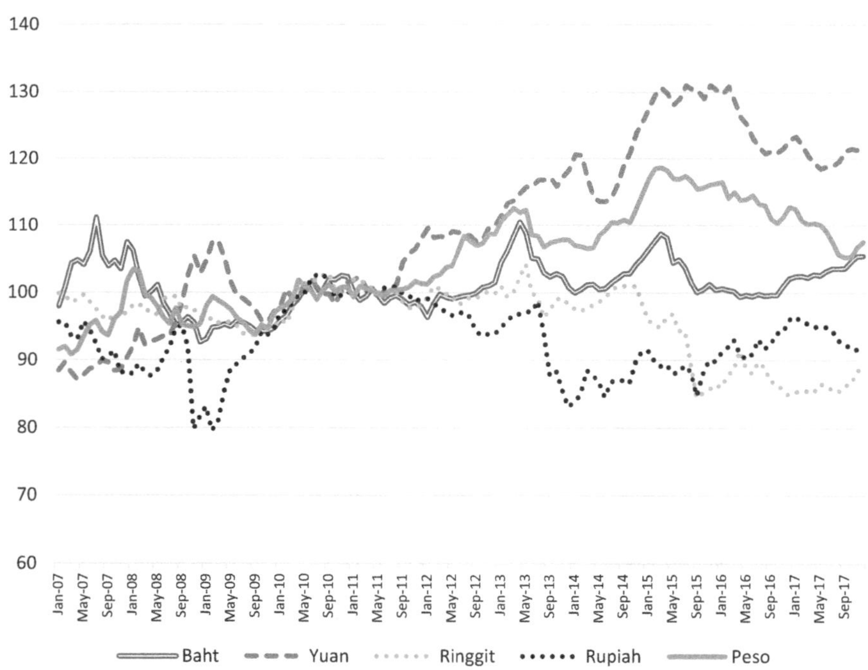

Figure 9.5 Real board effective exchange rates

Source: Federal Reserve Bank

during the same corresponding period. The appreciation of the ringgit reduced export growth from 14 percent to 3 percent. Despite the depreciation of the rupiah, Indonesia's exports growth collapsed from 29 percent to −3 percent. The appreciation of the peso decelerated the Philippines' export growth from 8 percent to 4 percent in 2013. These ASEAN countries had between 11 percent and 13 percent export exposures to the Chinese market. China's total imports growth declined from 25 percent to just 1 percent in 2014. Economic activity in China was affected by yuan appreciation, which therefore had strong repercussions on the growth performance of ASEAN countries.

3. Short-run and long-run impacts on output

The unconventional monetary policy conducted by the Fed since 2008 has affected long-term interest rates through quantitative easing. Low interest rates produced portfolio reallocations from the US markets. Kiley (2014) illustrated the co-movement between interest rates and equity prices caused by monetary policy changes. A decline in long-term interest rate induced by monetary policy statements associated with zero bound on the short-term interest rate had a positive impact on equity prices prior to 2009. Furthermore, the QE also influence equity prices in emerging economies. Because of an influx of capital inflows through portfolio investment, stock markets in Asia experienced strong performances. Thailand's level of international reserve reached 181 billion USD in May 2011, thanks to capital inflows induced by the QE. The rising international reserves implied that the BoT continued buying the dollar to prevent the baht from appreciation. Since then, the BoT stopped buying the dollar and started selling the dollar to prevent the baht from depreciation. As a result, the level of international reserve declined gradually as the baht depreciated to almost 33 baht at the end of 2014. The BoT intervenes regularly in both directions, indicating that the fear of floating still prevails in the mindset of monetary authorities.

It is difficult to find an optimum level of foreign exchange rate to achieve external equilibrium conditions. Encouraging exports and maintaining price stability simultaneously complicate the conduct of monetary policy. Adjusting the key policy interest rate may not achieve both targets. The rising amount of international reserve prior to the GFC, which continued into the QE episodes, implies a rapidly enlarging monetary base and money supply in emerging economies.

Thailand's stock prices rose in line with the expansion of money supply. Since the economy experienced growth slowdown, interest rates from bank deposit remained at low levels, increasing the attractiveness of portfolio investment. The rate of return from investing in the stock market and the expansion of money supply are related (Figure 5.6). The rise in the stock price in Thailand is partly due to investors' sentiment driven by share prices in Wall Street. Thus, the QE conducted in the US has direct and indirect impacts on Thailand's stock market. Other Southeast Asian stock markets also rose in line with the Dow Jones index because the region has become more closely related. As such, Asian share prices move in tandem with Wall Street.

Using 94 observations from January 2007 to December 2014, the hypothesis that growth rate of M2 Granger causes stock market returns cannot be rejected at a very high level of statistical significance, and the causation runs both ways. This evidence indicates that enlarged money supply leads to rising stock market prices in Thailand.

The stock prices are also determined by portfolio capital inflows. The QE in the US dampened the rate of return from investment in US corporate bonds (Figure 9.6), making it more attractive to shift portfolio investment away from the US markets. Had the BoT not intervened in the foreign exchange market, the money supply would not have grown at very high rate that subsequently led to asset price appreciation. The impact of the QE therefore depends also on a particular exchange rate policy setting. A more stable exchange with intervention regularity would lead to more expansion of money supply, notwithstanding the central bank's sterilization.

The cyclical components of stock prices, which are caused by random arrivals of good and bad news, can be removed from actual values by the Hodrick-Prescott filter (HP). The HP trend of annual rate of return in Thailand's stock market and US corporate bond yields are shown in Figure 9.6. The substantial gap between the two rates of returns explains portfolio investment flows to emerging markets, including Thailand. The low and declining yield from the US bond markets made Southeast Asian stock markets become relatively attractive and led to more capital inflows and rapid appreciation of the Asian currencies. The continued appreciation of the baht made Thailand's assets become even more attractive.

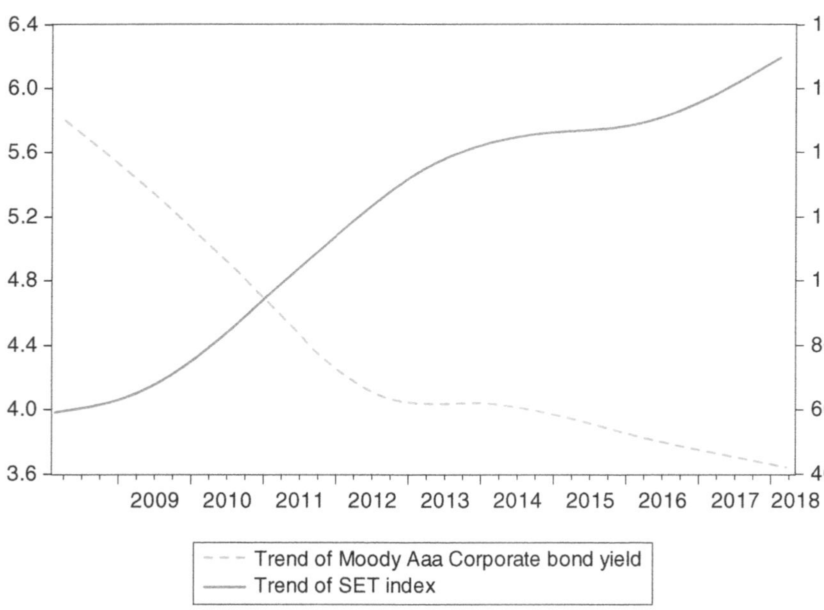

Figure 9.6 Trends of SET and Moody Aaa corporate bond yield

Source: Bank of Thailand, Federal Reserve Bank

Portfolio investment from abroad caused further appreciation of the baht. Other asset prices are also affected by these capital inflows.

Rising asset prices in the property sector leads to expansion in bank credit and vice versa (Figure 9.7). The steady rising level of property credit for real estate development and personal housing perpetuated asset price bubbles, aggravated by speculation in the property sector. We can measure degree of speculation by computing the ratio of personal housing credit and real estate development credit, which suggests a heightening degree of speculation in the real estate sector. The rising tide of speculation was apparent in 2001 and continued unabated up to 2010.

Using the dynamic ordinary least squares estimation method applied to monthly data from 2012 to 2017, it is found that changes in the level of property credit in the previous 36 months can explain variations of the change in current condominium prices. The price of a single unit house is highly correlated with condo prices, suggesting that current housing prices can be used as a proxy for expected change in the condo price level.

The amount of bank credit expanded to the property sector has been astronomically high, compared to the credit level during the period of the Asian financial crisis in 1997–1998. Excessive credit growth in the non-trade sector causes relocation of resources from the traded sector to the non-traded sector, thereby shrinking the export sector. The situation is akin to Dutch disease, when the real exchange rate appreciates, shifting resources from the traded sector to the non-traded sector. Seen in this light, the impact of QE conducted in high-income countries has a profound macroeconomic impact on emerging countries like Thailand. Amonhaemanon et al. (2014) showed that real estates in Thailand were

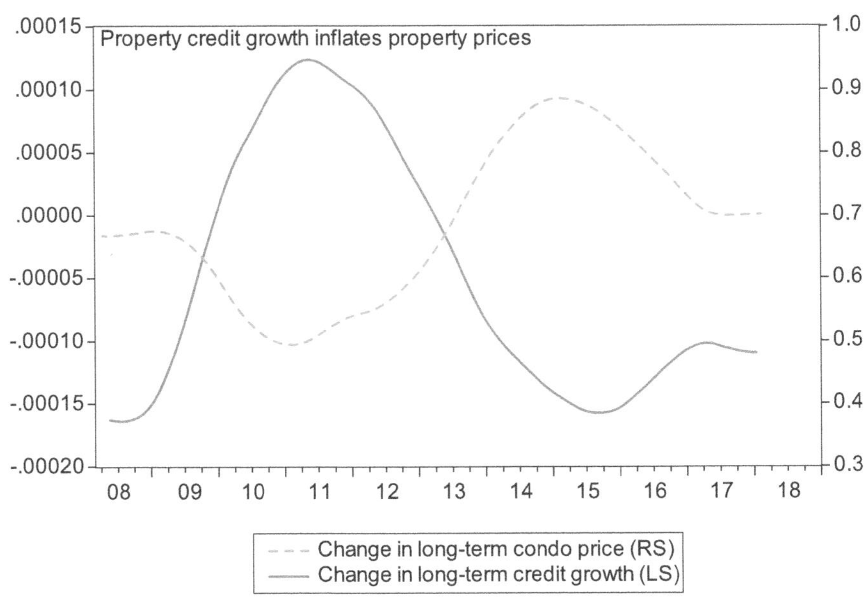

Figure 9.7 Lag effects of property credit growth on property prices

Source: Bank of Thailand

used to hedge against inflation during 1987–2011. The very high rate of return from the real estate sector after the GFC was the result of speculative demand fueled by personal housing credit (Figure 9.7). Asset prices are increasingly deviating from fundamentals. Household debts are increasing, while household incomes remain stagnant. Inevitably, the property bubble would burst unless the excess supply can be eliminated by massive price correction and contraction in residential supply in the long run.

Excessive reliance on unconventional monetary policy by the Fed has produced a boom in Thailand's asset prices. The increased asset values could have led to higher private spending for consumption and investment via wealth effect on consumption and Tobin's Q effect. The private investment index exhibits fluctuations: a sharp rebound after the GFC in 2009, a temporary shock due to the 2011 floods, and a V-shaped recovery in 2012. The political turmoil and the 2014 coup depressed investment sentiment. In addition to the sluggish growth in Europe and China, private investment, after a recovery in 2009 and 2012, had resumed its declining trend since 2013 (Figure 9.8).

Consumer spending and investment were depressed further by declining investor sentiment and deteriorating consumer confidence. From 2012 to 2017, there was a significant declining trend in private capital formation (HPCAPITAL) in manufacturing and real estate sectors (HPAREA) (Figure 9.8). The wealth effect on private spending, if any, would not be strong enough to offset the depressing impact of pessimistic expectations.

During recessions, consumers are trying to maintain their previous level of consumption through borrowing to smooth consumption expenditures. As a result, the level of Thai household debt increased considerably to 85 percent

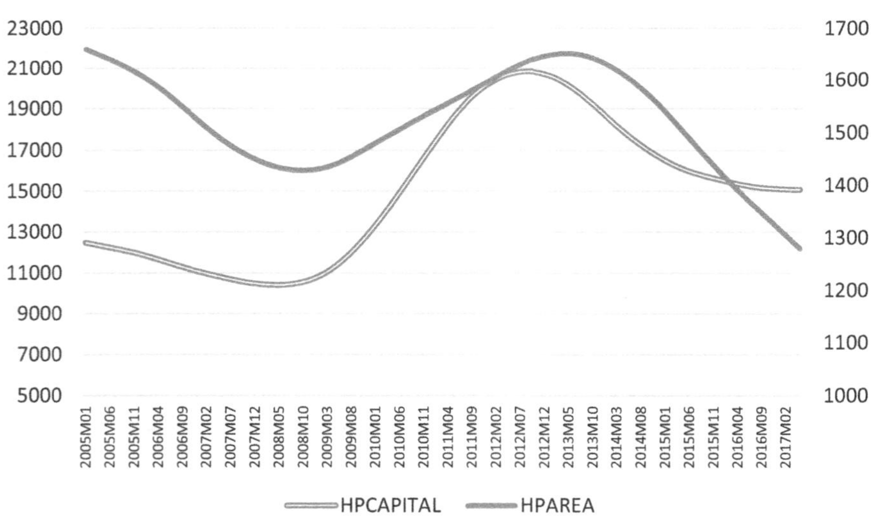

Figure 9.8 Trends of private investment in real estate and capital formation

Source: The Bank of Thailand

of GDP in 2015. Assets are concentrated on the top quintile of Thai population, which has a high marginal propensity to save. The wealth effect on consumption from QE-enhanced asset prices therefore remains weak. Household debts relative to income levels have been increasing considerably, limiting the wealth effect of asset price appreciation, the private consumption index remained flat from 2010 to 2017, while durable consumption declined sharply from March 2013 to February 2016, before it gradually regained its level in 2014 (Figure 9.9).

Unlike the instantaneous impact of the QE on exchange rates, its impact on output is not transmitted immediately as the pass-through effect on output is slow. The expansionary impact of QE is felt through credit availability and balance sheet effects. It takes considerable lags before consumption and investment expenditures respond to stimulus. Because of different financial structure, level of household debts, and trade structure in the US and Japan, the short-run and long-run impacts are dissimilar in directions and magnitudes.

In general, unconventional monetary policy to stimulate growth enlarged the monetary base in the US and Japan, resulting in capital outflows and depreciation of the dollar and the yen. Emerging countries received substantial flows of portfolio investment which raised stock prices in the Asian region. Undoubtedly, QE has increased the value of financial assets in these countries. On the other hand, QE has strong impact on exchange rates due to capital inflows. Table 9.1 summarizes the anticipated QE effects on Thailand's output and the direction of the baht exchange rates in the short run and long run. Expansion of the Fed's assets leads to baht appreciation against the dollar. Similarly, the BOJ's asset expansion causes the baht to appreciate against the yen.

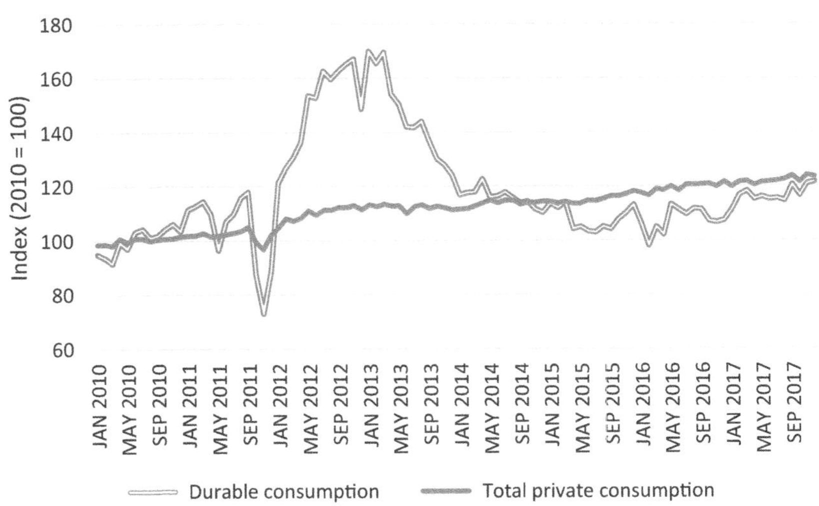

Figure 9.9 Private consumption expenditures

Source: Bank of Thailand

Table 9.1 Expected effects of QE on Thailand

Sources of external shocks	*Impacts of nominal Baht exchange rates*	*Impact on Thailand's output*	
		Short-run impact	*Long-run impact*
FED	Baht/USD appreciation	–	+
BOJ	Baht/Yen appreciation	–	+
Yuan appreciation against USD	Baht/Yuan depreciation	+	–

Thailand's manufacturing output responds negatively (positively) to baht appreciation (depreciation) because Thailand's manufacturing sector is driven by export demand. In the short run, the impact of QE is transmitted via substitution effect through exchange rate changes. In the long run, when output and employment increase in the US and Japan, we observe an increase in Thailand's output caused by rising demand for Thailand's manufactured goods. There is also a positive indirect output effect from network trade expansion when these two economies import more goods from other ASEAN countries. The short-run indirect impact of QE is on the appreciation of the yuan against the dollar and depreciation against the baht. In the medium run, the appreciation of the yuan against the dollar can retard the growth of the Chinese economy. In turn, the sputtering growth in China leads to a negative impact on Thailand's exports and GDP growth in the long run.

4. Examining QE impacts through VAR models

Casual empiricism cannot be used to answer questions regarding to the impact of QE on the Thai economy. A vector autoregression (VAR) model has been widely applied to analyze the impact of QE. Harada and Masujima (2009) employed a VAR model to answer the question whether an increase in monetary base raises aggregate output in Japan. Their model indicated that the impact of QE is primarily transmitted through the channels of asset prices and bank balance sheets. Their findings revealed that Japan's monetary policy has been effective in easing prolonged economic downturn. While the Fed and the BOJ acquired private assets through expanding the monetary base, the yen-dollar exchange rate would consequently be altered. Kano and Morita (2015) found evidence that money demand shocks were caused by the long-term interest rate differentials between the US and Japan. The depreciation of the yen-dollar nominal exchange rate after the Plaza Accord exhibited a common stochastic trend of the yen-dollar rate, which is dictated by the monetary base differential between the two countries. Fukuda (2015) advanced the hypothesis that the news shocks about Abenomics were successful in changing market expectations in stock prices and the yen-dollar rate. Favorable responses to news on Abenomics by foreign investors led to improving market sentiments despite revealing the news during the day. According to Fukuda (2015), foreigners' trade is conducted during nighttime, and the dramatic market responses happened only in time zones where foreign investors were active. Both stock prices and yen-dollar rates had structural breaks in daytime and nighttime. In sum, the QE has impacts on the exchange rates and asset prices in the US and Japan.

According to Kapetanios et al. (2012), the effects of the Bank of England's purchases of assets can be captured by using three different VAR models. The results indicate that QE has a peak effect on output and the price level around 1.5 percentage points. Sinclair and Ellis (2012) argue that the impact of QE in various countries can be different, depending on structure of the economy and the fiscal policy response. Since the world's financial markets are closely linked, the underlying drivers of movement of bond yields are not just domestic factors. In the UK context, international factors dominate local development in UK bond price movement, but not to the complete exclusion of domestic factors. A caveat that must be borne in mind when evaluating the impact of QE is to realize that a small open economy, abstracting from the impact of global movements in financial markets, can lead to very different conclusions. Menon and Hee Ng (2013) use global VAR to examine the impact of quantitative easing in the Eurozone. Although direct impacts are small, a further shock can lead to a much larger adjustment in risks and asset valuations. There is a real possibility that vulnerability in the Southeast Asian region increases following massive inflows of capital and buildup of debt, related to successive bouts of QE in the US and Japan. Joyce et al. (2012) point out that the Western economies remain weak and sluggish, indicating that, even if the QE programs work, they need to be supplemented by other measures, since the recessionary forces are very strong.

The VAR model constructed by Nidhiprabha (2016) indicates that QE implementation in the US and Japan led to an appreciation of the baht-dollar rate in the short run. In terms of the QE impacts on the baht-yen rate, we observe that it appreciates immediately after the BOJ's action. The appreciation continues to 4 months and disappears by the tenth month. The response of Thailand's exports to QE is transmitted via the movements of the two exchange rates discussed earlier. The impulse response function reveals that the contractionary impact on exports is more severe in the first 4 months before it dies off. This is a reflection of the undershooting of the baht exchange rate that would tend to gravitate back to its normal level after the shocks dissipates.

As far as the impact of the asset prices is concerned, the Fed's QE program caused a negative impact in the first 2 months, but began to push the stock price higher after 3 months. The lag effect of QE on American corporate bond yields and its announcement effect initially created market pessimism in the aftermath of the subprime crisis. As the yield curve becomes flatter, portfolio reallocation takes place, when investors try to seek a higher rate of returns in foreign stock markets. The accumulated response of the stock market becomes positive, albeit disappearing in three quarters. For the BOJ's QE, the positive impact on Thailand's stock price occurs immediately after the operation, although its impact dies off slowly after three quarters.

Since manufactured output amounted to more than 80 percent of Thailand's total exports, the exports contraction follows the decline in manufacturing

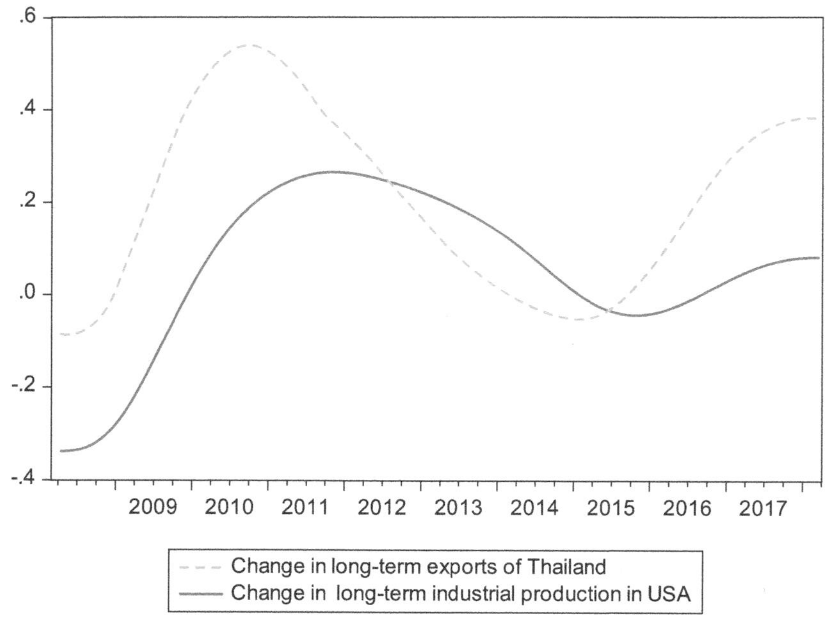

Figure 9.10 Long-term paths of Thailand's exports and US's industrial production

Source: Bank of Thailand

output. The QE by the Fed has stronger contractionary impact than the BOJ's action. This is due to stronger appreciation of the baht-dollar exchange rates and the fact that more than 85 percent of Thailand's international transactions are conducted in the dollar. Nevertheless, the output contraction decelerates after two quarters as the baht-dollar rate rebounds to the initial level. The coincident index is a measurement of the overall economic activity, and exhibits similar movements, because investment and consumption expenditures are primarily determined by output and income level.

We can conclude that QE launched by the Fed and the BOJ has contractionary impacts on the Thai economy in the short and medium run through the effect of baht appreciation which depresses Thailand's export demand. Unless the QE programs generate sustainable recovery in the US and Japan, Thailand's economic recovery will be protracted because of declining exports, plunging commodity prices, and sluggish consumption and investment expenditures. Figure 9.10 supports the prediction of the model that, in the long run, when the QE finally spurs output growth in the US, Thailand's exports would rebound accordingly.

5. Concluding remarks

If the export growth engine is damaged by the appreciation of the baht against the dollar, fiscal policy must be employed to counteract the economic downturn.

Given political instability and the loss of investor confidence, expansionary fiscal policy is less effective when undertaken during the absence of consumer confidence. Because the military coup in May 2014 disrupted the fiscal budget process, it was impossible to the employ fiscal policy to offset the collapse in exports growth. As a result, Thailand's exports barely grew in 2014 and output growth rate declined from 2.3 percent in 2013 to 0.7 percent in 2014. Notwithstanding the economic slowdown, the stock market and the property sector were booming, thanks to capital inflow from other parts of the world. One has to ask if Thailand is approaching the Minsky moment.

One of the adverse consequences of the QE conducted in industrial countries is the loss of Thailand's competitiveness due to real exchange rate appreciation. Thailand has shifted its resources from the traded to non-traded sector, which is buoyed by capital inflow. Dutch disease has eroded the international competitiveness of Thailand's export sector. Thailand's policy response to the adverse impact of the QE was too little and too late. The large interest rate differentials still remain. As long as the baht continues to appreciate against the dollar, the export sector will not be able to generate growth and produce a V-shaped recovery as it did in the aftermath of the 1997 Asian financial crisis. Furthermore, macro prudential policy must be urgently implemented to prevent asset bubbles. Allowing exchange rates to restore external equilibrium can mitigate the impact of external shocks that might lead to capital inflows or instigate capital flight. Even when the baht started to depreciate against the dollar in the second half of 2015, the expansionary effect of the baht depreciation was insignificant because other emerging economies' currencies were also depreciating against the dollar. Moreover, the slowdown in economic growth in China dramatically reduced the demand for imports from the rest of the world. The contractionary income effect on the demand for Thailand's exports was stronger than the offsetting expansionary effect of currency depreciation.

The conclusion is that a small and relatively open economy such as Thailand is vulnerable to unconventional monetary policy from the US and Japan. Not only the Thai baht appreciates against the dollar, the real effective exchange rate of the renminbi also appreciates considerably. Consequently, China's exports and output growth decelerate, further reducing China's demand for imports from the rest of the world. We cannot underestimate the indirect impact of QE that exerts negative impact of growth of China's exports. While fiscal policy is not operating effectively due to Thailand's political constraints, conducting monetary policy in increasingly volatile global markets is one of the greatest challenges faced by the Bank of Thailand.

Notes

1 Consumer confidence fell for the eighth straight month in September 2015.
2 In May 2015, the Bank of Thailand cut the key policy rate to 1.5 percent and maintained that rate throughout 2015.
3 ASEAN inter-country trade is low and is therefore unable to substitute for the loss of exports to developed economies (Simarmata, 2013).

References

Amonhaemanon, Dalina, Jan Annaert, and Marc De Ceuster. 2014. "The Inflation-Hedging Ability of Real Estate Thai Evidence: 1987–2011." *Advances in Management and Applied Economics*, 4 (1): 1–15.

Baumeister, Christiane, and Luca Bernati. 2010. "Unconventional Monetary Policy and the Great Recession-Estimating the Impact of a Compression in the Yield Spread at the Zero Lower Bound." Working Paper Series No. 1258, European Central Bank.

Breedon, Francis, Jagjit S. Chadha, and Alex Waters. 2012. "The Financial Market Impact of UK Quantitative Easing." *Oxford Review of Economic Policy*, 28 (4): 702–728.

Chung, H., J. P. Laforte, D. Reifschneider, and John C. Williams. 2012. "Have We Underestimated the Likelihood and Severity of Zero Bound Events?" *Journal of Money, Credit and Banking*, 44 (Supplement): 47–82.

Fukuda, Shin-Ichi. 2015. "Abenomics: Why Was It so Successful in Changing Market Expectations." *Journal of the Japanese and International Economics*, 37: 1–20.

Harada, Yutaka, and Minoru Masujima. 2009. "Effectiveness and Transmission Mechanisms of Japan's Quantitative Monetary Easing Policy." *Japanese Economy*, 36 (1): 48–105.

Joyce, Michael, David Miles, Andrew Scott, and Dimitri Vayanos. 2012. "Quantitative Easing and Unconventional Monetary Policy – An Introduction." *Economic Journal*, 122 (564): F271–F288.

Joyce, Michael, Matthew Tong, and Robert Woods. 2011. "The United Kingdom's Quantitative Easing Policy: Design, Operation and Impact." *Bank of England Quarterly Bulletin*, 51 (3): 200–212.

Kano, Takashi, and Hiroshi Morita. 2015. "An Equilibrium Foundation of the Soros Chart." *Journal of the Japanese and International Economics*, 37: 21–42.

Kapetanios, George, Haroon Mumtaz, Ibrahim Stevens, and Konstantinos Theodoridis. 2012. "Assessing the Economy-Wide Effects of Quantitative Easing." *Economic Journal*, 122 (564): 316–347.

Kiley, Michael T. 2014. "The Response of Equity Prices to Movements in Long-Term Interest Rates Associated with Monetary Policy Statements: Before and After the Zero Lower Bound." *Journal of Money, Credit, and Banking*, 46 (5): 1057–1071.

Menon, Jayant, and Thiam Hee Ng. 2013. "Impact of Eurozone Financial Shocks on Southeast Asian Economies." *Journal of Southeast Asian Economies*, 30 (2): 179–200.

Nidhiprabha, Bhanupong. 2016. "Impacts of Quantitative Monetary Easing Policy in the United States and Japan on the Thai Economy." *The Developing Economies*, 54 (1): 80–102.

Simarmata, Djamester A. 2013. "The Effects of Global Debt Problems on the ASEAN Economy." *Journal of Southeast Asian Economies*, 30 (2): 201–212.

Sinclair, Peter, and Colin Ellis. 2012. "Quantitative Easing Is Not as Unconventional as It Seems." *Oxford Review of Economic Policy*, 28 (4): 837–854.

Tharnpanich, Nat, and John S. L. McCombie. 2013. "Balance-of-Payments Constrained Growth, Structural Change, and the Thai Economy." *Journal of Post Keynesian Economics*, 35 (4): 569–597.

Warburton, Christopher E. S. 2013. "Monetary Policy and the Trade Weighted Dollar." *Studies in Economics and Finance*, 30 (2): 80–93.

10 China's business cycle and impacts on Thailand

1. Introduction

In this chapter, we examine how acceleration and deceleration of the Chinese economy influences the Thai economy. If China's rebalancing policy increases domestic consumption and reduces investment expenditure, the Thai economy is adversely affected by China's new normal growth if imports from China slow down. There are three major channels through which the Chinese economy affects the Thai economy: the international trade volume, the exchange rate, and the price transmission mechanism. We will explore the sensitivity of Thailand's exports and imports with respect to China's business cycle. Both commodity and services exports are equally important. Thailand's tourism industry depends heavily on Chinese tourists, which are expected to exceed 12 million people by the year 2020. The exchange rate between the baht and renminbi is also important for Chinese tourists in choosing their holidays. Exports and imports elasticities will be estimated to understand how Thailand's trade sector responds to price and exchange rate changes. We will compare and contrast the trade elasticities among major trade partners: China, Japan, US, and ASEAN countries.

There is also a question whether there is a business cycle synchronization between Thailand, China, and other ASEAN countries. If so, there would be a ripple effect of China's slowdown and China's recovery through indirect effects of China's imports from ASEAN regions. The synchronization would go beyond output cycles to price levels. Thus, we would examine exchange rate policy strategy to make the best out of the growing China factor.

2. China rising

It is evident that China's real GDP increased rapidly after embracing the market economy. From 1990 to 2016, the economy expanded about seven-fold (Figure 10.1). Output growth in Japan and US paled in comparison with China. China has become a new locomotive growth engine for the world.

If the year 2000 is used as a benchmark, China's rising influence on the world trade can be seen in Figure 10.2. While the US and Japan remains major traders in the world, China has risen more rapidly and dominated the roles of the

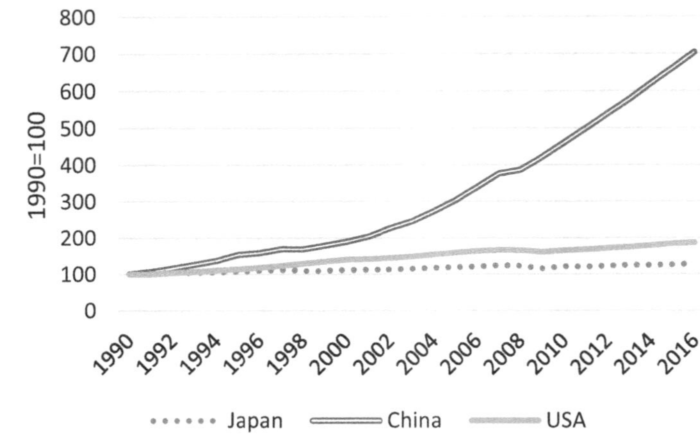

Figure 10.1 China rising: index of real GDP

Source: Federal Reserve Bank

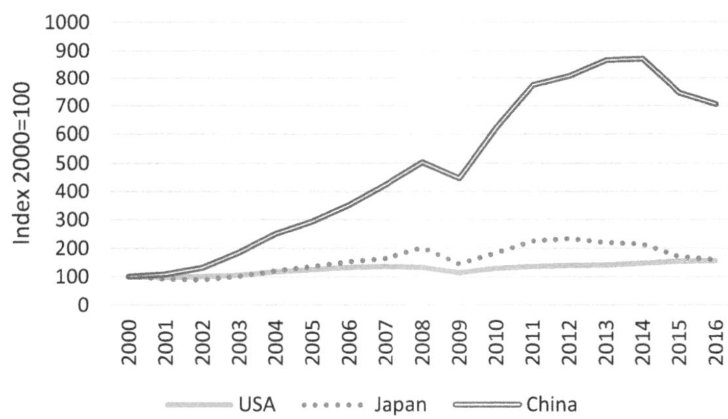

Figure 10.2 Real values of total imports from China, Japan, and the US

Source: Federal Reserve Bank

two countries. In 2009, the impact of the global financial crisis (GFC) can be observed by the shortfalls of imports from these three giant economies.

Because of China's V-shaped recovery after the GFC, China's world imports rebounded sharply after 2009. From 2015, the deceleration of China's growth resulted in the sharp decline of imports from the rest of the world, including Thailand.

For these locomotive growth engine countries, their income elasticities of demand for imports are huge (Table 10.1). More than the US, China and Japan's imports respond dramatically to changes in their output growth. Consequently,

Table 10.1 Import elasticities of the three largest world importers

	China	*Japan*	*US*
Real GDP	4.1	4.26	2.59
REER	-2.28	-0.03	0.20
Import price	7.32	5.14	0.348

Note: Estimated coefficients obtained from fully modified OLS, based on annual data from 2000 to 2016. All estimated coefficients are statistically significant, except the coefficients of real effective exchange rate (REER) for Japan and US.

Source of data: Federal Reserve Bank, Federal Reserve Economic Data (FRED)

growth swings in these three economies cause gyrating export growth to the rest of the world. Geographical diversification would not help reduce export instability, unless China can detach from the other two economies. Decoupling can take place if one of these economies effectively applies macroeconomic policy to decouple from the other two, such as when China successfully applied monetary and fiscal expansionary policy right after the GFC broke out in 2009. As a result, Asian economies were saved from a long duration of economic recession.

The loss of China's competitiveness is shown by the appreciation of the real effective exchange rate (REER), which weighs down China's exports. When China's exports decline, its imports also decline. This is why we observe that the estimated coefficient of the REER in China's imports is –2.28. For Japan and the US's import function, the estimated coefficients of the REER are not statistically significant. It should be noted that when import prices increase in China and Japan, the import values also increase. Unlike the case of the US, import price elasticities of import value function are much higher than the output elasticity. This can be explained by the fact that the two economies fundamentally rely on imported raw materials and intermediate inputs from the rest of the world. Import values in the US do not increase as fast as the increase at the price level, because the US relies less on imported raw materials and is less dependent on international trade.

The exports-led growth policy of China has been characterized by an artificially weak exchange rate and subsidized credit by a public-owned banking system. China has welcome FDI inflows in order to increase the strength of its industrial development, which has contributed to enormous capacity. When the world could no longer support of the growth of China's exports, they collapsed spectacularly after the V-shaped recovery in 2010 (Figure 10.2). Consequently, imports also declined as a result of the collapse in the network trade. The GFC caused a sharp export decline in 2009, but the sharp recovery in 2010 was not sustained. Since then both exports and imports started falling rapidly. Overcapacity among exporting firms would eventually lead to non-performing loans of banks which provided subsidized credit to the Chinese export sector.

Due to trade fragmentation, exports and imports are related. To export more, China needs to import intermediate products and raw materials. Hence, China's slowdown implies less importation from the rest of the world. Furthermore, growth deceleration implies declining growth of imported consumer products and capital goods. The percentage changes in China's exports and imports are closely related in such a way that there is a long-run relationship between them. China's imports from the rest of the world rise in line with its exports. During China's double-digit growth era, the rest of the world enjoyed high growth of exports to China.[1] The long-run relationship between exports and imports is also observed in Thailand.

In July 2015, China devalued the renminbi after its exports declined by almost 9 percent from the same corresponding period in 2014. The sharp fall was due to a strengthening US dollar and rising wages. China's devaluation was an attempt to compensate the strength of the yuan as it has been pegged with the dollar. This dramatic economic slowdown has led to substantial export shortfall in Thailand and other ASEAN countries.

3. China's influence on Thailand's economy

Trade is the most important channel that transmits impacts of China's business cycle to Thailand. As shown in Figure 10.3, Thailand's volatile growth of exports is closely related to China's imports. Although correlation does not necessarily imply causation, we shall examine if Thailand's exports are affected by China's trade volume.

In 2016, Thailand's exports to China represented 11 percent of Thailand's total exports. But Figure 10.3 suggests that Thailand's total exports moved in line with China's total imports. In 2001, the mild recession in the US resulted in a sharp drop of China's imports and Thailand's total exports. In 2009, the GFC led to a sharp contraction in China's imports and Thailand's exports. The

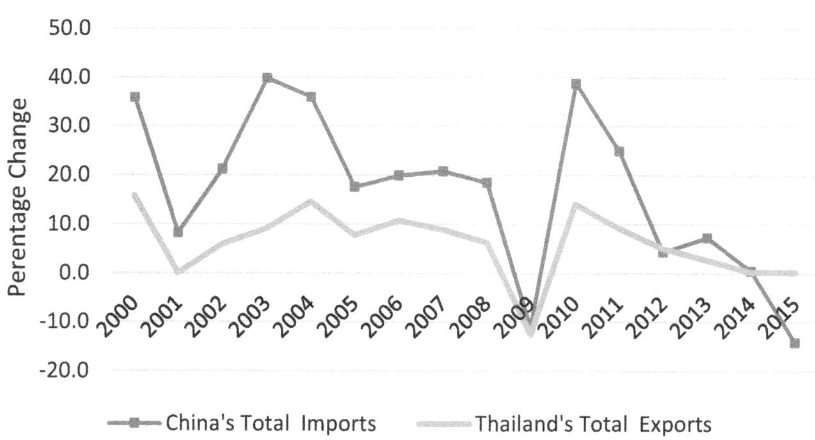

Figure 10.3 China's influence on Thailand's exports

Source: Asian Development Bank

correlates of the two series in Figure 10.3 can be attributed to a common factor. When China's trade volume experienced upturns and downturns, the peaks and troughs of Thailand's export growth rates coincide with it. The fact of the matter is that China is a huge importer from the rest of the world. When China slows down, the growth rate of the rest of the world also decelerates. The strength and weakness of the Chinese economy exerts impact directly on Thailand's exports, and also indirectly as the rest of world demands fewer imports from Thailand.

Table 10.2 shows Thailand's most important commodities in terms of value exported to China in 2016. Rubber exports to China amounted to 30 percent of the value of Thailand's rubber exports. Exports of wood and vegetables represented more than 50 percent of Thailand's exports in those categories. We can define revealed comparative advantage (RCA) with respect to China as the share of commodity X exported to China over the share of commodity X China imported from the world. An RCA index greater than unity indicates Thailand has comparative advantage; less than unity indicates comparative disadvantage. Table 10.2 shows that electrical and mechanical machinery are not produced with comparative advantage, as opposed to other primary commodities which Thailand specializes in producing.

To gauge the impact of China's business cycle on Thailand's total exports, we define business cycle as the output level which deviates from the long-run GDP path. The long-run path of China's real GDP is obtained by the Hodrick-Prescott filter. The hypothesis is that Thailand's exports depend on China's total imports (quasi-income effect) and China's business cycle. In other words, Thailand's exports level depends on China's total trade volume as well as the cyclical patter of China's output. The upturns and downturns of Chinese economic activity give rise to fluctuations in Thailand's total exports. Because of the increasing

Table 10.2 Thailand's exports to China in 2016

	Share of exports to China in Thailand's total exports, % (1)	*China's share in world imports, % (2)*	*Revealed comparative advantage index RCA (with respect to China) (3) = (1)/(2)*
All products	11	10	1.1
Rubber and articles	30	8	3.8
Electrical machinery and equipment	10	17	0.6
Machinery	8	8	1.0
Plastics and articles	23	11	2.1
Optical, photographic	31	17	1.8
Wood and articles	56	15	3.7
Organic chemicals	32	12	2.7
Vegetables	81	3	27.0

Source: International Trade Center

network trade among ASEAN countries, economic growth of ASEAN economies (excluding Thailand) should exert impact on the demand for Thailand's exports

In 2016, imports from Thailand amounted to only 2 percent of China's world imports. The estimated coefficients reported in Figure 10.4 confirm the hypothesis that China's import growth significantly impacts Thailand's exports, which are highly sensitive to China's business cycle. Deviation from China's stable growth path results in a larger swing on the demand for Thailand's exports. Nevertheless, growing reliance on interregional trade within ASEAN economies intensifies the interconnectedness of ASEAN economies through trade channels. Using the principle component of the GDP growth of four ASEAN countries—Indonesia, Malaysia, Singapore, and the Philippines—we can obtain the aggregate growth of ASEAN-4 countries. The estimated ASEAN-4 elasticity of 2.09 indicates a high sensitivity of Thailand's exports with respect to economic activities in ASEAN-4. The influence of China's economic activity is underestimated by the estimated coefficients reported in Figure 10.4, if we consider that ASEAN-4 countries have large market exposure to China.

Thailand's three largest export markets are the US, China, and Japan. In 2009, exports in these markets suffered from a shortfall due to the GFC. Thanks to China's fiscal stimuli and monetary expansion in response to the shock, the Chinese economy rebounded. Consequently, Thailand's exports to China rebounded substantially, whereas exports to Japan and the US remained stagnant (Figure 10.5).

China's elasticity of demand for imports from Thailand is 1.73, not as high as the corresponding magnitude in Japan and the US (Table 10.3). Nevertheless, the elasticity is larger than unity. On the contrary, the income elasticity in ASEAN countries is less than unity, suggesting that buoyancy in the ASEAN economy

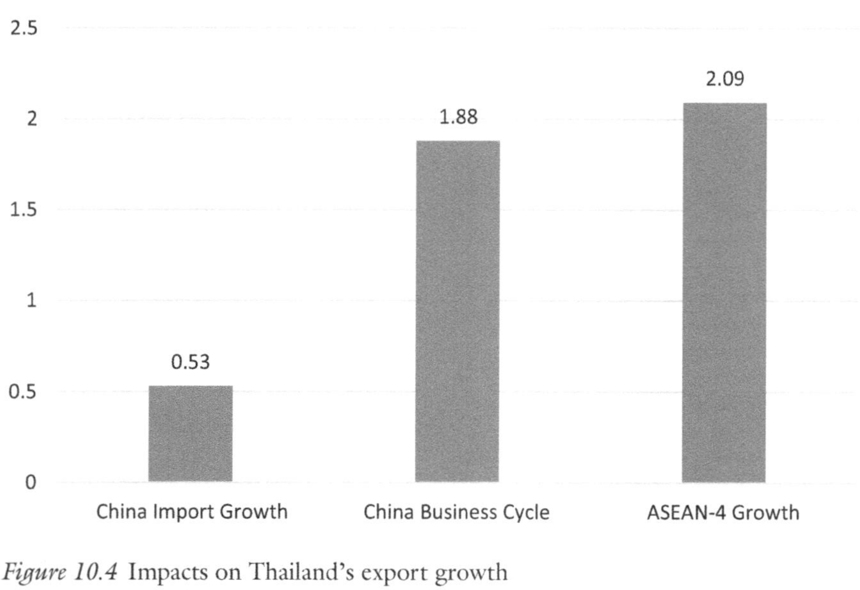

Figure 10.4 Impacts on Thailand's export growth

Source: FMOLS estimated coefficients annual data: 2003–2016

Table 10.3 Export values elasticities: 2003–2016

	China	*US*	*Japan*	*ASEAN*
Income ($)	1.73	1.29	2.11	0.60
Export price ($)	3.82	0.13	1.69	1.19

Source: Author's calculation: fully modified ordinary least squares (FMOLS)

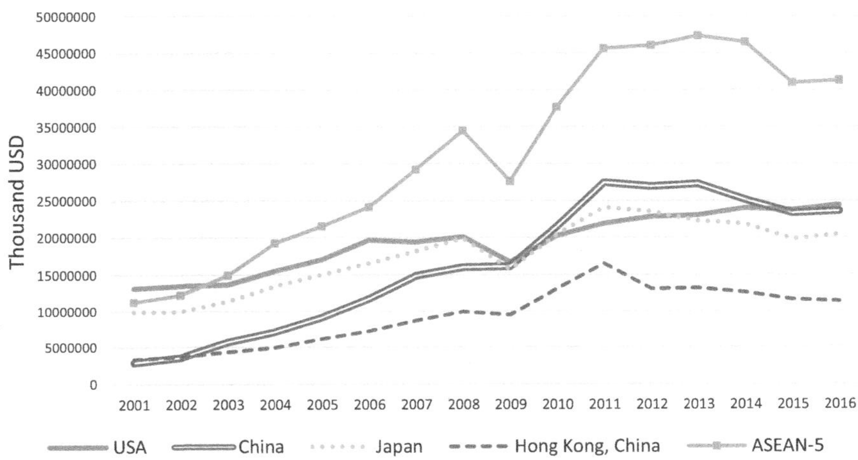

Figure 10.5 Thailand's major export markets

Source: Bank of Thailand

would not give rise to an export surge in Thailand. But when we examine the price elasticity for demand for export from China, it shows a very high degree of responsiveness of price changes, whether in terms of export prices or exchange rate movement. The strength of the substitution effect is more than twice that of the Japanese and ASEAN economies. To sum up, Thailand's exports to the Chinese market are very sensitive to China's economic cycles as well as price and exchange rate movements. Since exchange rates between the baht-dollar and the yuan-dollar are highly correlated, a slight movement between the two can lead to substantial effect on exports.

In 2009, Thailand's exports to ASEAN economies slumped due to the GFC (Figure 10.5). The ASEAN economies experience similar business cycles as exports and investment decline during uncertain times. Note that Thailand's exports to Vietnam and the Philippines remained strong compared to Malaysia, Singapore, and Indonesia, thanks to their robust economic growth. Thailand's exports to Malaysia, Singapore, and Indonesia experienced a slump after China's slowdown in 2015. These are the three economics which have a high degree of trade exposure and high dependency on China's imports.

The influence of China on Thailand's imports can be seen in Table 10.4. The value of the estimated income elasticity of Thailand's demand for imports from China is the highest among major trading partners, followed by ASEAN trading

Table 10.4 Import value elasticities from three major sources: 2002–2016

	China	*US*	*Japan*	*ASEAN*
Thailand GDP ($)	3.91	1.40	0.73	1.63
Import price ($)	0.65	0.10	1.32	0.85

Source: Author's calculation, fully modified ordinary least squares (FMOLS)

partners. It turns out that the income elasticity of the demand for imports from Japan is lower than that of the US by almost one-half. The estimated elasticity for imports from Japan is 0.73, while the estimated elasticities from other regions are greater than unity. Because of substantial Japanese FDI in Thailand, domestic markets are full of import-competing products from Japan. Unlike other regions, locally produced goods do not have stronger substitutability for imports from China, the US, and ASEAN countries. Consequently, we observe the greater than unity estimated value of import price elasticity from Japan. Other import price elasticities of import values from the China, the US, and ASEAN are less than unity.

Figure 10.6 shows that Thailand's imports from Japan declined from a peak in 2013 to a level a bit higher than the trough in 2009. The slowdown in the Thai economy is responsible for the decline.

The second channel through which China's economic activity affects Thailand is the price channel. If the baht-renminbi remains rather stable, inflation in China can be transmitted to Thailand and other ASEAN countries. Table 10.5 suggests that Thailand's imports of food items such as vegetables and fruits, clothing, textile, and footwear are dominated by China. These items, which Thailand has comparative disadvantage, have a large share in the consumer price index.

In the long run, the law of one price predicts that Thailand's inflation converges with China's. If this is the case, the role of monetary policy will be constrained by the price of traded goods, which are dictated by external forces. Nevertheless, monetary policy can still be used to affect non-traded-good prices. A more flexible exchange rate policy with less foreign exchange market intervention can enhance the central bank's ability to control inflation.

A large weight of food prices is put into Thailand's consumer price index. The global food crisis that broke out in 2008 caused a jump in the consumer price index in Thailand and China. When China and India experienced drought and rice shortage, coupled with export bans in China, rice price increased. The low interest rate prior to the GFC also led to speculation in grains. Once the global food crisis was over, the price of rice declined considerably in 2009. Inflation in Thailand and China dropped sharply but accelerated in the following 2 years before slowing down in line with China's growth deceleration. As a small and open economy, Thailand's price levels are dictated by price levels of its two major trading partners: China and the USA. As long as the baht exchange rate remains stable to the dollar and the renminbi, Thailand's inflation cannot deviate much from the two countries' inflation rates in the long run (Figure 10.7).

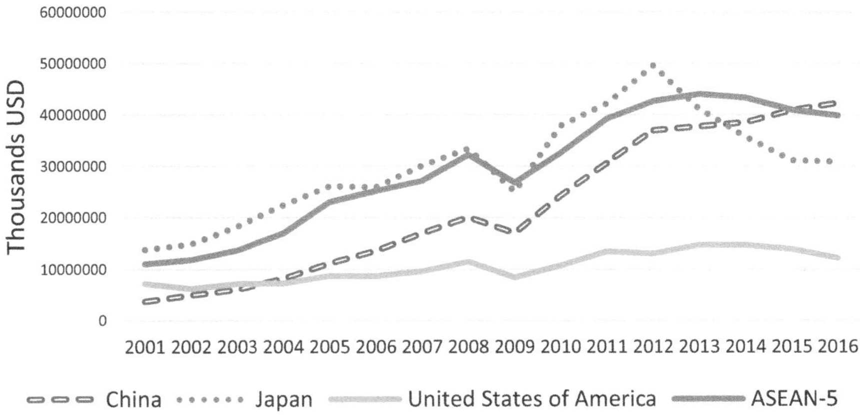

Figure 10.6 Sources of Thailand's imports

Source: Bank of Thailand

Table 10.5 Thailand's imports from China in 2016

	Share in Thailand's imports from China (1)	*Share in world exports of China (2)*	*Revealed comparative disadvantage: (1)/(2)*
All products	22	13	1.7
Electrical machinery	33	24	1.4
Machinery	28	18	1.6
Articles of iron/steel	40	20	2.0
Chemical products	27	8	3.4
Aluminum	26	13	2.0
Fruit and nuts	54	5	10.8
Apparel and clothing	54	33	1.6
Vegetables	39	15	2.6
Footwear	42	35	1.2

Source: International Trade Center

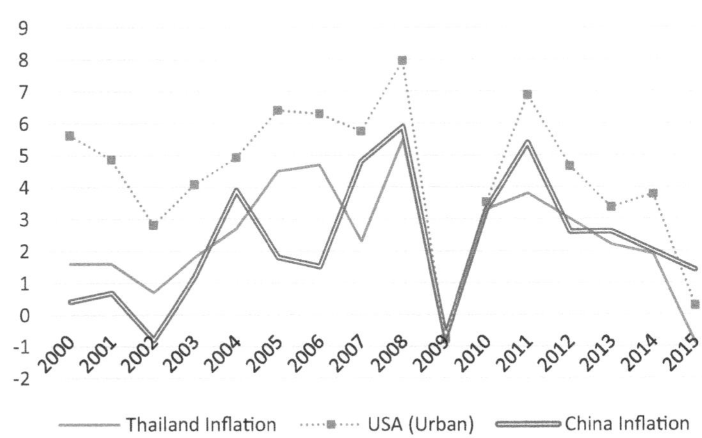

Figure 10.7 External influences on Thailand's inflation

Source: Federal Reserve Bank

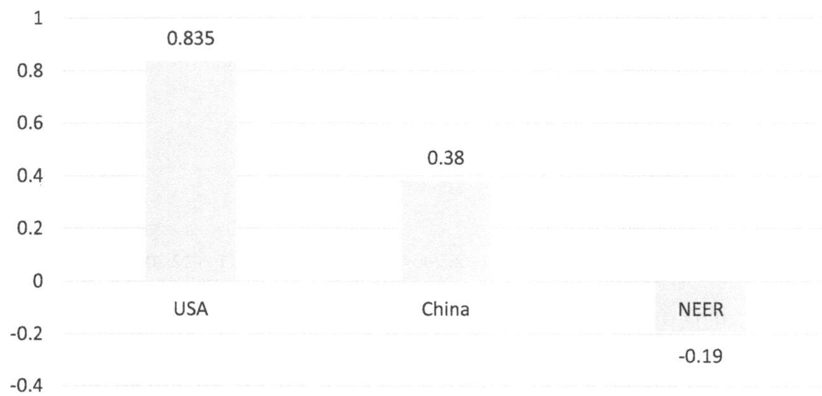

Figure 10.8 Thailand's consumer price elasticities

Source: Estimated coefficients obtained from canonical co-integrating regression (January 1994–May 2017)

Appreciation of the baht can reduce imported inflation, thereby reducing pressure on the domestic price level. A 10 percent appreciation of the NEER would lower Thailand's consumer price index by almost 2 percent (Figure 10.8). Nevertheless, the offsetting impact from exchange rate mechanism is small when compared to inflation transmitted from the US and China. A 10 percent increase in inflation in the US and China gives rise to 8.4 percent and 3.8 percent, respectively.

4. ASEAN business cycle and the China factor

Fragmentation-based specialization has become an integral part of the economic landscape of East Asia. Athukorala and Hill (2010) pointed out that dependence on this new form of international specialization is proportionately larger in ASEAN nations than in North America and Europe through the rapid integration of China into regional production networks. This development of regional production networks is a counterpoint to the popular belief that China's global integration would crowd out other countries' opportunities for international specialization.

Eichengreen et al. (2012) analyzed the incidence and correlates of growth slowdowns in fast-growing middle-income countries. They found that a larger group of countries is at risk of growth slowdowns, which are less likely in countries where the population has a relatively high level of secondary and tertiary education and where high-technology products account for a relatively large share of exports. Thus, moving up the technology ladder is vital to avoid the middle-income trap.

Utilizing data from 26 countries over the period 1981 to 2013, Cashin et al. (2017) found that a 1 percent permanent negative GDP shock in China had significant global macroeconomic repercussions, with world growth reducing by

0.23 percentage points in the short run. Moreover, there was a surge in global financial market volatility that translated into a fall in world economic growth of around 0.29 percentage points, but also had negative short-run impacts on global equity markets, oil prices, and long-term interest rates.

China, the world's second largest economy, experienced an economic growth rate fall from 10 percent in 2010–2011 to 7 percent in 2017. The economic slowdown and the renminbi depreciation had significant negative consequences on some ASEAN economies. Through vertical integration, foreign direct investment (FDI) has made ASEAN vulnerable to fluctuations in world trade volume. ASEAN business cycles are synchronized through regional trade linkages. On financial flows, synchronization of ASEAN-5 stock market has been well documented. Teng et al. (2013) reported that stock markets in traditional ASEAN countries are well aligned with economic activities in developed economies rather than those in emerging economies. Also, they do not react to external shocks originated in other ASEAN markets. Each stock market in ASEAN-5 responds differently in terms of direction and degree towards changing world economic conditions. In August 2015, the stock market crash in China led to fear of market meltdown. The China factor is significant to the rest of the world in the real and financial sectors, from commodity prices and exchange rates to stock prices.[2]

Because ASEAN economies have some degree of heterogeneity, some ASEAN countries suffer from the slowing growth of China more than others. Differences in the level of trade integration, export commodity concentration, and export market dependency lead to dissimilar impacts of China's new normal growth path. Furthermore, the quality of ASEAN institutions differs greatly from authoritarian to democratic regimes.

The quality of institutions can affect the attractiveness of FDI in ASEAN countries (Masron and Nor, 2013). The heterogeneity among ASEAN countries implies differences in the effectiveness and efficiency of macroeconomic policy in response to China's economic slowdown. China rising has caused a shift in global trade patterns, with China dominating Western markets at the expense of ASEAN countries (Napoli, 2014). Nevertheless, China's dominance does not appear to have had a significant negative effect on growth rates for ASEAN GDP, exports, or FDI stocks. While China is crowding ASEAN out of developed markets, increased Chinese demand for ASEAN imports has more than offset this effect. The impact of China's slowdown has become more pronounced in export sectors in US., Europe, and Japan. Since ASEAN's export sectors have market exposures to those markets, although they do not directly rely on China's imports, eventually they will be adversely affected by the growth slowdown in China.

We use principal component analysis to obtain the combined growth rates of four ASEAN nations: Indonesia, Malaysia, the Philippines, and Singapore. To obtain a proxy for business cycle, we employ the Hodrick-Prescott filter (HP) to separate cyclical components from the trend paths of China's GDP growth and ASEAN-4's HP growth path. Indeed, Figure 10.9 clearly demonstrates that China's business cycle is related to growth cycles in the ASEAN-4 economies.

ASEAN economies experienced similar shocks from the Asian financial crisis (AFC) in the period 1997–1998 to the GFC in the period 2008–2009. The

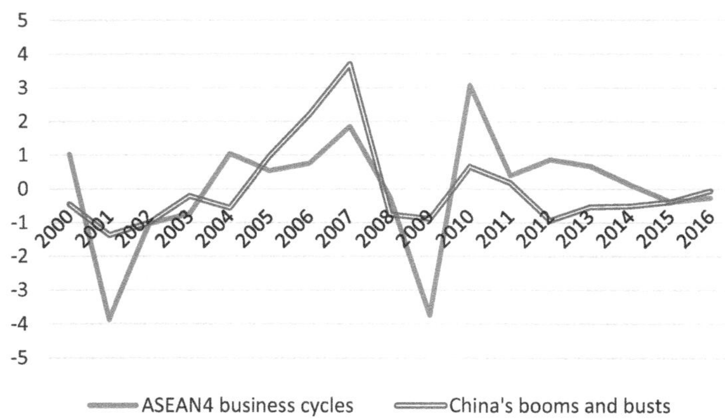

Figure 10.9 Business cycles in China and ASEAN-4 (deviation from trend growth path) (Indonesia, Malaysia, Singapore, and the Philippines)

Source: ADB Key Indicators

spectacular falls in output were followed by V-shaped recoveries. The reason behind this co-movement of output can be traced back to similar patterns of exports and investment cycles in ASEAN economies.

Not only their output growth paths are related, but also inflation, interest rates, and stock market performance tend to move together. Since the AFC, the saving-investment gaps in ASEAN economies widened as the current account deficit in the pre-AFC turned around into surplus.

China's major sources of imports are Japan and the US. Both Malaysia and Thailand are also important sources of China's imports, ranking among the top 10 countries. To gauge the impact of China's imports on ASEAN economies, we compare the movement of the business cycle in ASEAN economies with China's imports. There is a striking similarity between upturns and downturns of the two magnitudes. A long-run relationship between the two series is confirmed by the Johansen co-integration test. The Granger causality test indicates that the direction runs from ASEAN's business cycle to China's import growth. Booming economic activity in ASEAN countries can predict a rising demand for imports from China. On the contrary, there is no evidence of co-integration between the ASEAN business cycle and the US's imports. Indeed, the ASEAN business cycle is synchronized with Chin's economic activity, i.e., trade and output growth. After the establishment of ASEAN Economic Community (AEC) in 2016, with diversity in population and economic sizes, income levels, and natural resources, it is expected that synchronization of economic activity among ASEAN members will become more intensified through increasing trade within the AEC and with China.

Another explanation of the business cycle synchronization between ASEAN countries and China is related to the performance of the Japanese economy. The quantitative easing policy of the Bank of Japan, through its record US$665 billion annual asset-buying scheme, had only a limited impact on output growth and inflation. Japan suffered as exports to key trading partner China slumped. Japanese consumption spending was also sluggish as the result of an increase in sales tax in 2014. The deterioration in the global economic outlook, including developments in China, delayed Japanese companies in expanding business investment and raising wages. If the Japanese economy is in recession and deflationary mode, the demand for Japanese exports from China will also decline, implying a reduction in imported parts and components from ASEAN countries.

The synchronized business cycle is related to credit cycles and exchange rates. Mohan and Nandwa (2009) find evidence of co-integration among ASEAN interest rates and the direction of these interest rates is affected by China. This evidence points to a linkage among ASEAN-5 and China. The synchronization can also be explained by the exchange rate channel. ASEAN countries avoid currency appreciation when the dollar trends downward. China also tries to peg the yuan with the dollar. Thus, trade between ASEAN countries and China can be conducted within an environment of stable exchange rates. Tang (2014) shows that, because of the region's production networks, increasing intraregional exchange rate volatility among Asian economies leads to a decline in intraregional trade, in particular among ASEAN economies. Intraregional trade within ASEAN amounted to only 24 percent, compared to 69 percent among the European community. Ong and Habibullah (2012) found evidence of a continuous macroeconomic interdependence between ASEAN-5 and China, which led to successful ASEAN-China economic cooperation.

The macroeconomic interdependence between ASEAN and China can be demonstrated by co-movements of price levels in the two regions. Employing the principal component of ASEAN inflation rates in 10 member countries, we can obtain the proxy of inflation cycles, shown in Figure 10.10. When compared with China,

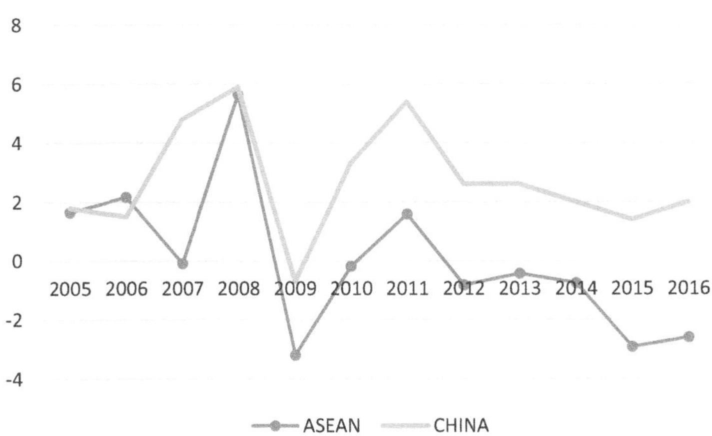

Figure 10.10 China and ASEAN inflation synchronization (principal component analysis of consumer price index)

Source: ADB Key Indicators

it is obvious price stability between China and ASEAN is related. The long-run relationship between China and ASEAN exists, with the causal relationship running from China's inflation to ASEAN's. The long-run relationship is confirmed by the Johansen co-integration test. The hypothesis that China's inflation rate does not Granger cause the inflation cycle in ASEAN countries is rejected at a statistically significant level. The global food crisis in 2008 led China to ban exports of rice and sent panic to Asia. The inflation rate temporarily skyrocketed because of food inflation, followed by export collapse caused by the GFC.

Tham and Kam (2014) employed a gravity model that captures the effects of trade in parts and components as well as final manufactured goods from ASEAN countries to China. Devadason (2011) also found evidence that China's integration in the ASEAN region increases the size of the ASEAN export market, rather than reducing ASEAN's export expansion. His results are in line with the fact that, although China has become an important export destination and an import source for individual ASEAN-5 countries, there is no reduction in intra-ASEAN-5 trade. From the literature, we can conclude that trade seems to be the most important channel explaining the synchronization between China and the ASEAN business cycle.

5. China's influence on baht exchange rates

Since correlations do not simply guarantee causation, we investigate further whether the baht REER is affected by the major world currencies (Figure 10.11). Using a dynamic least squares with double-log model based on monthly data from January 2000 to July 2017, the estimated elasticity of the REER of the baht

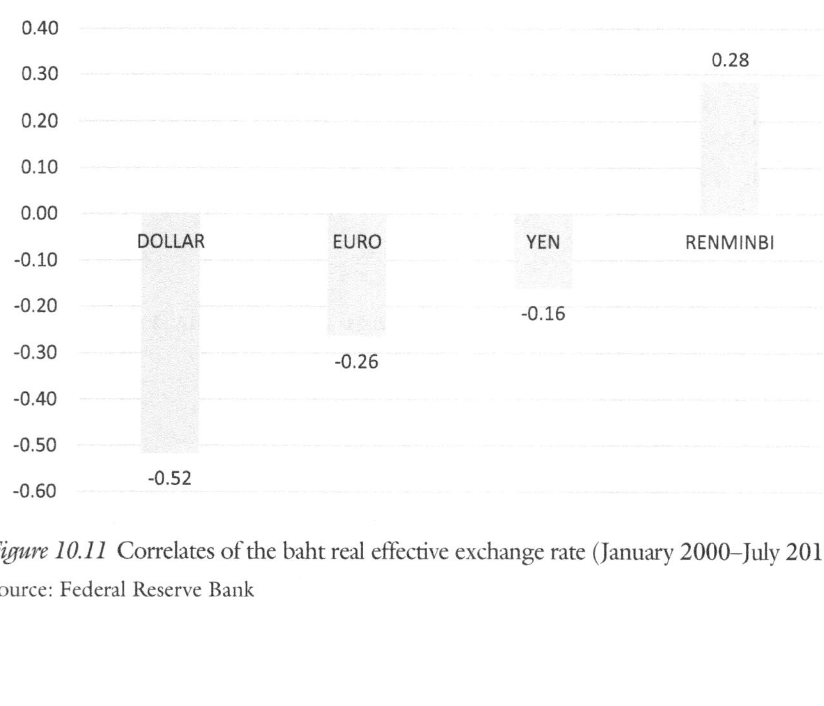

Figure 10.11 Correlates of the baht real effective exchange rate (January 2000–July 2017)
Source: Federal Reserve Bank

with respective to the REER of the dollar and the yen was -0.44. and -0.21, respectively. The model explains around 94 percent of the variations of the baht REER. Except for the euro, all estimated coefficients are statistically significant at 1 percent confidence level.

The result indicates that the movement of the baht exchange rate competitiveness is inversely related to that of the dollar and the yen. The impact of changes in the dollar REER is thrice as large as the yen. The baht gains competitiveness when the dollar and the yen lose their strength. On the other hand, the estimated coefficient of the baht REER is 0.28 with respect to the REER of the renminbi. Thus the competitiveness of the baht follows that of the renminbi, which is stronger than the yen in the opposite direction. It can be concluded that the direction of the baht is in line with the renminbi, as can be seen in Figure 10.12, showing a highly positive correlation (0.61) between the between the baht and the renminbi REERs. The renminbi REER moves in the opposite direction of world major currencies, while the baht REER exchange rate moves in line with the renminbi.

To conclude, China's exchange rate policy has an impact on the movement of the baht. This is precisely why China has a strong impact on the Thai economy, not just through income effect, but also on the substitution effect via exchange rate movements.

Hooy et al. (2015) found that the yuan real exchange rate has a significant positive impact on ASEAN's total exports to China. Parts and components exports are sensitive to yuan depreciation, because of the recent production relocations of multinational corporations (MNCs) in the ASEAN region to China and Vietnam. The huge capital inflows after QE operations prompted the ASEAN central banks to buy dollars and accumulate international reserves so as to prevent currency

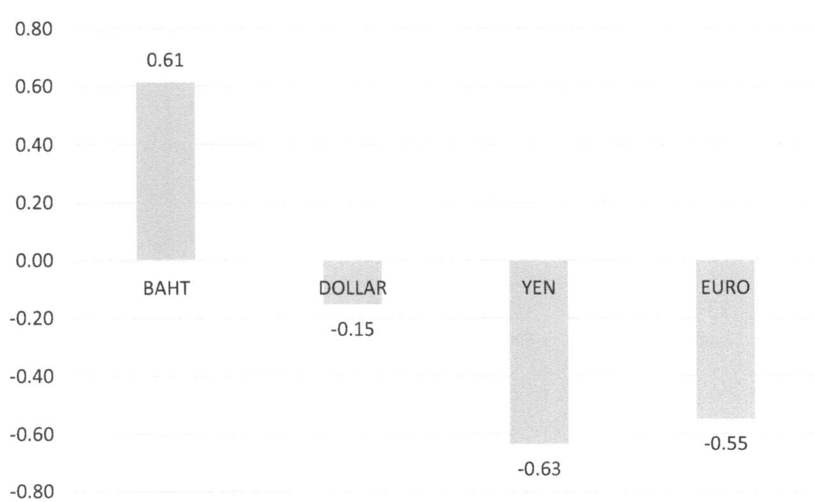

Figure 10.12 Correlates of the REER renminbi (January 2000–July 2017)

Source: Calculation based on data from Federal Reserve Bank

appreciation. By 2015, the dollar gained strength as the US economy rebounded and the anticipation of the Fed's interest rate hike led to fear of capital outflows from the ASEAN region.

Since China surprised world markets by devaluation of the yuan by 2 percent in August 2015, net capital outflows have reached $200 billion. The People's Bank of China was reported to have spent $229 billion in foreign exchange intervention to prop up the yuan in the third quarter of 2015. There was speculation that a Fed interest rate hike was imminent as the US economy approached the full employment level in the last quarter of 2015. While the economic recovery in the Eurozone is still protracted and fragile, due to a decline from Chinese imports, the European Central Bank (ECB) has maintained an easy monetary policy. As a result, the gap between the interest rates in the US and in the Eurozone widened in 2016. The dollar may continue appreciation. Because of the dollar-pegged renminbi, there could be speculation of another round of yuan devaluation. In the future, we may observer a similar pattern of Asian currency depreciation as shown in Figure 10.13. As it turned out, the renminbi and the baht appreciated against the dollar, while other ASEAN currencies, except the Singapore dollar, depreciated against the dollar. Indonesian rupiah depreciated by 1.6 percent, the ringgit 3.9 percent, the yen 6.9 percent, and the peso 9.7 percent. Note that, except for Japan, these economies grew faster than Thailand in 2017. The conclusion is once again, movement of the baht follows China's exchange rate.

Trade exposure to external shocks can be measured by the value of total trade volume relative to GDP (Figure 10.14). In general, the ratio can be thought of as a measure of the degree of openness, reflecting trade liberalization over time. The increasing trend of trade openness also implies increasing risk exposure to external shocks such as terms of trade and volume of trade shocks. Small countries

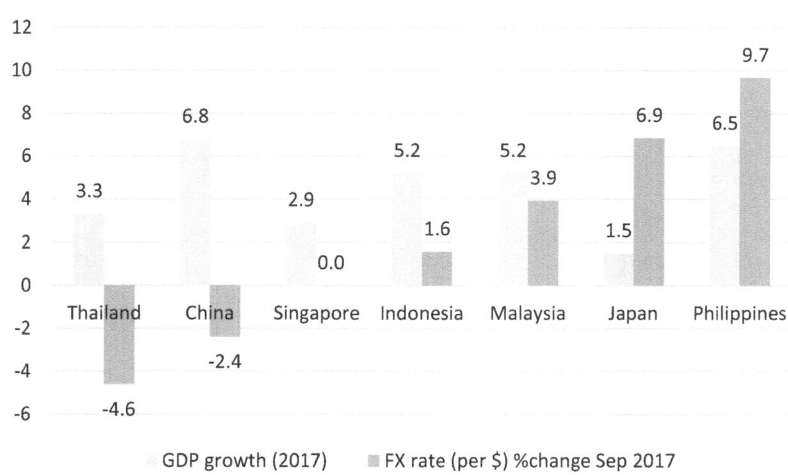

Figure 10.13 Asian GDP growth and currency movements (2017)

Source: ADB Key Indicators

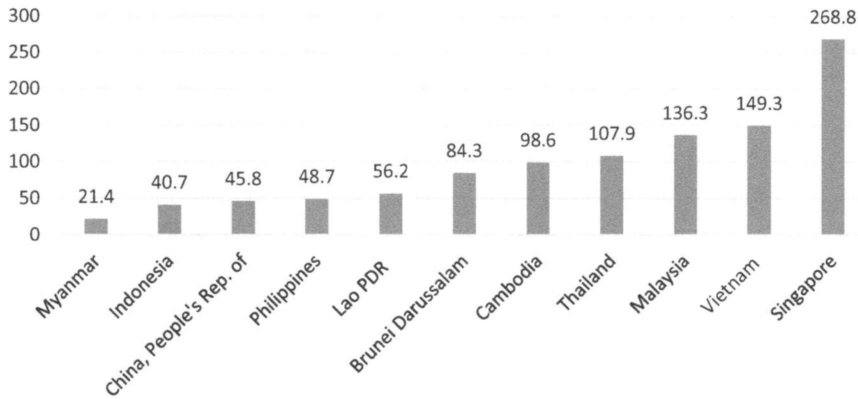

Figure 10.14 Trade exposure of Asian countries (period: average 2010–2014)

Source: ADB Key Indicators

tend to have higher trade volume relative to GDP, while large countries with large domestic markets tend to have lower exposure to trade shocks from the rest of the world. The high trade exposure ratio bodes well for the degree of trade integration, which can serve as an economic growth driver.

China's new normal growth implies that ASEAN economies' expansion should slow down. China's slowdown has reverberated around the world. Some ASEAN economies would not be affected unless public investment can be implemented effectively to induce growth via enhancing effect of public infrastructure, which can lead to crowding in effect on private and consumption expenditures. ASEAN countries are seemingly homogenous, yet each country has heterogeneity in trade exposure, export markets, and export products concentration. When China's growth declines, it adversely affects Asian countries, in particular, those with high trade exposure and heavy dependency on imports from China.

The adverse impact of China's slowdown would be less felt in the CLMV (Cambodia, Lao PDR, Myanmar, and Vietnam) countries. In particular, developing rapid transportation networks in the region can compensate for the declining volume of trade with China through increasing trade among ASEAN countries, which would be enhanced by reduced transportation costs. In addition, FDI outflows from ASEAN-5 countries into CLMV can offset declining export demand from China. Indonesia and the Philippines would suffer the least from China's slowdown. Market size and age of the population can ensure dynamism in investment and consumption expenditures. Thailand would be the laggard in the region unless a democratic government can be restored. Authoritarian rules reflect extractive institutions which create risks, and uncertainty can drive out investment and lower long-term growth. In the scenario of global growth slowdown, currency depreciation, and rising interest rates, the main challenge will be household and business sector debts that eventually impair the quality of bank loans and prolong economic recovery. The road to economic recovery will be hard unless the ASEAN community can increase its intraregional trade by improving regional connectedness through massive infrastructure investment to compensate for China's declining demand for their exports.

6. China and Thailand's tourism industry

During the time of Thailand's dismal exports growth between 2015 and 2017, Thailand's receipts from international tourists were dominated by Chinese tourists. In 2010, tourism income amounted to 10 percent of merchandise exports. In 2015, earnings from the international tourism industry increased to 18 percent. It can be said that Thailand's ability to avoid recession is partly due to the strength of the tourism industry. Figure 10.15 shows that also Thailand's tourism industry is the most competitive in the ASEAN region.

As can be seen from Figure 10.16, Bangkok has the highest rank among the world's top destination cities in 2017. There are many reasons why Bangkok attracted 20 million visitors in 2017, more than London and Paris. Cultural capital, perception of safety, and geographical locations are among the factors contributing to the competitiveness of Thailand's tourism industry. But one of the most important factors that determines the attractiveness for tourists is the cost factor. Closer distance to China means that Chinese tourists who are cost conscious in deciding holiday destinations choose to come to Thailand. Lower transportation costs also make Thailand more affordable to Chinese tourists.

The strengthening of the renminbi against the Thai baht makes holiday in Thailand cheaper than taking a holiday in Europe or Japan. Figure 10.17 shows

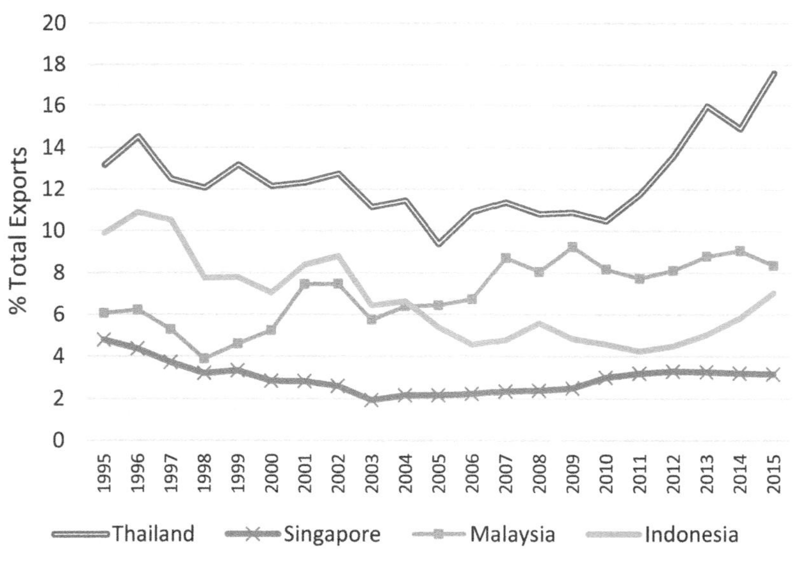

Figure 10.15 Receipts from international tourism

Source: ADB Key Indicators

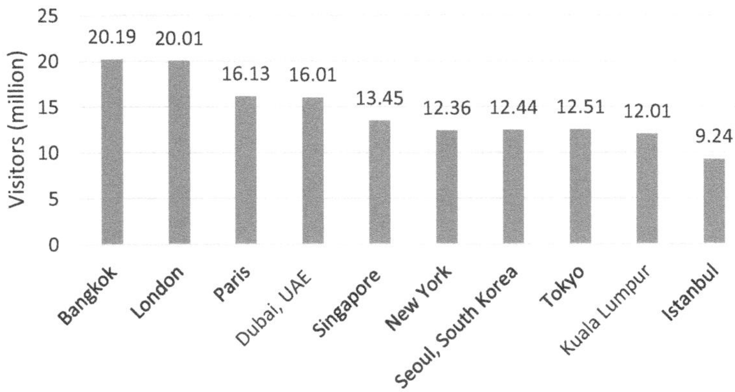

Figure 10.16 World top 10 destination cities in 2017

Source: Mastercard's 2017 Global Destination Cities Index

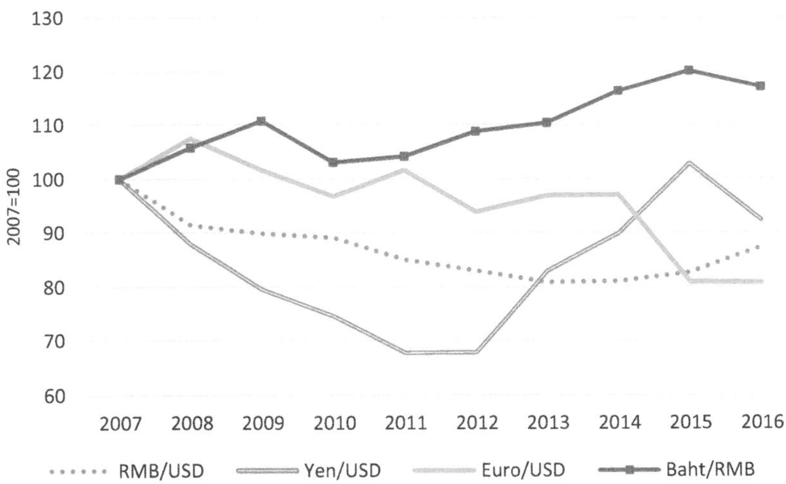

Figure 10.17 Baht depreciation against renminbi

Source: Federal Reserve Bank

that the renminbi (RMB) appreciated by 20 percent against the baht between 2007 and 2015, while the renminbi appreciated against the dollar by 20 percent. During the corresponding period, the yen and the euro also appreciated against the dollar, making a holiday in Europe and Japan more expensive.

It is evident from Figure 10.18 that Thailand's market share of Chinese tourists increased considerable from just 2 percent in 2007 to 5 percent in 2015. Moreover, the average spending of Chinese tourists in Thailand was the highest among Thailand's international visitors.

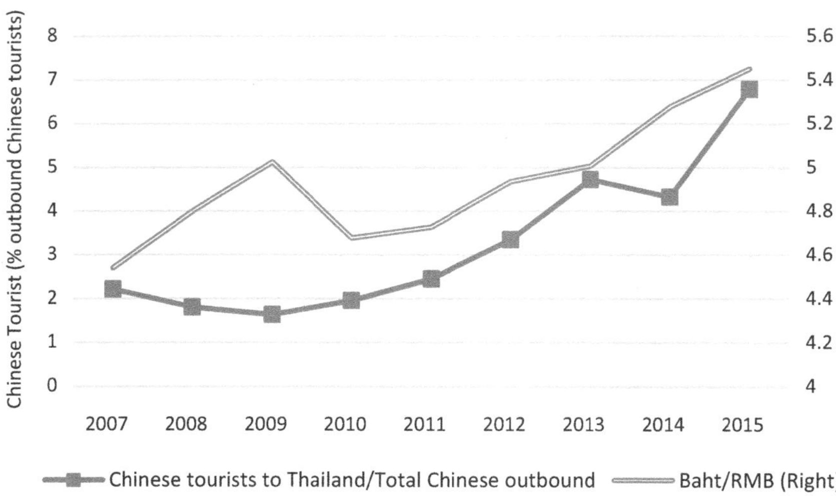

Figure 10.18 Exchange rate matters for Chinese tourists

Source: Federal Reserve Bank

The rapidly rising number of Chinese tourists was evident after the GFC in 2009. Only in 2014 did the trend of Chinese visitors remain flat. The impact of political unrest that culminated in the military coup in 2014 took a high toll on the tourism industry. By 2015, the recovery was underway. The number of Chinese tourists surpassed ASEAN visitors, thanks to the recovery of the Chinese economy. The exponential growth path of Chinese tourists offset the tourism revenue shortfalls from Europe and Japan.

There is a strong positive correlation (0.85) between the baht-renminbi exchange rate and the number of Chinese visitors to Thailand. Contrary to the renminbi, the baht-euro and baht-yen exchange rates are negatively correlated with the number of European and Japanese visitors to Thailand, at -0.78 and -0.45, respectively. The exchange rate is a factor contributing to the rising number of Chinese tourists in Thailand, but not for European and Japanese tourists. The Chinese tourists are more concerned about the cost of their holidays, while other tourists considered other factors such as safety and cultural capital offered by Thailand.

7. Concluding remarks

By 2018, China has become the second largest economy in the world, influencing the world trade and dominating the Asian emerging economies. It is shown in this chapter that fluctuations in China's economic growth rate are associated with the volatile export growth of emerging economies in Asia. Since China gained access to the WTO in the early 2000s, China business cycle has synchronized with the ASEAN business cycle. Not just output growth, ASEAN's exports, inflation, and investment synchronize with China.

Consequently, China's slowdown results in declining growth rate of exports of ASEAN countries. Thailand's exports to China are goods that Thailand has the comparative advantage, while Thailand imports goods which Thailand has the comparative disadvantage in production. In this sense, expansion of trading volume benefits both countries.

China's influence on Thailand and other emerging economies goes beyond trade volume effect. We have shown that there is macroeconomic interdependence between ASEAN and China. The baht exchange rate vis-à-vis the dollar moves in line with the renminbi, although at a lesser extent. As a result, the baht depreciates against the renminbi when the dollar appreciates against other key currencies, attracting Chinese tourists to Thailand.

By 2018, the world economy was in right conditions, buoyed by a synchronized acceleration in the US, Europe, and Asia. Exports from Thailand grew at 11.3% (year-on-year) in the first quarter of 2018, while imports increased by 16.2%. It was the fastest increase in exports in more than five years, due to the robust global demand. When China growth resumed in the third quarter of 2017, Thailand's exports rebounded, thanks to improved shipment orders and favorable commodity prices. Unless China maintains growth momentum, the Thai economy would still be growing below its potential output level.

Note

1 Except for the U.S., which has encountered enormous trade deficit with China, the escalating trade war between the two countries in 2018 stemmed from their inability to address the issue of "global rebalancing." Hill and Gochoco-Bautista (2013) argue that only those countries with large trade surplus and high trade dependent should reassess their export-led growth strategy.

2 China's Shanghai composite index rose by 150 percent (yoy) in June 2015. The sharp fall in August 2015 represented a 40 percent fall from the June peak.

References

Athukorala, Prema Chandra, and Hal Hill. 2010. "Asian Trade: Long Term Patterns and Key Policy Issues." *Asian-Pacific Economic Literature*, 24 (2): 52–82.

Cashin, Paul, Kamiar Mohaddes, and Mehdi Raissi. 2017. "China's Slowdown and Global Financial Market Volatility: Is World Growth Losing Out?" *Emerging Markets Review*, 31: 164–175.

Devadason, Evelyn S. 2011. "Reorganization of Intra-ASEAN 5 Trade Flows: The 'China Factor'." *Asian Economic Journal*, 25 (2): 129–149.

Eichengreen, Barry, Donghyun Park, and Kwanho Shin. 2012. "When Fast-Growing Economies Slow Down: International Evidence and Implications for China." *Asian Economic Papers*, 11 (1): 42–87.

Hill, Hal, and Maria Socorro Gochoco-Bautista. 2013. "Perspectives and Issues." In Hill, Hal and Maria Socorro Gochoco-Bautista (eds.) *Asia Rising: Growth and*

Resilience in an Uncertain Global Economy. Cheltenham, UK and Northampton, MA: Elgar; Manila: Asian Development Bank, 3–45.
Hooy, Chee-Wooi, Law Siong-Hook, and Chan Tze-Haw. 2015. "The Impact of the Renminbi Real Exchange Rate on ASEAN Disaggregated Exports to China." *Economic Modelling*, 47: 253–259.
Masron, Tajul Ariffin, and Eliza Nor. 2013. "FDI in ASEAN-8: Does Institutional Quality Matter?" *Applied Economics Letters*, 20 (1–3): 186–189.
Mohan, Ramesh, and Boaz Nandwa. 2009. "Examining Interest Rate Linkages Among ASEAN-5, China and India." *ASEAN Economic Bulletin*, 26 (2): 174–179.
Napoli, Christopher. 2014. "China's Economic Rise: Implications for ASEAN Trade Flows." *Journal of Southeast Asian Economies*, 31 (3): 345–360.
Ong, Hway-Boon, and Muzafar Shah Habibullah. 2012. "Is China Compatible With ASEAN-5? A Gradual Cointegration Analysis." *Journal of Economic Studies*, 39 (3–4): 356–367.
Tang, Hsiao Chink. 2014. "Exchange Rate Volatility and Intra-Asia Trade: Evidence by Type of Goods." *World Economy*, 37 (2): 335–352.
Teng, Kee Tuan, Siew Hwa Yen, and Soo Y. Chua. 2013. "The Synchronization of ASEAN-5 Stock Markets with the Growth Rate Cycles of Selected Emerging and Developed Economies." *The Journal of Applied Economic Research*, 7 (1): 1–28.
Tham, Siew Yean, and Andrew Jia Yi Kam. 2014. "Re-Examining the Impact of ACFTA on ASEAN's Exports of Manufactured Goods to China." *Asian Economic Papers*, 13 (3): 63–82.

11 Fiscal policy for long-term growth and stability

1. Introduction

Most Asian countries which suffered from the global financial crisis between 2007 and 2009 employed expansionary fiscal policy to counteract the shortfall in exports. Thailand's exports continued increasing in 2008 despite the impact of the global economic slowdown that began in 2007. The temporary commodity boom and the food price crisis gave rise to such impressive performance of Thai exports in 2008. From 2000 to 2008, there was an increasing trend of Thailand's exports. However, when the global financial crisis finally hit the Thai economy, exports declined sharply in 2009. This was also the period when domestic investment and consumer spending were subdued. Thus, the contraction of external and internal demand reduced real GDP growth to 2.3 percent in 2009, the lowest growth rate since the massive output contraction of 10 percent in the aftermath of the Asian financial crisis (AFC). The 1998 recession was short-lived, despite the massive destroyed value of financial assets during the meltdown of financial institutions. It was the rapid growth exports caused by currency depreciation that restored growth. Since the AFC did not spread to the rest of the world, Thailand was able to export its way out of recession through currency devaluation.

But the global economic environment was different in 2009, when developed economies cut down imports from Asia, as households in high-income countries were trying to restore wealth through raising savings and subsequently reducing imports. Furthermore, appreciation of the baht caused by quantitative easing in the US made it difficult for Thai exporters to reap the benefits they used to obtain in the aftermath of the AFC. During the 2009 global financial crisis episode, many Asian scholars started questioning the traditional model of export-led growth, arguing that Asian countries should depend less on exports and pay more attention to the role of domestic demand to minimize the impacts of the world business cycle. Monetary policy can be conducted through changing the domestic interest rate, but it has to be concerned with impact on capital flows and exchange rates. This is why fiscal policy is called upon during periods of sluggish demand growth. In developing countries where monetary policy instruments have some limitations, fiscal stimulus is the only policy measure available to compensate declining export demand.

2. Fiscal stance and macroeconomic variables

Whether the size of budget deficit or surplus differs from the planned level depends largely on how the budget interacts with output and price levels. If the planned budget surplus causes output contraction, the actual size of the surplus budget can differ significantly from the planned level. High inflation may lead to burgeoning budget deficit if the government insists on maintaining the level of real public spending. Thus, macroeconomic variables such as the price and output levels interact with fiscal stance.

The boom in the early 1990s was followed by growth collapse after the 1997 financial crisis. It took 7 years before the output regained its pre-shock growth path in 2004. Since then output had risen above the trend path until it sharply declined after the global financial crisis in 2008.

The impact of the global financial crisis has previously been overestimated. The robust growth of India and China generated strong export demand for goods from Thailand. A V-shaped recovery of exports was observed in 2010. The sustainability of export recovery depends on the strength of economic recovery in high-income countries. If developed economies experience prolonged recession, developing countries must brace for another round of export contraction and they must increase the volume of trade among themselves. There is a limited possibility for having a market substitution between advanced economies and Asian emerging economies, because a large part of the final import demand for manufactured goods originates from developed areas.

The role of domestic demand must be emphasized. In particular, if domestic investment and consumption are weak as a result of uncertainties and pessimism, the government must act immediately and stimulate the economy by appropriate strength of expansionary fiscal and monetary policy. However, when the world economy recovers, public spending must return to its normal pattern observed before the global financial crisis. The collapse of exports in 2009 can be thought of as a temporary shock. The long-term output level should not be affected once exports return to normalcy. The export shortfall in 2011 was mainly due to the supply shocks caused by floods that disrupted manufacturing production. However, in 2014 Thailand's exports grew less than 1 percent, which was the result of global economic downturn. Because of political turmoil and the 2014 military coup, investment uncertainty and pessimistic consumers further aggravated contraction in domestic demand

In the past decade, the Thai government did not employ fiscal policy to stabilize growth and price stability. The size of the government, measured by public spending, between 1996 and 2013, averaged 18.9 percent of GDP, while the average public revenue was 16.6 percent. During this period, the average budget deficit was 2.4 percent of GDP, which was relatively small and manageable. The size of the deficit was reduced from 4.2 percent between 1966 and 2003 to 1.3 percent on the average between 2004 and 2013.

As Figure 11.1 illustrates, the size of public spending relative to GDP increased gradually after 2006. There was no sign of countercyclical movement, unlike the

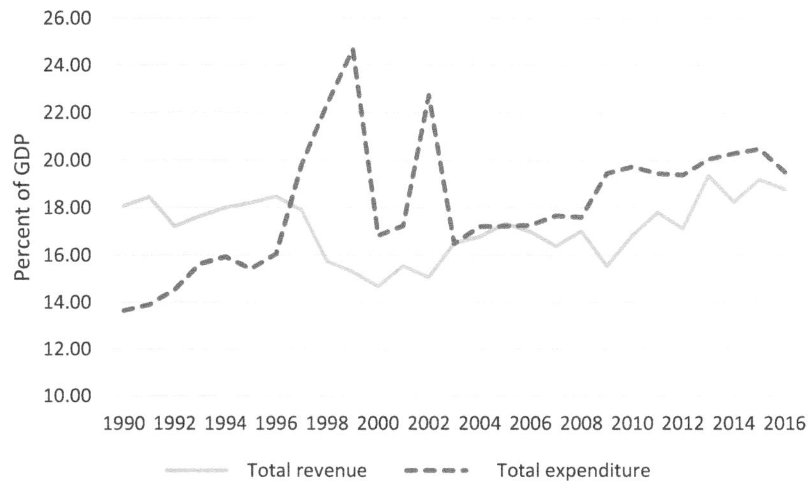

Figure 11.1 Public expenditure and revenue: 1990–2016

Source: Bank of Thailand

period between 1996 and 2002. During this period, there was a discretionary policy applied in response to economic recession in 1998, 2001, and 2009. In 1999, the spike in public spending was attributed to spending on economic services. The sharp increase in 2002 was due to increases in general public services. In 2009, a defense spending hike raised public spending to 19.6 percent of GDP. It is important to analyze what type of public spending categories gives the highest expansionary impact.

According to Afonso et al. (2010), government spending and revenue can be decomposed into three components: responsiveness, persistence, and discretion. Using data from 132 countries, they concluded that fiscal policy is more persistent than responsive to economic conditions, implying that the authorities have less leeway in the short run to curb spending. Less discretion and responsiveness reflect weak institutional capability. In the case of Thailand, the government was incapable of employing countercyclical policy measures, which were limited by political constraints such as unstable governments and political turmoil. However, the lack of discretionary fiscal policy can be mitigated by the working of automatic fiscal stabilizers.

Thailand's fiscal balance, measured as a percent of GDP, seems to be countercyclical (Figure 11.2). Public revenue might be countercyclical due to automatic tax stabilizers. The AFC in 1998 and the global financial crisis in 2009 resulted in growth collapses. The booms were associated with surplus budget, as tax revenue increased in line with economic activity. On the other hand, growth collapse led to a decline in tax revenue, resulting in budget deficit.

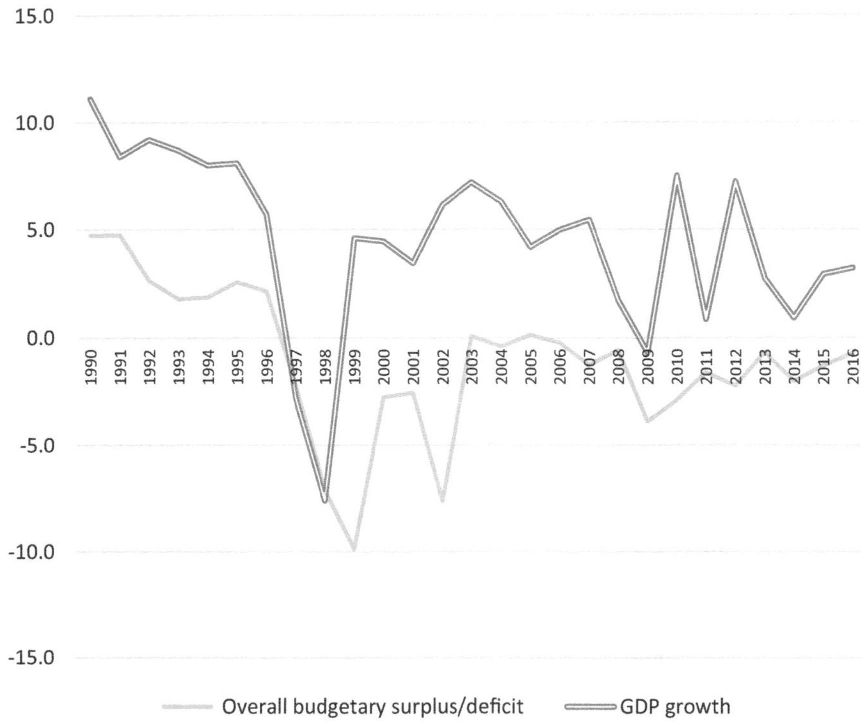

Figure 11.2 GDP growth and fiscal surplus

Source: Bank of Thailand

A severe contraction in aggregate demand led to a deep recession in 1998, causing revenue reduction and subsequent budget deficit. Similarly, in 2009, a mild recession resulted in enlarged budget deficit, which is a stabilizing feature of countercyclical fiscal policy. With growth acceleration, budget deficit tends to decline.

Hernandez and Moral-Benito (2013) argued that successful fiscal consolidation to reduce budget deficits and public debt requires growth-enhancing policies and cuts in public wages. If the government raises public wages in line with rising price levels, it will be difficult to curb budget deficit. It is not surprising to find that government spending rises as a result of rising price levels. In general, price stability is not a major threat to the Thai economy, where inflation from 1977 to 2017 averaged 4.2 percent, reaching an all-time high of 24.6 percent in June of 1980 and a record low of –4.38 percent in July of 2009. Inflation exerts its impact on public revenues and expenditures. Excluding years of unusually high inflation, budget balance seems to move in line with inflation.

From 1990 to 2012, fiscal surplus was negatively related to current account surplus. Current account deficit brings in more customs revenues as imports

Table 11.1 Correlates of fiscal surplus (percent GDP)

	Growth	*Inflation*	*Current account surplus*
1990–2012	0.66	0.55	-0.83
1990–1999	0.81	0.21	-0.87
2000–2012	0.44	0.65	-0.53
2013–2016	0.88	-0.11	0.06

Source: Calculation based on data provided by the Bank of Thailand

increase, implying that a deteriorating external balance does not exacerbate the fiscal position. Strong GDP growth leads to higher imports and current account deficit. As a result, high GDP growth is associated with strengthening fiscal position, with a correlation coefficient of 0.81 in the period 1990–1999 and 0.44 in the period 2000–2012 (Table 11.1). The decline in the correlation coefficient reflects continued trade liberalization which lowered tariff rates. Inflation rate is positively related to the size of fiscal surplus, with a correlation coefficient of 0.65 in the period 2000–2012. Inflation can lead to higher tax revenues through bracket creeps and higher corporate income tax revenues.

Although the correlates between fiscal surplus and output growth remained high in the period of 2013–2016, the strong positive correlations between fiscal surplus and inflation rate and negative correlation with current account surplus totally disappeared. This could be attributed to the flattening of the Phillips curve, when there is little trade-off between inflation and unemployment. China's slowdown, worldwide low inflation, and regional trade integration were the culprits. The crucial role played by automatic stabilizers was diminished. Before 2013, high inflation was associated with fiscal surplus. Similarly, current account deficit brought high customs tax revenue, leading to a negative correlation between current account deficit and fiscal position. This stabilizing feature of the interaction between fiscal policy stance and external imbalances and inflation has come to an end. The implication is that fiscal policy must be proactive. It cannot rely heavily on built-in stabilizers as it did in the past.

3. Analysis of public spending

Agnello et al. (2013), employing a panel data from 132 countries between 1960 and 2008, find that changes in government consumption lead to crowing-in effects in the short run, but crowding-out effects dominate the expansionary effect of fiscal spending in the medium run. This empirical evidence supports the hypothesis proposed by Barro (1990) that growth and saving rate fall with an increase in tax-financed government spending. However, the hypothesis of the negative impact of fiscal spending on output is far from being conclusive. DeLong and Summers (2012) argue that increased government purchases would be neither offset by the monetary authority, raising interest rates nor neutralized by supply-side bottlenecks. Moreover, expansionary fiscal policy is likely to be self-financing. Kandil (2009) shows that private consumption in developing countries depends on government spending due to the dominant role of government in providing employment. Crowding-out effect appears more prevalent in advanced countries. In addition, evidence from 10 developing countries in Asia shows that discretionary fiscal policy can effectively stimulate output. A deficit financed by tax cut can have positive impact on output (Jha et al., 2004). This evidence is in sharp contrast to Ricardian Equivalence proposition; thus there is a scope for countercyclical tax adjustments in Asia, so long as fiscal sustainability is not compromised.

The crowding-out effect from public spending implies that the expansionary impact of fiscal spending is offset by a rise in the interest rate, which would result in a fall in private spending. If public spending is money financed, rather than bond financed, the increased public expenditure would not lead to a rise in the interest rate. The fiscal multiplier associated with higher money supply would be larger than when the deficit budget is financed by issuing bonds. However, there can be a crowding-in effect of public spending. This is the case when public spending is complementary to private spending. For example, investment in public infrastructure encourages the private sector to invest more because more public infrastructure raises the expected rate of return of private investment through raising expected sales and because the new infrastructure reduces production cost in the private sector.

After using the Hodrick-Prescott filter (HP) to remove cyclical variations from actual values of public expenditure, private consumption, and private investment, we obtain the trend values of these magnitudes. Figure 11.3 shows

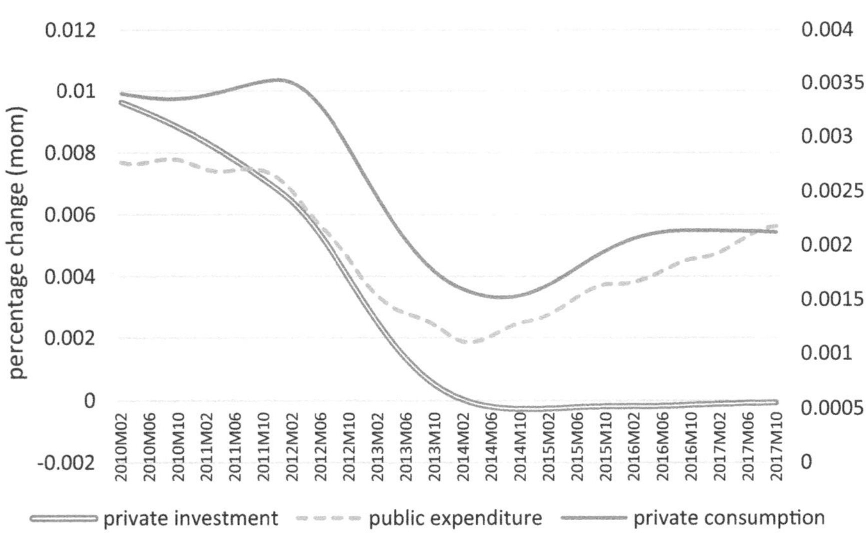

Figure 11.3 Public and private expenditures

Source: Bank of Thailand

month-on-month percentage changes of the trend magnitudes. From 2010 to 2017, public expenditure moved in line with private consumption. From 2010 to 2014, there was a sharp fall in private investment, which remained stagnant from 2014 to 2017. An increase in public spending did not stimulate growth in private investment and consumption. It is evident that the slowdown of Thailand's growth stemmed largely from contraction in private investment growth.

Interestingly, public expenditure also moved in line with private consumption. From Figure 11.3, we cannot make any definite conclusions about the crowding-out or crowding-in effect of public spending. Not until the third quarter of 2014 did the public spending started to rise. From 2011 to 2013, the Thai government was unable to use fiscal policy to offset the fall in private spending. Political unrest and unstable governments had precluded the government from effectively using fiscal expenditure to counteract the economic slowdown. Low-quality institutions in the form of ineffective government and a lack of rule of law hamper effective stabilization policy.

There is a negative correlation between changes in public expenditure and private investment trends from 1993 to 2006 (Figure 11.4). The investment trend is represented by the amount of new registered capital. Fiscal spending increased and decreased to counteract fluctuations in private investment (as measured by the amount of new registered capital). Nevertheless, after the 2006 coup, public spending became procyclical rather than countercyclical. In particular, new registered capital reached its peak in September 2011. The sharp drop in new investment was also followed by a sharp decline in public expenditures, rather than a boost in spending which could have offset declining in economic activity.

It can be seen from Figure 11.5 that between 2010 and 2017 government spending is complementary to private expenditure spending and negatively related to the price rises. Thus, public spending is procyclical. Public expenditure responds vigorously to private consumption, with an elasticity of 1.66. This can be explained by the fact that increased consumption raises tax revenue, which

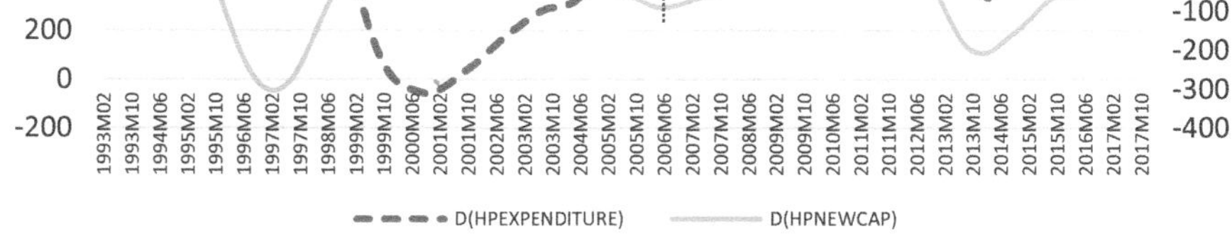

Figure 11.4 Countercyclical and procyclical public spending

Source: Bank of Thailand

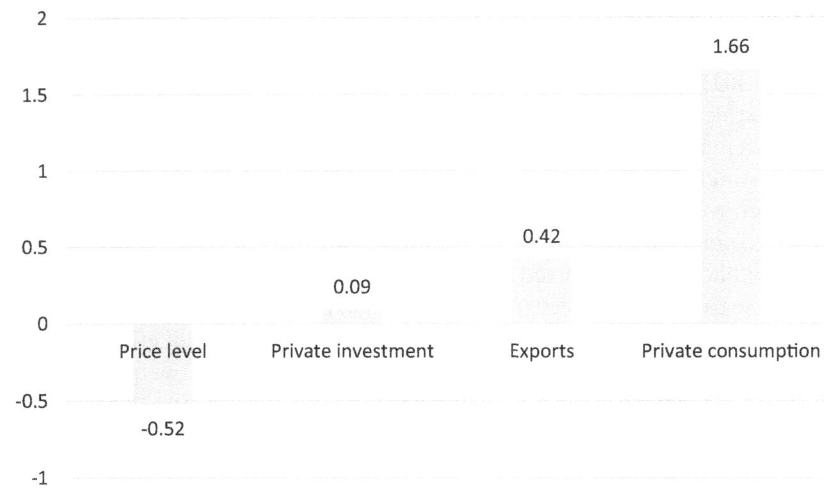

Figure 11.5 Response of public spending (2010–2017)

Source: FMOLS estimated elasticities based on monthly data 2000–2017

in turn gives rise to public revenue. The increased revenues enhance the ability of the government to spend more. Similarly, rising exports and private investment permit the government to spend more. Nevertheless, public expenditure response to surges in exports and private investment is not large. The reason why private consumption produces a stronger response from the government is the fact that private consumption is the largest component of aggregate demand. High consumption generates output expansion, which results in higher tax revenues, enabling the government to spend more. In addition, value-added tax is based on consumption expenditures. Since the consumption elasticity of public expenditure is greater than unity, a fall in private consumption implies a fall in public spending. Viewed in this light, fiscal expenditure can be destabilizing since public and private expenditure move up and down together over business cycles.

When price level rises, public spending declines. This has nothing to do with the government's desire to reduce pressure on the price level. Due to the fact that inflation reduces the purchasing power of the government, some public procurement cannot be implemented due to high cost. Cost overrun leads to delay of public spending. The fact that public spending in real terms declines during inflation implies that there will never be inflationary pressure from government spending, because the government does not try to maintain public spending in real terms.

The causation runs both ways from between public and private spending, but the impact of public spending lasts longer due to the multiplier effect. Rather than measuring the multiplier effects on output, we examine the short-run and long-run impacts of public spending on private investment and output. Figure 11.6

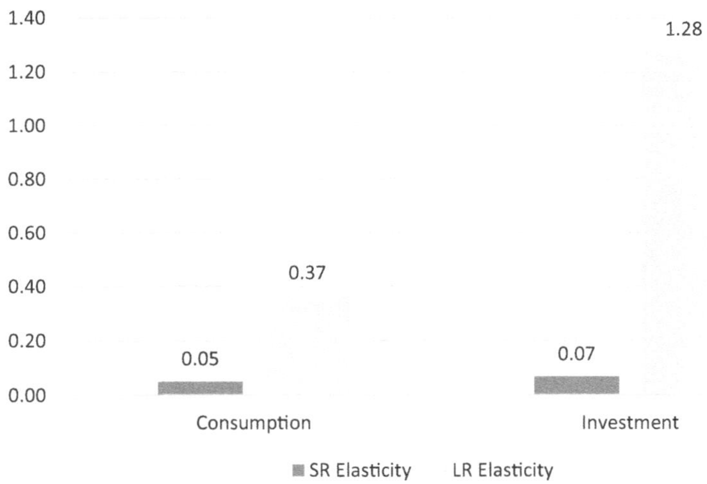

Figure 11.6 Short-run and long-run impact of public spending

Source: FMOLS estimates based on monthly data 2000–2017

provides the estimated coefficients from double-log linear equations. In the short run, the impacts of public spending on private consumption and investment is small and they are not statistically different from each other (between 0.05 and 0.07). Nevertheless, the long-run multiplier effect on investment (1.28) is larger than consumption (0.37). Seen in this light, public spending can mitigate the contractionary effect of global slowdown.

We can conclude that fiscal policy stimulus has a stronger effect on investment than consumption. Private consumption also depends on household debt and liquidity constraints, aside from the propensity to consume, which varies according to target groups of public spending. Furthermore, there is no evidence of a non-Keynesian effect on fiscal policy, where public spending leads to a contractionary impact on output. The presence of a non-Keysinan effect seems a remote possibility, because Thailand's level of public debt is relatively low. We can attribute the low level of public to rule of fiscal discipline. The issue of sustainability of public debt will be discussed in a subsequent section.

4. Automatic fiscal stabilizers and dynamic adjustments

By removing cyclical components from actual public spending and revenue, and by utilizing monthly data from January 1993 to November 2017, we can obtain the long-term trends of public expenditure and revenue. Using the first difference of these trend variables, we can approximate patterns of fiscal stance, which reflect the outcome of both discretionary fiscal policy and automatic fiscal stabilizers (Figure 11.7). Expressed in percentage, Thailand fiscal stance reflects

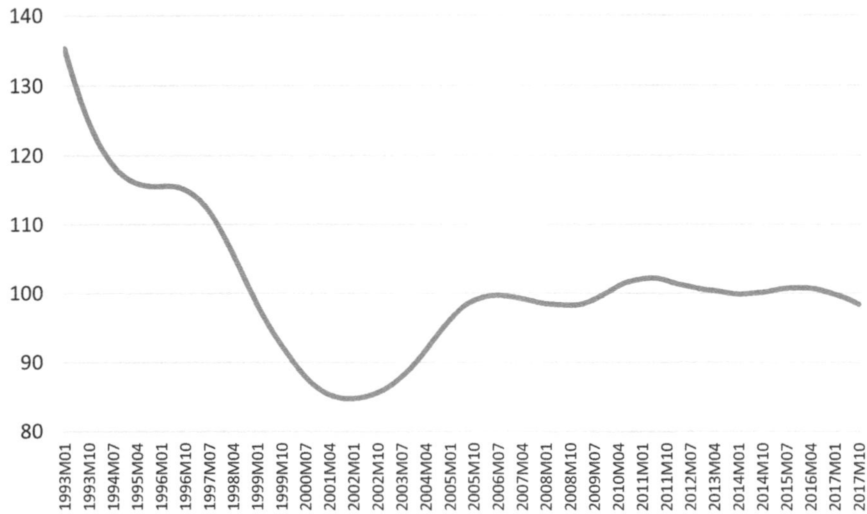

Figure 11.7 Fiscal stance: ratio of public revenue to expenditure trend values (percent)
Source: Bank of Thailand

the working of automatic stabilizers. During the boom years prior to the 1997 financial crisis, revenue exceeded expenditure more than 30 percent. However, the trend declined as the economy went into recession. Nevertheless, expenditure rose faster than the revenue when the economy rebounded. By 2006, the ratio of revenue to expenditure seemed to stabilize somewhat. This implies that from 2014 to 2017, the government failed to use discretionary fiscal policy to offset the collapse of growth in private expenditures.

When considering the movements of revenue and expenditure, the two series moved together closely (Figure 11.8). There is a long-run relationship between revenue and expenditure. The causation runs both ways. Higher revenues permit the ability to spend for the government, while higher public spending creates expansion output, providing higher tax bases. Hence, there will never be a runaway budget deficit, as financing is done through tax and bond financing. Public borrowing from the Bank of Thailand is minimal. Government bonds held by the central bank are small; hence the government does not finance budget deficits by printing money.

There is also a possibility that fiscal stimulus is self-financing in the long run, if fiscal stimulus packages can effectively raise the revenue. Ultraconservatism in conducting fiscal policy limits potential growth of the economy. Preoccupation with a low level of public debt leads to the opportunity cost of attaining a high income level.

Discretionary fiscal policy can be delayed because of implementation lags caused by a lengthy parliamentary process of budget approval. If a country has

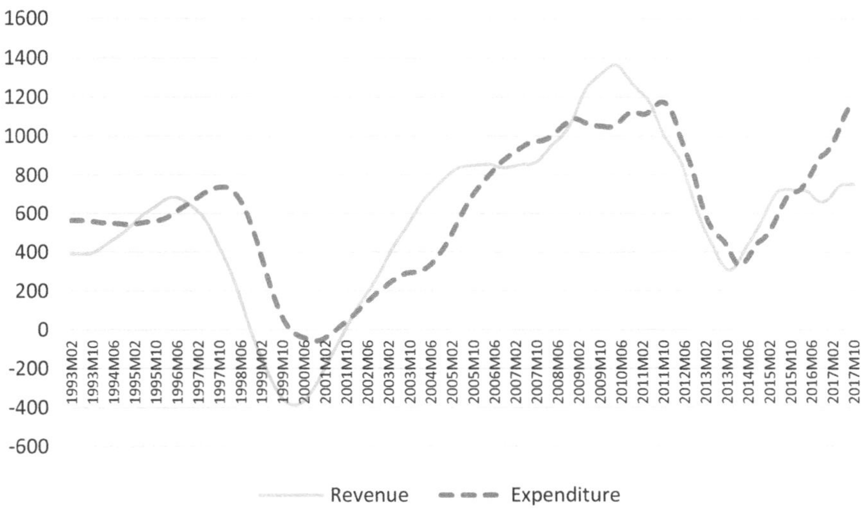

Figure 11.8 Changes in long-term public expenditure and revenue (changes from the previous month)

Source: Bank of Thailand

established fiscal automatic stabilizers, fiscal policy can be stabilizing, because it can do away with the long budgetary process.

Employing monthly data, whose cyclical components have been removed by HP filter, we can obtain the trends of surplus and output. Figure 11.9 depicts changes in the trend values of the two series. The first difference is used in order to remove spurious relationship between the level of budget surplus and output level. Similar to the observations of annual data in Figure 11.2, there is a strong correlation between output expansion and budget surplus. The output path shown in Figure 11.9 is represented by monthly data of the manufacturing production index. This confirms the earlier conjecture from annual data that the built-in-stabilizer operates to provide stability for fiscal position.

Fiscal stimulus can also be carried out through tax reduction in addition to increased spending, but the impact of the tax cut on public debt will be larger than increased spending. In theory, tax-financed budget deficit is less expansionary than bond-financed budget deficit. If bonds are net wealth and wealth has a significant impact on private consumption, bond-financed budget deficit can lead to more expansionary impact because bond holders will start spending more if they feel wealthier by holding more government bonds. The Thai military government attempted to sell government bonds to finance the budget deficit. Since some of the proceeds from selling government bonds will be used to increase current expenditures, instead of capital expenditures, there is also an issue of the burden of public debt for future generations.

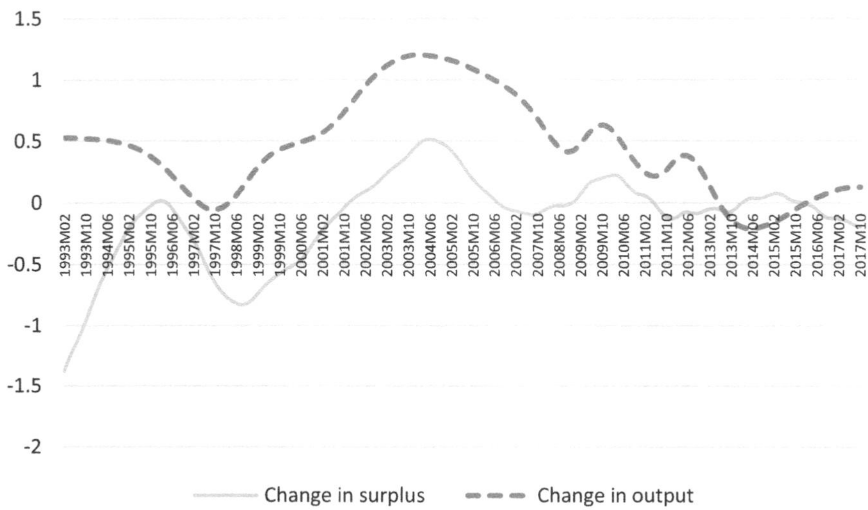

Figure 11.9 Budget surplus and GDP growth

Source: Bank of Thailand

Let us examine the role of automatic stabilizers in both taxation and expenditure when they change in response to changes in output and prices. Co-integration analysis indicates the existence of long-run relationships between fiscal variables, output, and the price level.

We obtain estimated coefficients from running a double-log regression of revenue and expenditure on manufacturing production and consumer price indexes. It takes longer for expenditure than revenue to respond to changes in prices and output. Twelve months are required for the response of revenue to changes in output and price level, while it takes 30 months before expenditure reacts to changes in output and the price level. A lengthy budgetary process causes longer adjustment of public spending, while revenue responds faster, although with a 12-month delayed adjustment due to a lag in tax collection. Both revenue and expenditure respond more to changes in the price level. The price elasticities range between 1.74 and 1.79 (Figure 11.10). Because of the value of the elasticities are greater than unity, fiscal variables respond more to price changes than output changes. Note that the price elasticity of spending is a bit higher on the expenditure side than revenue. It implies that inflation can make the budget deficit higher.

When examining the output elasticity, both revenue and expenditure elasticities are less than unity (Figure 11.10). The former is greater, implying that output expansion would tend to raise budget surplus. When output contracts, budget would tend to deficit because revenue elasticity (0.61) is higher than expenditure elasticity (0.34). This is a nice feature of automatic stabilizers. The main finding from this analysis is that Thailand's fiscal sustainability can be attributed to the

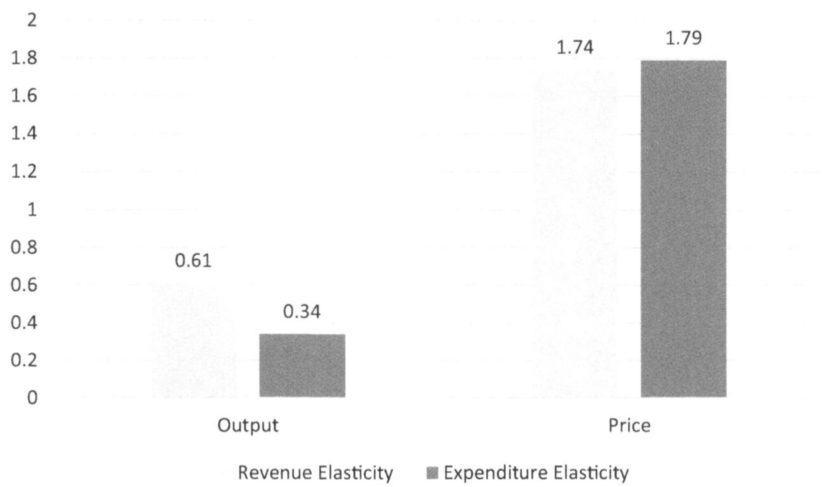

Figure 11.10 Dynamism of fiscal automatic stabilizers

Note: 12 month-lag for revenue, 30 month-lag for expenditure

Source: FMOLS estimates based on monthly data 1995 to 2017

working mechanism of the tax and public expenditure, which tend to offset the fluctuations of the aggregate demand over the course of volatile business cycles.

5. Impacts of specific public expenditures

Increasing government spending stimulates growth in private consumption and investment, which in turn give rise to output and expanding tax bases. In a dynamic framework, there is a feedback effect from public to private spending and vice versa with long-term lag effects. To examine these dynamic impacts of various types of public spending, a VAR framework is employed by using five variables: indexes of private consumption expenditure, private investment, and changes in the HP trends of public spending on economic service, health and education, and defense. Using monthly data from January 1993 to December 2017, impulse response functions of private investment and private consumption after an increase in the three types of public spending are obtained (Figure 11.11).

We can interpret the values of the responses of consumption and investment as fiscal multipliers of specific types of public spending. It is shown that health and education spending provide the highest expansionary impact on consumption and investment. On the other hand, defense budget generates a negative impact on private aggregate spending of the economy. Within a year after an increase in the spending, we have seen an increasing positive impact on private expenditures, which would imply higher output growth. Public spending on economic affairs raises both investment and consumption, although the short-run impact is not as strong as health and education expenditures. There might be a lag effect of this

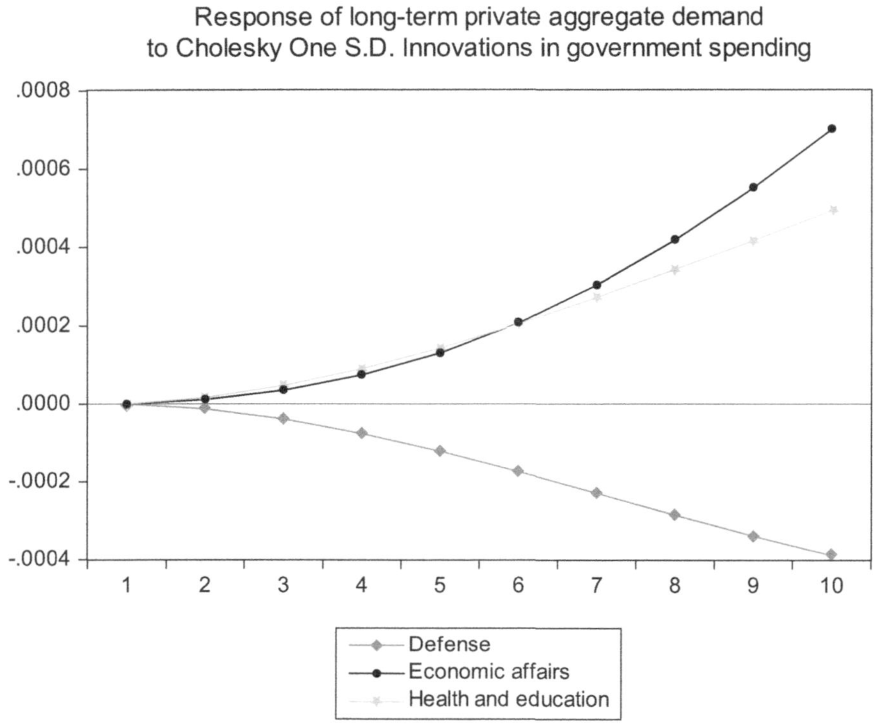

Figure 11.11 Impacts of public spending on long-term private consumption and investment

type of spending on the perception of consumers and investors. It is important to stress that the impact on output expansion is stronger in the medium term, because it takes time for the increased consumption and investment to work out their multiplier effects. The long-run impacts on output depend on the magnitudes of marginal propensity to consume and invest by investors.

The finding points out the danger of military coups which could harm long-term growth. The budget is diverted into defense spending rather than public investment in capital infrastructure and human and health capital. Public spending for economic activity produces a positive impact on long-term growth of the economy, while spending on defense has a negative impact. The reason can be attributed to import leakages and a corruption-prone type of defense budget. Neither business sentiment nor consumer confidence can be improved by enlarging military budget in the same fashion as other public outlays on economic services and social development. There is an opportunity cost of increasing the share of defense spending. Given the same level of budget, a rise in military spending implies a fall in budget for other more productive activities. After the 2014 coup, the defense budget hike was 5 percent in 2015 and 7 percent in 2016. For the 2017 fiscal budget, the defense spending was raised by 2 percent, while education budget was cut by 4.7 percent. The National Assembly approved the 2018 budget, increasing defense budget by 5 percent ($6.5 billion). Indeed, the coup has far-reaching impacts on the economy. If expenditures on economic services, health, and education are cut when military spending is raised, the impact on long-term growth is devastating because the contractionary impacts on output are larger. Fiscal austerity on education and health implies output contraction, while a defense splurge also intensifies output contraction.

The empirical evidence from this VAR framework supports the argument that fiscal policy can be used to stabilize the long-run output growth path. However, fiscal expenditure must be allocated to productive uses such as economic services, health, and education. There are some spillover effects of these categories of spending to private investment and consumption. The discretionary impact of increased public spending and tax cuts can be amplified if implemented when consumer confidence investor sentiments are high (Nidhiprabha, 2015).

6. Rules for fiscal sustainability

Financial discipline is required if a government wishes to maintain fiscal sustainability. Public debt must be contained by resisting runaway public deficit. Tax revenue must be enhanced to keep up with rising public expenditures. Nevertheless, the government must be forward-looking, aiming to strike a balance between long-term growth and public debt. Too high level of public debt would prevent the government from using fiscal stimulus during recession. On the other hand, too low public debt would preclude the government from financing infrastructure development, which would adversely put a limit on the long-term growth of the economy.

If primary deficit cannot be curtailed, public debt will keep rising and threaten the sustainability of the fiscal system. To stabilize the debt-GDP ratio, the primary deficit must be cut and the GDP growth rate must exceed the real rate of interest, which is the cost of public borrowing. Thus, during economic recession, the government must ensure that fiscal stimulus can bring about an economic growth rate that is higher than the real interest rate.

The ceiling on debt-GDP ratio was reduced from 60 percent to 50 percent in 2004, reflecting the conservative fiscal ideology. But the fear of global recession caused by financial crisis prompted the government to raise the ceiling back to 60 percent again in 2009 (Figure 11.12). Nevertheless, Thailand's actual debt-GDP ratio has never hit the debt ceiling. There is a need to recognize that some types of public spending can be self-financed, because if public debt can generate strong growth in GDP in the medium term, the debt-GDP ratio will be tend to be lower as the economy is driven by quality public spending.

The gap between the ceiling and actual level of debt-GDP ratio indicates fiscal space, which allows the government to pursue debt-financing budget deficit to spur growth. By early 2018, public debt was only at 41 percent of GDP, the level which is a far cry from the public debt in advanced economies. There has been ample fiscal space for the Thai government to embark on public infrastructure spending.

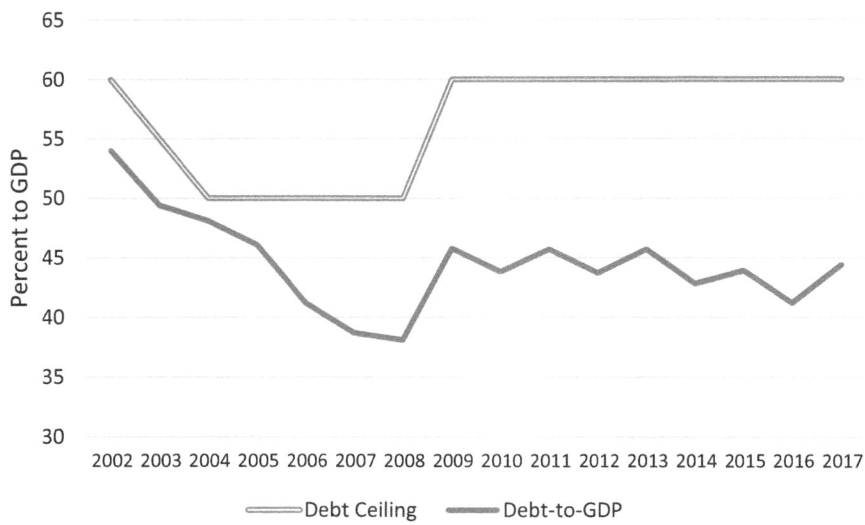

Figure 11.12 Ample fiscal space

Source: Bank of Thailand

Since high debt causes a rapid rise in interest payments, another rule of fiscal sustainability has been institutionalized by imposing a ceiling on debt service as a percentage of total budget. The ceiling was made more stringent after 2003 by lowering the maximum debt service from 16 percent to 15 percent of total budget. The Thai government was able to control the debt service within the ceiling without difficulty. The high liquidity in the money market during the economic downturn enabled the government to borrow at a very low interest rate.

As far as foreign borrowing is concerned, there is also a ceiling on foreign debt service to exports at 5 percent. Foreign borrowing declined while exports grew rapidly in the last decade. Therefore, there has been no problem in keeping the debt service to exports ratio within the permissible range (Figure 11.13).

There is another prudential fiscal rule to make sure that fiscal policy fosters long-term growth. This is the only sustainability condition that Thailand has failed miserably. The structure of government spending matters for long-term growth. If a large part of government spending is current rather than capital expenditure, it would be very difficult for the government to curtail total spending as it would affect those who used to receive such benefits. On the other hand, if a large portion of expenditures falls into capital goods, it would be relatively easier to cut down the budget deficit in the future. In other words, fiscal flexibility will be impaired with a higher proportion of current expenditure in total budget. Political consideration is involved when the government has to choose between capital goods and consumption goods which include military hardware.

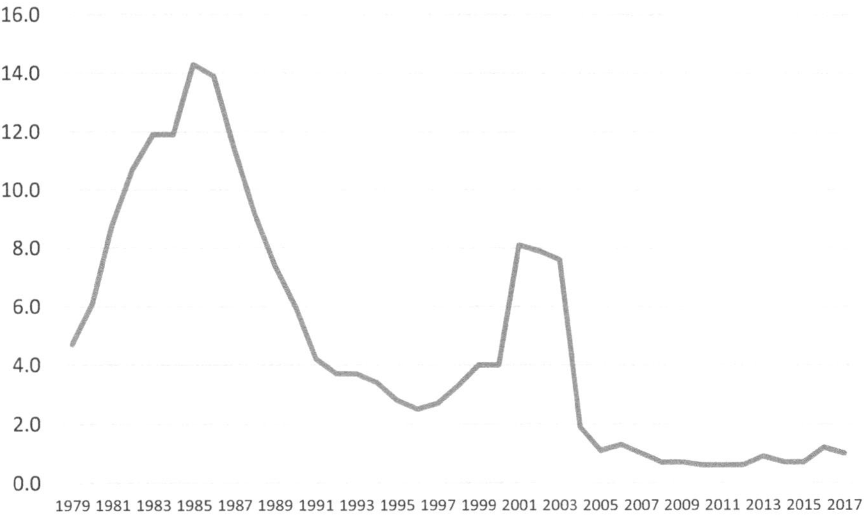

Figure 11.13 Government's external debt service ratio (percent exports)

Source: Bank of Thailand

Public investment in infrastructure projects can increase productivity in the private sector and raise the economy's long-term growth path. In particular, public investment in transportation and communication has a supernatural high rate of return to the economy. Such a kind of investment is complementary to private investment. Therefore, increased public investment has a crowding-in effect. In contrast, high public consumption relative to public investment can retard growth. Empirical evidence of cross-country investigation indicates that growth can be jeopardized if public consumption increases faster than public investment.

Thailand's rule of fiscal sustainability is also concerned with structure of fiscal expenditure. It imposes a minimum level of public investment, requiring that it must not fall below 25 percent of total budget. Since 2008 the budget allocated to public investment has fallen below the required level. The share of capital spending was 35 percent in 1997, declining steadily to 9 percent in 2013. With depreciation of existing public capital stock, the net public investment did not sufficiently raise public capital stock. Consequently, the long-term growth of the Thai economy has been adversely affected by the declining share of public investment. In the short run, we will not see the impact of a slowdown in public investment. However, in the longer term, the trade-off between output growth in the future and current consumption will become apparent in the forms of sluggish growth, low productivity, and deteriorating international competitiveness.

Using data on 42 developing countries from 1975 to 2001, Vergne (2009) found the evidence that election-year public spending shifts towards more visible current expenditures, in particular wages and subsidies, and away from capital expenditures. Ehrhart (2013) investigated panel data from 56 developing countries over the 1980–2006 and concluded that indirect tax revenue in election years is estimated to be lower by 0.3 percent of GDP than in other years. His result supports the opportunistic political budget model.

Viewed in this light, fiscal variables are affected by political and economic factors. Fiscal sustainability is ensured if rules and regulations are strictly observed. Time inconsistencies can occur in conducting monetary and fiscal policy. The government and people who are receiving the benefits of present consumption through populism programs are happy in the short run, but in the long-run fiscal policy that departs from the rule of adequate capital spending will retard growth.

Figure 11.14 suggests a rise in the current-capital spending ratio. It will be difficult to cut down current spending let alone maintain its level. Using the year 2000 as a benchmark, the current spending kept rising and quadrupled by 2016, while capital spending was maintained at the same level as in 2000 and even declined in 2016. The fiscal spending structure has changed in such a way that the long-term growth path has been compromised. The rise in current expenditure relative to capital spending is related to political economy and the economics of the coups.

For Thailand, there was no specific election year, which varies according to the years of military coups and the length of time spent on drafting a new constitution. But it can be observed that current expenditures, in particular defense spending, increase after the military coups. Yakovlev (2007) provided empirical evidence that increasing defense budget at the expense of budget for other development goals can be detrimental to economic growth. Similarly, Hou and Chen (2013) applied the augmented Solow growth model to examine the influence of military expenditure on economic growth for 35 developing countries

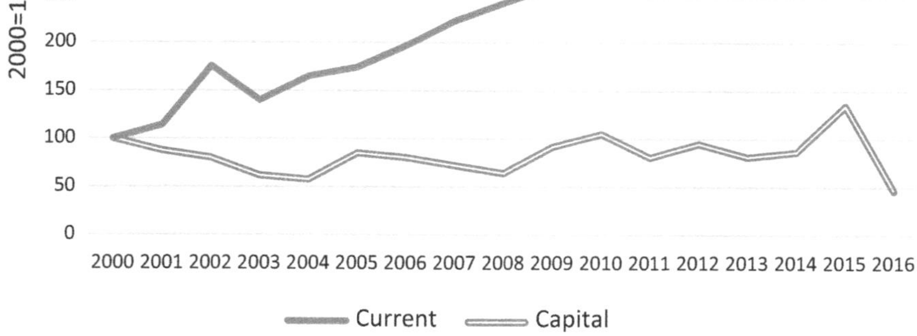

Figure 11.14 Current and capital expenditures

Source: Bank of Thailand

over the period 1975–2009. The empirical results from the system of generalized method of moments (GMM) estimators indicate that defense has a negative and significant effect on economic growth. In 2014, Thailand's military government proposed a purchase of submarines for protecting natural resources and preventing human trafficking in the gulf of Thailand. The detrimental impact of increased defense spending on long-term growth is imminent when share of public expenditure on economic services declines, as happened after the 2006 military coup (Nidhiprabha, 2009).

Expansionary fiscal policy through tax cuts and increased spending can effectively increase output, but its impact on inflationary pressure cannot be ignored. The timing of the policy implementation is important. If the fiscal stimulus is carried out during the period of oil price decline and exchange rate appreciation, the inflationary impact of running budget deficit can be mitigated. Carrere and de Melo (2012) analyzed data from 140 countries over 1972–2005 and concluded that the probability of occurrence of growth in the years following a fiscal stimulus is greater the lower the level of fiscal deficit. The success of a growth-oriented fiscal expenditure reform is associated with a stabilized macroeconomic environment.

Vera (2009) pointed out that the conventional arguments against fiscal activism are based on simple monetarism assumptions, ignoring developing countries' economic structures and causation mechanisms. The expansionary impact on the output of fiscal stimulus suggests that the Thai economy could have returned to the pre-shock growth path had fiscal stimulus been earnestly implemented. The fear of excessive budget deficit inhibits output stabilization and incurs opportunity cost of high growth in the long run.

7. Concluding remarks

This chapter provided evidence that Thailand's fiscal policy can be employed to stabilize short-term fluctuations of output and maintain price stability. There are several lessons from Thailand's fiscal experience. To stimulate growth in the aftermath of the global recession, sufficient fiscal space is needed to carry out fiscal expansionary policy. If the rules of fiscal sustainability are observed, available fiscal space permits effective fiscal stimulus.

Fiscal stimulus must not be applied too late and too little after the collapse of exports and domestic demand. The empirical evidence from this Chapter points out that fiscal policy instruments are effective tools when the economy experiences external and internal shocks. With ample fiscal space, discretionary fiscal policy can be undertaken to achieve long-term growth. Unwarranted fear of unsustainable public debt and ultra-conservative fiscal policy has cost the country an opportunity for achieving long-term growth.

After the military coups in 2006 and 2014, the Thai economy experienced the lowest economic growth in ASEAN region. To make matters worse, budget spent on economic services was diverted into current spending such as defense and income transfer payments. The opportunistic political budget models predict fiscal spending before an election to gain votes by incumbent governments.

However, in the case of Thailand, such opportunistic spending comes after military coups, akin to military business cycle spending.

Expansionary fiscal policy employed to counteract short-term fluctuations must be withdrawn after the economy is on its recovery path. If not, it can be a burden to the government and result in adverse impact on the economy, as people gradually become addicted to populism policy, such as proving cash handouts to rice farmers and rubber tree growers when the world commodity prices are declining. The political risk and adverse consequences of withdrawal of fiscal spending consequences must be considered before implementing fiscal expansion in response to insufficient aggregate demand.

Tax revenue increases faster than expenditure during economic upturns, mitigating the inflationary pressure by enlarging budget surplus. During economic downturns, tax revenue declines faster than public expenditure, leading to budget deficit to reduce the deflationary gap. When the economy experiences rising price levels, public spending tends to increase faster than public revenue. When formulating countercyclical fiscal policy measures, the role of automatic stabilizers must be taken into account. Any new measures of fiscal policy applied in response to economic slowdown must consider the impact of such a policy on the working process of automatic stabilizers. For example, the tax exemption for high-income taxpayers in long-term savings in the forms of investment in capital markets as LTF (long-term funds) and RMF (retirement funds) has eroded the effectiveness of automatic stabilizers and created income inequality.

Income tax-allowance schemes intended to spur private consumption expenditures up to 15,000 baht before the year ends, 3 years in a row from 2015 to 2017, are prime examples of short-termism. Because of their temporary nature, they have no permanent effect on the economy. At worst, they raise vertical inequity, because only those who pay income tax receive that kind of tax benefit. Stimulus fiscal packages should focus on capital spending, rather than current spending, so as to maintain fiscal flexibility of spending and to promote long-term growth.

If public spending goes to infrastructure rather than a wage hike in the public sector, the economy's output capacity can be enhanced. Thus, raising the share of capital expenditure in the total budget is important to promote long-term growth with price stability. It is imperative that current spending be curtailed once the economy regains its pre-shock growth path. Since 1997, the share of capital spending has declined so much that it reduced the long-term growth rate.

The expansionary impact of increased public spending and tax cuts would not be effective during the period of political turmoil and uncertainty. Countercyclical policy can lead to output expansion provided that the government is able to maintain consumer confidence and restore business sentiment.

References

Afonso, Antonio, Luca Agnello, and Davide Furceri. 2010. "Fiscal Policy Responsiveness, Persistence, and Discretion." *Public Choice*, 145 (3–4): 503–530.

Agnello, Luca, Davide Furceri, and Ricardo M. Sousa. 2013. "Discretionary Government Consumption, Private Domestic Demand, and Crisis Episodes." *Open Economies Review*, 24 (1): 79–100.

Barro, Robert J. 1990. "Government Spending in a Simple Model of Endogenous Growth." *Journal of Political Economy*, 98 (5): 103–125.

Carrere, Celine, and J. de Melo. 2012. "Fiscal Spending and Economic Growth: Some Stylized Facts." *World Development*, 40 (9): 1750–1761.

DeLong, J. Bradford., and Lawrence H. Summers. 2012. "Fiscal Policy in a Depressed Economy." *Brookings Papers on Economic Activity*, 2012 (1): 233–297.

Ehrhart, Helene. 2013. "Elections and the Structure of Taxation in Developing Countries." *Public Choice*, 156 (1–2): 195–211.

Hernandez de Cos, Pablo, and Enrique Moral-Benito. 2013. "What Drives a Successful Fiscal Consolidation?" *Applied Economics Letters*, 20 (7–9): 748–753.

Hou, Na, and Bo Chen. 2013. "Military Expenditure and Economic Growth in Developing Countries: Evidence from System GMM Estimates." *Defiance and Peace Economics*, 24 (3): 183–193.

Jha, Shikha, Sushanta K. Mallick, Donghyun Park, and Pilipinas F. Quising. 2014. "Effectiveness of Countercyclical Fiscal Policy: Evidence from Developing Asia." *Journal of Macroeconomics*, 40: 82–98.

Kandil, Magda. 2009. "Public Spending and the Macroeconomy: Evidence from Developing and Developed Countries." *International Journal of Business and Economics*, 8 (2): 133–158.

Nidhiprabha, Bhanupong. 2009. "The Thai Economy After the Coup." In Funston, John (ed.) *Divided over Thaksin, Thailand's Coup and Problematic Transition*. Singapore: Institute of Southeast Asian Studies, 172–188.

Nidhiprabha, Bhanupong. 2015. "Lessons From Thailand's Fiscal Policy." *Asian Economic Papers*, 14 (3).

Vera, Leonardo. 2009. "Reassessing Fiscal Policy: Perspectives from Developing Countries." *Development and Change*, 40 (4): 611–643.

Vergne, Clemence. 2009. "Democracy, Elections and Allocation of Public Expenditures in Developing Countries." *European Journal of Political Economy*, 25 (1): 63–77.

Yakovlev, Pavel. 2007. "Arms Trade, Military Spending and Economic Growth." *Defense and Peace Economics*, 18 (4), August: 317–338.

12 Macroeconomic perspective of poverty and income distribution

1. Introduction

Social upheaval and political turmoil are rooted in countries with injustice and income inequality. Macroeconomic policies which provide inclusive growth would be more likely to sustain growth in the long run. Uninterrupted growth over many decades is a prerequisite to a high standard of living. As discussed in earlier chapters, political unrest stalled Thailand's stable growth path, notwithstanding several major external shocks. High output growth generates employment, thereby reducing poverty. Similarly, high crop prices can reduce poverty and improve income disparity between rural and urban areas. Thus, exchange rate policy that affects commodity prices has a far-reaching effect on poverty and income inequality. High growth of wage rates in urban areas brings about labor migration. With plenty of job opportunity, urban areas generate employment and attract labor from rural areas. Urbanization therefore has an impact on poverty reduction.

There has been a disputable fact on the issue of the trade-off between growth and income inequality. Evidence in some high-income countries shows that their development paths did not undergo deteriorating income inequality. We will examine the existence of such a trade-off and explain why there is a declining trend of poverty and income equality. We will explore how fiscal policy can exert influence on poverty and income distribution.

2. Economic growth benefits the poor

Warr (2007) stated that the long-term economic performance of Thailand has been remarkable, as reflected in life expectancy, infant and maternal mortality, and literacy. Although poverty has declined dramatically, economic inequality has increased. Ten years have passed since the dire remarks by Warr, and Thailand has come a long way since then. In this chapter, we explain the tendency for poverty eradication and inequality improvement in Thailand over the last two decades, despite a slowdown in economic growth. Kurta and Kurosaki (2011) observed that inequality in Thailand and the Philippines reduced the growth rate of per capita consumption. Differences in income inequality in both countries explain how the two countries have different outcomes in output growth and poverty reduction since the late 1980s. Thailand escaped the poverty trap, partly because of the declining fertility rate in the last five decades.[1] The downward trend continues so much that the country will be facing an aging problem in the near future. According to Day (2015), declining fertility rates in developing countries occur simultaneously with rising per capita income. As a result, the fraction of skilled workers increases with economic growth. The rising opportunity cost of having children and the high cost of childrearing inputs make the fertility rate decline further.

Strong economic growth generates high employment. The poor, who are largely unskilled, earn a higher income share from job creation during economic booms. If growth continues without disruptions, the poverty level declines. Thailand's level of poverty was cut by half from 70 percent in the early 1980s to 35 percent in 1996. The panacea for poverty is the ability to maintain strong and steady economic expansion. In 1997, the Thai economy succumbed to the Asian financial crisis, and the poverty headcount reverted to 43 percent in 2000 (Figure 12.1) before gradually declined to 7.2 percent in 2015, thanks to economic recovery.

The poverty gap (percent of the difference between the poverty line and consumption expenditures of the poor) also replicates the movement of the poverty headcount. It can be said that Thailand's economic development succeeded in reducing poverty; the poverty gap dropped dramatically from 24 percent in 1988 to just 1.1 percent in 2015 (Figure 12.1).

An important contributor to this poverty eradication was the ability to maintain price stability. The poverty line climbed up from 879 baht in 1988 to 2,644 baht in 2015. As a food-exporting country, Thailand does not have problem with famine and food security. The ability to keep food prices low helps alleviate the plight of the poor, who live below the poverty line. Macroeconomic stabilization

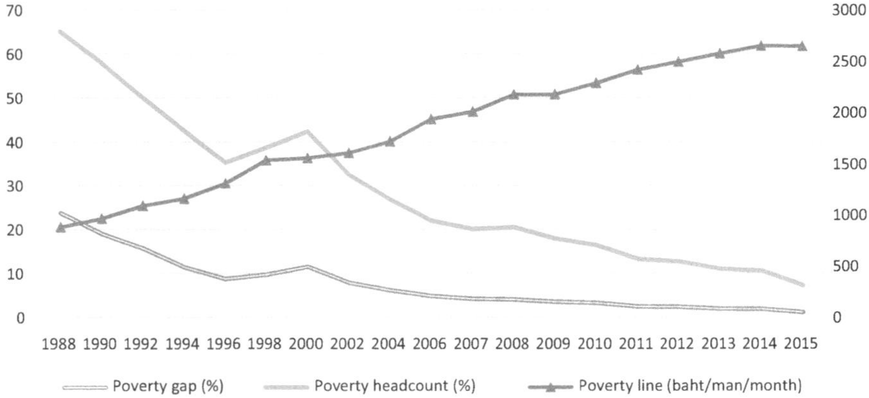

Figure 12.1 Declining poverty incidence

Source: NESDB

policy therefore has an indirect impact on poverty reduction by maintaining high employment and price stability.

There is a relationship between output growth and changes in unemployment rate (Okun, 1962). In the case of the US, a 1 percent reduction in the unemployment rate corresponds to a two percentage point growth that is faster than the potential output growth. Since high growth raises the demand for labor, it must also provide jobs for the poor and reduce the poverty level. Consequently, there must be a positive relationship between the speed of poverty reduction and GDP growth.

The period of high economic growth between 1990 and 1996, was also the period of the fastest speed of poverty reduction. Thailand's per capita income grew by 7 percent, while poverty declined by 22.7 percent (Figure 12.2). Then came the Asian financial crisis during 1997–1998, when per capita income contracted by 10.2 percent and the poverty rate increased by 3.4 percent. Recession depressed the demand for labor and the poor bore the brunt of economic crisis. As the Thai economy slowly rebounded and was bouyed by the export boom during 1999–2004, per capita income rose 4.3 percent. The progress on poverty reduction resumed as the unemployment rate declined, resulting in a 11.9 percent decline in poverty level between 1999 and 2004.

After that episode, the Thai economy suffered from a slowdown in GDP growth due to the global financial crisis during 2008–2009; exports declined but rebounded sharply. Income per capita continued growing but at a low level of 3.2 percent. Consequently, the poverty level dropped by 10.4 percent from 2005

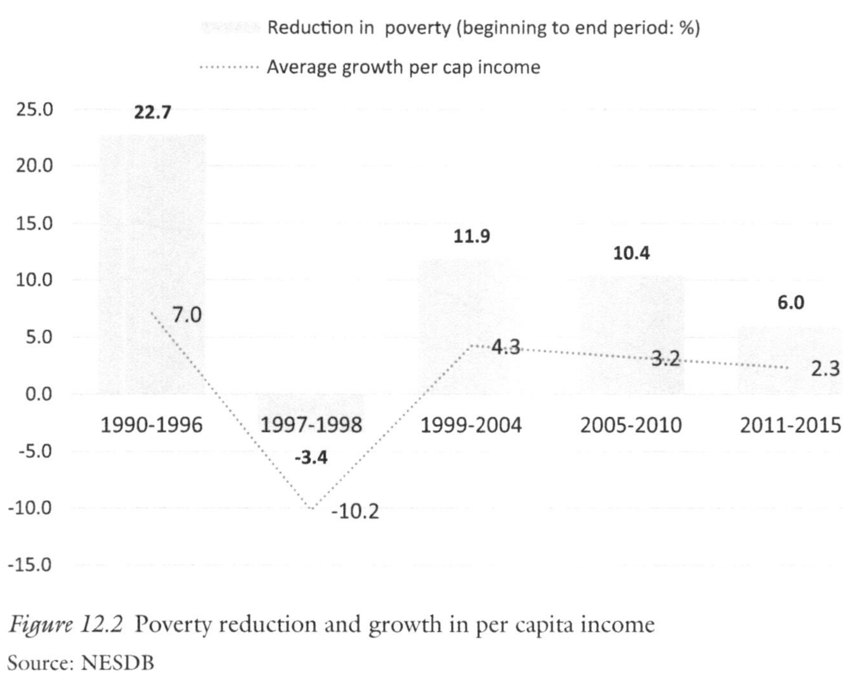

Figure 12.2 Poverty reduction and growth in per capita income

Source: NESDB

to 2010. Nevertheless, the downward trend of poverty began when the economy entered a new growth episode – slowing down the potential growth path. By 2015, the poverty rate was reduced 6 percent from the level in 2011. This is because the continued slowdown of the GDP growth of the Thai economy, thanks to China's slowdown, could not provide sufficient strength to reduce poverty as it did in the past. Per capita income grew only by 2.3 percent, the lowest period of positive growth, which corresponds to the period of the slowest poverty reduction.

It is now obvious that external factors indirectly impact poverty level. Through commodity booms and busts, changing export demand for Thailand's agricultural commodities can therefore affect farmers' incomes in rural areas. Thailand's main agricultural export commodities are rice, rubber, and tapioca. Figure 12.3 illustrates the correlates of poverty reduction and changes in the global prices of rice and rubber. Interestingly enough, Lin and Fu (2016) provide evidence in small developing countries showing that trade leads to a significant reduction in income inequality in autocracies, since they export more primary products. On the contrary, income inequality increases in democratic countries, because they are more active in trade through manufacturing outsourcing.

Between the periods 1990–1996 and 2005–2010, global prices of rice and rubber were favorable to Thai farmers. The speed of poverty reduction was strong. On the contrary, commodity slumps during the periods 1997–1998 and 2011–2015 resulted in decelerated poverty reduction. Most of the time, the prices of rice and rubber moved in tandem. However, between 1999 and 2004, they moved in an opposite direction. Rubber price went up by 12.4 percent and the rice price went down by 2.3 percent. Yet poverty continued to decline by 11.9 percent, thanks to the high export prices of maize and tapioca during the

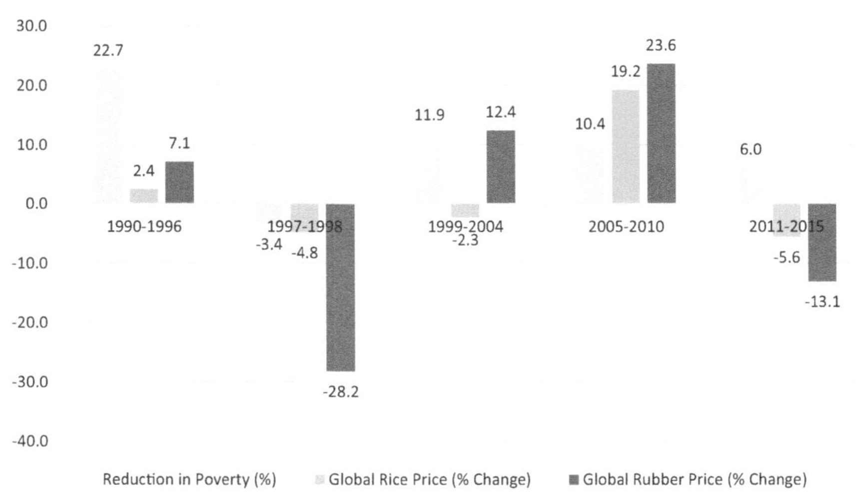

Figure 12.3 Global commodity prices and poverty reduction

Source: NESDB

corresponding periods. Indeed, poverty reduction depends partly on the strength of commodity prices.

The percentage changes of the global export prices of rice and rubber shown in Figure 12.3 were based on the values in the US dollar. The baht-dollar exchange rate movements can thwart or propel commodity booms and busts. As such, exchange rate policy indirectly influences the welfare of the poor. A change in the level of exchange rate exerts impact on every commodity the poor consume, both in rural and urban areas. Since Thailand is a net importer of crude oil, exchange rate depreciation also affects farm input prices, including transportation costs. Not just price stability is required for poverty reduction; an appropriate exchange rate management is needed because the exchange rate policy has a far-reaching effect on poverty eradication.

3. Rural vs. urban income disparity

The gap between rural and urban poverty can be seen as a spatial inequality. Unlike farmers in the central plain, the northeastern farmers do not have abundant water resources. Farmers in the northeastern provinces cannot grow rice twice a year. Hence their income is lower than other farmers in the country. Figure 12.4 illustrates that, despite the co-movements of the poverty incidence, the poor in the rural northeast experienced extremely poor living conditions more than the poor in other parts of the country.

The declining trend of urban and rural poverty mirrors the rising per capita income discussed in Figure 12.2. The disparity between the rural and urban poor can be measured by the gap between urban and rural poverty rates.

Since rural poverty declined faster than urban poverty, the gap between poverty in urban and rural areas has narrowed (Figure 12.4). Poverty rate declines slower in urban than rural areas. Access to credit markets and labor mobility are

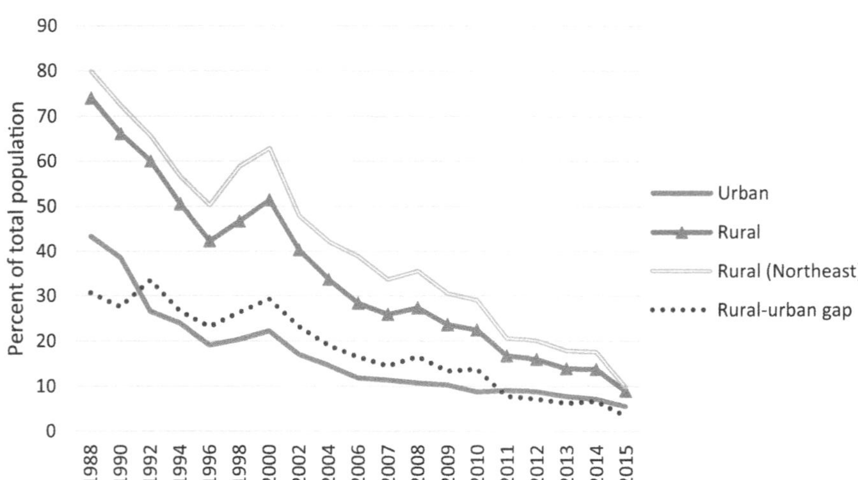

Figure 12.4 Poverty in rural and urban areas

Source: NESDB

contributing factors to reducing the poverty gap between the two sectors. The wide gap of 30 percentage points in 1988 was reduced to just 3.4 percent in 2015. The implication is that there is no evidence of urban bias in the case of Thailand. Furthermore, the evidence suggests that urbanization in Thailand is sustainable, for the disparity between rural and urban areas has diminished over time. However, there are existing large gaps on the regional level. The northeastern region is still the poorest in the country. Farming in the northeast has changed gradually. Farmers do not have to rely solely on growing paddy and glutinous rice. Other agricultural crops have emerged, including cassava, sugarcane, maize, and rubber. Crop diversification may reduce the risk of heavy reliance on monocropping. Figure 12.5 shows the correlation coefficients of the fragrance paddy price and other crop prices in the northeast. The strong correlation of these farm prices indicates that crop diversification does not help farmers to stabilize their income. Northeastern farmers are still vulnerable to abnormal weather conditions and price fluctuations. There is a limit to risk diversification because different outputs in the same areas can be destroyed by unpredictable weather conditions; crop prices can move up and down together. Diversification can reduce risk only when there is no price correlation or there is a negative correlation between commodity prices.

The income of the urban poor would be more stable than the rural poor. Services and industrial sectors are in urban areas. There is a strong correlation between output growth rate in the manufacturing and service sectors, but agricultural growth correlations with services and manufacturing growth are insignificant. This is because of the lack of linkages between agriculture production and other sectors. Growth in the manufacturing sector can stimulate activity in the service sector – not the agricultural sector. To raise income in rural areas, a

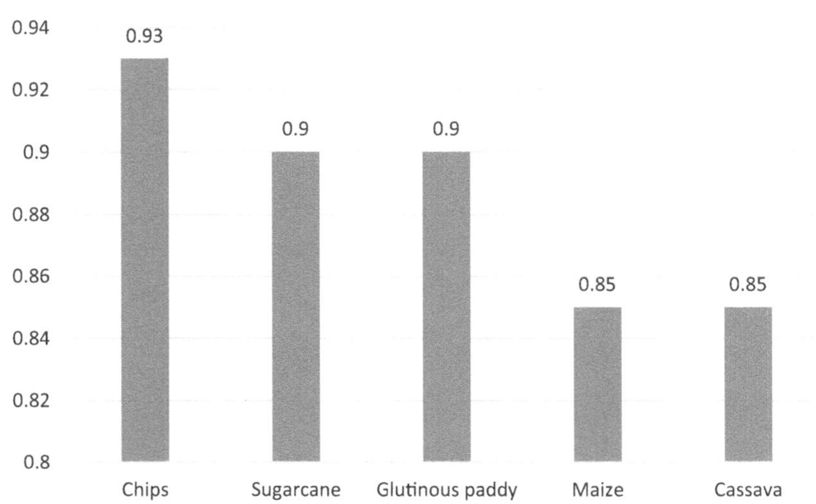

Figure 12.5 Correlates of crop prices and fragrance paddy

Source: Author's calculation

specific policy targeted to the plight of the poor is needed, because the trickle-down effect of the growth in manufacturing and service to the agricultural sector is low.

There is a strong negative relationship between urbanization and poverty (Figure 12.6). The faster farmers move from rural to urban areas, the faster the rate of poverty reduction. The most effective way to maintain income level for the poor is to transfer agricultural labor to service or manufacturing sectors in urban areas. There is a caveat here. The fast rate of urbanization can have an undesirable effect, because the country would have less time to establish urban infrastructure, including laws and regulations, to pave the way for high quality urbanization, which includes the exploitation of economies of scale of expanding cities. Traffic congestion within the inner cities, long commuting hours, and pollution are forces counteracting the expansion of the city.

Despite the pull factor of higher wages in cities, traffic congestion and low quality of urban life hinder the transfer of labor from rural areas. The push factors from rural to urban labor are farm mechanization and improved farm productivity. Public infrastructure investment in the agricultural sector can strengthen the push factor and speed up the transfer of rural labor. However, some problems remain, for example, how to equip agricultural labor with new technology or provide employment training for them in the modern sector. This is possible for the young in rural areas, but not for the limited skilled elderly, who cannot be retooled to fit in the service and industrial sectors. The average age of Thai farmers is above 50 years and they would probably be happy remaining in the rural areas.

Thailand has a larger labor force in the agricultural sector when compared to other countries at the same level of income. Thailand's idiosyncrasy of labor employment structure affects poverty and income distribution. The process of

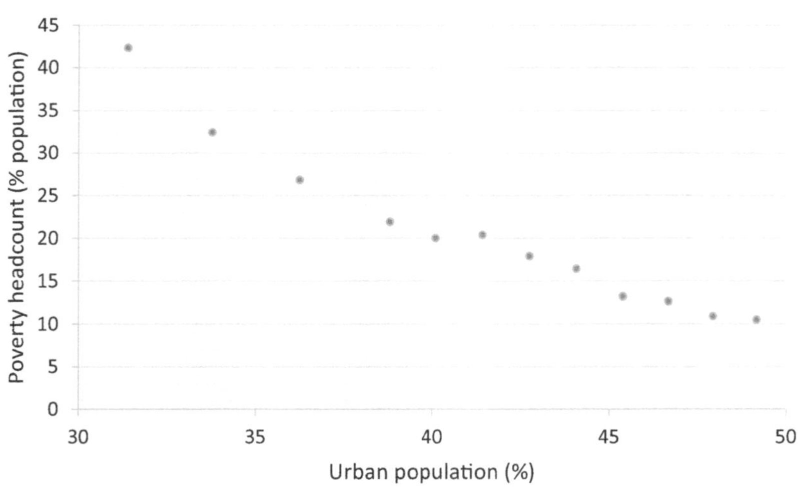

Figure 12.6 Poverty reduction and urbanization (2000–2015)

Source: NESDB

poverty eradication can hit a snag if the urbanization rate decelerates. Basically, urbanization and poverty reduction have a two-way relationship. On the one hand, urbanization attracts people from rural areas by the lure of high wages and high employment. Overall poverty can be reduced by rising high wages in both rural and urban areas. The dual economy described by Lewis' model has become a blur, due to labor migration and agricultural labor productivity improvement, which tend to equalize the wage rate between the two sectors. On the other hand, when poverty is reduced substantially and income inequality is narrowed down, there is less incentive to move into urban areas, thereby slowing down the urbanization rate. This is what is happening in high-income countries, where the rate of urbanization has plateaued after achieving a certain per capita income level.

Gerschenkron (1962) espouses the idea that economic backwardness is due to the lack of financial institution development. The more economic backwardness of the country, the more it needs the intervention of the public to establish financial institutions. If the poor are excluded from formal credit markets, this can exacerbate the poverty problem. In particular, if banking activities concentrate in certain regions of the country, the poor are alienated and have difficulty obtaining credit to finance their consumption and investment. They remain in the poverty trap because they rely on exorbitantly high rates of interest in the informal money markets. With a higher degree of urbanization, an increasing number of bank branches provide financial access to the poor. For Thailand, bank branches are not heavily concentrated in the primal city – Bangkok. Bank branches are geographically distributed according to intensity of economic activities. The pattern of regional distribution of bank branches in 2006 was not different from the pattern in 2016. About 33 percent of all bank branches were located in Bangkok, 30 percent in the central region, and roughly 12 percent the northeast, the north, and the south. Hence, the hypothesis of financial urban bias and financial concentration in urban areas does not explain the rural-urban disparity. In Thailand, the financial factor does not impede the poverty reduction process. It can be concluded that financial institution development that began earnestly in the 1970s helped rather than hindered poverty eradication.

4. Kuznets hypothesis revisited

The relationship between income level and income inequality was examined by Kuznets (1955). As an economy develops from predominantly rural agriculture to an industrialized urban economy, income inequality rises up to a threshold level before it starts to decline. The Kuznets curve hypothesis can be illustrated by the nonlinear relationship between the Gini coefficient and income per capita over the course of economic development. But the relationship between economic growth and income distribution is more complex than can be captured by the inverted U-shaped curve. The causation is bi-directional, with a feedback effect from inequality to growth.

In a study of 109 developing countries observed between 1981 and 2008, Amini and Bianco (2016) found evidence that poverty is negatively related to growth and positively related to income inequality. They also found that human capital in terms of education and health facilitates the effect of GDP growth on poverty reduction. This finding is consistent with Kuznets curve hypothesis regarding worsening income distribution at the early stages of economic development. The validity of Kuznets curve theory has been questioned by Fields (2001), whose empirical work is based on large panels of countries or time series data. The inverted U-shaped curve relationship between income inequality and per capita income seems to disappear. More recently, Piketty (2014) argued that the return to capital is rising faster than the economic growth rate. The resulting concentration of wealth implies that the relation is U-shaped rather than the inverted U-shape curve observed by Kuznets. Tridico (2010) examined the relationship between inequality within 50 emerging and transitioning economies from 1995 to 2006. He finds that growth did not reduce property while income inequality intensified. Nevertheless, countries with high public spending on education and health did not experience worsening income inequality. Perara et al. (2013) observed that economic growth leads to poverty reduction. Furthermore, poverty can be further reduced in countries with stable governments and law and order. Improvements in corruption, democratic accountability, and bureaucratic quality reduced poverty but raised income inequality. Recent research on the nexus between growth, poverty, and income inequality points to the importance of quality institutions. Whether a growing economy experiences poverty reduction and improvement in income inequality depends on the quality of institutions. Institutional changes can take the form of market liberalization and trade reform, which are handmaidens of economic growth. Lin and Fu (2016) examined how trade affects income inequality in small developing countries. They attributed rising income inequality to trade under autocracies. For democratic societies, trade can reduce income inequality through activity in manufacturing products via production fragmentation and network trade. Increasingly, the role of institutions, including administrative regimes and the quality of the government, has been emphasized as a factor influencing how a country's inequality evolves along its development path.

An increasing degree of trade openness since the early 1980s has made Thailand more vulnerable to external shocks. A change in the terms of trade of agricultural products and manufacturing exports can alter income shares between people in rural and urban areas. The trickle-down effect of economic development can be captured by the inverted U-shaped curve of the relationship between income inequality and the level of per capita income. When Thailand's economy adopted an infrastructure-led growth development policy in the 1960s, per capita income started to rise rapidly. Many critics of Thailand's economic development argued that income disparity was widening. In some countries, stylized facts of economic development do not match with the prediction of Kuznets. Fiscal measures such as a progressive income tax and a high level of public expenditure on education enable some countries to enjoy the benefits of economic development without experiencing higher income inequality.

An analysis of the relationship between per capita income and the Gini coefficient reveals that Thailand has already passed the threshold income level, where the trend of declining income inequality continues if per capita income keeps rising (Figure 12.7). Due to limited data availability on the Gini coefficient in the 1960s, we can infer that inequality must have been rising in the1960s up to the late 1980s. Nevertheless, there is a measurement problem associated with using income to calculate Gini coefficients. Because income comprises savings and consumption, the income Gini coefficient also reflects inequality in savings. The rich have a tendency to save more than the poor; therefore, we should calculate inequality based on consumption expenditures, which can be measured with more accuracy than income.

The Gini coefficient measured from consumption expenditures suggests that there is a case to support Kuznets hypothesis. As the Thai economy expanded rapidly during the first three decades of economic development, income inequality rose before it exhibited a downward trend starting in the early 1990s. Figure 12.8 suggests that Thailand experienced Kuznets inverted U-shaped curve.[2]

During the period of 2014–2017, income inequality reduced and poverty decelerated as the economic growth rate declined sharply, compared to the period before political upheaval and regime changes. There have been changes in the quality of governing institutions. According to worldwide governance indictors, Thailand's institutional quality deteriorated sharply from 2005 to 2015, due to the lack of political stability, voice, and accountability, rising violence, terrorism, and rampant corruption. If the quality of institutions matters for growth, it would also indirectly impact poverty and income distribution. The downward trend of poverty and inequality continues, notwithstanding the deteriorating quality of institutions. We cannot discern that an autocratic regime is consistent with improving living standards and reducing inequality. Without the effectiveness and commitment of the pro-poor policy, the autocratic government's

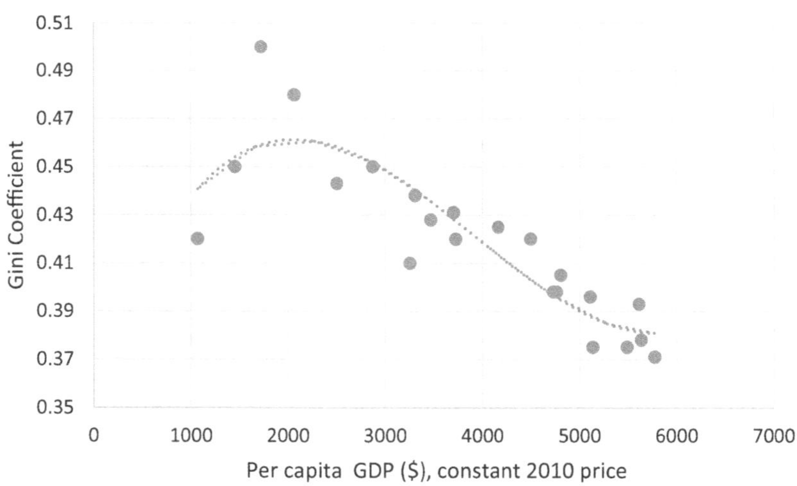

Figure 12.7 Kuznets curve: 1975–2015

Source: NESDB

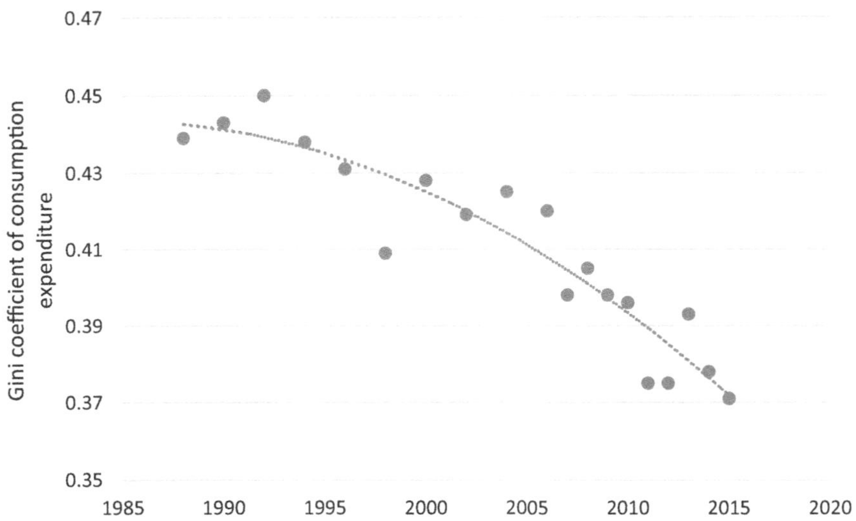

Figure 12.8 Declining consumption inequality

Source: NESDB

economic policy programs would prolong and complicate the path to solving social inequality. There are other contributing factors that lift up the poor and reduce income inequality after the regime changes.

Whatever the political regime, if the aim is to reduce poverty and income inequality, the policy focus must be on reducing rural poverty. There is a significant positive relationship between the Gini coefficient and the level of poverty in rural areas (Figure 12.9). This is hardly surprising since poverty concentrates in rural areas, where the majority of the poor are in the bottom 10 percent of the social strata. The policy implication from the positive relationship between rural poverty and Gini coefficient is quite clear: if we succeed in reducing rural poverty, our objective of more equitable income distribution can be achieved.

The main source of rural income is agriculture. Fluctuations in farm output and commodity prices result in a high proportion of transitory income in total income. With a low proportion of permanent income in total income, rural households tend to save less. When experiencing shocks from unfavorable weather conditions, rural farmers take on debt and become trapped in poverty cycles. When rural poverty declines, the income share of people in the bottom 10 percent increases. Stable commodity prices and stable growth of agricultural output would allow farmers to get out of poverty as permanent income from farms will rise. Public policy which aims to stabilize output and income in rural areas will have a favorable impact on income distribution.

The long-term impact of agrarian structure on income inequality has been scrutinized by Oyvat (2016). Land inequality increases income Gini coefficients

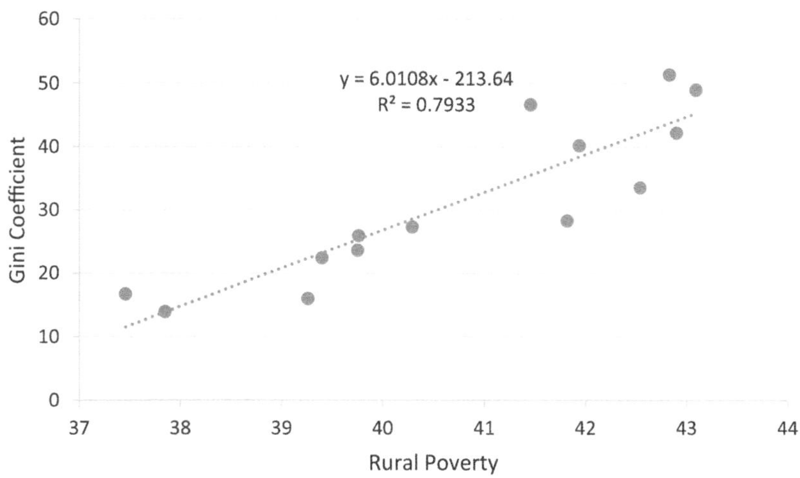

Figure 12.9 Inequality and rural poverty relationship

Source: NESDB

in both urban and rural sectors. The existence of land inequality has a significant impact on the level of urbanization and overall income inequalities. Oyvat argues that progressive land reform and subsidies to small farmers can reduce inequality and poverty in the long run. It seems that land reform programs in Thailand have not been successful. There is very large inequality of land holding in Thailand. This may be a stumbling block that slows down income inequality in Thailand. About 27 percent of the population holds 15 rai (2.4 hectare), while 4 percent hold more than 100 rai (16 hectare) of land. The existence of numerous small farms inhibits efficient farm mechanization as it does not permit exploitation of economies of scale of heavy farm machinery. As a result, farm labor productivity remains low. Only 10 percent of Thais own about 70 percent of the nation's total land. To solve the problem, farm lands were allocated to farmers by the Agricultural Land Reform Office. The problem is that allocated land can be sold to wealthy landowners and speculators. This scheme actually has intensified asset inequality in the country. In 2014, the National Committee on Land Policy was established with a mandate to allocate land of 4 million rai (640,000 hectare) to the poor in the form of cooperatives, instead of granting individual rights of ownership. The progress has been slow and there are no effective fiscal measures to cope with land speculation. Income inequality is directly caused by asset inequality, which has remained a perennial problem underlying the structure of Thailand's inequality. In effect, there is a lower bound level of the Gini coefficient (Figure 12.8). To pass that threshold level, the country needs a long-term solution for asset inequality, and the solution might lie in the area of fiscal policy.

5. Fiscal policy and income inequality

The structure of Thailand's sectoral employment is different from other countries with the same level of per capita income. The share of agricultural labor in total employment has been considerably higher than in other countries at the same level of economic development. This idiosyncrasy is due to the lack of farm productivity improvement, which can release agricultural workers to other sectors. On the demand side, the manufacturing sector's share of employment was sluggish from 2000 to 2010 (Figure 12.10). Employment generated by other sectors has been stagnant since 2012. The agricultural labor transformation process is painfully slow, because farm labor productivity increases gradually over the years. The limited ability to transfer labor out of agriculture affects the speed of poverty eradication and income inequality reduction.

The growth in manufacturing output did not lead to substantial transfer of labor from farm land to factories in urban areas. One of the reasons is the low level of human capital formation in the agricultural sector. Despite a high percentage of budget allocated to education, the outcome from human capital investment is disappointing.[3] Moreover, the high capital-labor ratio in the manufacturing sector precludes the sector from sufficient absorbing labor from the agricultural sector. The capital-labor ratios in the manufacturing and financial sectors are higher than agriculture (Figure 12.11). As a result, output expansion in this capital-intensive sector does not generate substantial employment. Industry-led growth does not generate employment fast enough to pull agricultural labor. FDI that keeps flowing into the manufacturing sector is the main cause of substantial differences in the capital-labor ratio between the two sectors. While investment in agriculture

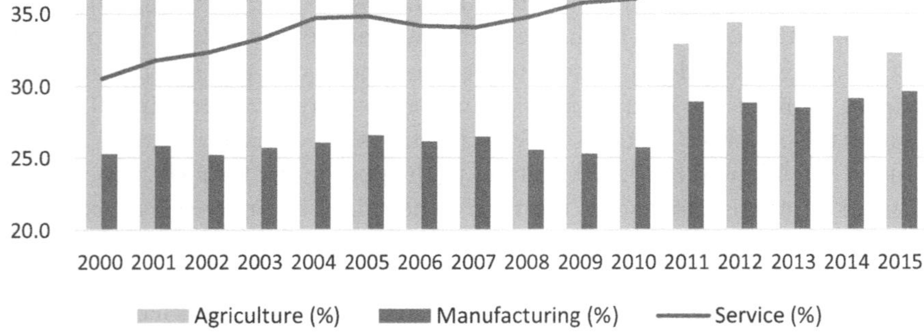

Figure 12.10 Employment share by sector

Source: NESDB

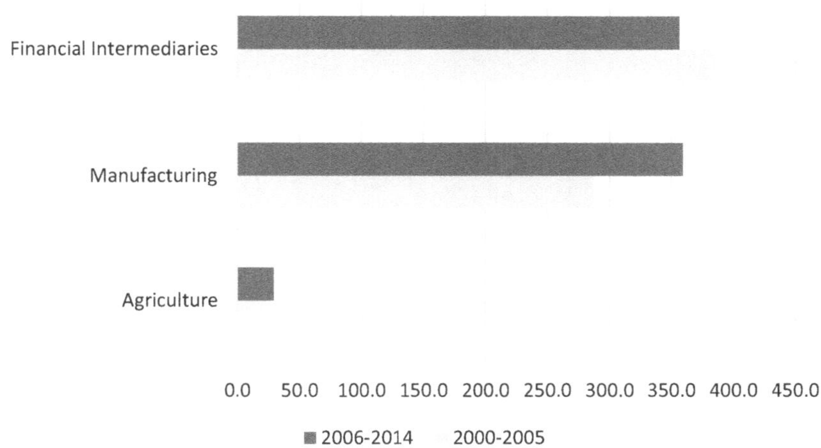

Figure 12.11 Sectoral capital-labor ratios

Source: NESDB

has been ignored, foreign investors are attracted to only the financial and manufacturing sectors. Thanks to the Asian financial crisis, which made asset prices of the banking sector cheap, considerable FDI inflows enhanced commercial banks' capital funds. Moreover, the Board of Investment provides tax incentives to foreign investors in such a way that FDI concentrates in certain industries, ignoring low profitable agricultural investment.

The low capital-labor ratio in the agricultural sector explains the productivity gap between the manufacturing and financial sectors. Because the real wage rate depends on the value of marginal productivity, the demand for farm labor cannot increase as much as other sectors if there is no improvement in agricultural technology and favorable farm prices. In turn, the higher productivity in the manufacturing and financial sectors leads to wage pressure in the farming sector. Farm input prices also rise during commodity booms, making it difficult for farmers to make a profit and retain sufficient investible funds for improving farm productivity. As long as labor productivity gaps remain wide, rising national wage rates would exacerbate the plight of the farmers, because net farm income will be squeezed by the rising agricultural wage rate (Figure 12.12). Small-scale farmers would remain in debt and it would be impossible for them to have ability or incentives to improve human physical capital investment.

The relative labor productivity index (Figure 12.13) reveals that between 2000 and 2005, agricultural labor was well below the overall labor productivity – only 21.7 percent of the national level. And there was only a slight improvement between the period 2006 and 2015. During the same corresponding period, the average labor product in the service sector was about 63 percent and 42 percent higher than the economy-wide level. The relative average productivity of labor

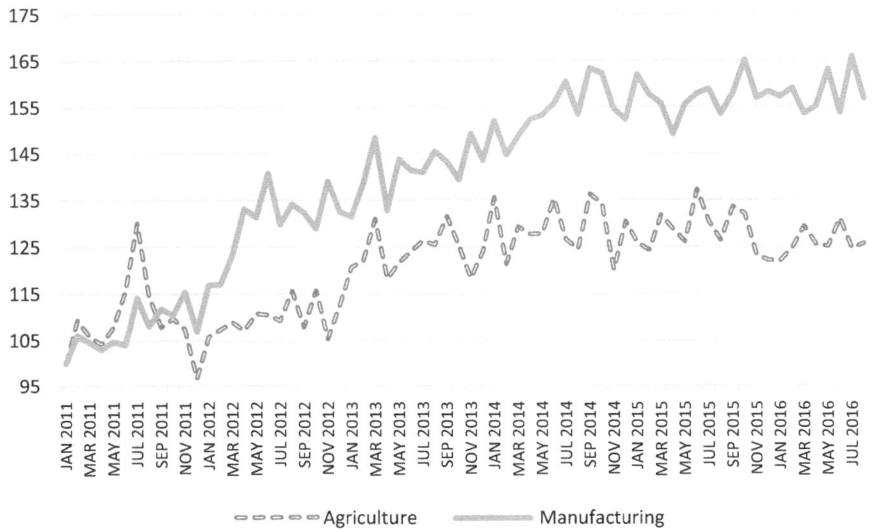

Figure 12.12 Widening wage gap

Source: NESDB

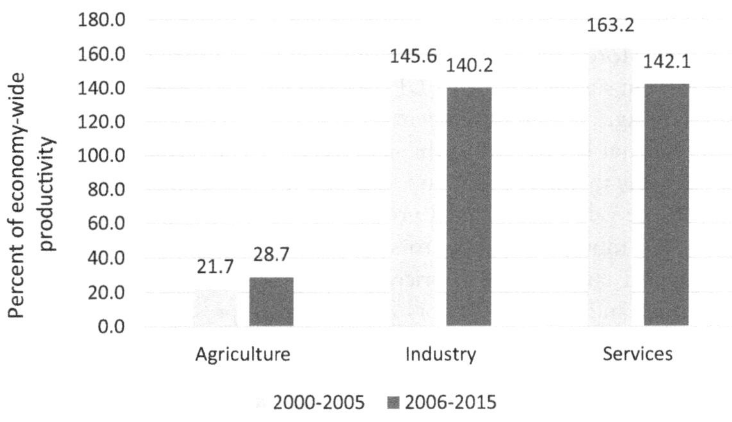

Figure 12.13 Relative labor productivity index (sectoral output share/employment share)

Source: NESDB

in industry was also roughly 45 percent and 40 percent higher than the national productivity average, but it also trended downward after 2014. The low level of private investment, including FDI, was the main culprit for the decline. Consequently, there was less pressure on manufacturing wage rate. But as shown in Figure 12.12, the wage rate in the agriculture sector was stagnant, reflecting

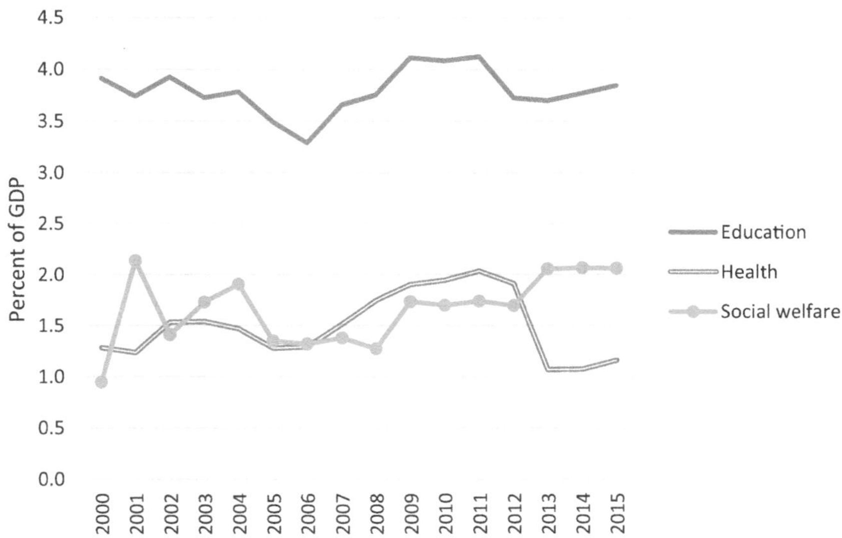

Figure 12.14 Public expenditures on human and health capital

Source: NESDB

low improvement in the productivity of agricultural labor. It is also difficult to relocate a large number of farm workers to other sectors, but this difficulty can be addressed by fiscal policy. Public investment in irrigation, transportation, and farming technology can enhance productivity in the agricultural sector, thereby raising the marginal productivity of farm labor. That particular form of public investment can lower poverty in rural areas and at the same time improve income inequality. Furthermore, higher productivity can release farm labor to the service sector and speed up the process of urbanization.

6. Other dimensions of inequality

Empirical evidence provided by Pickett and Wilkinson (2015) strongly suggests that large income differences have damaging health consequences, causing violence and other social problems. As such, reducing income inequality will improve overall health and well-being. It is argued in this chapter that the causation runs both ways. A low stock of health capital results in poverty and income inequality. On the other hand, increasing inequality brings about poor health.

If an educated and healthy labor force contributes to high labor productivity, public spending to raise human and health capital is crucial for sustainable long-term growth of the economy. However, the multiplier effect of such public spending will be small in the short run. Only in the long run will the country benefit from such long-term investment. Because of myopic behavior, governments might not see the long-term beneficial impacts of maintaining expenditures for health and human capital investment. Public spending on education and health should not be affected by political and military business cycles. Public spending on schools and hospitals should not be used to stabilize the economy; it should meet a minimum requirement of a certain percentage of GDP to assure that long-term growth of the economy is not adversely affected by fiscal austerity during economic downturn.

Gaiha et al. (2012) employed data from Asian countries during the period 1991–2007 and found that poverty reduction is larger if the fiscal stimulus is directed to social spending in health and education. Unfortunately, Thailand's budget allocated to education and health seems to be procyclical. The education budget declined from 3.9 percent of GDP in 2000 to 3.7 percent during the mild recession in 2001(Figure 12.4). From the high level of 3.7 percent in 2002, it continuously declined, reaching 3.3 percent in 2006. The declining trend reversed as the economy gradually recovered, plateauing around 4.1 percent between 2009 and 2011. When the economy was on the way to economic trough, education spending was reduced to around 3.7 percent of GDP. A similar procyclical pattern can be observed for budget allocated to strengthen health capital. Social welfare spending should be countercyclical to offer a cushion for the poor in times of crisis and disaster. It can also serve as a built-in fiscal stabilizer during economic downturn.

It is imperative that budget on education and health be maintained at a certain minimum requirement to ensure long-term growth of human and health capital. Furthermore, it is very important to realize that cutting health and education budgets has long-term consequences on poverty and income distribution. Health and education spending is similar to merit goods; the government sometimes fails to understand their significance.

In the classic work of Mincer (1958), there were substantial returns to schooling in the form of higher wages. Evidence illustrated in Figure 12.15 supports Mincer's hypothesis. For people without education attainment, their level of poverty incidence is the highest level among all education attainment classes. The higher the level of education, or the longer they invested time in schooling, the lower their percentage of living below poverty lines. The level of poverty incidence declines as the level of education goes up. Note that over time, from 2008 to 2015, there was a declining trend of poverty in particular for the less educated, reflecting the economic gradual recovery after experiencing the brief recession in 2009.

To elucidate the point that poverty and education are related, we examine the level of poverty in the three southernmost provinces: Pattani, Yala, and Narathiwas. These are the lowest income provinces in the country. When compared to other southern provinces, whose poverty rate has been steadily declining, these three provinces' poverty fluctuated substantially between 2000 and 2015. The fluctuations of the poverty rate reflect output volatility. Other, less poor southern provinces earn steady income from the tourism industry, but these three southern provinces suffer from perennial problems of terrorist activities, threatening a favorable environment for trade and investment. Falling rubber prices and high unemployment gave rise to poverty, underground activities, and violence. In turn,

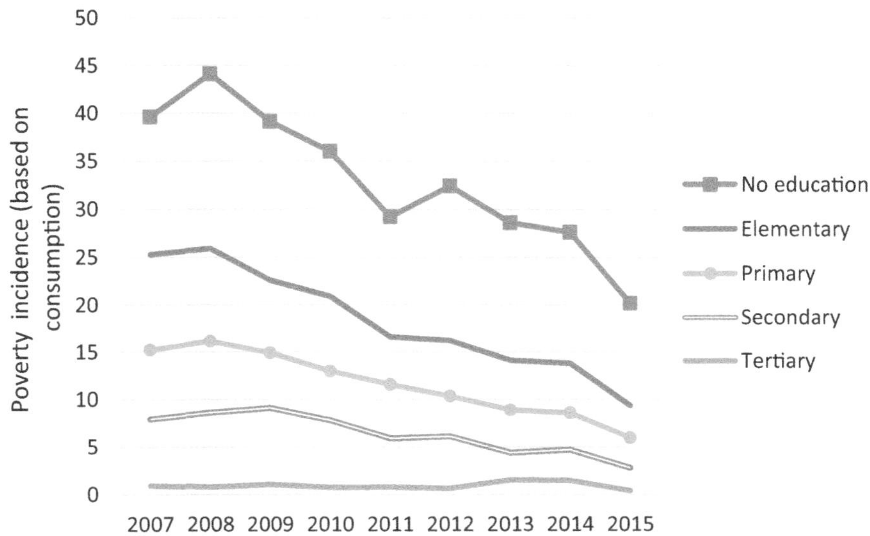

Figure 12.15 Educational attainments and poverty

Source: NESDB

economic and social instability gave rise to low quality of schooling and shorter time spans children spent in school. The number of years spent in school in these three provinces was on average 8 years – 3 years lower than the level in Bangkok.

Poverty and income distribution is a multi-faceted problem, encompassing factor endowment, social, and political issues. Nevertheless, one of the basic factors contributing to income inequality is the shortage of human capital, which must be addressed by an appropriate education policy that fits into local culture and social values. There are other non-monetary aspects of poverty that pertain to quality of life. The maternal mortality ratio declined from 36 (out of 100,000 born) in 1990 to 20 in 2015 (Figure 12.16). Admittedly, the rate is still high, but substantial progress has been made. Notice that the large reduction was made during the economic boom in the early 1990s, reaching its trough at 22 around the 1997–1998. When the economy suffered from the financial crisis, the ratio rose again and peaked at 28 around 2003–2004 before it gradually declined. Thailand did not experience as sharp a decline in mortality ratio as it achieved during the boom. It is hard to dispute that GDP growth is good for the poor, but business cycles do have real impacts on the well-being of the poor.

Another non-monetary measure of the well-being of the poor is the prevalence of underweight children. In the first 5 years of life, malnutrition can lead to poor cognitive and non-cognitive abilities. The malnourishment of children adversely affects the ability to learn and negatively relates to health capital. In the long run, poor health conditions in workers preclude productivity improvement and long-run economic growth.

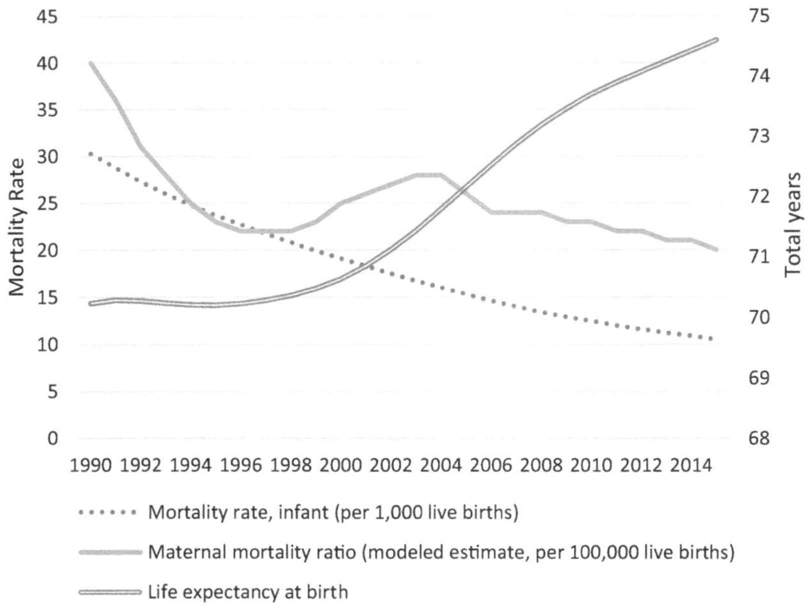

Figure 12.16 Mortality and life expectancy

Source: World Development Indicators

Life expectancy at birth rose from 70 years in 1990 to 74.6 years in 2015 (Figure 12.16). Castello and Domenwxh (2008) argued that the life expectancy mechanism explains a large part of the relationship between inequality and human capital accumulation. When individuals invest in education, they take into account their life expectancy, which depends on the human capital of their parents. The initial inequality of education creates a poverty trap in which children raised in poor families have low life expectancy and work as unskilled labor.

The prevalence of underweight Thai children under 5 years of age had declined slowly but steadily to 15.4 percent in 1995. By 2006, the percentage of underweight children declined sharply by half to just 7 percent, thanks to public budget allocated to health services. Nevertheless, there was a slight rebound to 9.2 percent in 2012. Growth slowdown and the healthcare and social welfare budget were reallocated to other priorities. Growth is good for the poor, but an inclusive and sustainable growth requires a good government that prioritizes the plight of the poor.

7. Concluding remarks

Macroeconomic policy must preserve and maintain macroeconomic stability, while taking into consideration on the impact on the poor. Exchange rate policy adjustments to correct disequilibrium in the balance of payments must be accompanied by fiscal policy to mitigate adverse consequences on the poor, who would suffer from price changes induced by exchange rate depreciation. On the other hand, fiscal policy which stimulates or deflates the economy must take into account unintended impacts of public expenditures and tax burdens on the poor.

Macroeconomic policy must take into account the long-term impact on growth by designing economic stabilization policies with the strategy of pro-poor policies. Fiscal policy focusing on education and health can stimulate long-term growth and reduce poverty. These are specific sets of pro-poor macroeconomic policies, encompassing the well-coordinated fiscal, monetary, international trade, and exchange rate policies. In the case of fiscal sustainability, the government must maintain a minimum 25 percent of total budget allocated to capital expenditures to maintain long-term growth trajectory. Similarly, there must be a lower bound for public spending on health and social welfare. Because investment in human and health capital should not be procyclical, the minimum requirement should be based on the minimum percentage of GDP. Historical patterns of spending in this category (Figure 12.14) suggest that public spending on education should not go below 4 percent of GDP, while the minimum public spending on social welfare and health should not be less than 2 percent of GDP for each category. This public spending rule can prevent myopic behavior of the government which mainly focuses on current spending. It is a dangerous economic consequence when self-interest and short-termism undermine long-term growth.

Notes

1 In 1967, the fertility rate was 6 births per woman. By 2015, it declined to 1.5.
2 Jitsuchon (2014) observes that Thailand has passed Kuznets' turning point since the mid-1990s.
3 The 2013 national average of PISA scores of Thai students in reading, mathematics, and science are equivalent to one proficiency level – much lower than the OECD average.

References

Amini, Chiara, and Silvia Dal Bianco. 2016. "Poverty, Growth, Inequality and Pro–Poor Factors: New Evidence from Macro Data." *Journal of Developing Areas*, 2: 231.

Castello, A., and Rafael Domenech. 2008. "Human Capital Inequality, Life Expectancy and Economic Growth." *Economic Journal*, 118 (528): 653–677.

Day, Creina. 2015. "Skill Composition, Fertility, and Economic Growth." *Review of Income and Wealth*, 61 (1): 164–178.

Fields, Gary. 2001. *Distribution and Development, A New Look at the Developing World. Russel Sage Foundation*. New York, Cambridge, MA, London: The MIT Press.

Gaiha, R. et al. 2012. "Fiscal Stimulus, Agricultural growth and Poverty in Asia." *World Economy*, 35 (6): 713–739.

Gerschenkron, Alexander. 1962. *Economic Backwardness in Historical Perspective*. Cambridge, MA: Harvard University Press.

Jitsuchon, Somchai. 2014. "Income Inequality, Poverty and Labor Migration in Thailand." *The Singapore Economic Review*, 59 (1).

Kurta, K., and Takashi Kurosaki. 2011. "Dynamics of Growth, Poverty and Inequality: A Panel Analysis of Regional Data from Thailand and the Philippines." *Asian Economic Journal*, 25 (1): 3–33.

Kuznets, Simon. 1955. "Economic Growth and Income Inequality" *American Economic Review*, 45: 1–28.

Lin, Faqin, and Dahai Fu. 2016. "Trade, Institution Quality and Income Inequality." *World Development*, 77: 129–142.

Mincer, Jacob. 1958. "Investment in Human Capital and Personal Income Distribution." *Journal of Political Economy*, 66 (4): 281–302.

Okun, Arthur M. 1962. *Potential GNP, Its Measurement and Significance.* Cowles Foundation, Yale University.

Oyvat, Cem. 2016. "Agrarian Structures, Urbanization, and Inequality." W*orld Development*, 83: 207–230.

Perara, Liyanage, Devangi H., and Grace H. Y. Lee. 2013. "Have Economic Growth and Institutional Quality Contributed to Poverty and Inequality Reduction in Asia?" *Journal of Asian Economics*, 27: 71–87.

Pickett, Kate E., and Richard G. Wilkinson. 2015. "Review: Income Inequality and Health: A Causal Review." *Social Science & Medicine*, 128: 316–326.

Piketty, Thomas. 2014. *Capital in the 21st Century.* Cambridge, MA: Harvard University Press.

Tridico, Pasquale. 2010. "Growth, Inequality and Poverty in Emerging and Transition Economies." *Transitions Studies Review*, 16 (4): 979–1003.

Warr, Peter G. 2007. "Long-Term Economic Performance in Thailand." *ASEAN Economic Bulletin*, 24 (1): 138–163.

13 Conclusions

Lessons for emerging economies

Thailand's macroeconomic management experience in the past six decades provides valuable lessons for emerging economies. Although developing economies are heterogeneous, they share some common conditions and situations which require similar policy responses. Some successful macroeconomic policies employed in Thailand may work effectively in other emerging and transitional economies. This book argues that macroeconomic policies which did not achieve desirable results would not likely work in other emerging countries. As history repeats itself, we can learn from the success and failure of Thailand's macroeconomic management.

The first three decades of Thailand's economic development, between 1961 and 1990, we can characterize as a high-growth episode when the economy grew on the average of 7 percent with price stability. Trade liberalization undertaken in this period brought along rapid growth, which transformed Thailand from a primary commodity export-dependent economy to a manufacturing export-led growth economy. During this period, the economy experienced two oil price shocks in the 1970s, causing double-digit inflation. Nevertheless, the economy adjusted back to price stability within a year after the shocks, which led to output growth slowdown and large current account deficits. The overvalued exchange rate, caused by the fixed exchange rate, contributed to unsustainable current account deficits. Two major unavoidable devaluations took place in 1981 and 1984 to correct the balance of payments difficulties. Despite adopting a basket of currencies system to determine the baht-dollar exchange rate, the Thai monetary authorities gradually returned the baht-dollar rate to a fixed exchange rate system, in which the dollar had gained more weight in the currency basket over the years. Although this practice promoted a stable environment for international trade, it paved the way to problems in the following decades.

There exists a trade-off between growth, inflation, and current account disequilibrium. High growth stemmed from expansionary aggregate demand, resulting in high inflation and current account deficit. When the economy was expanding rapidly, high GDP growth rate became unsustainable. We can measure growth sustainability by employing a disequilibrium-adjusted growth index, which takes into account both internal and external imbalances. The new measurement of growth provides an early warning indicator of the likelihood of unsustainable growth. If the disequilibrium-adjusted growth rate is negative, despite a positive actual GDP growth rate, the economy would eventually succumb to macroeconomic instability unless some macroeconomic policy measures are taken to address the fundamental disequilibrium problems.

During the period 1990–2005, the disequilibrium-adjusted growth rate turned negative in 1995, indicating imminent required adjustments. Similarly, the index went into negative territory again in 2005, suggesting that the growth sustainability was threatened and required a serious macroeconomic policy adjustment. Aside from the aforementioned years of difficulties, the economy remained robust with strong growth and price stability. Inflation was mainly driven by food prices and inflationary expectations were kept low, thanks to the temporary price controls and energy price subsidies. Food and energy prices are key commodity prices which directly affect how people formulate and expect future price trends.

During economic booms, the saving ratio increased because of the positive income effect of growth on financial savings. Low inflation enabled interest rates to remain low, which in turn decreased the user cost of capital. As long as inflation was sufficiently low, low nominal interest rates still generated positive real interest rates, thereby attracting financial savings. There was no sign of Dutch disease during the period of high growth and low inflation, because export prices rose faster than prices in the non-traded sector. Consequently, the real exchange rate depreciated and the export sector benefited from industrial output expansion. As a result of long-term political stability and a stable macroeconomic environment, substantial FDI flows were attracted into the manufacturing sector.

After the Asian financial crisis, Thailand's exports responded rapidly to the massive baht depreciation. The Thai economy was resilient enough to export its way out of recession, since the rest of the world did not suffer from global recession. Expansion in world income and substitution effects from currency depreciation boosted Thailand's exports. Between 1995 and 2005, exports of electronic products, vehicles, steel, jewelry, and textiles increased substantially. The export boom was followed by jumps in imports, because production of exports requires importation of raw materials and intermediate products.

It is obvious that Thailand's exports cycle is dictated by the world business cycle. World economic expansion translates into Thailand's export booms, while slowdown in world trade is associated with meager export growth. It seems that changes in the exchange rate are not as important as changes in the world trade volume in determining the Thailand's export growth. Nevertheless, when the exchange rate is seriously overvalued, exchange rate misalignments could destroy the export growth engine as they did prior to 1997. After 2002, the baht regained strength and continued appreciating against the dollar thanks to capital inflows. Fear of depreciation has turned into fear of appreciation, with a firm belief that baht strength can harm exports.

The economic slump after the 2006 coup led to a loss of opportunity to obtain FDI and technology spillover effect. Without sufficient technology transfer from FDI, the Thai economy got stuck in low productivity and a dismal growth path. Private investment also remained low after the 2006 coup. Very often, investors and consumers make spending decisions based on animal spirits and emotions rather than being rational.[1] When confidence is low, and when perception of corruption and social unfairness increases, animal spirits make investors and consumers become more pessimistic, depressing their spending and moving the entire economy from an equilibrium with a high growth path to another equilibrium with a low growth path. In addition to rising wages due to shortages of skilled labor, low investment and dismal output growth further dampened FDI. Consequently, insufficient capital formation reduced export capability and eroded international competitiveness. Long gone were the growth engines which worked diligently in the high growth and low inflation episode. When investment and exports collapsed, consumption expenditure slowed down accordingly.

FDI in the manufacturing sector depends, among other factors, on how the domestic market absorbs output produced by multinational corporations. Neighboring countries' output grew more rapidly because of strong domestic demand generated by rising income and population growth. Economic growth therefore is crucial for attracting FDI. Some multinational corporations have been relocating production bases from Thailand to other ASEAN countries to take advantage of their lower operating costs and political stability, avoiding Thailand's political uncertainty and precariousness.

The Thai economy is vulnerable to external shocks because of its high exposure to trade and capital flows. Despite its adverse consequences on the real sector of the Thai economy in 2009, the global financial crisis had little impact on the Thai financial sector. The healthy performance and resilience of Thai financial institutions can be attributed to the financial reform undertaken after the Asian financial crisis and the favorable macroeconomic environment. Improving macroeconomic conditions in the country lifted up bank profitability. Thai banks have performed well under volatile GDP growth by raising labor productivity. To survive fast-changing and disruptive banking technology, most banks have enhanced operating efficiency by cutting costs and embracing new digital technology. At the same time, commercial banks have become more conservative by raising capital funds and providing ample reserves for non-performing loans. Bank liquidity is raised higher than the requirement of the central bank's strengthened prudential regulations. As long as banks have some monopoly power, profitability can be achieved. Their conservative strategy and continued improvement in efficiency would make them well prepared for future macroeconomic disturbances.

There is an intricate nexus between the level of output, aggregate private expenditures, and the stock market liquidity. The stock market provides a linkage between the real and financial sectors. A boom in the stock market is transmitted into a high level of spending in the real sector through the wealth effect on consumption. In turn, the stock market boom gives rise to private investment and improved business sentiment. A boom in Thailand's stock market occurs because of the rise in liquidity and optimism in Wall Street. In addition, Thailand's stock market price is also influenced by expectations from the private sector and expansion of domestic money supply. The optimistic view of the business sector provides impetus for private spending on durable goods and stimulates private investment in new capital and construction in the real estate sector. With strong liquidity in the stock market, the baht-dollar exchange rate tends to appreciate. On the contrary, pessimistic expectations on the state of the economy lead to deteriorating business sentiment, depressing investment and consumption. Liquidity in the stock market is low and the baht tends to depreciate. The case of Thailand illustrates that exchange rate movements are related to performance in the stock market. Emerging economies whose capital markets are open to foreign investors are likely to be affected by liquidity in the stock markets, which in turn indirectly impacts the real sector through its impact on the trade sector.

Expectations about the future state of the economy affect private expenditure. The expectation effect is stronger than the current income effect from the expanding economy, in particular the impact on demand for durable goods. Similarly, expectations about the future growth path are the strongest driving force for investment growth, more powerful than the contemporaneous output growth which accelerates current investment. The spillover effect from the stock market and its interaction with the expectation effect have ripple effects on the real economy. Because money supply affects stock market prices, by controlling the level of money supply, the central bank can exert impact on stock market liquidity and indirectly influence the real sector through the stock market liquidity channel.

Based on the saving-investment framework, during the course of rapid economic growth, capital inflows finance deficit current account, because savings do not rise fast enough to provide sufficient financial resources for domestic investment. Capital inflows lower domestic interest rates, enabling domestic investment and output to expand beyond the level permitted by available domestic savings. When exchange rate adjustments are not allowed to perform their role to equilibrate current account imbalance, because of the Bank of Thailand's attempt to maintain baht stability, adjustments have to take place through output to restore external equilibrium. Current account deficit is a problem associated with a booming economy, while current capital surplus is observed during economic slowdown. The problem of external disequilibrium in Thailand arises from imbalances between savings and investment, rather than fiscal imbalances. When the current account is surplus, the government experiences fiscal deficit. This is in contrast to the twin deficits hypothesis, which states that current account deficit is caused by the investment-saving gap and government budget deficit. While growth induces current account deficit, strong growth also tends to improve fiscal balance. Therefore, Thailand's current account deficit is associated with budget surplus, thanks to the working of fiscal automatic stabilizers. On the other hand, when growth slows down, fiscal budget turns deficit, while the current account balance also improves.

The movement of the real exchange rate also matters for current account position, although not as much as the impact of changes in output level. There are feedback effects from real exchange rate movements on changes in current account balance. Current account surplus tends to cause baht appreciation, while deficit causes baht depreciation. Movements in the real exchange rate, if permitted, would smooth adjustment of the external imbalances. With a higher degree of currency movements, output fluctuations can be minimized. Viewed in this light, there is a trade-off between variabilities in the output growth rate and the real exchange rate.

Empirical findings provided in this book show that capital inflows are affected by interest gaps between domestic and foreign interest rates. This is not surprising as the Thai economy has a high degree of capital mobility. Because capital flows are also influenced by exchange rate expectations, anticipation of baht strengthening would lead to more capital inflows, given other factors remain constant. One of the detrimental impacts of the military coup is clearly demonstrated by capital outflows. Indeed, political stability affects perception of risks. Thailand's long absence of military coups before 2006 sustained business sentiment and optimism about democracy. International investors did not require compensation for higher risk premiums during the period of political stability.

Thailand's exchange rate policy exhibits long-term consistency in the sense that the central bank prefers a weak baht. It should be emphasized again that high export growth is not inconsistent with strong baht. A weak currency does not necessarily imply strong export growth. Because the current nominal exchange rate is determined by the expectations of the future real exchange rate, the current nominal exchange rate can appreciate because of the expectation of the appreciation of the future real exchange rate. The latter is determined by real conditions in the economy, i.e., the productivity and productive capacity of the country. In the short run, the central bank can maintain exchange rate competitiveness by keeping the inflation rate lower than trading partners. Consequently, exchange rate competitiveness declines if the real exchange rate appreciates if the central bank cannot keep inflation lower than trading partners. Money illusion complicates exchange rate policy management. It has become more challenging when money illusion occurs in the goods market as well as in the foreign markets. Market participants think of nominal rather than real exchange rate changes. They perceive nominal exchange rate appreciation as real exchange rate appreciation and thereby react as if the real exchange rate appreciates. The real exchange rate appreciates less than the nominal exchange rate appreciation if inflation in Thailand is lower than inflation in trading countries.

If the world economy recovers slowly, getting out of recession requires consumers to resume normal spending patterns, which fundamentally depends on the level of consumer confidence. In times of political uncertainty and various external shocks, it is difficult to boost investor sentiment and raise the morale of consumers. During periods of domestic demand contraction, exports are the only remaining growth driver in Thailand, but exports are mainly determined by conditions in the world market – not the weak currency. Thailand's exchange rate policy has influenced the effectiveness of macroeconomic policies over the past decades. One of the prime examples of disastrous policies were the capital controls adopted in December 2006. In formulating the exchange rate policy, monetary authorities must understand that the baht-dollar exchange rate fluctuations are mostly influenced by movements of the dollar rate vis-à-vis other major currencies. The Singapore dollar, in particular, has strong influence over the movement of the Thai baht against the US dollar. A higher degree of the baht flexibility is preferable to having rigidly controlled movements. The private sector will eventually have to learn and adjust to changing the dollar price. There are always requests from exporters for weakening the currency. Lessons from Thailand's erroneous choices of exchange rate system should not be repeated. Thailand's exports are fundamentally determined by world income rather than the exchange rate. Any attempt to create undervaluation is counterproductive and costly. The Bank of Thailand cannot lean against the wind of key currency movements and speculative attacks. Sterilization of currency does not work either. Admittedly, it is in the mindset of monetary authorities – fear of floating and burning desire to intervene in the markets without thinking carefully about the short-run and long-run costs and benefits of intervention.

There is a long-run relationship between output and monetary aggregates. Monetary policy can stabilize the economy to achieve stable long-term growth and price stability. Changes in the monetary base influence cyclical movements of real output. If the broad money supply grows at a stable rate corresponding to output growth, monetary authorities can avoid deep recessions and excessive booms. In general, for all emerging economies, controlling the monetary base can be done by reducing intervention in the foreign exchange markets and refraining from printing money to finance budget deficit. In the case of Thailand, monetary base expansion is caused by the central banks' purchase of the dollars to prevent baht appreciation – not the central bank buying government bonds to finance budget deficit. Lessons from past experience should be learned and not forgotten.

Overlending to the property sector leads to asset price bubbles. Due to linear perception of property market participants, the private sector always underestimates the risk of the Minsky meltdown. Thus, macro prudential policy has been installed by the Bank of Thailand. Loan-to-value ratio and loan-to-income ratio are examples of instruments to curb household debts and speculation in the property markets.

The key policy rate of the Bank of Thailand responds more to inflation than economic growth and real exchange rate appreciation. It is possible to conduct an independent monetary policy to stabilize the economy, but there are some side effects on the real economy. Furthermore, unlike the federal funds rate, there is a rather loose link between the central bank's key policy rate and commercial banks' lending rate. Emerging markets' monetary policy instruments are not as powerful as in the US, because of the weak link between underdevelopment capital markets and money markets. Short-term and long-term interest rates do not move together, because emerging economies rely heavily on bank loans rather than raising funds from capital markets. They also suffer from the original sin, because they cannot borrow from foreign markets in their own currencies. The monopolistic commercial structure enables banks to earn profit higher than the normal rate of return. The minimum lending rate of Thai commercial banks is determined by deposit interest rates, thereby weakening the central bank's ability to control the magnitude and direction of commercial bank lending rates.

Changes in interest rates influence the levels of consumption and investment, but banks' lending volumes exert stronger impact on private spending more than the cost of funds. Thus, the credit availability channel is the main transmission mechanism of monetary policy. This is the case for all bank-based emerging economies. It boils down to the ability to control the monetary base to influence the economy. The effectiveness of inflating targeting pales in comparison to monetary base control. And the ability to control the latter depends crucially on the degree of intervention in the foreign exchange markets. The lesser the degree of intervention, the higher the degree of monetary base control.

There is a trade-off between inflation and unemployment. For Thailand, the cost of pushing the economy to full employment is not high in terms of sacrificing price stability. Nevertheless, persistence of inflation is a factor that makes it difficult to subdue inflation once it starts accelerating. Policies which affect inflation expectations include temporary price ceilings and subsidies during the period of price shocks. Nevertheless, these measures are temporary in nature to cool down inflationary expectations. Permanent price distortions result in inefficiency and lower potential output growth in the long run. There is also another challenge in commodity price, which tends to be stabilized for a period of time. If prices are maintained for too long, households tend to experience money illusion. For example, if energy prices are adjusted upward due to rising crude oil prices in the world markets, households perceive the nominal rise in the price level by the same percentage as the real price hike and they react by cutting down consumption accordingly. Had the households experienced price movements in both directions more often, they would not overreact as they would be able to distinguish between real and nominal changes in the price level.

Quantitative easing monetary policy conducted by the Fed and the BOJ has significant impact on the Thai economy. The strength of the first-round impact of the QE policy depends on Thailand's export exposures, trade, and financial linkages with US and Japan. In the short run, the QE impact can be either expansionary or contractionary, depending whether the baht depreciates or appreciates against the dollar and the yen. In the medium run, the QE impact is related to the appreciation of the yuan and the slowdown of the Chinese economy, which further depresses Thailand's exports and prolongs Thailand's output recovery. In the long run, when the QE stimulates economic recovery in the US and spurs global output expansion, Thailand's manufactured output and exports respond positively to world economic recovery. The long-run impact of the QE will be positive. This is evident in 2018 after the global recovery became more pronounced in the US, Japan, and China, resulting in a higher growth rate of Thailand's exports.

The QE measures also have impact on local asset prices. The QE had lowered corporate bond yields in US, thereby making investment in emerging markets more profitable. The huge capital inflows into emerging economies created local currency appreciation. The stock market boomed and property prices increased rapidly, as an influx of foreign capital flooded local stock markets and the property sector. Another undesirable impact of the QE is the problem of emerging Dutch disease, which causes real exchange rate appreciation when the price of non-traded goods rises faster than traded good prices. It is a great challenge to central banks in emerging economies to prevent asset price bubbles and deterioration of international competitiveness, while maintaining the strength of the private spending.[2]

The situation is more complicated when the Fed's quantitative monetary easing becomes quantitative monetary restricting; its impacts will be the opposite. Fear of rising world interest rates and normalizing of interest rate policy in advanced countries has already caused a concern among central banks in emerging countries.[3] By 2018, the yield of the 10-year US treasury bills is higher than Thailand's government bond yield, reflecting higher inflation in the US and the anticipation of the baht appreciation. As inflation in the US is trending up, while unemployment is well below the natural rate, there is a heightened fear of rising interest rates in the US. Conducting monetary policy in uncertain times has become increasingly difficult as monetary authorities in emerging economies must have certain instruments to delay the impact of the shocks transmitted from the conduct of monetary policy in advanced countries.

The Thai economy has been integrated to the global economy through expanding trade relations and increasing openness to FDI. Consequently, the rising volume of trade networks has deepened the economy's interconnectedness with China and other ASEAN countries. Trade intensity between Thailand and other ASEAN members has also been rising, thanks to the formulation of free trade agreements decades earlier. This book points out that business cycles in ASEAN economies are synchronized with China's. The booms in Thailand's exports and tourism industry are closely related with China's GDP and import growth. Not only regional GDP growth synchronized with China's business cycle, inflation rate in China and ASEAN countries are also closely related. The Thai economic is directly influenced by China's new normal growth and more importantly by the indirect effect of China's growth impact on other ASEAN economies, whose trade intensity with Thailand is growing over time through development of the ASEAN Economic Community.

Thailand's consumer price indexes are influenced significantly by the price level in the US, but China's price level also has an impact on Thailand's via the trade channel. The baht-yuan exchange rate is another factor leading to rapid flows of trade and services from China, due to baht depreciation against the yuan. The boom in Thailand's tourism industry has been the influx of Chinese tourists, offsetting the decline of Thailand's exports between 2014 and 2016. The baht-dollar exchange rate moves in line with the yuan, but the baht moves in an opposite direction with the dollar and the yen.

As China's growth slows down, adverse consequences on ASEAN economies have become more pronounced. The extent of the adverse effects depends on Thailand's trade exposure and China's dependency. The slowing down of the Chinese economy undoubtedly results in a decline in Thailand's exports and ASEAN's long-term growth, unless appropriate fiscal and monetary policy responses are implemented.[4]

Fiscal policy stimulus is required during a repressed economy. Thailand's fiscal policy can only be an effective means to spur growth during times when consumer and investor confidence remains strong. When business sentiment is low, the expansionary impact of fiscal deficit will be low. Maintaining a favorable business environment is important in preventing the propagation of global recession into severe output contraction.

Unwarranted fear of unsustainable public debt and ultra-conservative fiscal policy have prevented the country from achieving a high-growth trajectory. Fiscal deficit can be paid off by the helping hand of automatic fiscal stabilizers, because revenues grow faster than expenditures during economic upturn. As long as fiscal deficit can stimulate the economy, the fear of unsustainable public debt is exaggerated. Public spending should be countercyclical, rather than procyclical as it was in Thailand after 2006. Empirical evidence provided in this book indicates that investment responds to public spending more than consumption. In particular, expenditures on economic affairs and health and education can raise growth trajectory in the long run, whereas defense budget decreases it. After the military coups in 2006 and 2014, the Thai economy experienced the lowest economic growth in the ASEAN region. Thailand has been mired in meager growth. Budget spent on economic services was diverted into defense, public sector wage hikes, and income transfer employed for popularity.

To stimulate growth in the aftermath of the global recession, sufficient fiscal space is needed to carry out fiscal expansion. If the rules of fiscal sustainability are observed, available fiscal space permits effective fiscal programs. Fiscal stimulus must not be applied too late or too little after the collapse of exports and domestic demand. It is imperative that current public spending be curtailed once the economy regains its pre-shock growth path. The caveat is that the public can become addicted to subsidies offered by government programs in such a way that when the economy regains strength, the government dares not trim down these programs in order to maintain popularity among voters.

There is a complex relationship between economic growth, poverty, and income distribution. We have established that, with some certain conditions, macroeconomic policy can be used to stabilize income growth and maintain price stability. Because growth and price levels affect income of the poor, macroeconomic policy can directly and indirectly affect poverty and income inequality. It is found that growth is good for the poor. Poverty in Thailand has been declining and so has income inequality. The faster the reduction in rural poverty, the more equitable income distribution would be. Priority must be given to rural poverty reduction, as it will eventually improve income distribution for the whole country.

There are factors contributing to declining poverty and improving income inequality. It is argued that the speed of poverty reduction is related to the GDP growth rate. Other factors that matter for poverty reduction are commodity prices and urbanization. Clinging to traditional commodity exports, which are subject to virulent terms of trade shocks and climatic conditions, hurts long-term growth and delays the speed of poverty reduction. Some of those public subsidies on primary commodities could have been put toward more productive uses for long-term capital formation in rural areas. We have observed that poverty reduction slowed down during commodity slumps.

Transforming the agricultural sector in a rural economy to manufacturing and service sectors in urban areas can reduce poverty. But efficient farm mechanization is required to release labor from the agricultural sector, while non-agricultural sectors must generate employment high enough to absorb rural workers. A particular set of fiscal policies can improve income inequality and improve labor productivity, which in turn sustain high income level growth. Policies which enhance investment and productivity in the agricultural sector are required. Promoting foreign direct investment in the agricultural sector is necessary. For human capital investment in agriculture, the policy of free education up to 12 years is not enough for raising quality human capital. There must be a requirement level for public budget of at least 4 percent GDP on education, and also 4 percent of GDP for combined public expenditures on health and social welfare.[5] In addition, these types of public expenditures should not be procyclical. In other words, they should not be cut during economic downturns, because they have a long-term impact on development of health and human capital, which are crucially important for maintaining long-term growth.

Thailand has been cursed by twin traps: the middle-income and the military coup traps. The problem of the middle-income trap is not independent of the military coup trap. The 2006 military coup enabled the hike of defense budget at the expense of public capital deepening. The coup had a detrimental impact on domestic and foreign investment. Subsequent rises in corruption further reduced the rate of return on private investment, hampering the economy from gravitating back to pre-coup growth.[6] Low levels of capital investment reduce the chance of getting out of the middle-income trap and keep the country forever in the military coup trap. Low income levels and income equality are perpetuated by the lack of sufficient human and health capital investment, and the lack of willingness to uphold and respect the rule of law.

In 2007, the military government stayed in power until the general election took place under a newly drafted constitution. The defense budget rose considerably during the military-backed regime. Nevertheless, the share of defense spending in total government budget gradually declined after a democratic government was established. A similar pattern of military business cycles can be observed after the 2014 coup. The destruction of rule of law and degenerating quality of government led Thailand into ineffective macroeconomic policy management to respond to external shocks. In a state of unfavorable investment environment, due to risks and uncertainties of political upheavals and social conflict, the Thai economy remains in the low growth and high power of an autocratic regime. The other equilibrium state of the economy will be in high growth and high respect for rule of law and democracy. This is the state of the economy which corresponds to optimistic expectations. In the low growth, low quality of institution equilibrium, pessimistic expectations dampen investment and consumption.[7] Credit and output growth remain sluggish. This book highlights the important role of expectations which can alter the level of private spending and monetary aggregates.

It is a vicious cycle in Thailand's politics, where general elections are followed by elected governments. It does not matter whether or not an elected government is too weak, because of coalition of many parties, or too strong because of majority of the governing party in the parliament – when a military coup takes place, the governing constitution is abolished. Then a new constitution is drafted; the country temporarily returns to democracy until a new coup is staged and a new constitution is proclaimed. In the short history of Thailand's nascent democracy since 1922, there have been 19 constitutions in total. The return of the coup in 2006 affected the business environment. The military-installed government engineered a policy that destroyed investment sentiment and consumer confidence. The 2014 coup differs significantly from the 2006 coup. The 2014 coup leader stayed in power more than 4 years – much longer than the 2006 coup leader. The longer the military junta stays in power, the higher the damages inflicted on the economy. The general election has been postponed four times, causing anxieties and uncertainty to investors. The fundamental message from Keynes' general theory is that the private sector's decision on spending depends crucially on the perception of risk and uncertainties. The long-term impact of the 2014 coup will go beyond 2020. For some quarters in Thai society, there has been a mindset that democracy cannot solve corruption and elected governments cannot bring economic prosperity, but only chaos and political turmoil. There are groups of people who are willing to sacrifice freedom of expression and voting rights for the absence of violence and terrorism. International evidence does not support benevolent autocracy. Repressive regimes and violation of human rights would bring a calamitous effect on long-term development.[8] Indeed, Thailand will get stuck in both middle-income and military coup traps as long as Thai society remains divided by their political views and their respect for the rule of law.

Notes

1 Akerlof and Shiller (2010) extend Keynes' concept of animal spirits to include confidence, fairness, corruption and bad faith, money illusion, and stories shared among particular groups of people. With this broader definition of animal spirits, the whole economy can be moved by a change from an optimistic to pessimistic view on the economy.
2 See Nidhiprabha (2017) for the discussion of the effectiveness of monetary policy in CLMV countries under dollarization.
3 In December 2008, the federal funds rate was set at its lowest level of 0.25 percent. After normalization of the interest rate, the federal funds rate was gradually raised to 1.75 percent by May 2018.
4 The resurgence of Thailand's exports growth in 2018 can partly be attributed to the expansion of the Chinese economy.
5 Obviously, these ceilings must be applied to the actual level of spending, net of corruption.
6 The 2016 corruption perceptions index, compiled by Transparency International, deteriorated by three points from the level in 2014. By 2017, it improved by two points – to 37 points, the same level it was in 2012 before the coup took place.
7 The EU suspended the signing of a partnership agreement with Thailand following the May 2014 coup. Similarly, the free trade agreement between Thailand and the

US has been postponed. While some other developing countries still receive Generalized System of Preferences (GSP) benefits from the EU, the withdrawal of the GSP for Thailand could have been compensated by a partnership agreement with the EU.

8 See Easterly (2014) for evidence from various countries under the hands of military rulers.

References

Akerlof, George A., and Robert J. Shiller. 2010. *Animal Spirits: How Human Psychology Drives the Economy, and Why It Matters for Global Capitalism.* Princeton: Princeton University Press.

Easterly, William. 2014. *The Tyranny of Experts: Economists, Dictators, and the Forgotten Rights of the Poor.* New York: Basic Books.

Nidhiprabha, Bhanupong. 2017. "Economic Growth, Monetary Policy, and Dollarization in CLMV Countries." In Kubo, Koji (ed.) *Dollarization and De-dollarization in Transitional Economies of Southeast Asia.* Cham: Springer International Publishing, Macmillan, 167–196.

Index

Note: Page numbers in *italic* indicate a figure and page numbers in **bold** indicate a table on the corresponding page.

For Product Safety Concerns and Information please contact our
EU representative GPSR@taylorandfrancis.com Taylor & Francis
Verlag GmbH, Kaufingerstraße 24, 80331 München, Germany